CONCISE COLLEGE TEXTS

TORT

OTHER BOOKS IN THIS SERIES:

AUSTRALIA
The Law Book Company Ltd.
Sydney

CANADA
The Carswell Company Ltd.
Toronto, Ontario

INDIA
N.M. Tripathi (Private) Ltd.
Bombay
and
Eastern Law House (Private) Ltd.
Calcutta
M.P.P. House
Bangalore
Universal Book Traders
Delhi

ISRAEL
Steimatzky's Agency Ltd.
Tel Aviv

PAKISTAN
Pakistan Law House
Karachi

CONCISE COLLEGE TEXTS

TORT

by

C.D. BAKER, B.C.L., M.A.
of the Inner Temple, Barrister
Practitioner of the Supreme Court of Australia;
Senior Lecturer in Law,
University of Adelaide

FIFTH EDITION

LONDON
SWEET & MAXWELL
1991

First Edition 1972
Second Edition 1976
Second Impression 1978
Third Impression 1979
Fourth Edition 1986
Fifth Edition 1991

Published in 1991 by
Sweet & Maxwell Limited of
183 Marsh Wall, London E14 9FT
Laserset by
P.B. Computer Typesetting, N. Yorks
Printed by
Richard Clay Limited, Bungay, Suffolk

*A CIP catalogue record
for this book is available
from The British Library*

ISBN 0–421–432705

PREFACE

By far the most important developments in the law of tort since the last edition of this book are the House of Lords decisions in *Murphy* v. *Brentwood D.C.* (1990) and *Caparo Industries plc* v. *Dickman* (1989). The former overrules *Anns* v. *London Borough of Merton* (1977) as far as its own duty-situation is concerned. The latter effectively gets rid of the *Anns* two-tier test as a means of solving the question of duty of care in negligence in general, though it is predictable that the new criteria provided may create confusion, and the author does not share the belief that the two-tier test was obviously unsatisfactory. The implications of these decisions are spelled out in detail in the chapters on duty of care in negligence and on liability for defective premises. The negligence chapter also is updated in the light of significant developments relating to liability for misstatements, for causing nervous shock and for allowing the causing of damage by a third party. There have been other important judicial clarifications of the law in relation to causation in fact, liability for animals, the pleading rules in relation to the defences to defamation of justification and fair comment, and the economic torts. The present edition contains a full account of these, though as far as the economic torts are concerned the addendum at the foot of this preface should be noted. There is also a full account of the statutory innovations in the Latent Damage Act 1986 and the Consumer Protection Act 1987.

The whole of the present edition was prepared while on study leave in Britain in the Institute of Advanced Legal Studies, and to that remarkable institution the author expresses the appropriate measure of thanks, as also to the publishing representatives of Sweet & Maxwell for their prompt and efficient handling of the text. The book was prepared in accordance with materials available to me in the Institute at the end of March 1991. The two addenda below concern matters which occurred too late for incorporation in the text.

David Baker   *July 26, 1991*

ADDENDA

In *Lonrho plc* v. *Al Fayed* (*The Times*, July 3, 1991) the House of Lords, reversing the Court of Appeal, concluded that Lord Diplock's speech in *Lonrho Ltd.* v. *Shell Petroleum Co. Ltd. (No. 2)* (1982) A.C. 173, with which all the other members of the House of Lords concurred, was not intended to remove the distinction between the conspiracy to commit a lawful act, where a predominant purpose to injure the plaintiff was required in the conspirators, and the conspiracy to use unlawful means, where no such predominant purpose was required. This (to this author at least) rather surprising interpretation of Lord Diplock's speech equates the intention requirement in the conspiracy to use unlawful means to that required in the other economic torts, a matter fully considered in the text. It also revives the doctrine espoused by *Rookes* v. *Barnard* (1964) under which a threat of an unlawful general withdrawal of labour made by chosen defendants is actionable on the basis that those defendants are liable for the whole of the damage produced or threatened by the strike, even though not all the strikers are sued.

In *R.* v. *Deputy Governor of Parkhurst Prison, ex p. Hague* and *Weldon* v. *Home Office* (*The Times*, July 25, 1991) the House of Lords, in each case reversing an earlier decision of the Court of Appeal, held that imprisonment of a lawfully detained prisoner under intolerable conditions could not amount to the tort of false imprisonment, though where injury resulted an action for negligence might lie. It is now clear, therefore, that neither an imprisonment constricting an interference with the prisoner's "residual liberty" nor an imprisonment under intolerable conditions amounts to false imprisonment.

CONTENTS

TABLE OF CASES

ix

TABLE OF STATUTES

1. INTRODUCTION

DEFINITION OF "TORT"; PURPOSE OF THE LAW OF TORT

The difficulty of defining the word "tort" is well recognised. In the words of an American authority (*Prosser on Torts* (4th ed.), p. 1), "the numerous attempts which have been made to define the term [*i.e.* tort] have succeeded only in achieving language so broad that it includes other matters than torts, or else so narrow that it leaves out some torts themselves." The main reason for this difficulty is the extreme variety of behaviour which may constitute a tort. Intentionally or negligently to cause physical injury to another, to interfere with his enjoyment of his land, to defame him, or to conspire with another to cause him financial loss are examples of such behaviour. Such cases appear to have three elements. The first is behaviour by a human being (the defendant) considered by the law to be wrongful. Generally speaking torts are committed only by wrongful behaviour, *i.e.* by intentional wrongdoing or negligent conduct, but there are a few torts in which that is not so and in which the defendant is liable without fault. These are the so-called torts of strict liability. The second element is that the behaviour must infringe another human being's [the plaintiff's] interest, which the law regards as being worthy of protection against that form of behaviour. Some interests are regarded as so important by the law that they receive protection against both intentional and negligent infringement and even in some cases against conduct in which there is no element of fault.

Such are the interests in the security of one's person and property. Other interests are much less well protected. The interest in one's economic well-being, for example, is protected against a number of torts requiring an intentional act, is less well protected against negligence (although during recent years that position has been in the course of rectification) and is not protected by any of the torts of strict liability. The third element is that the plaintiff is entitled to obtain compensation from the defendants in the form of damages by taking action in a civil court. The compensatory function of the law of torts is that which distinguishes it from criminal law which exists to satisfy the public interest in the redress and suppression of crime by the prosecution of offenders. Many torts arise out of behaviour which is also criminal and it is perfectly possible for two sets of proceedings, civil and criminal, to be brought in relation to the same wrongful act.

The above paragraph suggests a state of the law of tort as one showing considerable logical force and symmetry. This is undoubtedly true at the present day, but it tends to disguise the somewhat unprincipled and haphazard process of evolution underlying the present system. For example, for several centuries the law drew a not altogether rational distinction between direct injuries to person or property which were actionable as trespass, and indirect injuries which were actionable under the so-called action on the case. The distinction between direct and indirect harm has today lost most of its importance with the result that we now have a much more cogent distinction between injuries to person or property inflicted intentionally (most examples of which are still called trespass) and those inflicted through negligence (which are actionable under the tort of negligence). Again nuisance grew up as a tort regulating the mutual obligations of adjacent landowners and it seems that little thought was given originally to the question of what sort of wrongful conduct was necessary on the part of the defendant to render him liable in the tort. Only in the present century has it been clearly recognised that wrongful conduct is generally necessary for liability in nuisance to arise and that this sort of behaviour even by a person who is not an occupier of land may give rise to liability if it disturbs another person in the enjoyment of his land. This process of rationalisation may be seen also in cases such as the liability of the occupier of premises towards his visitors for defects in the premises and the liability of the person who puts a dangerous chattel into circulation. These cases were once subject to complicated special rules but are now regarded as mere applications of the general principles of negligence to a particular field.

Unliquidated damages

Winfield (Province of the Law of Tort) took the view that the right to claim unliquidated damages was an important indication that the action was one of tort. Unliquidated damages may be defined as damages which are not a specific, predetermined sum but are measured by the amount of loss or damage suffered by the plaintiff through the wrong done to him. They compare with liquidated damages which are awarded when the plaintiff claims a specific sum of money arising, for example, from a debt owed to him by the defendant whether of a contractual or a quasi-contractual nature. But unliquidated damages are not exclusive to actions in tort. They certainly may be awarded in an action for breach of contract, they seem to be possible in the case of liability of the trustee for breach of trust, and Winfield himself admitted that in certain cases they might be awarded in actions for quasi-contract. The invariable right to claim unliquidated damages for a tort, however, enables us to say with confidence that where such a right exists, and other civil wrongs are excluded, the case is one of tort. Tort, with its lack of a central identifying principle, acts as a residual category for civil wrongs which are hard to classify. Equally, absence of the right to claim unliquidated damages excludes the case from tort, even though a civil remedy exists for the wrong in question. A few doubtful cases of this sort which are potential torts but have not yet been admitted into the category are considered in Chapter 26.

Tort and contract

The right to sue in tort and the right to claim unliquidated damages for breach of contract are similar in purpose and effect. Both actions have a clear compensatory function, distinguishing them from claims for breach of trust, or quasi-contract, where the chief purpose of the claim is to seek restitution of money or property. In claims for tort and contract, also, there is no doubt about the plaintiff's right to recover damages for consequential loss arising from the wrong, provided that the loss complies with the requirement that in law it is not too remote. Finding any absolute difference between tort and contract seems to be impossible apart from the formal difference that one suing in tort does not have to prove a contract and its breach. Even so, in certain cases of tortious liability arising under the case of *Hedley Byrne & Co.* v. *Heller* (1964), the existence of the contractual agreement is clearly relevant to the establishing of liability. There is no reason why breach of contract should not be regarded as a special type of tort, but there are a number of typical differences between them, which continue to hold true in general.

First, the parties to a contract in effect make law for themselves when composing their contract, though the obligation to perform the contract is imposed by the law itself. Tortious rights and obligations on the other hand are imposed by law. Many contractual obligations are, nevertheless, of a mandatory nature imposed by the law. For example, the obligation in a contract of sale of goods for a seller to supply goods of merchantable quality arises by law rather than by agreement between the parties (Sale of Goods Act 1979, s.14(2)) and cannot be excluded by contractual provision (Sale of Goods Act 1979, s.6(2)). And of course the basic obligation to carry out contracts is imposed by law.

Secondly, the rights created by the law of torts, for example a person's right to the physical safety of his person, are available against all persons. They are *iura in rem*. Contractual rights are available only against particular persons. They are *iura in personam*. In fact, however, the *iura in rem* protected by the law of torts, such as the right to the physical safety of one's person or property are only protected against particular persons at particular times and in respect of particular conduct. So that the generalised *iura in rem* protected by torts are for practical purposes just as particularised as the *iura in personam* protected by the law of contract.

Thirdly, it is possible to point to what may be regarded as an essential difference between the nature of tortious and contractual rights. The tortious right is one of exclusion, of freedom from interference with a particular interest. The holder of this right seeks to hold on to what he has already got, rather than to obtain a new thing. The contractual right is a right to performance. The whole purpose of it is that it should change the plaintiff's position to one which he considers to be better. The interest it protects is generally an expectation of future benefit. This points to a further difference. Tort liability is concerned with misfeasance, that is, with positive actions causing damage. Contract liability is for nonfeasance, in other words, for failing to perform the contractual promise. Nevertheless, these differences are typical rather than categorical. In particular, a tort may be committed in numerous circumstances by nonfeasance, including the cases of omission to act and of positive action failing to achieve a required result. Also, tort may in a number of cases protect expectations of future benefit. One tort, inducement of a breach of contract, actually protects the plaintiff's interest in the performance of a contract made between himself and another person. There has been an increase in recent years in cases in which an action in tort has been found to lie where previously it had been thought that, in the absence of a contract, no action was available. Thus, actions in negligence have been allowed to succeed where that negligence caused the plaintiff's expectation of benefit under a contractual arrangement with a third party to be defeated (*Ross* v. *Caunters* (1980); *Junior Books Ltd.* v. *Veitchi* (1982)). So also an action in tort has been found to lie for the negligent failure to perform a non-contractual promise (*Meates* v. *Att.-Gen.* (1983)—A New Zealand decision). There is, however, still an element of controversy about these decisions. The matter is considered in detail in relation to liability under the *Hedley Byrne* case in Chapter 6.

Since there is no absolute qualitative difference between tort and contract, the position may well arise that the same facts may give rise to overlapping claims under both heads. Judicial recognition of the phenomenon of overlap between claims in tort and contract has been rendered possible by two leading House of Lords decisions. *Donoghue* v. *Stevenson* (1932) held that a contracting party may owe a duty of care in the performance of the contract which does not derive from the contract itself but from the law of tort. *Hedley Byrne & Co.* v. *Heller* (1964) went further in that, in recognising the existence of a duty of care under the law of tort with regard to the making of statements, it opened up the way to actions in tort lying against contractual advisers for the giving of negligent advice where exactly the same liability existed under a contract. That there may be identity between the two causes of action has recently been accepted after some earlier doubt in

Midland Bank Trust Co. v. *Hett, Stubbs & Kemp* (1979) in which it was found that alternative claims in contract and tort arose out of the negligent performance by a solicitor of his contract with his client (followed in *Bell* v. *Peter Browne* (1990)). Classifying the claim as contract or tort or contract and tort is not purely an academic matter. Limitation periods differ significantly according to whether the claim is in contract or tort, an important point in recent years. The measure of damages is different. Contributory negligence is a defence to an action in tort but not to one in contract generally.

CLASSIFICATION OF TORTS

Something must be said about classification in order to explain the order of treatment in this book. The emphasis of the courts has tended to be placed on the interest that is infringed, and on whether this was worthy of being protected against the defendant's conduct. This book has therefore adopted a classification of torts based upon the interest protected, beginning with the tortious infringement of the most important interests, those in personal security and property, and continuing with the protection of interests in reputation, in economic security, in not being maliciously prosecuted and in various miscellaneous matters such as the right to vote. In view of the central importance at the present day of the tort of negligence, a classification based upon the mental element involved in the defendant's conduct into torts of intention, negligence and strict liability might seem logical. But negligence is preeminently of importance in protecting interests in person and property. It will therefore be treated as a whole in the part of the book dealing with torts to person or property, though this leads to a discussion of the negligent infringement of economic interests before such interests are dealt with as a whole. Otherwise, however, the classification of torts by reference to the interest protected is maintained.

Motive and malice

Motive in general is irrelevant in the law of tort. As in the case of criminal law, an intention to do the wrongful act is generally sufficient, whatever the motive, and clearly the question of motive is quite irrelevant in the case of torts based on negligence. The tortfeasor's reasons are of course relevant to the assessment of damages against him. A person who sets fire to a house because he is an incendiarist is likely to be treated quite differently in the matter of damages from one who does so under a mistaken belief that he has the authority of the owner of the house. In particular, the incendiarist is likely to have to pay aggravated and possibly exemplary damages, *i.e.* compensation going beyond the damage done to the house. A question arises whether the existence of a malicious motive is relevant to establish liability in tort in those cases where the mere intention to inflict loss is insufficient, for example, in the case where the defendant has intentionally inflicted economic loss upon another person without committing any of the existing economic torts (*infra*, Chapter 22). Put more generally, is the malicious infliction of actual damage always sufficient to establish liability in tort? The answer, perhaps surprisingly, is that it is not. Malice is relevant in the case of those torts requiring proof of malicious intention (for example, malicious prosecution, injurious falsehood); for rebutting a defence based on qualified privilege (defamation); or to show that the defendant behaved unreasonably (nuisance). But there is no general principle of liability for the malicious infliction of harm. Two cases illustrate the point. In *Bradford Corporation* v. *Pickles* (1895) the defendant had caused to be stopped underground water flowing under his land for the purpose as the Court found of depriving the plaintiffs of the flow of water to their land and so compelling them to buy his land at an inflated price. The landowner has in general a right to take as much water from water in undefined channels beneath his land as he wishes, even if this completely deprives his neighbours of any flow. The House of Lords found the defendant not liable here and dismissed as irrelevant the question of his motive. It is true that the defendant was not malicious here, and was merely acting to protect his economic interests, but Lord McNaghten expressly stated that no difference would have resulted even if he had been found malicious. *Allen* v. *Flood* (1898) is a more conclusive illustration of the general rule. In that case a threat was made by the defendant to the plaintiff's employer to call a strike among boilermakers (the strike was assumed by the House of Lords not to be a breach of the boilermakers' contracts of employment) unless the employer dismissed the plaintiffs, which he did. The threat was made for the purpose of punishing the plaintiffs for having engaged in ironwork for another company, that being regarded as the exclusive province of the boilermakers. The jury found the defendant to have acted maliciously in causing the dismissal of the plaintiffs but the House of Lords found that no cause of action existed in the absence of any unlawfulness in the threat itself or the means used to carry it out.

Civil trials and actions in torts

Questions of evidence are dealt with in detail in Chapter 10. At this stage it may be noted that the plaintiff has the burden of proving all the factual allegations necessary to prove the commission of the tort on which he is relying. He must prove these facts on the balance of probabilities, a lesser standard of proof than that required of the prosecutor in a criminal trial who must prove the relevant facts beyond a reasonable doubt. The plaintiff's action in tort may still fail because the factual allegations on which he is relying, even if he is capable of proving them, do not establish the existence of a cause of action in tort. That will be because the facts do not fall within any of the existing recognised torts, though it is possible but extremely unlikely that the plaintiff will persuade the court to recognise a new tort on the facts alleged by him (a feat nevertheless achieved by the plaintiff in *Thomas* v. *N.U.M.* (1985) *infra*, p. 30). Even if the plaintiff's allegations do disclose a cause of action in tort, the defendant may be able to plead a defence to that tort which if established will enable him to succeed. Reliance on a defence constitutes in effect an admission that the allegations of the plaintiff show prima facie the commission of a tort by the defendant and requires the proof by the defendant of other facts which give him an excuse in law. The defendant accordingly has the legal burden of proving on the balance of probabilities the facts necessary to establish the defence. A defence of this sort (called confession and avoidance and on which the defendant has the legal burden of proof) may be pleaded in the alternative to an outright denial of the plaintiff's allegations (called a traverse, and on which the defendant clearly does not have the burden of proof).

Jury trials are now rare in actions in tort. They can be demanded by either party in actions for libel, slander, malicious prosecution, or false imprisonment, and by the defendant when the action against him contains an allegation of fraud. In all these cases the court may refuse jury trial if it considers that the trial will involve a prolonged examination of documents or accounts or a scientific or local investigation. In all other cases the court has a discretion to order trial by jury but this discretion is exercised sparingly especially in actions for personal injury. In the case of these the Court of Appeal in *Ward* v. *James* (1966) laid down that there must be special circumstances before the court may order jury trial. The reason for this was the fear of excessive awards of damages against defendants on the ground that they were insured. *Ward* v. *James* also laid down as a general rule that the discretion to order jury trial is not a completely unfettered discretion but is one that must be exercised judicially. As a result of this case, jury trial in actions of tort, already uncommon, will become increasingly so, a result strengthened by the enactment of section 69(3) of the Administration of Justice Act 1981 which has further emphasised the leaning against jury trials in actions for personal injury which judges ought to show in exercising their discretion (*H.* v. *Ministry of Defence*, *The Daily Telegraph*, April 1, 1991).

FAULT AND COMPENSATION

In the majority of cases under English law, the plaintiff must show fault on the part of the defendant or someone for whose acts the defendant is in law responsible. Despite the advent of the age of machinery, and such inherently dangerous objects as industrial plant and high-speed locomotives, the courts have not adopted the view that those who carry on enterprises or activities in which such machinery plays a part should be liable without fault for the damage they cause. "Our law," said Scott L.J. in *Read* v. *Lyons* (1945, in the Court of Appeal), "is concerned not with [the defendant's] activities but with [his] acts." This rejection of enterprise or activity liability seems doubly unfortunate. First, it discards the justice of holding liable those who, though no fault can be proved against them in the individual case, have increased the risk of injuries by carrying on a certain activity. Secondly, the enterprise is normally in a better position than the victim to absorb the loss suffered by having to pay damages, either by passing it on to the public in the form of prices it charges for its product or by insuring against it. *Read* v. *Lyons* is significant in this respect. In it, the House of Lords rejected an attempt to argue a principle of strict liability for the carrying on of hazardous activities postulated on the basis of the rule of *Rylands* v. *Fletcher* (1868) which established that under certain conditions strict liability existed for the escape of dangerous things from the defendant's land. From the time of this decision, therefore, strict liability in the English law of tort could only exist in the logically unsatisfactory form of the rule in *Rylands* v. *Fletcher* itself, and in a few other unconnected instances.

Another problem which the law of tort has to face is that though liability in tort may be established, the means of the defendant may be insufficient to satisfy the judgment. Although no general rule of English law exists to avert this possibility, there are rules which ensure that in the large majority of tortious claims for personal injury the judgment will be satisfied. Under the provisions of various Road Traffic Acts the owner of a motor vehicle is compelled to insure against tortious liability to third parties. The master of a servant is at common law liable for torts committed by that servant in the course of his employment. An employer is compelled by the Employers' Liability (Compulsory Insurance) Act 1969 to insure himself against his liability for personal injury to his employees. These rules have the desirable effect of ensuring that in road and industrial accident cases, numerically the most important area of tort, the tortfeasor's liability will normally be met by a solvent person. These provisions do not cover the whole of tortious liability, and they are only applicable when tortious liability can be established.

The Royal Commission on Civil Liability and Compensation for Personal Injury was appointed in 1973 under the chairmanship of Lord Pearson. It published its report in 1978. Its terms of reference were: to consider to what extent, in what circumstances and by what means compensation should be payable in respect of death or personal injury (including antenatal injury) suffered by any person:

(a) in the course of employment;
(b) through the use of a motor vehicle or other means of transport;
(c) through the manufacture, supply or use of goods or services;
(d) on premises belonging to or occupied by another;

(e) otherwise through the act or omission of another where compensation is recoverable only on proof of fault or under the rules of strict liability, all this having regard to the cost and other implications of the arrangements for the recovery of compensation, whether by way of compulsory insurance or otherwise.

The Commission was appointed in the wake of the disaster caused by the drug thalidomide. Its function was clearly to review the whole of the present system of compensation in tort for personal injury. The tort system has been criticised on the ground that it is expensive to operate, that it compensates only a small proportion of accident victims, and that the difficulty of proving fault makes it an arbitrary process (see, for example, Atiyah, "Accidents, Compensation and the Law"; Elliott and Street, "Road Accidents"). To abolish the action in tort would have the effect of freeing financial resources which could be used for the compensation of all accident victims. The figures quoted in the Pearson Commission Report tend to confirm these criticisms. They show that the cost of obtaining tort compensation is considerably greater than that of administering the social security system; that only a very small proportion of persons injured in accidents recover tort compensation; that over 90 per cent. of tort payments are for less than £2,000 which presumably means that most tort actions are brought for pain and suffering over a fairly limited period, there being little in the way of residual disability affecting future earning power. The Commission, however, found itself unable, because of its terms of reference, to recommend abolition of the action in tort altogether in cases of personal injury. Instead it recommended a strengthening of the system of social security payments for the two main classes of accident victims under which the present scheme of compensation for industrial injuries would be improved and extended to the victims of road accidents. The Commission recommended a limited increase in the amount of strict liability in tort, by the introduction of strict liability for the manufacture of products, for medical experiments on volunteers producing severe injury, for vaccine damage caused by authorised vaccinations, and for certain "extra-hazardous" activities. Despite their recommendation that the action in tort should be retained, the Commission made two proposals which would markedly reduce its scope as a means of compensating minor injuries. The first is that damages for pain and suffering in the first three months after the injury should be abolished. The second is that there should be a total offset of social security benefits to the victim against damages in tort. Some parts of the Commission's recommendations have become law and are considered at the appropriate parts of this book. Its recommendations on damages for personal injury are considered in Chapter 20.

There is interesting evidence from New Zealand not available to the Pearson Commission about the actual working there of a no-fault compensation scheme. Such a scheme was introduced in New Zealand in 1972 and subjected to minor amendments in 1982. The scheme is a comprehensive one comprising all accidental injury, though excluding disease other than occupational diseases. The common law action in tort is abolished. Benefits are provided mainly in the form of replacement of lost earnings (generally at 80 per cent. of the earning rate). Lump sums are provided but are low, $17,000 being the maximum payable in the case of permanent disability and this amount is not indexed for inflation. In 1982 none of the major interest groups, including employers, and employees, trade unions and the legal profession, supported a reversion to the tort system in their submissions to the Parliamentary Committee which was considering changes.

2. INTENTIONAL INTERFERENCE WITH THE PERSON

In this chapter the law concerning intentional interferences by the defendant with the plaintiff's person will be considered. The law on this subject is still to some extent bound up with the former distinction between the action of trespass and that of case. It is therefore necessary as a preliminary matter to consider the distinction between the two.

TRESPASS AND CASE

Trespass and case were forms of action by which a claim for injury or damage wrongfully inflicted on the plaintiff by the defendant could be made. The form of action in trespass always contained an allegation of the use of force by the defendant (*vi et armis et contra pacem regis*) though that was often a fiction. An action in case required merely a statement of the facts upon which the plaintiff relied to show that the defendant was responsible for his injury. The main difference between the two was that trespass lay where the injury to the plaintiff arose directly from the defendant's positive act, while an action in case was actionable where it arose indirectly or consequentially, whether from his act or omission to act. For example, if the defendant threw a log into the highway, striking the plaintiff, trespass was the appropriate action; if the log lay in the highway and the plaintiff rode his horse into it, the proper action was case. Under the old system of

13

pleading it was essential to choose the correct form of action. A plaintiff who could establish facts which would justify the bringing of trespass would therefore be non-suited if he relied on case, and vice versa. This might cause problems since it was not always easy to classify the claim. In the well-known case of *Scott* v. *Shepherd* (1773) the defendant threw a lighted squib into a crowded market-place. The squib was thrown on by two persons acting in preservation of person or property and then exploded, putting out the plaintiff's eye. The majority of the court, in holding the defendant liable, found that the action was correctly brought as one of trespass. Blackstone J. dissented on the ground that the intervening acts of the two other persons determined that the action should have been brought in case.

The distinction between trespass and case was not of significance merely from the point of view of procedure. Trespass was actionable *per se*, that is on proof of bodily contact without proof of actual physical injury or damage; case needed such proof. No particular state of mind on the part of the defendant is associated with either trespass or case. Trespass may have been originally a tort of strict liability. However, the most likely interpretation of the cases up to the nineteenth century is that the plaintiff succeeded by proving the commission of a trespassory act by the defendant unless the latter succeeded in showing that that act was committed without any fault on his part, *i.e.* that his act was involuntary or that he neither intended the interference with the plaintiff's person or property nor was negligent in producing it (the so-called defence of inevitable accident—see *Weaver* v. *Ward* (1617)). Case generally required proof of fault in the form of intentional or negligent wrongdoing on the defendant's part but occasionally might lie in circumstances where liability was strict. Trespass retained its requirement of a positive act and could not be committed by omission. Case was available in certain circum-stances in relation to an omission to act.

TRESPASS AND NEGLIGENCE

In the nineteenth century legislation was passed abolishing the forms of action and allowing a plaintiff merely to recite the facts of his case in his statement of claim. Provided these facts disclosed a cause of action, the plaintiff could no longer lose by making an incorrect choice of the form of action. From then on the term "trespass" came to be used in a substantive rather than a procedural sense; to describe a tort, rather than the form of action for enforcing the tort. There have been two important developments in the tort of trespass since that time. The first is that a number of cases have decided that trespass with the possible exception of trespass to land is no longer, if it ever was, a tort of strict liability (decided for trespass to the person by *Stanley* v. *Powell* (1891); for trespass to chattels by *National Coal Board* v. *Evans* (1951). Furthermore, it has been decided that the onus of proof is upon the plaintiff to show that the defendant either intended the trespass or was negligent in committing it, rather than upon the defendant to show that he acted without fault. In *Fowler* v. *Lanning* (1959) the plaintiff in his statement of claim alleged that "the defendant shot the plaintiff." It was held that the fact stated did not disclose a cause of action. The plaintiff also needed to allege (and therefore to prove) that the defendant shot him either intentionally or negligently.

The second development concerns the relationship between trespass and negligence. The frequency of actions in which negligence is the gist of the action, due to the increased mechanisation and industrialisation of society and the consequent multiplication of cases of personal injury caused by negligence, has led to the idea of negligence as a tort in itself, and not simply as a means of committing trespass or case. The tort of negligence has thus taken over much of the former area of trespass, namely, where it lay for personal injuries caused negligently though directly. Although trespass has been recognised as theoretically still available in such cases as the causing of personal injuries through the negligent driving of a motor vehicle, in practice such actions have usually been described as actions of negligence. Furthermore, the phrase "trespass to the person" has been more commonly applied to intentional invasions of the interest in bodily security such as assault, battery, and false imprisonment. In *Letang* v. *Cooper* (1965) this distinction gained Court of Appeal approval. The plaintiff was sunbathing in the car-park of a hotel. The defendant drove his car over her legs injuring her. Over three years later the plaintiff sued the defendant in negligence and trespass. There was no doubt that the claim in negligence was barred by the lapse of over three years after the accident under section 2(1) of the Law Reform (Limitations of Actions etc.) Act 1954 (now replaced), which set up a three-year limitation period on actions for negligence, nuisance, or breach of duty, when the plaintiff had suffered personal injuries. The question in the action was whether the plaintiff's action in trespass, to which a six-year limitation period under a different Act applied, was also barred under this subsection.

The Court of Appeal found that it was barred on the ground that: (1) it was an action for breach of duty within the meaning of the subsection; (2) it was also an action for negligence within the meaning of the subsection. For present purposes only the second *ratio decidendi* is of importance. Lord Denning M.R. (with whom Danckwerts L.J. agreed) said that it was no longer possible to sue in trespass where negligent conduct was relied on by the plaintiff. The old distinction between trespass and case had been replaced by a distinction between trespass, which lay for intentional, direct invasions of the plaintiff's interest and which was actionable *per se*, and negligence, which lay for all negligent invasions direct or indirect and which was actionable only upon proof of actual injury or damage. Diplock L.J. held that though it was possible to call an action based on negligent, direct invasion, trespass, that did not change the nature of the cause of action which was an action for the tort of negligence with its requirement that there should be a duty of care on the part of the defendant and that actual damage needed to be shown. That action, also, was an action for negligence within the meaning of section 2(1) of the Law Reform (Limitation of Actions) Act 1954 since the law looked to the substance rather than to the form.

There is nothing to choose between the views of Lord Denning and Diplock L.J. here. On the latter's view, the plaintiff can gain no advantage from suing in trespass rather than negligence even though it may still be possible for him to do so where a direct invasion is in question. Despite some initial academic protest at the liberties the judgments in the Court of Appeal take with the former law, there have been no later decisions indicating disapproval (although we shall see in Chapter 4 that trespass to land remains a tort which may be committed by negligence).

The old forms of action of trespass and case are the progenitors of all the torts that are covered in this book. The three forms of trespass, trespass to the person, to chattels and to land, cover the case of intentional, direct interferences with the plaintiff's person or his tangible property. All other torts are descendants of the action on the case.

TRESPASS TO THE PERSON

In the remainder of this chapter, various forms of intentional interference with the person will be considered. Of these, battery, assault, and false imprisonment are forms of trespass. Liability under the *Bird* v. *Holbrook* (1828) principle (*infra*, p. 29) is on the other hand derived from the action on the case.

Assault and battery are both crimes as well as torts. It does not appear that the criminal law on what constitutes an assault or a battery differs from the civil, with the exception that it is certain that neither crime can be committed negligently and that the law relating to consent and other defences is different. Consequently many of the relevant precedents in civil actions of assault or battery are decisions in criminal cases.

Battery

Where the defendant, intending this result, does an act which directly and physically affects the person of the plaintiff, he commits battery.

It will be noticed that battery is here defined as an intentional tort, in line with the decision of the Court of Appeal in *Letang* v. *Cooper* (1965).

Intention in battery

Battery like other forms of trespass does not require an intention to commit a battery, merely an intention to commit the requisite interference with the plaintiff's person. Mistake of fact or law is in general no defence, however reasonable the mistake. So battery may operate as a tort of strict liability (as also may the other forms of trespass to the person, *i.e.* assault and false imprisonment).

Hostility

Prior to the case of *Wilson* v. *Pringle* (1986) it was thought that any intentional contact with the person of the plaintiff was prima facie a battery, though this was subject to a broad exception in the case of those contacts which were part and parcel of everyday life, for example, jostling in a street crowd, or touching another person in order to gain his attention (to which contacts the plaintiff is conclusively deemed to consent as a matter of law). *Wilson* v. *Pringle* adds the requirement that the touching be hostile. In that case the defendant schoolboy had pulled a sports bag from the shoulder of the plaintiff, another schoolboy, in the course of what the defendant alleged was horseplay. The plaintiff fell and suffered an injury to his hip. The Court of Appeal held that this was not battery unless the contact with the plaintiff's person was hostile. The requirement of hostility sits uneasily with previous case law, more particularly with *Collins* v. *Wilcock* (1984) upon which, and in particular the judgment of Goff L.J., the Court of Appeal relied. In Collins it was held that a police officer, who stopped an accused person by taking hold of her arm but did not arrest her, committed battery. Again, it has always been thought to be the law that a surgeon who exceeds the plaintiff's consent in the course of an operation commits battery and this has recently been confirmed in *T.* v. *T.* (1988) where the court refused to follow *Wilson* v. *Pringle* as being inconsistent with *Collins* v. *Wilcock*. *Wilson* v. *Pringle* may rest on the inarticulated premise that the defendant should not be made to pay for the unforeseeable consequences of a relatively innocent act, but the question of remoteness of damage was not an issue in the case itself and the law affecting remoteness of damage in battery has not been authoritatively settled (*infra*, this chapter).

The battery need not be forcible but must be direct

Battery can be committed without the use of force, though under *Wilson* v. *Pringle* the contact with the plaintiff's person must be hostile. But the requirement of directness excludes from the category of battery many intentional inflictions of physical harm upon another person. Thus it is not battery to poison another's drink, or to dig a hole intending another to fall into it, even though in each case the intended harm occurs. These cases are, however, clearly remediable by action based on the principle of *Bird* v. *Holbrook* (1828) (*infra*, p. 29).

Method of commission of battery

The battery need not be committed with the person of the defendant; it is battery to strike the plaintiff by throwing a stone at him. Equally provided the force used has its effect against the person of the plaintiff, it is not necessary that it should be aimed against his person, though to satisfy the definition of battery given above, the effect on the plaintiff's person must be intended by the defendant. For instance, it would be battery to throw over the chair in which the plaintiff is sitting. Equally it is probably sufficiently direct to constitute battery to remove the chair on which the plaintiff is about to sit, or to cut the rope up which he is climbing. There seems no less reason to find a battery where the plaintiff has used the force of gravity than where he has used the force of the explosive contained inside a gun.

A positive act by the defendant is needed for the commission of a battery. Trespass could not be committed by an omission to act. In *Fagan* v. *Metropolitan Police Commissioner* (1969) the defendant accidentally drove his car on to the foot of a police constable. He then delayed in reversing the car, thus preventing the constable from escaping, and knowing that his foot was trapped. The majority of the court held the accused liable for criminal assault, but Bridge J. dissented on the ground that at the time the accused did the act complained of, he had no *mens rea*, and after he had formed the *mens rea*, he did not act. The decision seems justifiable, however, on the ground that at the time the accused formed a wrongful intention, the effects of his act in the form of physical contact with the constable's person still persisted (though the majority in the case found the accused liable on the basis of a continuing act, a difficult reason to support).

One situation that may cause difficulty arises where A intends to commit battery against B, but instead and by mistake strikes C. In criminal law, it appears that a battery is committed (in *R.* v. *Latimer* (1886) it was held that in similar circumstances the crime of malicious wounding was committed by the accused). In America such conduct is regarded as tortious on the ground that A's wrongful intent towards B is transferred to C. But it is doubtful whether English courts should adopt this doctrine. In every case, it appears, A's conduct will be negligent towards C. The doctrine of transferred intent, though necessary in criminal law because of the absence of a general principle of criminal liability for negligence, is unnecessary in tort.

Assault

A person commits assault if he intentionally and directly causes the plaintiff to apprehend that he is going to commit a battery against the plaintiff. As in the case of battery, it is suggested that after *Letang* v. *Cooper* (1965) assault can only be committed intentionally. The interest protected by assault, that is, freedom from apprehension of a battery, is unusual. The reason for the existence of a tort of assault separate from battery is that, where two persons have fought, the law may regard the aggressor as a tortfeasor and the other as acting in self-defence, even though the aggressor does not succeed in landing the first blow.

Can assault be committed verbally?

In *Meade's Case* (1823) which was a criminal prosecution for murder, it was said, "no words or singing are equivalent to an assault." It seems unsatisfactory to exclude the mere threat as a means of committing assault, on the basis of this flimsy *obiter dictum*, although if assault by threat is held actionable it would be a question of fact in each case whether the defendant intends to implement the threat. In *Read* v. *Coker* (1853) the defendant, who had paid rent on behalf of the plaintiff, visited the plaintiff with some of his workmen, and threatened the plaintiff with physical violence in order to make him leave the premises. The workmen clustered round the plaintiff and committed such threatening actions as tucking up their sleeves and aprons. This was held to be an assault, but in the judgment of Jervis C.J. there is no indication that the threat by itself was not enough. He said, "There was a threat of violence, exhibiting an intention to assault, and a present ability to carry the threat into execution." In *Barton* v. *Armstrong* (1969) the court refused to strike out as revealing no cause of action, an action for assault in relation to threats of violence over the telephone, on the ground that such threats might give rise to a sufficiently immediate apprehension of their implementation. If the plaintiff has acted on the threats to his loss, there may be an action for intimidation in this case (*infra*) but there seems no good reason why the threat should not be actionable in the absence of that.

Words may qualify or explain an otherwise threatening action, so as to render it no assault. In *Tuberville* v. *Savage* (1669), the defendant did not commit assault by placing his hand on his sword in the plaintiff's presence, because he said the words, "If it were not assize-time, I would not take such language from you." Where, on the other hand, the words take the form of a conditional threat ("Your money or your life"), this seemingly constitutes assault, at least where it appears there is a present intention to carry the threat into execution. There is New Zealand authority for this in *Police* v. *Greaves* (1964). In that case the accused's threat of committing a knife attack on certain policemen if they should approach nearer to him, or did not leave his premises immediately, was held to be an assault.

Must the defendant intend to commit battery?

The old view of assault was that it was an incomplete battery. The question arose, if the defendant did not intend to commit battery, but nevertheless induced a belief in the plaintiff's mind that he was about to do so, would this amount to assault? The usual example is that of the defendant who points an unloaded gun at the plaintiff. This behaviour complies with the definition of assault given above, and in principle it seems that it ought to amount to assault. It is therefore to be hoped that a criminal case, *R.* v. *St. George* (1840) which holds it to be assault, should be preferred to a civil case, *Blake* v. *Barnard* (1840) which holds it not to be. The analogy between assault and battery can, it seems, be overstated. Battery, for instance, can take place without prior apprehension of harm by the plaintiff, as, for example, where he is struck from behind. If battery is not necessarily a completed assault, there is no reason why assault should necessarily be an inchoate battery. (Australian authority supports *R.* v. *St. George—McLelland* v. *Symons* (1951)).

What must the plaintiff apprehend?

Suppose the plaintiff to be an unusually timorous person in whom the defendant has induced the fear of an imminent battery, though a reasonable man would not have feared in such circumstances. Does the defendant commit assault? The better view here appears to be that the test is based on the subjective intention of both parties—there is an assault if the defendant intends to create in the plaintiff fear of the commission of a battery, whether or not the defendant knows of the plaintiff's timorousness, and the plaintiff actually has this fear. In other words the reasonableness or otherwise of the plaintiff's apprehension is irrelevant. It is also clear that, provided the plaintiff apprehends the immediate commission of a battery, it does not matter that the defendant does not have the power to carry it out (*Stephens* v. *Myers* (1830)—defendant who approached plaintiff with raised fist but was stopped well short of the plaintiff was held liable in assault). In *Smith* v. *Superintendent of Woking* (1983) 76 C.A.R. 234 the defendant was convicted of a criminal assault when he entered the grounds of a private house and appeared at the window of a bed-sitting room for a few seconds, seriously frightening its occupant, who was getting ready for bed. The conviction is supportable on the ground that the defendant intentionally aroused apprehension and that apprehension could only have been of an immediate act of violence.

Clearly, however, the plaintiff must apprehend a battery. So it is not assault to stand still at the door to a room barring the plaintiff's entry (*Innes* v. *Wylie* (1844)). It would also not be assault if the defendant falsely cried, "Fire!" in a crowded theatre (*cf.* the facts of *R.* v. *Martin* (1881)). If, on the other hand, the plaintiff apprehends an injury to himself, without knowing the circumstances that would cause the injury if it occurs to be a battery, then it seems likely that assault is committed (for example, the plaintiff sees a missile approaching him but does not know it has been thrown by the defendant).

Damages in assault and battery

Both torts, being forms of trespass are actionable *per se*. Where the defendant's act has caused no damage to the plaintiff, the plaintiff may in fact get only nominal damages. But it is quite possible for the court to give high damages in such a case because, the tort being actionable *per se*, damages are at large and the court may award aggravated damages because of the injury to the plaintiff's feelings arising from the circumstances of the tort's commission. In a suitable case an additional award of exemplary damages might also be made. So in *Loudon* v. *Ryder* (1953) the defendant entered the plaintiff's flat through a window. He then beat the plaintiff on her shoulders and dragged her downstairs but she sustained no serious injury. The following damages were awarded: £1500 for the trespass; £1000 for the assault and battery; £3000 as exemplary damages.

A large component of the award made here for trespass, assault and battery was aggravated damages. Exemplary damages could not now be awarded on these facts (see the judgment of Lord Devlin in *Rookes* v. *Barnard* (1964). For the power to award aggravated and exemplary damages generally, see p. 411 *et seq.*).

INJUNCTION

An injunction may be awarded against the commission of a future assault and battery (*Egan* v. *Egan* (1975)).

Remoteness of damage in trespass to the person

The rule determining whether damage suffered as a result of the trespass is too remote is not authoritatively settled for trespass to the person, nor indeed for other forms of trespass. The requirement of *The Wagon Mound* (No. 1) that the damage must be foreseeable may be limited to torts of negligence and may not extend to intentional wrongdoing. Authority prior to *The Wagon Mound* decision suggested that the defendant was liable for all the direct consequences of the trespass. In *Nash* v. *Sheen* (1953) the defendant, a ladies hairdresser, applied a tone-rinse to the plaintiff's hair without her consent. He was held liable for a rash that the tone-rinse caused to the plaintiff's scalp even though this was not reasonably foreseeable. That decision was made at a time when *Re Polemis* (1921) laid down a different rule in general for remoteness of damage than foreseeability, the test of direct consequences. There is, however, Canadian authority (post *Wagon Mound* (*No. 1*) which effectively removed *Re Polemis*) in *Bettel* v. *Yim* (1978) and *Allen* v. *Mount Sinai Hospital* (1980) that the defendant is liable for all the direct consequences of an intended battery, whether these are intended or reasonably foreseeable or not. English law, however, with its adoption of the general principle that liability should not extend beyond those consequences for which the defendant may be adjudged at fault may not follow these cases.

FALSE IMPRISONMENT

This tort is committed by one who intentionally and directly places a total restraint upon the liberty of the plaintiff. It is a form of trespass to the person, and is actionable *per se*.

Intention and directness

The tort is defined to exclude negligent imprisonment of another person. This is a reflection of the views of the Court of Appeal in *Letang* v. *Cooper* (1965). There is also a requirement that the tort should be committed directly. This is of course a requirement of trespass to the person. Where for either reason the plaintiff cannot establish false imprisonment, an action in negligence may still be available. Thus in *Sayers* v. *Harlow U.D.C.* (1958) the plaintiff became imprisoned inside the defendants' toilet because of the negligent maintenance of the door lock by the defendants' servants. In trying to climb out of the lavatory, she fell and was injured. She recovered damages from the defendants because it was a reasonable act on her part to attempt to escape from the situation in which the defendants by their negligence had placed her. An action for false imprisonment would not have been available because there was no direct act of imprisonment. False imprisonment may operate as a tort of strict liability where the defendant intentionally and wrongfully imprisons the plaintiff, unreasonably believing in his right to do so.

Where the plaintiff has been imprisoned by the negligence of the defendant, but has suffered no damage, it seems that he has no remedy if we define false imprisonment to exclude negligence since negligence is actionable only upon proof of damage. This may cause hardship to a person who has suffered a fairly lengthy period of imprisonment. Even if such a person has suffered financial loss, for example, in the form of loss of wages, it seems that he could not recover these in an action of negligence since negligence will not lie for purely pecuniary loss. The solution may be to regard the period of imprisonment itself, if it is not of merely trivial duration as damage, loss of wages being then recoverable as consequential loss. Some support for this exists in the case of *De Freville* v. *Dill* (1927). The defendant, a doctor, negligently certified the plaintiff to be insane, as a result of which she was detained in a lunatic asylum for two days. The action for false imprisonment was not available because the plaintiff had not been directly imprisoned by the defendant. Nevertheless, the plaintiff's action succeeded and she recovered £50 in damages. Since no damage other than the actual detention was suffered, the court seem to have regarded this as sufficient damage to support the action. The action was said to be on the case, but since it was based on negligence, the case may seem authority for a general right of recovery in the tort of negligence for being imprisoned. It is noticeable that the actual damage necessary to sustain an action for malicious prosecution includes the imprisonment of the plaintiff. At the same time there is a considerable difference between being arrested as a result of malicious prosecution, or locked up in a lunatic asylum, and merely being negligently imprisoned.

The act of imprisonment

There must be a total restraint placed upon the plaintiff's freedom of action. In *Bird* v. *Jones* (1845) the defendant closed off the public footpath over one side of Hammersmith Bridge. The plaintiff, wishing to use the footpath, was prevented by the defendant. In the plaintiff's action one of the questions it was necessary to decide was whether the defendant's act amounted to a false imprisonment. The court held that it did not since the defendant had not placed a total restraint on the plaintiff (the blocking-off of part of the public highway might well be a public nuisance for which the plaintiff could bring an action in tort if he could show special damage arising from it).

Provided the area of restraint is total, it does not seem to matter that it is very large. False imprisonment on a large estate or in a town seems possible. But there must be limits to this. A wrongful deportation order which has the effect of excluding the deportee from a particular country could hardly be regarded as false imprisonment in the rest of the world. There has been a difference of opinion between the Court of Appeal and the Divisional Court as to the circumstances in which a person already lawfully imprisoned in a prison may be regarded as falsely imprisoned (*Wheldon* v. *Home Office* [1990] A.C.; *R.* v. *Deputy Governor of Parkhurst Prison* [1990] D.C.) There was agreement that imprisonment under intolerable conditions would amount to false imprisonment. The Court of Appeal required knowledge of those conditions by the defendant, but the Divisional Court did not (the latter view seems correct since false imprisonment is a tort of strict liability). The Court of Appeal thought that a deprivation of the prisoner's residual liberty (*i.e.* where the type of imprisonment was not justified by prison regulations) would constitute false imprisonment whereas the Divisional Court thought that a defence would exist here under section 12 of the Prisons Act 1952. There is of course false imprisonment where a prisoner is detained beyond the legal date for his release (*Cowell* v. *Corrective Services Commissioner* (1989)).

Despite the fact that false imprisonment is a form of trespass to the person, it does not require a physical act aimed against the person of the plaintiff. Imprisonment by show of authority is sufficient, for example, arrest by a police-constable or restraint by persuasion used by a Commissioner of Lunacy to prevent the plaintiff, whom he believed to be insane, from leaving the room (see *Harnett* v. *Bond* (1925)).

Reasonable escape

There is no false imprisonment if a reasonable escape route is available to the plaintiff. In *Wright* v. *Wilson* (1699) false imprisonment was not committed where the plaintiff could escape by trespassing on the land of a third party.

What is a reasonable escape route depends upon the circumstances of the case. The mere fact that the plaintiff is *able* to take advantage of an escape route does not mean that he should do so. An expert swimmer might be justified in not taking advantage of an escape route offered by swimming if he thought that release by other means would soon become available.

Although an escape route which involves a risk of injury to the plaintiff may be regarded as unreasonable for the purpose of establishing the tort of false imprisonment, it appears that an imprisoned person may not have acted unreasonably in taking that means of escape and suffering injury as a result. Thus in *Sayers* v. *Harlow U.D.C.* (1958) (*supra*) though it was regarded as reasonable, and therefore not a "new cause" for the plaintiff to attempt to escape from a lavatory in which she was locked by climbing over the wall, it seems likely that such an escape route would not have been held a reasonable one for the purpose of preventing her detention from amounting to false imprisonment. A person locked by the defendant in a room from which the only possibility of escape is a hazardous climb down a drain-pipe, is falsely imprisoned, and yet if he risks the climb and suffers injury, it seems that he might be held to have acted reasonably and therefore recover damages from the defendant. But whether he has acted reasonably depends upon a number of factors, in particular the possible duration of his detention and the degree of risk involved in trying to escape.

False imprisonment by omission to act

In *Herd* v. *Weardale Steel, Coal and Coke Co.* (1915) the plaintiff miners refused to complete their shift because they considered the work to be dangerous. The defendants' manager refused for some time to allow the lift to be used to take the men up the lift-shaft. The defendants were not in breach of contract because there was no obligation to remove men from the mine except at certain times.

The House of Lords held that this did not amount to false imprisonment since the defendants had committed no positive act of detention upon the plaintiffs (they clearly consented to being taken down to the lift originally) and the manager's refusal to work the lift at a time not required by the contract of employment did not amount to false imprisonment. The doctrine of *volenti non fit injuria* was relied on by Viscount Haldane as the main ground for his decision. From this it seems to follow that a failure to release the miners at the contractually agreed time would have amounted to false imprisonment and that the ratio of the case does not therefore exclude liability for omission to act. Even so, the decision in the case does not seem satisfactory, since, although the miners consented to their initial imprisonment and may have been contractually bound to complete the shift, it seems wrong to infer from the latter point a consent on their part to being imprisoned for the duration of the shift. (For a convincing criticism of the *Herd* decision, which he thinks is wrongly decided, see Glanville Williams, "Justice, Equity and the Law," *Essays in Tribute to G. W. Keeton*, p. 47).

What interest does this tort protect?

Although the obvious answer to this question appears to be, the interest in freedom, there is some force in the idea that it is the plaintiff's belief in his freedom that is protected. If the defendant informs the plaintiff that he is to be confined to his house, and that armed guards are placed outside the house with instructions to shoot the plaintiff if he attempts to leave, this appears to be false imprisonment even if no armed guards are present. Clearly, also, a wrongful arrest may be constituted by mere show of wrongful authority to make the arrest—there is no need for an actual restraint to be placed on the plaintiff's person.

More difficult is the case where the plaintiff does not know that he is imprisoned. In *Meering* v. *Graham-White Aviation Co.* (1919) the plaintiff was being questioned at the defendants' factory in connection with certain thefts from the defendant company. He did not know of the presence outside the room in which he was being questioned of two works police who would have prevented his leaving if necessary. He succeeded in an action of false imprisonment against the defendants. It seems that *Meering's* case is correct in principle and that it may be supported on the ground advanced by Atkin L.J. in his judgment in the case that an actual imprisonment may damage the plaintiff's reputation or cause him other loss. *Meering's* case was approved *obiter* by the House of Lords in *Murray* v. *Ministry of Defence* (1988). Damages have been awarded in false imprisonment where the imprisonment injures reputation (*Walter* v. *Alltools* (1944)) or has caused the plaintiff business loss (*Childs* v. *Lewis* (1924)—plaintiff forced to resign from board of directors by his co-directors).

Justification of imprisonment

It is clear that it is not in every case in which one person detains or imprisons another that such detention is wrongful. The detention may be justified because of a lawful arrest, or because there may have been a consent to the detention by the person detained.

There is, however, no power to arrest for a purely civil offence, for example the non-payment of a debt (*Sunbolf* v. *Alford* (1838)—defendant landlord committed false imprisonment by detaining guest for non-payment of his bill). The action was in fact brought for battery. The defendant innkeeper had forcibly removed the plaintiff lodger's coat in order to hold it as security for an unpaid bill. He was held liable. Clearly an action for false imprisonment would have lain had the plaintiff himself been detained. The case of *Robinson* v. *Balmain New Ferry Co.* (1910) does not conflict with this principle—the defendant's forcible refusal to allow the plaintiff through the turnstile on its wharf unless he paid a penny was not false imprisonment since the plaintiff was attempting to leave the wharf by the exit on the side he had entered and in the words of the Privy Council "there is no law requiring the defendants to make the exit from their premises gratuitous to people who come upon a definite contract which involves their leaving by another way." Since the "other way" merely involved a 20-minute wait for a ferry-boat to arrive, and since no penny was payable on exit at the other side, the case is an illustration of the principle stated earlier that the restraint must be total.

INTENTIONALLY CAUSING PHYSICAL HARM

In *Bird* v. *Holbrook* (1828) a trespasser succeeded in an action on the case against an occupier of land who had set a spring-gun on his land and thus caused injury to the trespasser. The principle underlying the case must have been liability for intentionally causing injury—there could have been no question of liability for mere negligence towards a trespasser. The principle the case establishes may be stated as one of liability for the intentional, indirect infliction of physical harm upon the person of the plaintiff. Since the tort is not trespass, actual injury must be proved as part of the cause of action.

A similar principle was applied in *Wilkinson* v. *Downton* (1897). The defendant, as a joke, told the plaintiff falsely that her husband had been seriously injured in an accident and that she was to take a cab with two pillows to fetch him home. The plaintiff suffered severe nervous shock as a result. The defendant was held liable under a principle which Wright J. thought to be that where the defendant has wilfully done an act calculated to cause physical harm to the plaintiff, and in fact causes physical harm, the plaintiff has a good cause of action. Wright J. went on to say: "This wilful iniuria (*injury*) is in law malicious, although no malicious purpose to cause the harm which was caused nor any motive of spite is imputed to the defendant."

The principle on which the case was decided gives rise to difficulty. The main trouble is with the words "calculated to cause." If these words mean no more than that harm was foreseeably likely as a result of the act or statement, there is great difficulty in distinguishing the *Wilkinson* v. *Downton* (1897) principle from negligence. If the words mean more than foreseeable, such as certain or substantially certain, there is difficulty with the case itself since nervous shock, as distinct from mental distress, though a foreseeable result of the news imparted to the plaintiff, was hardly a certain or a substantially certain result. Only if the case is interpreted in this way, however, does it seem that the principle can have a separate existence independent of the tort of negligence.

It is clear that the law must impose liability for the intentional, non-trespassory infliction of personal injury, *i.e.* the *Bird* v. *Holbrook* situation. It is also clear, however, that with the present day development of the tort of negligence, there is no need for a principle of liability for foreseeable harm of the type that Wright J.'s judgment envisages. The principle may have, however, a continuing importance in relation to statements made by the defendant since it is still the law that in general there is no liability in negligence for statements which foreseeably produce nervous shock (*infra*, p. 129 *et seq.*). Even so, the principle as it relates to statements needs some reformulation to exclude conduct that is merely negligent. The defendant should be liable only if he has maliciously (*i.e.* dishonestly or without proper motive) made a statement to the plaintiff intending to frighten him in circumstances where it is foreseeable that the statement will cause shock and where the plaintiff actually suffers nervous shock. This formulation would also explain the only other English decision on the principle, *Janvier* v. *Sweeney* (1918) in which the plaintiff recovered damages from the defendants for nervous shock she suffered when the defendants told her a false story that she was wanted by the police because of her correspondence with a German spy.

English law has at the moment no equivalent of the American liability in tort for inflicting distress through insulting behaviour, that liability having arisen by way of an extension of the *Wilkinson* v. *Downton* principle. *Thomas* v. *N.U.M.* (1985) held that pickets outside a colliery, who subjected other workers entering or leaving the colliery to verbal abuse, committed a tort analogous to private nuisance in the harassment of persons in the exercise of their lawful rights. The same tort would be committed by one who followed and verbally abused a pedestrian on the highway. The principle laid down confuses rights with privileges (or liberties). But it is not clear that, apart from this, it is wrong.

3. INTENTIONAL INTERFERENCE WITH CHATTELS

The term "chattel" is generally taken to mean all forms of tangible property not regarded as realty, including goods, money, cheques and other negotiable instruments and animals.

The law relating to interference with chattels is full of difficulties, many of them arising from its evolution from three different forms of action, trespass, detinue, and conversion. Although each of these actions had a different function, there was a great deal of overlapping between them, and particularly in the case of detinue and conversion it was often a moot point whether the rules of one tort or the other should be applied. Much of this uncertainty has been removed by the Torts (Interference with Goods) Act 1977. Section 2(1) abolishes the tort of detinue. Section 2(2) preserves the liability it embodied as conversion. Section 1 of the Act defines the torts of conversion, trespass to chattels, negligence or any other tort that results in damage to chattels or to an interest in them as wrongful interference. Wrongful interference is regulated by the rest of the Act. It seems an unfortunate omission that the common law remedy of the bailor against the bailee does not seem to fall within Section 1 and is therefore not regulated by the Act. The effect of the Act will be considered in the course of this chapter. It should be mentioned that although the Act refers to "goods," the more precise term "chattel" will be used in this book except when dealing with the Act's provisions.

31

There is no doubt that the person principally protected by these tortious remedies is the owner of the chattel. He will normally be the person with a right to the immediate possession of the chattel as is required in conversion. He will also normally, though less often, be the person in actual possession of it as required in trespass. But the emphasis of the law on possession rather than title means that many others besides the owner of the chattel can sue in tort for interference with the chattel. These may include the wrongful possessor, even the thief. The extent to which the law has gone in protecting actual possession may be derived from the fact that such possession is a means of establishing a right to the chattel's possession, so that the person deprived of it may bring conversion.

TRESPASS TO CHATTELS

The tort may be defined as an intentional and direct act of interference by the defendant with a chattel of which the plaintiff is in possession at the time of the interference.

Plaintiff's interest: possession

The defendant's act must disturb the plaintiff in his possession of the chattel. Therefore it will be necessary for the plaintiff to prove his possession in order to succeed in trespass. Generally, in order to prove possession of a chattel, it is necessary to prove that it is within one's control, either because it is in one's physical grasp or by other means. Thus a person continues to possess the goods that he has left in his house or car despite the fact that he himself is not in the house or car. It is also possible for possession to exist through another person; thus a master is in possession of goods held on his behalf by his servant.

It appears to be the law that there is no requirement in trespass that the possession should be lawful. Thus a thief may sue in trespass. But there must be some limits to this. The owner, or one with some genuine proprietary right over the chattel, cannot be successfully sued in trespass by a thief. This does not mean that an owner can never commit trespass to his own chattel. In *Rose* v. *Matt* (1951) the purchaser of some goods pledged his clock with the seller of the goods as security for a loan of the purchase price. Later he returned and took the clock away secretly. The owner of the clock was convicted of larceny. Since larceny (now called theft) was an offence which involved a trespassory taking, there is no doubt that the owner of the clock could have been sued in trespass by the pledgee.

Exceptions to the rule that the plaintiff must have possession

(i) Bailment is a transaction by which A, the bailor, transfers possession of a chattel to B, the bailee, both intending that at some future date, it should be transferred back to A. If no term is fixed for the bailment, it is said to be at will, and the bailor can demand possession from the bailee at any time. If a term is fixed, the bailor cannot demand possession from the bailee until the term has expired (or the bailment has otherwise been determined).

The bailor-at-will is allowed to sue for trespasses to his bailee's possession (*Lotan* v. *Cross* (1810); *Johnson* v. *Diprose* (1893)). The justification of this is normally expressed to be that the bailor here has a right to the immediate possession of the chattel, and in consequence may be regarded as being in actual possession through his bailee. (*Wilson* v. *Lombank* (1963)). The bailor for a term, who has no right to immediate possession of the chattel, cannot sue in trespass (*Gordon* v. *Harper* (1796)). It seems contrary to principle that the bailor can ever sue his bailee in trespass for doing an act contrary to the terms of the bailment, since there can be no question of the bailee infringing his own possession. There is support for this view in the judgment of Dixon J. in the Australian case of *Penfold's Wines Pty.* v. *Elliott* (1946), but in the English case of *Burnard* v. *Haggis* (1863) the court held that an act of the bailee which was not merely a wrongful performance of the bailment but went completely outside its terms was trespassory at the suit of the bailor. The case seems difficult to support.

(ii) The title of executors and administrators of estates relates back to the death of the deceased. This is the case with possession of chattels forming part of the estate. They are thus enabled to sue for trespass to such chattels committed before they actually take possession of the estate.

(iii) The owner of a franchise in wrecks has been allowed to sue in trespass one who seized a cask of whisky from the wreck (*Dunwich Corporation* v. *Sterry* (1831)).

(iv) A trustee may sue for trespass to chattels in the possession of a beneficiary.

Jus tertii

Jus tertii may now be a defence to trespass to chattels under section 8 of the Torts (Interference with Goods) Act 1977. Its effect is considered on p. 43.

Acts constituting trespass

The defendant's act need not dispossess the plaintiff. A mere moving of the chattel, called an asportation, is sufficient.

In *Kirk* v. *Gregory* (1876) the defendant, the sister-in-law of a person recently deceased, removed his jewellery from the room where he lay dead to another room in the house, in order to safeguard it. The jewellery was stolen by some unknown person. She was sued successfully in trespass by the executor of the estate, although the damages awarded against her were nominal, no doubt on the ground that the theft was not a foreseeable result of moving the chattel from one room to another. Clearly a dispossession of the plaintiff will amount to trespass. Mere touching of the chattel without dispossessing the plaintiff, asporting the chattel or damaging it is a trespass, though this sort of trespass is unlikely to produce litigation. Repeated, deliberate and unwarranted handling of a chattel might, however, move the plaintiff to sue for an injunction.

Defendant's act must directly cause the trespass

If the defendant has put poison down for the plaintiff's dog which the dog consumes, or placed a barrier across the highway into which the plaintiff drives his car, damaging the car, these acts will not amount to trespass because they are insufficiently direct (though in the Australian case of *Hutchins* v. *Maughan* (1947) it was thought to be sufficiently direct to feed an animal though not to lay baits. Yet there is clearly liability here under a similar principle to that underlying *Bird* v. *Holbrook* (1828), that is, for the intentional, indirect infliction by the defendant of actual damage upon a chattel.

As in battery, there is no need for the defendant himself to come into physical contact with the chattel. To throw a stone at a window and break it is therefore a trespass.

State of mind of defendant

It is suggested that after *Letang* v. *Cooper* (1965) this form of trespass requires an intentional act on the defendant's part. It is true that *Letang* v. *Cooper* (1965) concerned trespass to the person, but there seems no reason why this should be treated differently from trespass to chattels. The New Zealand case of *Everitt* v. *Martin* (1953) supports *Letang* v. *Cooper* in this respect (unintentional touching of car without damaging it was not trespass even if it was negligent).

National Coal Board v. *Evans* (1951) is authority for the proposition that in the absence of intention or negligence on the defendant's part, trespass to chattels will not lie. In that case the defendants' servant in the course of excavating the foundations of a building damaged the plaintiff's cable which was situated beneath the land surface. Because the presence of the cable could not have been foreseen by the servant, the defendants were held not liable in trespass.

It is assumed that after *Fowler* v. *Lanning* (1959) the burden of proving fault in this form of trespass rests on the plaintiff.

Damages in trespass to chattels

The successful plaintiff who has actually been permanently deprived of the chattel by the defendant is entitled to its full value (even where as in *Wilson* v. *Lombank* (1963) the plaintiff has no title to the chattel, and the defendant's trespass involves restoring the chattel to its true owner). It may be assumed that consequential loss due to the plaintiff's being deprived of the chattel will also be awarded in trespass. Where the defendant has not deprived the plaintiff of the chattel, but has damaged it, the damages awarded will be measured by the extent of the damage. This may be the cost of repairs or the loss in value of the chattel in the discretion of the court. Damages may be awarded for loss of profits caused by the loss of a profit-earning chattel (*The Liesbosch* (1932)), although there is a principle of uncertain extent (*The*

Llanover (1947)) which deprives the plaintiff of loss of profits where the plaintiff has already received compensation for loss of profits in the form of the increased valuation to be placed on a chattel which is profit-earning. As in other forms of trespass, there is the possibility of an award of aggravated damages in the appropriate case and also, though less likely, of exemplary damages.

CONVERSION

This tort requires an intentional dealing with a chattel by the defendant which constitutes a sufficiently serious infringement of the plaintiff's right to possess that chattel as to amount to a denial of it.

Conversion is both more various in its methods of commission than trespass, and more exacting in its requirement that the defendant's act must amount to a denial of the plaintiff's right to possess the chattel. Thus an infringement of actual possession is always trespass, but whether it is conversion depends upon the seriousness of the infringement. Conversion may, of course, take many forms other than an infringement of actual possession.

Conversion is the primary remedy by which proprietary interests in chattels are protected. Its reputation for difficulty owes something to this, since many disputes over title to chattels involve complex questions of commercial law. Although it is largely an accident of history that proprietary claims to chattels are protected by actions in tort, the tortious aspect of conversion causes it to have characteristics which a purely proprietary action would not possess. Thus the judgment in conversion is for the value of the chattel, rather than for the return of the chattel itself. Where the plaintiff is the owner of the chattel, his title in the chattel passes to the defendant when the latter satisfies a judgment obtained against him in conversion; for this reason conversion operates like a compulsory sale of the chattel to the defendant. Conversion is not unique in this respect. If a judgment is obtained in trespass for the whole value of the chattel, the same will apply. A further feature of conversion is that it lies against anyone who has had dealings with the chattel provided they are sufficient to amount to conversion; a purely proprietary action would lie only against the actual possessor of the chattel.

It must also not be overlooked that because the interest protected in conversion is the plaintiff's right to possess the chattel rather than his title to it, and because such right to possess may be established in other ways than by showing title to the chattel (*infra*), the interest protected is more extensive than a merely proprietary one.

The distinction between right to possession and title can be observed in those cases where the owner has no right to possess his own chattel. On the facts of *Rose* v. *Matt* (1951) (*supra*, p. 33) for instance, the pledgee could certainly have sued the owner of the clock in conversion. This is because the pledgor, as a bailor for a term, had lost the right to possess the clock for the period of the pledge.

Plaintiff's interest: concept of right to possession

The plaintiff in conversion must have a right to the chattel's immediate possession. The force of the word "immediate" is that it serves to exclude cases where the plaintiff has some right over the chattel which will entitle the plaintiff to its possession at some future date. For example, the bailor for a term of a chattel will eventually become entitled to its possession. Since, however, his right is to eventual rather than immediate possession, he cannot sue in conversion.

The plaintiff may prove his right to immediate possession of the chattel in one of two ways:

1. He may show that he was in actual possession of the chattel at the time of the defendant's act. The mere fact of possession peacefully held is usually enough to confer a right to possession as against one who disturbs it. But this will not be the case where the person interfering with possession is the true owner or some other person with a title to the chattel which entitles him to its immediate possession. In some cases, however, even the owner can commit conversion against one in actual possession (the facts of *Rose* v. *Matt* again present an example).
2. Where the plaintiff was not in possession at the time of the defendant's act, he must show that he has some right in relation to the chattel, entitling him to its immediate possession. Again ownership is the best example, with the

proviso that as already explained, the owner does not always have the right to immediate possession of his chattel. Holders of a special property in a chattel deriving from a transaction with its owner, such as bailees, pledgees and lienees also may bring conversion, though not against the owner himself unless, as in *Rose* v. *Matt*, he has lost the right to possession as against the plaintiff.

The following examples show the working of the law:

1. A bails a chattel for a term to B. It is stolen by C who sells it to D.
   Under the principles laid down above, A has no action in conversion against anyone. B can sue either C or D in conversion (the receipt by D under a sale amounts to conversion).
2. A buys a chattel from B. It is stolen from B by C. The buyer of a chattel normally acquires ownership once the contract of sale has been concluded (Sale of Goods Act 1979, section 18) and therefore has the right to possession of the chattel. But he only has this right if he has paid or tendered the purchase-price to the seller; until that time the seller has a lien over the chattel. In the above example B could sue C in conversion, since C has infringed his actual possession. A could sue C in conversion if he had paid or tendered the purchase price to B, since only then does B's lien over the chattel terminate, (*cf. Lord* v. *Price* (1874) where the facts were similar to this example).

Although the bailor for a term of a chattel has no right to its immediate possession during the term, at the end of the term or at the termination of the bailment, for example, where the bailee has committed an act repugnant to the bailment, the bailor acquires the right to the immediate possession of the chattel and can sue in conversion. If, for example, the bailee sells the chattel, the bailor may sue the bailee or the buyer in conversion. In a hire-purchase contract, for example, sale of the goods by the hire-purchaser will expose both himself and the buyer to an action for conversion. The doctrine of termination of the bailment contract by virtue of the bailee's inconsistent act may operate even though there is express provision in the contract for its determination as, for example, by notice given by the bailor (*Union Transport Finance* v. *British Car Auctions* (1978)). The Court of Appeal in that case was in agreement that it would require very clear language in the contract to exclude the bailor's common law rights. The case leaves uncertain the question of the effect of the doctrine upon rights in the contract upon which the bailor wishes to rely.

Apart from these specific cases, there appears to be a general rule that possession of a chattel confers a right to possession of that chattel as against a later possessor. The clearest example of the so-called possessory title is that of the finder, but the doctrine does not appear to be limited to this case. So if A is in possession of a chattel, he has a right to its possession, not only against B who steals it from him but as against C who buys it from B. (*Buckley* v. *Gross* (1863); *Russell* v. *Wilson* (1923)).

Right to possession of a wrongdoer

There appears to be no English authority upon whether a thief and other wrongful possessors can sue in conversion, but academic opinion leans in favour of their being able to do so where the thief is suing for an infringement of his actual possession, but less so where they are suing on the basis of a possessory title. In the Canadian case of *Bird* v. *Fort Francis* (1949) the plaintiff who had found money on land while trespassing on that land, was allowed to recover its value from the defendant in an action of conversion. The court thought that whether or not he committed larceny as a finder was immaterial, since a thief could sue in conversion on the basis of his possessory title where the defendant had no superior claim to possession.

Finder

The finder is a somewhat special case. In those cases in which he gets possession, he can sue in conversion for an infringement of his actual possession, or on the basis of his possessory title.

In *Armory* v. *Delamirie* (1721) a chimney-sweep's boy found a jewel and handed it to the apprentice of a goldsmith for valuation. The latter extracted the jewel from its setting and, handing back the setting to the boy, offered him 1½d. for the jewel. This offer the boy refused and later sued the goldsmith in conversion. This action was successful, the court ruling that "the finder has such a property as will enable him to keep it against all but the rightful owner."

This went further than was necessary for the decision. In the first place, by property the courts clearly meant possession. In *Armory* v. *Delamirie* (1721), for example, there was an infringement of an existing possession, which the plaintiff had not surrendered by handing over the jewel for valuation. Secondly, the finder's possession will not always avail against all but the owner; for example, a previous lawful possessor from whom the goods had been stolen previous to the find would have a title superior to the finder's. Finally the courts have limited the possession of finders to cases where the finding is on the surface of land. Thus in *Bridges* v. *Hawkesworth* (1851) the plaintiff, a customer in the defendant's shop, found some banknotes on the floor of the shop. He then handed them to the defendant for the purpose of trying to discover the owner, but the notes were never claimed. The plaintiff successfully sued in conversion for the notes. The facts clearly illustrate the underlying principles. The plaintiff had obtained possession of the notes by finding, and although he surrendered them under a bailment to the defendant for the purpose of discovering the owner, the bailment became determinable on demand by the bailor when it was clear that the owner would make no claim. The defendant, therefore, committed conversion by refusing the plaintiff's demand for the banknotes. To the same effect was *Hannah* v. *Peel* (1945), in which the Court of Appeal held that a soldier who found a brooch in a house which had been requisitioned by the military authorities was entitled to it as against the owner of the house.

On the other hand, where the chattel is attached to or lying beneath the surface of land, the possessor of land has possession of it. On this ground the possessor of land has been held entitled as against the finder to a pre-historic boat buried beneath the land surface (*Elwes* v. *Brigg Gas Co.* (1886), two rings lying in the mud at the bottom of a pool (*South Staffs. Water Co.* v. *Sharman* (1896)) and banknotes found by workmen in the wall safe of demolition premises (*City of London Corporation* v. *Appleyard* (1963)). It should be emphasised that possession of the land *at the time of the finding* may not be necessary. Thus in *Elwes* v. *Brigg Gas Co.* (1886) the boat was found by the actual possessor of the land who had possession under a lease from the plaintiff. As it was clear, however, that the boat had been under the land at the beginning of the lease, the plaintiff was entitled to it.

The "attachment" cases clearly turn upon the greater degree of control that the possessor of land is here able to show. This distinguishes the case from that where the chattel is found lying on the surface of land, but the difficulty arises that some private land is so exclusively within the control of the occupier of it that it might well be thought that he was in possession of chattels lying upon it. *Bridges* v. *Hawkesworth* was a case where the chattel was found in the shop part of the premises to which the public had access. *Hannah* v. *Peel*, though a finding on private property, was a case where the property was not in the possession of its private owner at the time of the finding. In *Parker* v. *British Airways Board* (1982) the Court of Appeal approved a distinction between a finding on land to which the public had general access and a finding on private land over which the occupier exercises exclusive control. In the latter case the occupier obtains possession of the chattel as against the finder. Applying that to the facts of the case the court found that the plaintiff passenger who found a bracelet in the executive lounge of the defendant's airport was entitled to it as against the defendant. The lounge was reserved for first-class passengers and employees of the airport but that was not sufficiently exclusive control to entitle the defendant to possession. The Court of Appeal found *Hannah* v. *Peel* distinguishable on the ground that the house in that case was occupied by the military authorities rather than the defendant, and approved the decisions in *Bridges* v. *Hawkesworth* and the "attachment" cases. Donaldson L.J. added that a trespasser would in no circumstances acquire finder's title against the occupier of land (this would not of course preclude him establishing a title based on actual possession against other third parties). In terms of policy, the distinction created by the Court of Appeal's decision is satisfactory. In general, in order to ensure the return of the chattel to its true owner, the occupier of land on which the chattel is found seems to be the most appropriate person to be awarded possessory title. Where the finding is on land to which the public has access, however, there is an increased risk of the finder disappearing with his find and this may be sufficient for the law in this case to offer an inducement to him to be honest and to report his find by awarding him a possessory title prevailing against the claim of the occupier of the land.

Finder an employee

In his judgment in *Parker* v. *British Airways Board*, Donaldson L.J. said *obiter* that a finder's title to objects found by employees while acting in the course of their employment vested in their employer, though it would vest in the employee where the finding was "wholly incidental" to the employment. This is generally thought to state the law correctly, though it does not explain why the employer should obtain a possessory title through his employee where the employment does not relate to the finding of objects.

Treasure trove

The Crown has a prerogative right to any gold or silver in coin, plate or bullion found in circumstances such that the owner is unknown but had hidden rather than lost or mislaid the goods (*A.-G. of the Duchy of Lancaster* v. *G. E. Overton Farms* (1980); *R.* v. *Hancock* (1990)).

Right of a proprietarynature

Whether the plaintiff's right to immediate possession of the chattel is based upon a right of property in it, or a right deriving from previous possession of it, it seems clear that a right of a proprietary nature is necessary—a mere contractual right to obtain immediate possession is not sufficient (*Jarvis* v. *Williams* (1955); but *cf.* the disagreement of two members of the Court of Appeal on this point in *International Factors* v. *Rodriguez* (1979)).

Jus tertii (right of a third party)

In certain circumstances the defendant could rely as a defence to an action for trespass or conversion on the fact that a third party had a better title to the chattel than the plaintiff. In such circumstances the defence was successful even though the plaintiff had a better title than the defendant. At common law the defence was only clearly available in three situations: (1) where the defendant acted under the authority of the third party in committing the act complained of; (2) where the defendant defended the action brought against him under the authority of the third party; (3) where the defendant had been evicted by the third party's title paramount. *Jus tertii* was no defence, apart from these cases, where the defendant had infringed the plaintiff's actual possession, nor by a bailee against his bailor. It is a matter of academic dispute whether it was available where the plaintiff was relying on a right to immediate possession at the time of the defendant's act. The absence of the defence meant that the defendant might be subject to a double liability if he were sued first by one with a possessory title and later by the true owner. To allow the defence against one with only a possessory title would, however, be unfair if the true owner never made a claim for his chattel, since this would mean that the defendant succeeded against one with a better right to possession than himself. Section 8 of the Torts (Interference with Goods) Act 1977 attempts to resolve the problem. Section 8(1) allows the defendant to plead the defence that a third party has a better title than the plaintiff in all actions for wrongful interference. Section 8(2) provides for the making of Rules of Court to apply in proceedings for wrongful interference, requiring the plaintiff to give particulars of his title, and to identify any person who has or claims any interest in the chattel, and authorising the defendant to have the third party joined as a party to the action, and the court to deprive the third party of his right of action against the defendant if he fails to appear in the action. This has now been done (R.S.C. Ord. 15, r. 10A, 11A).

The effect of section 8 on double liability must be considered in connection with section 7. This regulates the case where two or more persons have interests in a chattel, but the court would be entitled to award the full value of the chattel to either party as damages for conversion. The example may be taken of the finder (who has a possessory title) and the true owner. The finder could undoubtedly recover the full value of the chattel in conversion or trespass from a third party on the basis of his possessory title. The position now is that the defendant is entitled under section 8 to have the true owner joined as a party. If the defendant complies with the requirements of section 8 and the true owner fails to appear, the court may deprive him of any further right of action against the defendant. Double liability is thus avoided. If the true owner appears as a party, section 7(2) provides that the relief shall be such as to avoid double liability of the wrongdoer as between those claimants. The effect of this would be that the defendant would have to pay damages to the true owner alone, since a person with a possessory title could not succeed in conversion once the defendant has satisfied the true owner. Section 8 and section 7(2) depend upon the true owner being identifiable. Where this is not the case, double liability would still be possible since the defendant might be held liable in successive actions by the finder and the true owner. To avoid this, section 7(3) provides, in effect, that the finder has an obligation to account for what he has recovered in damages to the true owner, and section 7(4) that the true owner, if at that time he also has recovered damages from the defendant, must account to the defendant to the extent of the amount by which he is unjustly enriched. It should be noted that bailment does not present this problem of double liability, since satisfaction made to the bailee bars the bailor's action. The bailee has, however, a common law duty to account to the bailor.

The continued existence of the action on the bailment outside the bailment may cause a problem. The defence in section 8 only applies to an action for wrongful interference. Nor does section 7(2) apply since that is limited to actions for wrongful interference. Where the bailor and a third party made conflicting claims for the chattel against the bailee, the bailee ran the risk of converting it by delivering it to whichever had not got the superior title. His solution was to institute interpleader proceedings, the effect of which was that title to the chattel was determined by the court, and the bailee was protected from an action in conversion by handing over the chattel in accordance with the court's order. Interpleader proceedings are only available where the third party makes a claim. The absence of the machinery in sections 7 and 8 may therefore penalise the bailee where he is being sued on the bailment by the bailor, and a third party, whom he suspects to be owner, makes no claim (but the bailor's action against the bailee is an action for tort (*American Express Co.* v. *British Airways Board* (1983)) so may fit within the definition section in section 1 of the Act—is it, however, an action for damage to an interest in goods (section 1(d))?

Mental state of defendant in conversion

The defendant must intend to do the act which is relied on by the plaintiff as a conversion. This is quite different from intending to commit conversion. Where A does an act amounting to a conversion of B's chattel, in the mistaken belief that it belongs to him, he commits conversion. For this reason, conversion often operates as a tort of strict liability, in the sense that the defendant may be altogether free from fault.

Acts amounting to conversion

In order to constitute a conversion, the defendant's act must deny the plaintiff's right to possess the chattel. Around this somewhat vague requirement have centred most of the difficulties of conversion. Although there will be no argument about most of the forms that conversion may take, there will always be a peripheral category of acts about which doubt must be felt. The main problem in defining conversion arises from the fact that some of the cases proceed on the basis that it is the denial of the plaintiff's title that is the gist of the tort; for others it is the denial to him of possession. In fact both seem true for their respective cases. The only problem caused by this is the difficulty in framing a definition of conversion. The following is an account of the chief ways in which conversion can be committed. It is recognised that conversion may take other forms not here described.

Dispossession

Dispossession of another person is normally both a trespass and a conversion, since an infringement of another person's possession is usually sufficient to amount to a denial of that person's right to possess the chattel. Thus a thief commits both torts. Joyriding a car is also a conversion (*Aitken Agencies Ltd.* v. *Richardson* (1967)). Asportation, though invariably a trespass is not necessarily a conversion. Thus in *Fouldes* v. *Willoughby* (1841) the defendant, in order to induce the plaintiff to leave the defendant's ferryboat, removed the plaintiff's horses from the boat to the shore. The plaintiff remained in the boat and was transported across the river. This did not amount to a conversion; the defendant had done nothing inconsistent with the plaintiff's right to possess the horses. Where loss of the chattel is foreseeably likely as a result of the asportation, however, the defendant will be liable in conversion if such loss occurs. Thus, in *Forsdick* v. *Collins* (1816) the defendant took possession of land on which was lying a block of Portland stone belonging to the plaintiff. He removed the stone off the land to another place, and subsequently the stone was lost. The defendant was held liable in conversion to the plaintiff.

Destruction

Intentional and total destruction of another's chattel is a conversion. Partial damage or negligent destruction will normally be actionable either in trespass or in negligence, but not conversion. Consumption of the chattel by user is also conversion (*Lancashire & Yorkshire Ry.* v. *MacNicoll* (1919)).

Dealing

1. *After obtaining possession.* A sale and delivery of another person's chattel by one who is in possession of it is a conversion. Since the sale purports to transfer a title to the chattel to the buyer it is clearly inconsistent with the rights of the true owner. Nor does it matter that the defendant acquired possession innocently, and was quite ignorant of the fact that he was acting inconsistently with the rights of the owner. Conversion merely requires the intentional sale and delivery of the chattel by the defendant. It does not require that he should know this to be wrongful. The liability of the seller is in principle established by the decision of the House of Lords in *Hollins* v. *Fowler* (1875), although the case does not concern a sale as such. The defendant cotton broker had bought and delivered to his principal some cotton belonging to the plaintiff taking his usual commission on the transaction. The cotton was bought from a rogue who had obtained it fraudulently from the plaintiff. Despite his good faith, the defendant was held liable in conversion. Since he had acted without prior authority, it was found that he had acted as a principal, not an agent, so the transaction was equivalent to a sale of goods. It follows *a fortiori* from this case that a sale and delivery of another person's chattel is a conversion of it. This was accepted in later cases concerning the liability of auctioneers though they are undoubtedly acting as agents rather than principals; (*Consolidated Co.* v. *Curtis* (1892); *Barker* v. *Furlong* (1891)).

The rigour of this principle is to some extent mitigated by the fact that it appears that the defendant is only liable if he himself has negotiated the transaction under which the goods are disposed of to a third party. Where he has only acted to facilitate another's transaction he is not liable in conversion, despite the fact that he knows the transaction affects the title to the goods. In *National Mercantile Bank* v. *Rymill* (1881) goods were given to the defendant, an auctioneer, for sale at his auction. The goods were sold privately by the seller himself, and the defendant handed them over to the buyer on the seller's instructions, knowing they had been sold. He was held not liable in conversion to the true owner of the goods. This case has been criticised by Lord Denning M.R. and Roskill L.J. speaking *obiter* in *R. H. Willis & Son* v. *British Car Auctions Ltd.* (1978) as being inconsistent with the principles laid down in *Hollins* v. *Fowler*. It seems correct that where the defendant delivers the chattel to a third party under a transaction which he knows is intended to transfer title to it, it should make no difference that he did not negotiate that transaction. A carrier of goods does not convert them by his delivery of them (*Sheridan* v. *New Quay Co.* (1858)) but possibly it makes a difference where he knows he is purporting to effect a transfer of title (as Blackburn J. thought in *Hollins* v. *Fowler* relying on the early case of *Stephens* v. *Elwall* (1815). It is clear, however, that a misdelivery by a carrier constitutes a conversion even if it is done in good faith and without negligence (*Youl* v. *Harbottle* (1791); also by a bailee (*Devereux* v. *Barclay* (1819)).

Sale and hire-purchase are clear examples of transactions which deny the title of the true owner of the chattels because in the one, the defendant is purporting to convey an immediate title to the buyer, and in the other he is entering into a transaction which envisages the eventual passing of title to the hire-purchaser. The same is true of the pledging of a chattel, since ultimately on non-redemption of the pledge, the pledgee acquires title (see *Parker* v. *Godin* (1728)). In the case of most bailments, however, which consist in a mere temporary transfer of possession, there is no such denial, and the parties to them do not commit conversion.

2. *Disposition without physical dealing.* A mere sale of another person's chattel without a physical dealing with it is not normally a conversion, though it may amount to slander of title to goods (*Lancashire Waggon Co.* v. *Fitzhugh* (1861)). Where, however, the sale has caused the plaintiff to be deprived of a possession he enjoyed or was entitled to, this is a conversion. *Van Oppen* v.

Tredegars Ltd. (1921) illustrates the point. In this case the plaintiff delivered goods by mistake to a firm. The defendants' managing director sold the goods to the firm, claiming falsely that they belonged to the defendants. The firm used and disposed of the goods in the course of their business. The defendants were held vicariously liable for their servant's conversion of the goods. In this case, although the managing director did not physically deal with the goods, he clearly caused their ultimate loss, since he induced a belief in the firm that it could deal with the goods as its own. (The case of *Douglas Valley Finance Co.* v. *Hughes* (*Hirers*) *Ltd.* (1969) is less easy to explain because there the sale did not effect a transfer of possession of the chattel from seller to buyer).

Receipt

To receive another's chattel under a sale amounts to a conversion of it, even though the recipient is ignorant of the other's right. This rule clearly reflects the view on which the tort of conversion is based, that ownership, even of chattels, should be inviolable. In a predominantly commercial society, however, a parallel need is felt to uphold transactions, to protect the person who for value and in good faith has acquired the chattel. Thus numerous exceptions to the principle that receipt is a conversion have been established, principally by statute. For example, section 25(1) of the Sale of Goods Act 1979, allows a seller of goods who has remained in possession of them to transfer a title to the goods under a disposition to one who takes them in good faith with the result that such a person is protected against an action of conversion by the buyer.

Receipt under a transaction which does not involve the assertion of any proprietary right over the chattel is not a conversion. For example, a carrier or warehouseman does not convert the chattel he receives. The doubt that existed whether receipt by a pledgee was conversion has now been stilled by section 11(2) of the Torts (Interference with Goods) Act 1977, which makes it conversion if the pledgor himself committed conversion by making the pledge. An unauthorised pledge of another's chattel clearly constitutes conversion, so that the pledgee also commits conversion by receipt.

Involuntary receipt

Where the defendant has come into possession of a chattel involuntarily (for example, unwanted goods sent through the post), he is called an involuntary bailee of it. The term excludes persons on whose land the chattel is placed without their consent (*cf. British Economical Lamp case, infra*).

The legal position of the involuntary bailee is a question of some importance in view of the increasing use of high-pressure salesmanship of the practice of sending unwanted goods through the post and then claiming their price if they are not returned. The involuntary bailee does not commit conversion by his receipt of the goods. He is not bound to take steps to return the goods, nor by failing to return the goods does he become bound to pay for them. He is not liable for negligence in their safekeeping (*Howard* v. *Harris* (1884)) though *Newman* v. *Bourne & Hollingsworth Ltd.* (1915) held an involuntary bailee liable for "gross negligence." He converts if he unreasonably refuses to return the goods to the sender on request by the latter. He formerly had no right to use or dispose of the goods, but now under section 1 of the Unsolicited Goods and Services Act 1971, he has a right, after six months from receipt, or 30 days after giving notice to the sender, to use, deal with or dispose of the goods as if they are an unconditional gift to him (he must be the intended recipient of the goods—the Act does not cover cases of mistaken delivery).

An involuntary bailee who takes reasonable steps to return the goods to the sender is not liable if they are lost. In *Elvin and Powell Ltd.* v. *Plummer Roddis Ltd.* (1933) the delivery by the bailee to a rogue who posed as the plaintiff's agent for collection of the goods was held not to be conversion since the bailee had acted reasonably and without negligence. But in *Hiort* v. *Bott* (1874) where goods had been sent to a railway station, and were deliverable to the order either of the plaintiff or defendant, the defendant committed conversion by indorsing the delivery order to a rogue who posed as the plaintiff's agent. The defendant was here not in the position of an involuntary bailee, and his intermeddling had caused the plaintiff to lose the goods. It was irrelevant that his action may have been reasonable.

Interference with the exercise of the plaintiff's rights

It is clear that the defendant's act may be a conversion even though the defendant has not physically dealt with the plaintiff's chattel (see *Van Oppen & Co. Ltd.* v. *Tredegars Ltd.* (1921) (*supra*)). But in such a case it must be quite clear that the defendant's act constitutes a denial of the plaintiff's right to possess the chattel. In *British Economical Lamp Co.* v. *Mile End Theatre* (1913) the defendant's refusal to allow the plaintiff to enter their premises and remove some lamps belonging to the plaintiff which their tenant had left behind at the termination of the lease, was held to be neither conversion nor detinue. The lamps were not present by the defendants' act and the mere refusal to allow the plaintiffs to enter their land was not sufficient denial of the plaintiff's title to the lamps. It is important that the defendant was not regarded as being in possession of the lamps. Had he been so, there would have been a conversion by him (see below under conversion by demand and refusal; and *Moffatt* v. *Kazana* (1969); see also pp. 86–88 for the right of recaption of chattels). *Oakley* v. *Lyster* (1931) shows that a refusal to allow the plaintiff to exercise his rights over the chattel coupled with other acts of the defendant may be conversion. The plaintiff had leased some land for the purpose of depositing on it a quantity of hard core which he owned. The defendant acquired the freehold, and subsequently wrote to the plaintiff, informing him that he would not be allowed to remove the material, claiming that it belonged to the defendant; he also used part of the material. The Court of Appeal held that he had converted all the hard core. He clearly converted the material he had used, but the judgments in the case do not make clear on what basis he converted the rest of the hard core. The defendant's actions went beyond that of the defendant in the *British Economical Lamp* case, because his letter amounted to an interference with the plaintiff's possession. But *England* v. *Cowley* (1875) shows that an interference with possession is not necessarily a conversion (defendant landlord wrongfully prevented the plaintiff from removing furniture belonging to her tenant and of which the plaintiff was in lawful possession under a Bill of Sale, from the premises. This was held to be no conversion). The defendant in *Oakley* v. *Lyster* had also denied the plaintiff's title to the material, but at common law it was not conversion merely to deny the plaintiff's title, even by asserting one's own inconsistent title, and this receives confirmation in section 11(3) of the Torts (Interference with Goods) Act 1977. The case may therefore be authority only for what it actually decided: that to prevent the plaintiff from exercising an existing possession of his chattel, at the same time denying his title to it by asserting one's own inconsistent title to it and backing this up by using it is conversion (alternatively the case could be explained on the basis of the second ratio of Greer L.J. that the defendant had *dispossessed* the plaintiff of the hard core.

Demand and refusal

An action of conversion can be based on a demand for the return of the chattel, and a refusal to surrender it by the defendant. The action of detinue was the more typical remedy in this situation, and it was only by treating the defendant's refusal as evidence of a conversion by him that the availability of conversion could be justified by the courts.

Two conditions are necessary for the defendant's refusal to operate as a conversion:

1. The defendant must be in possession of the chattel. Where the defendant has lost possession, this may be because of his prior act of conversion. In such a case, the conversion dated for the purpose of the limitation period on the action from the act of conversion, detinue only from the demand and refusal (but see Limitation Act 1980, *infra*, pp. 436–437). Where the defendant has lost possession in circumstances not amounting to a conversion by him the plaintiff's only possibility was detinue, since merely losing possession, even if negligently, is not conversion.
2. The defendant's refusal to surrender the chattel to the plaintiff must be unreasonable. In *Clayton* v. *Le Roy* (1911) where the defendant refused to return the plaintiff's watch on demand to the managing clerk of the plaintiff's solicitors, it was held that the refusal was not unreasonable because the clerk had shown no evidence of authority from the plaintiff to make the demand.

Conversion and detinue

The tort of detinue was abolished by section 2(1) of the 1977 Act. The essence of detinue lay in the defendant's wrongful refusal of the plaintiff's demand for his chattel. Detinue lay in two cases. Where the defendant was in possession of the chattel at the time of the demand, his refusal to return it would be detinue in the same circumstances as it would be conversion. In fact detinue and conversion were here identical, and with the abolition of detinue the only remedy here is conversion. Detinue was also available against a bailee who was unable to restore the chattel to the bailor on the latter's demand because of his earlier wrongful loss of possession of the chattel, for example, by his disposing of, destroying or losing it. Conversion was not available here in relation to the refusal to restore the chattel although the earlier act of disposing of his possession may have constituted conversion. But detinue was also available in relation to the mere negligent loss of possession whereas conversion always requires an intentional act. This case of detinue was of further importance in that the bailee, although not liable in the absence of negligence, had the burden of proving that he took due care, whereas, if the action were brought in negligence, the plaintiff would have the burden of proving lack of care (*Houghland* v. *Low* (*Luxury Coaches*) (1962)). The case of detinue where the bailee of a chattel has wrongfully allowed it to be lost or destroyed without converting it is now expressly provided to be conversion by section 2(2) of the 1977 Act.

Howard E. Perry v. *B.R.B.* (1980) is an instructive case illustrating the effect of the Torts (Interference with Goods) Act 1977 in this area of the law. The defendants were in possession of some 500 tonnes of steel belonging to the plaintiffs. The plaintiffs asked the defendants to allow them to take away the steel but the defendants refused to comply with their request because they feared that compliance would cause industrial action to be invoked against them by reason of the national steel strike. The plaintiffs' action against the defendants for conversion of the steel was successful. The court found: (1) the refusal to return the steel for the duration of the strike was a sufficient denial of the plaintiffs' rights to possession to amount to conversion; (2) the power to order specific restitution in a case of wrongful interference with goods under section 3(2)(*a*) of the Act should be exercised in the plaintiffs' favour. Damages were an inadequate remedy because the steel strike had caused a shortage of steel and an equivalent amount was unobtainable on the market.

User

There is a certain amount of ancient authority (for example, *Petre* v. *Heneage* (1701)) to the effect that to use another's chattel without destroying or consuming it is conversion, and an Australian case provides support (*Penfold's Wine Pty. Ltd.* v.

Eliott (1946)). The desirability of following these cases seems doubtful. Where the defendant has innocently used the chattel, even if this is done in the belief that he has title to the chattel, his act does not seem to be sufficiently inconsistent with the owner's right to possess the chattel to be regarded as a conversion of it. It would be quite different if the user were mala fide. The problem of use is more difficult in the case of bailment because of the introduction by the courts of the nebulous concept of an act repugnant to the bailment. If such an action of user is committed by the bailee, this terminates the bailment and the bailee can be sued for conversion. If the bailee's user is not repugnant to the bailment but is contrary to its terms, it is actionable by action on the bailment provided it causes damage (*Donald* v. *Suckling* (1866)).

Conversion and negligence

Conversion requires an intentional act of dealing with the chattel; an unintended act, even though negligent, is not sufficient. Where, however, a foreseeable consequence of an intended dealing with a chattel not in itself a conversion is the ultimate loss of the chattel, it is clear that there may be a conversion if that loss occurs. This looks rather like conversion through negligence. The early case of *Forsdick* v. *Collins* (1816) has already been mentioned as a possible example of this liability (*supra*, p. 45). The asportation of the stone was conversion only because it caused its loss and this was foreseeable. Another such case is *Moorgate Mercantile Co.* v. *Finch and Read* (1962). The defendant's driving of the plaintiff hire-purchase company's car for the purpose of carrying in it some watches which had been smuggled through customs was found to be a conversion of the car, when it was lawfully confiscated by the customs authorities and permanently lost. The Court of Appeal treated this as an intentional conversion. This, however, seems only possible if it was shown that the defendant actually had the permanent loss of the car in mind when driving it and was therefore reckless as to that consequence, which seems unlikely.

Effect of judgment in cases of wrongful interference

Section 5(1) of the Torts (Interference with Goods) Act 1977 provides that where damages for wrongful interference are being assessed on the footing that the claimant is being compensated for the whole of his interest in the chattel (or for the whole subject to a reduction for his contributory negligence), payment of the damages, or the settlement of a claim for damages, extinguishes the claimant's title to that interest. This section reproduces, with slight extensions, the common law rule concerning the effect of satisfaction of a judgment in conversion. Under section 5(4) the same effect is produced as regards a third party's interest in a chattel where a claimant has accounted to him under section 7(3) of the Act.

REMEDIES FOR WRONGFUL INTERFERENCE

The primary remedy in those torts representing the present wrongful interferences is the action for damages. Where the tort has caused the loss of the chattel to the plaintiff, damages are based on the value of the chattel together with any consequential loss suffered by the plaintiff. In conversion and trespass, the measure of damages was based on the value of the chattel at the date of the wrong. Since the wrong was complete at that time and the plaintiff in neither action could get his chattel back, the plaintiff would be expected to mitigate his loss by purchasing a replacement. In detinue, on the other hand, which was based on a continuing wrongful detention of the chattel until the date of judgment (which might take the form of an order for specific restitution of the chattel), the chattel was valued at the date of judgment. These differences were less absolute than theory might suggest. For example, it would not be reasonable to expect a plaintiff to mitigate his loss if he did not know his chattel had been converted. In such circumstances in *Sachs* v. *Miklos* (1948) the plaintiff was allowed as damages for conversion the higher value of the chattel at the date of the judgment. In detinue also the notion of a continuing wrongful detention of the chattel until the date of judgment was a fiction in cases where the defendant had lost the chattel or negligently allowed it to be destroyed. The two supposed rules were probably no more than pointers to the court, the true rule being that the chattel was valued at the time most appropriate to compensate the plaintiff for his loss. This was the view of the Law Reform Committee on whose report the 1977 Act was based (Eighteenth Report, para. 88). The silence of the act on this point seems also confirmation, since if it were assimilating two torts (*i.e.* conversion and detinue) with different rules as to their measure of damages, it would surely have stated which was to apply. The compensatory role of the law relating to damages for conversion is emphasised also by the hire-purchase cases. The finance company, although absolute owner of the chattel before the completion of payment of the hire-purchase payments, may claim only the value of unpaid instalments rather than the value of the chattel when suing in conversion (*Wickham Holdings* v. *Brooke House Motors* (1967)), though when the amount of unpaid instalments exceeds the present value of the chattel, the defendant's liability is to pay only that value (*Chubb Cash* v. *John Crilley* (1983)).

Section 3(2) of the Torts (Interference with Goods) Act 1977 deals expressly with the remedies available where the defendant is still in possession or control of the goods. The plaintiff may here be entitled to one of three remedies: (*a*) an order for delivery of the goods, and for payment of any consequential damages; or (*b*) an order for delivery of the goods, but giving the defendant the alternative of paying damages by reference to the value of the goods, together in either alternative with payment of any consequential damages; or (*c*) damages. Specific restitution under subsection (*a*) thus survives as a remedy despite the abolition of detinue. Whether to grant it lies within the discretion of the court (see the judgment of Diplock L.J. in *General and Finance Facilities* v. *Cooks Cars* (*Romford*) (1963) for the principles governing the exercise of the discretion). The plaintiff may, however, choose either subsections (*b*) or (*c*) as a matter of right. One point that clearly emerges from this is that the successful plaintiff is entitled to refuse return of the chattel in mitigation of damages, although the common law power to stay an action of conversion where the defendant offers return of the chattel may still be available (*Fisher* v. *Prince* (1762)). It is unlikely that much reliance will ever be placed by plaintiffs on section 3(2)(*b*), since the option it gives to the defendant will mean that the latter will always choose the more financially advantageous course.

Munro v. *Willmott* (1948) was authority to the effect that where the defendant had in good faith improved the chattel, the expense of this was deductible from damages in conversion. Section 6 of the 1977 Act provides that in proceedings for wrongful interference against the improver, if the improver acted in the honest but mistaken belief that he had a good title to the chattel, an allowance must be made in assessing damages to the extent of the increase in value attributable to the improvement. Section 6(2) extends this protection to bona fide purchasers from the improver. Section 6 narrows the protection available to the improver at common law, since the defendant in *Munro* v. *Willmott* had no honest belief that he owned the car. The allowance is available only to a person who is a defendant in proceedings for wrongful interference (though the improver may establish a quasi-contractual claim against the owner in other cases—*Greenwood* v. *Bennett* (1973)). It is not discretionary, and is available for the whole value of the improvement even though this exceeds expenditure.

Damages could be awarded in conversion, detinue or trespass for consequential loss, and this continues to be the law. In *Bodley* v. *Reynolds* (1846), a carpenter was awarded damages for loss of earnings caused by the conversion of his tools of trade. Normally, however, the plaintiff will be required to mitigate such consequential loss by purchasing a replacement chattel. It may sometimes be excluded also on the ground that it was unforeseeable by the defendant and too remote (for example, loss of profit on a lucrative sale of the chattel by the plaintiff—*The Arpad* (1934)). In *Strand Electric* v. *Brisford* (1952), the defendants, who were in possession of the plaintiff's electrical equipment, wrongly refused to deliver it to the plaintiff on his demand. They were held liable to pay a reasonable hiring charge for all the equipment even though it was unlikely the plaintiff could have hired it all to customers. The profit-earning potential of the equipment was here obvious, and the plaintiff could not be expected to mitigate his loss by purchasing a replacement when the defendant was actually in possession of the equipment and refusing to give it back. At one time it was doubted whether a similar claim to that in the *Strand Electric* case could be made in an action for conversion, perhaps on the ground that conversion did not involve a continuing wrong but was complete with the act of conversion. With the disappearance of detinue, the matter has become of greater importance and was put to the test in *Hillesden Securities* v. *Ryjak* (1983). The defendants had converted a Rolls-Royce car by buying it from its lessee during the term of the lease. The owner some time after the conversion made a formal demand for the return of the car and, this having failed, assigned all rights in the car to the

plaintiff finance company. Eventually the defendants admitted
liability after legal proceedings for conversion had been commenced by the plaintiff and the car was returned. The defendants
argued that their liability was limited to the value of the car at the
date of the conversion (£7500) plus interest. The court, however,
awarded damages to the plaintiff on the basis of the lost hire
charge over the period from the initial conversion to the return of
the car, an amount of £13,282. The difference in amount is the
more striking in view of the fact that if the first amount had been
chosen the defendants would have acquired title to the car. In
detinue the plaintiff would only have been entitled to the hire
charge from the date of the formal demand, whereas on these facts
the liability in conversion to pay hire applied from the date of
initial receipt. That would seem reasonable against a mala fide
converter, but no finding seems to have been made that the
defendants were in bad faith at the time they received the car.

In the *Strand* and *Hillesden* cases, the chattels in question were
profit-earning chattels. In *Brandeis Goldschmidt* v. *Western
Transport* (1981) the defendants had wrongfully detained copper
belonging to the plaintiffs for a period during which the market
value of the copper fell by £3588. The plaintiffs claimed this fall in
an action of detinue (the facts occurred before the 1977 Act).
Refusing to allow them this amount, the Court of Appeal found
that there was no fixed rule that loss of market value was awarded
as damages in a case of detinue, and that since the plaintiffs
wanted the copper for use in production rather than for resale as
an investment, they were entitled to nominal damages only. There
is, however, no doubt that the courts may award damages for
tortiously causing the plaintiff to be deprived of possession of his
chattel even if that loss has caused the plaintiff no financial loss.
(*The Mediana* (1900); *Birmingham Corp.* v. *Sowsberry* (1969) 113
S.J. 877). The *Brandeis* case was distinguished in *B.B.M.B. Ltd.* v.
E.D.A. Holdings (1990) where it was held that a converter of
shares which it held on trust for the plaintiffs must pay as damages
the market value of the shares at the date of the conversion less
the value of replacement shares the defendant had purchased, even
though the shares at the time of the action were worthless, and the
plaintiffs had had no intention to sell before discovering the above
facts. The *Brandeis* case was distinguished on the ground that it
involved a mere temporary deprivation of possession, but this is

not entirely convincing. Cases such as those involving deliberate wrongdoing causing no actual loss would seem to be candidates for a rap over the knuckles in the form of a smallish award of examplary damages, but neither case would seem to qualify for exemplary damages under the present rules (*infra*, p. 412).

Contributory negligence and wrongful interference with goods

Section 11(1) of the 1977 Act provides that contributory negligence is not a defence to an action for conversion or for intentional trespass to goods. The effect of section 47 of the Banking Act 1979, however, is to preserve the defence in a case where is had been found to apply before the Act, that is, in an action against a negligent banker for conversion of a cheque (*Lumsden* v. *London Trustee Savings Bank* (1971)).

Plaintiff with possessory title

It is established law that the bailee, who is suing in conversion either on the basis of an infringement of his possession, or on the basis of his possessory title, may recover the whole value of the chattel despite the fact that his interest in the chattel is limited to the value of his services in relation to it (*cf. The Winkfield* (1902)). The same rule no doubt applies to persons in a comparable position, for example, carriers or pledgees. It is both just and convenient to allow the bailee, despite his limited interest, to recover the full value of the chattel, both because of his possible liability to account for its loss to the bailor under the contract of bailment and because of the desirability of finally disposing of the defendant's liability in one action. It is also clear that the holder of possession, or of a possessory title, which is not limited by any contract with a third party, is *a fortiori* entitled to recover the full value of the chattel in conversion. There is, however, a difference in the rule about satisfaction made by the defendant to the plaintiff. If the defendant makes satisfaction to the bailee by paying him the value of the chattel, this bars an action by the bailor against the defendant (no doubt because of the bailee's liability to account to the bailor for value of the chattel less the amount of his interest in it). In the case of a mere possessor, or holder of a possessory title, satisfaction made to him by the defendant does not bar action by the owner of the chattel (*Attenborough* v. *London & St. Katharine Docks* (1878)—this is the common law rule. Whether it will change in the light of section 7(3) of the 1977 Act which requires the holder of a possessory title to account to the owner for damages recovered is a matter of conjecture).

RESIDUAL FORMS OF TORTIOUS INTERFERENCE WITH CHATTELS

Trespass, conversion, and detinue do not exhaust the forms which a tortious interference with chattels may take. In these torts the plaintiff must prove either an infringement of his possession or a denial of his right to possession by the defendant. Where the plaintiff cannot fulfil these requirements, he may still be able to sue. Thus, if the defendant has damaged or destroyed the chattel, the owner may sue for the damage to his reversionary interest in the chattel. This rule may be of benefit to the bailor for a term (*cf. Mears* v. *L. & S.W. Ry.* (1862)), the purchaser of a chattel where the seller has a lien over it for its price, and other holders of reversionary interests in chattels. Under a similar principle, the bailee who has deviated from the terms of the bailment and thereby caused damage to the chattel may be sued by the bailor by what was formerly action on the case (*supra*, p. 53). Case was also stated by the court to be in principle available on the unusual facts of *England* v. *Cowley* (*supra*, p. 50), *i.e.* for damage caused by a wrongful act aimed at preventing the plaintiff from making use of the chattel in a particular way, and not constituting any of the existing torts of trespass, conversion or detinue.

Where the owner has no reversionary interest in the chattel (*i.e.* is not entitled in future to its possession), he may be able to rely on negligence. *Lee Cooper* v. *Jeakins* is an example of this. The plaintiffs, who had sold goods to a firm in Eire, arranged with X, another firm, for the reshipment and delivery of the goods, on arrival in port in England, to Eire. The defendants, who were road-haulage contractors, agreed with X to carry the goods from the English port of arrival to X's warehouse. The defendant lost the goods through their negligence. It was held that this negligence was actionable by the plaintiffs. Detinue was not available because the plaintiffs had lost the right to immediate possession of the goods, but their property in the goods enabled them to succeed in negligence.

Replevin: distress

The existence of these should be noted. Distress refers to any right which the law confers to seize and detain another's chattel as a means of enforcing a debt. Where the plaintiff complains of a wrongful distress, he may apply to the registrar of the county court who will restore possession of the chattel to him on his giving security to bring proceedings in replevin. Replevin is thus a means of contesting the legal validity of a distress, and this is now its only function although originally it was wider. There is now a general power under section 4 of the Torts (Interference with Goods) Act 1977 for a county court or the High Court to restore possession of a chattel to a claimant pending the bringing of proceedings for wrongful interference relating to the chattel. Wrongful interference with a lawful distress is actionable as rescous or pound breach.

4. TRESPASS TO LAND

This tort, which is also called trespass *quare clausum fregit*, is committed by one who intentionally or negligently makes entry on the land of a person in possession of that land. It is also committed by one who enters in circumstances not amounting to a trespass, but who commits a trespassory act while on the land, for example, by refusing to leave when required to by the occupier. Like other forms of trespass, trespass to land is actionable *per se*.

Plaintiff's interest: actual possession of the land

The plaintiff must show that he was in actual possession of the land at the time of the defendant's act. It is clear, therefore, that the remedy of an owner of land out of possession of it against one who has entered it cannot be trespass. In this situation the owner must sue the intruder with the action of ejectment (*infra*, p. 67 *et seq.*). The requirement of possession of the land in the plaintiff means also that trespass is available to persons other than the owner of the land. For example, a lessee who under the lease has possession of the demised premises may sue for trespass to them. So also may a mortgagee in possession of mortgaged land.

The law does not insist upon any legally recognised interest in the land entitling the plaintiff to possession of the land. To put the plaintiff to proof of his title to the land would penalise many persons whose peaceable and long-enjoyed occupation of land has been disturbed by a third party. But the wrongful possessor gets the benefit of the same rule, even seemingly the person who gained possession by his ejection of another person, except against that person. Thus in *Graham* v. *Peat* (1861) the plaintiff who was in possession of land under a lease which was wholly void by statute was allowed to sue in trespass. But there are limitations to this doctrine. An unlawful possession, though sufficient against a third party, is not so against the true owner of the land. In *Delaney* v. *T. P. Smith & Co.* (1946) the plaintiff and defendant had orally agreed that the plaintiff was to acquire the tenancy of the defendant's premises. The plaintiff entered the premises secretly before a tenancy agreement had been executed, and was ejected forcibly by the defendant a week later. The plaintiff's action against the defendant in trespass failed. The oral agreement could not be relied on by the plaintiff as giving him the right to the possession of the premises since it was not evidenced by writing as required by section 40 of the Law Property Act 1925. Furthermore, the plaintiff's actual possession of the premises did not justify him in bringing an action of trespass against the owner of the premises.

Title to the land, though not conferring a right to bring trespass, is therefore nevertheless relevant in providing the holder of such title with a defence to an action of trespass. This does not mean that an owner of land cannot commit trespass thereto, *e.g.* a lessor can trespass against his lessee. Another limitation upon the rule that possession of the land confers title to bring trespass is that actual possession gained as a result of ejecting another may not be sufficient to allow the possessor to treat a later entry of that other as trespass. The law allows the ejected person a reasonable time to reinstate himself in possession. If he succeeds in this, he does not commit trespass.

Title to the land also appears to be relevant where the exclusiveness of the plaintiff's possession is disputed by the defendant; if the plaintiff has title it will be more readily assumed in his favour that his actions in relation to the land show him to be in possession of it. Thus in *Fowley Marine (Emsworth) Ltd.* v. *Gafford* (1968) the plaintiffs were seeking an injunction against the defendant's trespassing on their tidal creek. Having found first of all that the plaintiffs could not establish a "paper title" to the creek, the court then ruled that the plaintiffs' actions in relation to the creek did not establish them to be in exclusive possession so that their action of trespass failed.

A licensee of land does not have possession of it, and his licence is revocable by the licensor at any time. Accordingly he is unable to sue in trespass. On the other hand the licence may be irrevocable by the licensor on the ground of estoppel, acquiescence, the fact that a proprietary interest is conferred or that the licence is contractual. It does not necessarily follow that in these cases the licensee can bring trespass against third parties, although *Mason* v. *Clarke* (1955) allowed such an action where the licensee had a proprietary interest in the land. Provided, however, that licensees of this sort have a sufficiently exclusive occupation of the land, they can probably bring trespass.

The act of trespass

The defendant by his act must cause a direct invasion of the plaintiff's land. Where the invasion is indirect, trespass will not lie, although nuisance or negligence may be available. In *Lemmon* v. *Webb* (1894) roots and branches of the defendant's trees projected from the defendant's land on to the plaintiff's. This was regarded as nuisance and not trespass. In *Esso Petroleum Co.* v. *Southport Corporation* (1956), oil discharged from the defendant's ship in order to lighten it was carried by the tide on to the plaintiff's foreshore where it caused damage. In the Court of Appeal, Lord Denning M.R. thought that this was too indirect to amount to trespass. Morris L.J. thought that it would be trespass to deliberately make use of the forces of nature, such as wind and tide, to cause the invasion or even to discharge the oil without good reason with the same effect. This view is open to the objection that it confuses the issue of directness with that of the state of mind required to commit the tort. The House of Lords left the question open, not having to decide it.

The entry on the land need not be that of the defendant. If he has thrown a stone on the land this is a trespass. But there must be some entry. In *Perera* v. *Vandiyar* (1953) the defendant turned off the plaintiff's gas and electricity from the meter in the defendant's cellar. This was not trespass because the defendant had caused no entry of anything into the plaintiff's premises although the effects of what he did were experienced there.

Trespass to the highway

The highway is in legal analysis a public right of way over land which remains in the ownership and possession of the adjoining landowners (although by statute ownership and possession of the surface and so much of the land above and below the surface as is necessary for the effective maintenance of the highway is often vested in a highway authority).

The public right over the highway is one of passage merely. One who uses the highway for a purpose other than that of passage may thereby commit a trespass against the adjoining landowners. Thus in *Harrison* v. *Duke of Rutland* (1893) the defendant who had scared off grouse as they were approaching a shooting-party on the Duke's land was successfully sued in trespass by the Duke. In *Randall* v. *Tarrant* (1955) the parking of a car on the highway was held not to be a trespass to the highway despite the fact that the occupants of the car after parking it committed trespasses on the plaintiff's adjoining land. The test appears to be whether the act committed on the highway can in itself be fairly objected to by the adjoining landowner.

State of mind of the defendant

The entry by the defendant on to the plaintiff's land will normally be intentional. This will be a trespass even if the defendant is under a reasonable though mistaken belief that he is entitled to enter (for example, because he thinks the land belongs to himself). The judgments in *Esso Petroleum* v. *Southport Corp.* (1956) are consistent with the possibility that trespass to land may also operate as a tort of strict liability where the defendant intentionally does an act resulting directly in an invasion of land. That, however, did not need to be decided and may be to adopt a view that is too strict. Where the consequence is both direct and intended by the defendant, he is clearly liable for trespass and that liability according to a recent case extends to the situation where he is reckless as to the consequence and even where he is merely negligent in failing to avoid them. So in *League Against Cruel Sports* v. *Scott* (1985) it was held that the master of hounds was liable in trespass to land for entry by those hounds into the land of the plaintiff if he intended their entry, or persisted in hunting in an area where he knew it to be impossible to restrain their entry, or, where there was a real risk of entry, was negligent (either personally or through his servants or agents) in failing to prevent that entry. If the judgment is correct it follows that trespass to land is an exception to the decision in *Letang* v. *Cooper* that an action for negligent trespass is no longer possible but it is a little difficult to see what purpose such an action serves. If the entry causes actual damage then an action of negligence is of course available. Trespass to land always requires a voluntary act by the defendant. So it was not committed by one who was thrown by another person on to the plaintiff's land (*Smith* v. *Stone* (1647)).

Subject-matter of trespass

The subject-matter of this form of trespass is land. This is wide enough to cover buildings, rooms in buildings, plants and vegetables; indeed, anything attached to the land and capable of being separately possessed.

Possession of land was once thought to be *usque ad coelum, usque ad inferos, i.e.* extending to the air-space above the land as well as to the land beneath the surface. The latter proposition has not been tested in England but *Bernstein* v. *Skyviews Ltd.* (1977) has caused a modification of the *usque ad coelum* principle. That case held that the landowner's rights in the air-space above his land extend only to such height as is necessary for the use and enjoyment of the land. So the defendant's flight by aeroplane over the plaintiff's land for the purpose of photographing it was not trespass though repeated flights might be nuisance. The defendant also had a defence under the present section 76 of the Civil Aviation Act 1982, which provides that no action shall lie in respect of trespass by reason only of the flight of an aircraft over any property which, having regard to wind, weather and all the circumstances of the case, is reasonable. The Act applies to aircraft belonging to the Crown, except for military aircraft.

Trespass ab initio

Under the common law doctrine of trespass *ab initio*, one who has entered land under authority of law is liable as a trespasser in respect of his original entry if he commits some act on the land not justified by the authority under which he entered.

There is no doubt that the doctrine at its genesis was intended as a means of restraining abuse of power by officials who had a legal right to enter premises, and in particular sheriffs and bailiffs appointed to levy a distress on property within the premises. The fact that they could be treated as trespassers from the time of entry justified the award of greater damages. The same purpose can in many cases be achieved by the award of exemplary damages (*infra,*

p. 412). The only importance of the doctrine apart from this is to make trespassory what is not in itself trespassory. So in *Oxley* v. *Watts* (1785) the defendant had worked a horse which he had taken as a lawful distress. It was held that this made him a trespasser *ab initio*, although the working of the horse was not trespass to chattels. But where the wrongful conduct is an omission, trespass *ab initio* cannot apply (*Six Carpenters' Case* (1610)). It is also ruled out where a ground justifying entry remains, despite the misfeasance (*Elias* v. *Pasmore* (1934)—police lawfully entered premises to arrest plaintiff, and while there took documents some of which they were not entitled to take, but were not trespassers *ab initio* because of the arrest of the plaintiff). In *Chic Fashions Ltd.* v. *Jones* (1968) it was held that seizure by police lawfully on premises of goods on the premises reasonably believed by them to have been stolen was not trespass to chattels and the police were therefore not trespassers *ab initio*. The Court of Appeal appeared to doubt whether the doctrine of trespass *ab initio* had any continuing existence.

Defences

It is a defence that the defendant was on the land by permission or licence of the occupier. Such licence may be revoked by the occupier, and the entrant, having been given reasonable time to remove himself, ejected as a trespasser (the problems arising from revocation of contractual licences are not considered in this book).

The entrant also may have a legal right to enter, apart from the occupier's permission. This may be conferred by statute (for example, the powers given to officials of Gas and Electricity Boards), or may exist at common law (for example, public and private rights of way, and the right of recaption of chattels).

Jus tertii is no defence to trespass to land, except where the defendant acted under the third party's authority (*Nicholls* v. *Ely Beet Sugar Factory* (1931)).

Remedies

The action of trespass to land, like that of conversion, is not a means of recovering the plaintiff's property. The remedies available to the plaintiff for trespass, damages, or an injunction, will not suffice to restore possession of the land to the plaintiff if at the time of the action the defendant rather than the plaintiff has possession. Furthermore, the measure of damages in trespass to land assumes the plaintiff either to have or to be able to recover possession of the land, since the plaintiff gets not the value of land but the damage to it resulting from the trespass. The difference between conversion, on the one hand, where the plaintiff recovers the whole value of his chattel, and trespass, where he recovers only for the damage to his land, derives from the difference between chattels and land. Land is always identifiable—the plaintiff out of possession cannot therefore get the value of the land from the defendant but must bring action for the recovery of the land itself. All this points to the existence of another remedy if the plaintiff wishes to recover possession of the land rather than damages for an infringement of possession. This is the action of ejectment. It may be combined with an action for damages, called an action for mesne profits, which is merely another form of trespass *quare clausum fregit*. Where, therefore, the plaintiff is out of possession at the time of the action, even where he has been dispossessed by the defendant's act of trespass, he will sue in ejectment for recovery of the land and claim damages in the action of mesne profits. Where, on the other hand, he has possession at the time of the action, he will sue in trespass, claiming damages from the defendant, combined with, if necessary, an injunction against further disturbance of his possession.

Measure of damages in trespass

The rule is that the plaintiff recovers from the defendant the loss he has suffered as a result of the trespass. Where damage has been done to premises, he may recover for the cost of repairing the property if he is acting reasonably in having it repaired (see, for example, *Hollebone* v. *Midhurst and Fernhurst Builders* (1968); *Dodd Properties* v. *Canterbury City Council* (1980)); *Ward* v. *Cannock Chase D.C.* (1985)). In *Dominion Mosaics Ltd.* v. *Trafalgar Trucking Ltd.* (1989) the court went further and allowed the plaintiffs the cost of leasing new premises where rebuilding the existing premises was impracticable and taking the lease would reduce damages for loss of profits. But in some cases, his damages may be limited to the reduction in value of the property, particularly where it is held primarily as an investment (*Hole & Son.* v. *Harrisons of Thurscoe* (1973); *Taylor (Wholesale)* v. *Hepworths* (1977)); or where the plaintiff has sold it at the time of the trial (*Murphy* v. *Brentwood D.C.* (1990)—the Court of Appeal decision in that case). The plaintiff is further entitled to a reasonable rental for the land where the defendant has been in occupation of the land and has made use of it (*Whitwham* v. *Westminster Brymbo Coal and Coke Co.* (1896)—the two claims are cumulative—thus in the case itself the defendant had tipped refuse on part of the plaintiff's land. It was held that he must pay damages for the depreciation in the value of the land plus a reasonable amount of rental for that part of the land which the defendant had made use of for tipping). A claim to rental may also arise in a case where the plaintiff's land has suffered no damage. It is unnecessary for the plaintiff to bring evidence to show that he could or would have let the property (*Swordheath* v. *Tabet* (1979)).

In trespass to land, as in other cases of trespass, the damages are at large and there is a possibility of the award of aggravated or exemplary damages. In *Drane* v. *Evangelou* (1978) in which the plaintiff tenant was evicted by the defendant landlord who considered he would gain financial advantage by this action, the case was found to be an appropriate one for the award of exemplary damages under the second category stated by Lord Devlin in *Rookes* v. *Barnard* (*infra*, p. 412).

Injunction

In *Patel* v. *W. H. Smith Ltd.* (1987) the court held that a plaintiff whose title to land is undisputed is entitled to an interlocutory injunction against trespass as of right and with no inquiry as to the balance of convenience between the parties, unless there are exceptional reasons for not allowing it. (In *Woollerton & Wilson Ltd.* v. *Costain* (1970) an interlocutory injunction against trespass to the plaintiffs' airspace was suspended until the defendant contractors had finished their work-*sed quaere*).

Ejectment and the action for mesne profits

In all cases in which the plaintiff wishes to recover possession of his land from the defendant, he must use the action of ejectment. The action is wider in scope than trespass since it lies against a defendant who has come into possession of the plaintiff's land by other means than by committing trespass. The plaintiff must show that he has a right to immediate possession of the land. Proof of his title to the land will of course satisfy this requirement but it is a moot point whether the plaintiff may succeed on the strength of a previous *de facto* possession. It is also not clear whether *jus tertii* is a defence to an action of ejectment.

The action for mesne profits, as already pointed out, is merely a form of trespass *quare clausum fregit*. It is a claim in respect of damage of a trespassory nature done to the land by the defendant, together with a claim for profits taken from the land by the defendant during his occupancy, but unlike trespass is available where the plaintiff had a right to possession rather than possession at the time of the defendant's act. Since it is available in similar circumstances to the action of ejectment, it is normally combined with that action. The theoretical justification for allowing the plaintiff to sue in the action of mesne profits, which is a form of trespass, for acts of the defendant committed when the plaintiff had not possession of the land, is the doctrine of trespass by relation. Under this doctrine, the possession of one with a right to possession of land, who has recovered possession of it, is deemed to extend back to the date when the right to possession came into existence with the result that such a person can sue for trespass committed during the interim period. The theoretical objection against combining the action of mesne profits with the action of ejectment, namely that possession of the land is not recovered until *after* the action of ejectment, with the result that the doctrine of trespass by relation cannot then operate, is overlooked by the courts.

It may be helpful to set out the possibilities of action available to a person whose possession of land has been disturbed (it is assumed that he also has title to the land):

1. Trespass *quare clausum fregit* lies against the person who has actually infringed the plaintiff's possession, whether his act has dispossessed the plaintiff or not, and, if he has dispossessed the plaintiff, whether or not he is now in possession.
2. Where the plaintiff has been dispossessed of his land, it will be more usual to sue the person now in possession with the action of ejectment for recovery of the land, combining this with an action for mesne profits which lies against the present possessor, whether or not he is the person who dispossessed the plaintiff.

3. Where the plaintiff has recovered possession of his land without suing in ejectment, or where he did not claim damages in the action of ejectment, it seems that he may proceed in a claim for damages, either, in the case of the dispossessor, by an action of trespass, or against subsequent possessors, by the action for mesne profits.

4. Finally, there is a summary procedure for the recovery of land laid down by R.S.C. Order 113 (see also C.C.R. Order 26) and appropriate for the recovery of land from squatters. Where a person or persons have entered into or remained on land of which they are in *sole* occupation, a person claiming possession of such land may do so by means of an originating summons supported by an affidavit. This procedure is not only much quicker than the more traditional methods outlined above, but it has the advantage of being available against unidentifiable defendants (one of the features of the "squatters" cases being that the defendants refused to identify themselves thus making it impossible or at least very difficult for proceedings to be commenced against them). However, when recovery of land is sought by this method, no other claim, *e.g.* for mesne profits or damages, can be joined with the originating summons, and the procedure is in any case not available against a tenant holding over after the expiration of the tenancy.

Actions by those without possession or a right to immediate possession of the land

The typical case is that of the reversioner, for example the landlord or the person with an interest in remainder in land. The landlord has contractual protection against the tenant under the lease for damages to the premises. The remainderman is protected against damage done by the tenant for life under the rules of waste. Reversioners also have an action against third parties who have damaged the land in such permanent fashion that the reversioner's interest is prejudiced.

Declaratory judgment

If for any reason it is impossible to prove the requirements of the tort of trespass, it may still be possible for a plaintiff to obtain a declaration of his rights in a declaratory action. A declaratory judgment, though not enforceable by the plaintiff, is of use in cases where the parties are in genuine doubt about their rights and wish the courts to remove this doubt. It therefore may be of use in disputes over title to land. In *Acton Borough Council* v. *Morris* (1953) the defendant locked the door of his house thereby depriving the plaintiffs of access to their flat on the upper storey of the house. The defendant's act was not trespass, but the plaintiffs obtained a declaration from the court of their right to access to the flat.

5. DEFENCES TO THE INTENTIONAL TORTS TO PERSON AND PROPERTY

The defences that will be discussed in this chapter are those available where the defendant has committed an intentional invasion of the plaintiff's interest. Although some of these defences (for example, consent, contributory negligence) are equally applicable in the case of negligence and other non-intentional torts, most of the defences discussed here assume an intentional act by the defendant. The effect of the defence is that the defendant while admitting the commission of what would be a tort seeks to adduce in evidence additional facts which will excuse what he has done. For this reason the burden of proving the facts that establish the defence rests on the defendant.

CONSENT

Consent is the term used to describe the defence that may be available to one who is sued on the basis of his having committed an intentional tort. *Volenti non fit iniuria* is the appropriate term where the plaintiff's consent is relied on in an action brought for negligence or a tort of strict liability by him. The principles applying to the two defences are, however, the same. The consent must be actual in the sense that it is based upon the subjective state of mind of the plaintiff. It may be express or it may be implied from the plaintiff's conduct. The burden of proving the facts necessary to establish the defence rests on the defendant. *Volenti* is considered separately as a defence at pp. 193–198.

In order that consent should operate as a defence to an intentional tort, it must be given to the act complained of, it must not be vitiated by factors such as fraud, duress or undue influence, and the plaintiff must in law be capable of giving a binding consent. The first requirement is illustrated by *Nash* v. *Sheen* (*supra*, p. 23)—(the plaintiff consented to permanent wave, but not to tone-rinse) and by *R.* v. *Williams* (1923) (no defence where a naive teenage girl consented to sexual intercourse on the faith of the defendant's dishonest assurance that it was an operation of benefit to her vocal chords). The case also is an example of a consent vitiated by fraud. On duress the marginal decision in *Latter* v. *Braddell* (1881) is of interest. The plaintiff, a maid-servant, was found to have given a valid consent to an examination by a doctor at the insistence of the defendant, her employer, to find whether she was pregnant. Because the plaintiff believed that the employer had a right to compel her to have the examination, there was found to be no duress. On the third requirement, it is clear that certain persons such as lunatics and infants of tender years do not possess the capacity to give a valid consent. It is still not clearly settled whether the consent of the parents of an infant may operate in law as a defence, for example, when a medical operation has been carried out on the infant (see the *obiter dicta* in favour of allowing the defence in *S.* v. *McC.* (1972).). In any case the defendant here might be able to rely on the defence of necessity (as in the Canadian case of *Marshall* v. *Curry* (1933)). On the other hand it is clear that older infants may be able to give a binding consent on their own behalf and that whether they can do so depends upon the nature of their understanding of the matter and is a question of fact (*Buckpitt* v. *Oates* (1968)—17 year old validly consented to exclusion of liability displayed in car—see also *Gillick* v. *West Norfolk Health Authority* (1985), and the presumption of consent in certain cases of medical treatment under section 8(1), Family Law Reform Act, 1969). The *Gillick* case makes it clear that a consent given by an infant of sufficiently mature understanding cannot be rendered ineffective by parental refusal).

Provided the plaintiff has consented to an act the nature of which he knows, it does not matter that he does not know the quality of it, even if it is clear that had he known he would not have consented. In *Hegarty* v. *Shine* (1878) no battery was committed by one who had sexual intercourse with the plaintiff with her consent without disclosing to her his syphilitic condition and who had thereby infected her. Of course it would have been possible to maintain an action for negligence on these facts but the plaintiff sued in trespass. Some of the judgments in *Hegarty* indicate that it would have been different if the defendant had fraudulently misrepresented his condition, but they are not of one voice on this and the case is not like *R.* v. *Williams*, since there was no misrepresentation as to the nature of the act to be performed. In any case an action for deceit would lie. In the same way, a plaintiff who has consented to a medical operation the nature of which he understands will not be able to sue in battery on the basis that he claims to have been insufficiently informed about the risks of the operation (*cf. Chatterton* v. *Gerson* (1981); *Freeman* v. *Home Office* (1984); *Sidaway* v. *Bethlem Royal Hospital Governors* (1985). Whether such a person could succeed in negligence is considered later in the book (p. 158).

There is authority though of a slender nature that the legal burden of proof on the consent issue lies on the plaintiff, who must plead and prove his own lack of consent (*Christopherson* v. *Bare* (1948); *Freeman* v. *Home Office* (1983)). This does not seem satisfactory. At the very least the defendant has an evidential burden of proving facts which go towards establishing plaintiff's consent, even though the legal burden rests with the plaintiff.

MISTAKE

Mistake is in general no defence to an action brought for an intentional tort such as trespass or conversion. Thus it is trespass to land to enter it believing mistakenly that one has a right to do so, however reasonable that belief. Equally it is trespass or conversion to take away another person's chattel under a mistaken belief it is one's right to do so. A reasonable mistake is in certain circumstances a defence to an action in tort alleging a wrongful arrest (*infra*, this chapter).

INEVITABLE ACCIDENT

In an action of trespass, it appeared to be the law that the burden of proving that he acted neither intentionally nor negligently rested on the defendant—he had to prove inevitable accident. After *Fowler* v. *Lanning* (1959) (*supra*, p. 15) this defence is no longer necessary in an action of trespass to the person (nor probably the other forms of trespass).

SELF-DEFENCE: DEFENCE OF PERSON

The fact that the defendant was acting in the defence of his person may be a valid defence to an action of battery brought by the plaintiff. The defence is made out if the defendant shows that he used no more than reasonable force in the protection of his person. Force may be unreasonable either because it is more than necessary to repel the plaintiff's attack, or because though necessary it is disproportionate to the harm the plaintiff threatened to inflict on the defendant.

Thus, suppose that the plaintiff repeatedly ruffles the hair of the defendant, a much smaller man, against his will, and the defendant eventually stabs the plaintiff. Although there is no authority on the use of disproportionate force, it seems doubtful whether the defendant could here rely on self-defence.

A case for self-defence must exist; a reasonable though mistaken belief by the defendant in his right to act in self-defence is not enough. But it may in this connection be pointed out that one who intentionally induces in another a belief that he is about to use force against him, even if he does not intend to use that force, commits assault. In such a case there is no doubt that a right of self-defence exists, as when a plaintiff has pointed an unloaded gun at the defendant, and the defendant has then used force against the plaintiff.

R. v. *Bird* (1985) holds that there is no rule of law that in order to rely on self-defence the defendant must have demonstrated an initial unwillingness to fight, still less that he must have retreated before the plaintiff's attack.

The courts have also recognised that a person may be justified in acting in the defence of his wife, his family, and his servants. Whether this would be extended to other persons is doubtful. The rule is probably that provided the defendant has acted reasonably in defending another person, he can use this is as a defence.

DEFENCE OF PROPERTY

(i) Ejection of a trespasser

It is well established that reasonable force may be used by one in possession of land to eject a trespasser from that land. The privilege of using force to eject trespassers is limited to the person in possession of the land (*Holmes* v. *Bagge* (1853); *Stroud* v. *Bradbury* (1952)). An owner out of possession must attempt to establish the defence of defence of property which would mean establishing that the property is endangered rather than merely being trespassed upon. In *R.* v. *Chief Constable of Devon and Cornwall* (1982) the Court of Appeal seemed to think *obiter* that an Electricity Board had power at common law to remove demonstrators who were obstructing it in the exercise of its statutory powers, even though the Board did not have possession of the land in question. But the actions of the demonstrators were probably breaches of the peace, and the private citizen may take reasonable steps to prevent another person from committing a breach of the peace (*Albert* v. *Lavin* (1982)).

(ii) Defence of property generally

As a matter of principle, it seems right that force might legitimately be used in the defence of one's own property in other cases than the ejection of a trespasser; for example against one who threatens a trespass, or where an owner of property not in possession of it uses force in its defence. The only decisions appear to be on the defence of property against the attacks of animals.

Thus in *Cresswell* v. *Sirl* (1948) the defendant, acting under the authority of the owner of livestock, shot the plaintiff's dog, which he believed to be about to renew an attack on the livestock. The court held that if the defendant's belief was reasonable, and if he acted reasonably in regarding the shooting as necessary to protect the livestock, he had a good defence. Under section 9(3)(*b*) of the Animals Act 1971, the defendant is also provided with a defence if he has killed or injured a dog when it "has been worrying livestock, has not left the vicinity and is not under the control of any person and there are no practicable means of ascertaining to whom it belongs." *Cresswell* v. *Sirl* remains authority for a common law defence of defence of property. The case seems to be authority for the latter defence rather than for the wider defence of necessity, since the plaintiff would have been liable under the Dogs Act for any injury to the sheep, though in *Rigby* v. *Chief Constable of Northamptonshire* (1985) it was regarded by the court as authority for the existence of the defence of necessity.

Force used must be reasonable

As a general proposition it seems true that reasonable force in the defence of property means something less than reasonable force in the defence of person, but there is very little authority on how much force may be justifiable. In *Collins* v. *Renison* (1754) in which the defendant pulled away a ladder on which the plaintiff, a trespasser, was standing this was held to be an unreasonable use of force. In *Bird* v. *Holbrook* (*supra*, p. 29) in which the defendant set a spring gun on his land which went off and injured the plaintiff, a trespasser, the force clearly was not used for the purpose of ejection, and was therefore unreasonable. The defendant was therefore held liable. On the other hand, in *Ilott* v. *Wilkes* (1820) where the plaintiff, a trespasser, knew of the presence of spring guns on the land, recovery against the defendant was not allowed. In so far as this case suggests that any amount of force is reasonable provided the occupier gives prior warning of it or the trespasser has notice that it may be used, it seems to go too far. The use of a spiked wall or one with broken glass seems, however, clearly justifiable. The purpose is deterrent not retributory and the trespasser has only himself to blame if he takes the risk (as to keeping a savage dog, see, *infra*, p. 295).

NECESSITY

This defence differs from defence of person and property in that it purports to justify the infliction of harm on a person who is not himself threatening the person or property of the defendant. Nor is it necessary for the defendant himself be endangered.

It is an important defence although its scope is not very well-defined. Certain invasions of the plaintiff's person may be justified by reason of the necessity of preserving the plaintiff's own life. For example, force-feeding of the plaintiff prisoner who was on hunger strike in a prison was held not to be a battery (*Leigh* v. *Gladstone*

(1909)). Necessity may also excuse a surgeon who while operating on the plaintiff discovers a condition requiring immediate surgery that goes beyond the terms of the plaintiff's consent to the original operation and who proceeds to perform that surgery (*cf.* the Canadian case of *Marshall* v. *Curry* (1933)). Where, as in the case of a sterilisation operation to be performed on a mental patient, there is no emergency, necessity may still serve as a defence to an action for battery though here it is desirable that a declaration is obtained from the court as to the necessity of the operation prior to its being performed (*Re F.* (1989)).

It is settled law that necessity may successfully be pleaded as a defence where property is destroyed in order to preserve human life. The original authority is the ancient decision in *Mouse's* case (1609). The plaintiff complained that his property had been thrown overboard by the defendant from a ferry-boat travelling up the Thames. The defendant's plea of necessity succeeded, since he established that a need to lighten the ship had arisen because of a storm which threatened the lives of the passengers. *Rigby* v. *Chief Constable of Northamptonshire* (1985) provides modern confirmation of the availability of the defence where property is destroyed in order to save human life. It also shows that the defence is not available to a negligent defendant. In that case the police had fired a canister of CS gas into the premises of the plaintiff in order to flush out a dangerous armed psychopath who had taken refuge there and who was feared to present an immediate danger to the public. The premises as a result caught fire and were destroyed. Holding that in principle necessity was available as a defence here, the court nevertheless held the defendant liable on the ground that the police should have fired the canister only when fire-fighting services were in attendance, and were negligent in failing to do so. The need to preserve human life does not extend to the relief of homelessness so as to make the defence of necessity available to squatters who had entered private property (*London Borough of Southwark* v. *Williams* (1971).

Where the defendant has acted to save property, necessity may be a defence. In *Cope* v. *Sharpe* (No. 2) (1912) the Court of Appeal excused for this reason the action of a gamekeeper who set fire to heather on the plaintiff's land in order to prevent a fire on that land from spreading to land over which his master had shooting rights. The case is unsatisfactory since the question of liability of the plaintiff for the fire on his land is not considered so that defence of property cannot be ruled out. As a decision on necessity the case appears to be authority for three principles. The first is that the court will make a value-judgment as to which property deserved protection—the shooting-rights were valuable, the heather far less so. Secondly, it was important that the defendant was not a mere volunteer, being treated as having the same right to act as his master. It is uncertain whether a mere volunteer could ever rely on necessity as a defence in these circumstances. The third point is that the necessity of the defendant's action is judged at the time it is committed. If it appeared to be reasonably necessary at that time, it is irrelevant that it is later shown to have been unnecessary (as was the case in *Cope* v. *Sharpe (No. 2)*—the fire burned itself out).

The law of tort is very likely to follow the criminal law and reject necessity as a defence where human life is sacrificed in order to preserve other human life (*R.* v. *Dudley and Stevens* (1884, the cannibalism case). There is, however, a principle of uncertain extent under which a person may take purely defensive measures against a danger even though the inevitable or likely result is harm to another person. This certainly is true where property damage is the result. So, although the defendant who discharges flood-water from his land on to that of another person is liable in tort (*Whalley* v. *Lancashire & Yorkshire Ry.* (1880), it is otherwise if he merely erects barricades on his land against the flood causing the flood-water to collect on his neighbour's land (*Nield* v. *L. & N.W.Ry.* (1874); *cf. Greyvensteyn* v. *Hattingh* (1911)). What would have been the position in *Scott* v. *Shepherd* (1773) if the plaintiff had sued the two persons who threw on the squib, one of whom acted in self-preservation, the other merely to protect his property? The answer is complicated by the fact that neither person had time for due consideration of the priorities.

There is some suggestion that a defendant who has established a successful plea of necessity should nevertheless be required to pay compensation to the person who has suffered (*Winfield and Jolowicz on Tort* (13th ed.), p. 709). Requiring the payment of compensation would effectively override the defence and it is difficult to see on what principle it could be ordered (*Burmah Oil Ltd.* v. *Lord Advocate* (1965) merely established that the Crown must pay compensation for acts committed under the royal prerogative).

DISCIPLINE

It is recognised that parents and schoolteachers have a common law power, for the purposes of discipline, to inflict corporal punishment on children within their care. In all cases the force used must be for the purposes of discipline and correction and must be reasonable.

POLICE AND CRIMINAL EVIDENCE ACT 1984

Under this Act, which is one of vast importance and complexity, there is provided for the first time a comprehensive definition of the powers available to the police, and in some instances to private citizens, in the effort to deal with crime. Previously, there had been the powers contained in various separate Acts and the common law. The police powers that are most relevant for present purposes are the power to enter and search vehicles and to search persons (section 1); the power of entry on premises and search under search warrant (section 8); the power of entry on premises without a search warrant for the purpose of effecting an arrest or a recapture of an escaped person (section 17); the power of entry on and search of premises after making an arrest (section 18); the power of seizure by a constable lawfully on premises (section 19); the power of arrest without warrant for arrestable offences (section 24); the power of search upon arrest (section 32); the power of continued detention after arrest (section 34) and the power of questioning suspected persons (Part V). Clearly an account of these powers is beyond the scope of the book. The important point to note is that the various powers where they are lawfully exercised will operate as defences to torts. The most likely of the torts to be used in circumstances where the powers are relied on as defences are the various forms of trespass, trespass to the person (especially false imprisonment), to land and to chattels. The following is an account of the most important police power, that of arrest, a power which in certain circumstances is also available to the private citizen.

ARREST

Lawful arrest operates as a defence to certain torts, primarily battery and false imprisonment. It should be noted that there is no tort of "wrongful arrest" although belief in the existence of such a tort seems to be prevalent at the present day. The plaintiff proves a prima facie false imprisonment and or battery by proving the fact of his detention. The burden of proof then switches to the defendant to establish the defence of lawful arrest. The arrest power is now entirely statutory apart from the common law power of any person to take measures (which include arrest) reasonably thought to be necessary to prevent another person from committing a breach of the peace (*Albert* v. *Lavin* (1982)).

Under the Act the power of arrest without warrant is limited to arrestable offences which are defined in the Act (section 24(1) and (2)). The Act retains the distinction between the powers of arrest of the police constable and the private citizen originally drawn by the decision in *Walters* v. *W.H. Smith* (1914). They share the power of arrest on reasonable suspicion that a person is in the act of committing an arrestable offence (section 24(4)). In the case of arrest for an offence which has been committed, however, the private citizen may only arrest a person whom he reasonably suspects to have committed that offence if it is also shown that the offence has actually been committed—in the case of the police constable it is enough if he has a reasonable suspicion on the latter point (section 24(4) and (5)). Also, the police constable has a power of arrest of a person whom he reasonably suspects to be about to commit an arrestable offence—the private citizen has no statutory power of arrest in this case. "Reasonable suspicion" is not defined in the Act. It is objectively tested—it means something less than a prima facie case that the arrested person has committed the offence, or is committing it, or is about to commit it. (*Hussein* v. *Chong Fook Kam* (1970)).

When a private citizen lawfully arrests, he must bring the arrested person before a police officer or magistrate as soon as it is reasonably practicable to do so and if this is not done the arrest becomes unlawful (*John Lewis & Co.* v. *Tims* (1952)). A police officer, on the other hand, was held in *Dallison* v. *Caffery* (1965) to have a power to take a person arrested for theft to his house to search for stolen property. (This power is preserved by section 30 of the 1984 Act).

Under section 28 of the Act, the arrested person must be informed of the fact of his arrest and the ground for the arrest as soon as is reasonably practicable after the arrest, and in the case of arrest by a police constable this must be done even though the fact of the arrest and the ground for it may be obvious. During the period in which it is still reasonably practicable to inform the arrested person of the ground for his arrest, the arrest is lawful even though the arrested person is not informed at the time when it is reasonably practicable to do so (*D.P.P.* v. *Hawkins* (1988)). An arrest that is originally unlawful because of a breach of section 28 becomes lawful from the moment the breach is repaired (*Lewis* v. *Chief Constable of the South Wales Constabulary* (1991)). When informing the arrested person of the ground for the arrest, it is not necessary to use technical legal language nor to precisely define the offence for which the arrest is made. In *Abbassy* v. *M.P.C.* (1990) it was held that where a person who had refused to answer questions about his ownership of the car he was driving was arrested for "unlawful possession," this was a lawful arrest even though the words could have referred to three different offences (distinguishing *Christie* v. *Leachinsky* (1947) on the ground that the reason given for arrest in that case was spurious). Breach of section 28 renders the arrest unlawful so that an action for false imprisonment will succeed (*Lewis's* case, above). On the other hand where unreasonable force is used in effecting arrest, this does not make the arrest unlawful—the plaintiff must rely on battery rather than false imprisonment (*Simpson* v. *Chief Constable of South Yorkshire Police* (1991)).

CONTRIBUTORY NEGLIGENCE

On one possible view, contributory negligence was not available as a defence to the intentional torts as a matter of law, and the Law Reform (Contributory Negligence) Act 1945, which allows a reduction of damages recovered by the plaintiff because of his contributory negligence, does not alter the position because it applies only to "fault which apart from this Act gives rise to the defence of contributory negligence." No case has adopted this position but the application of the defence to intentional torts and the consequential reduction of damages that then occurs seems unlikely. In *Lane* v. *Holloway* (1968), the Court of Appeal refused to make any deduction for contributory negligence where the plaintiff, a man of 64, had insulted and made a feeble attempt to strike the defendant in answer to which the defendant, aged 24, struck the plaintiff a very severe blow thus injuring him. The defendant acted disproportionately to the provocation received. In the case of a lesser blow the requisite causal connection between the provocation and the blow might have been established. On the other hand, the Court of Appeal thought it possible that a reduction for contributory negligence might be made in an action by the estate of a deceased person who had formed a plot with others to beat up the defendant and as a result the deceased met his death at the hands of the defendant (*Murphy* v. *Culhane* (1977)): accepted in principle also in *Tumelty* v. *M.O.D.* (1988); *Wasson* v. *Chief Constable R.U.C.* (1987)).

Section 11(1) of the Torts (Interference with Goods) Act 1977 provides that contributory negligence is no defence in proceedings founded on conversion or intentional trespass to goods.

TORTS WHICH ARE ALSO CRIMES

It is now not a defence that criminal proceedings are yet to be instituted in relation to the tort (the common law rule which made this a defence where the crime was a felony has disappeared with the abolition of felonies under the Criminal Law Act 1967).

In certain circumstances it is a defence to a civil claim for assault or battery that criminal proceedings in relation to the assault have been taken against the defendant. The circumstances are:

1. The criminal proceedings must have been summary.
2. The justices must either have convicted the defendant, and he must have served a term of imprisonment or have paid a fine, or they must have dismissed the complaint against him on the merits of the case. Such certificate of dismissal may be granted because the assault was not proved, or was justified or was too trivial to merit punishment (Offences against the Person Act 1861, s.45).

A convicted person is not able to collaterally challenge the validity of his conviction in a civil action brought by himself, on the ground that the action is an abuse of the process of the court (*Hunter* v. *Chief Constable of the West Midland Police* (1982)). Thus an action for battery was not allowed to proceed where the criminal court had decided that battery had not been committed against the plaintiff in deciding on his guilt on the criminal charge.

ILLEGALITY

The principle of this defence is that no one can establish a cause of action if to do so it is necessary to rely on his own illegal act or one contrary to the public policy. The authorities on this matter are difficult to harmonise and there have been a number of different approaches by the courts to the problem, though at the end of the day it seems that the single question must arise whether as a matter of public policy the plaintiff's action should be allowed to succeed. The defence seems to be raised with increasing frequency at the present day, possibly because of the courts' reduction in status of the defence of *volenti non fit iniuria*. The defence is less likely to succeed in tort than in contract where it is strictly applied. This is because of the fact that the interests protected by torts are more fundamental than those protected by contract; also, since torts occur unexpectedly, the illegal behaviour is less likely to have a relation to the conduct producing the tort.

Some cases fall readily enough on one side of the line or the other. In *Thackwell* v. *Barclay's Bank* (1986) the plaintiff was not allowed to succeed in an action brought against the bank for conversion of a cheque, since the cheque was obtained by means of a fraud to which the plaintiff was a party. To have allowed the plaintiff to succeed would have allowed him to have obtained the fruits of the fraud, but the court expressed the opinion that the plaintiff would not have succeeded even if he had been innocent in the matter. The case throws some doubt on the earlier Privy Council decision in *Singh* v. *Ali* (1960) (a party to an illegal transaction could bring an action for conversion based on his property rights) and on the generally understood rule that a thief can succeed in trespass or conversion against a third party. The distinction may be that in *Thackwell* the plaintiff needed to obtain the assistance of the bank to obtain the value of the cheque. On the other side of the line is *Saunders* v. *Edwards* (1987). In that case the plaintiff was held to be able to recover damages in an action of deceit brought against the vendor of a house who had fraudulently represented that the house had a roof terrace, even though the plaintiff had been guilty of evading stamp duty in connection with the transaction. The plaintiff's misconduct was minor compared to that of the defendant and was also quite unconnected with the cause of action.

Three main, alternative approaches to the problem of illegality as a defence have been displayed by the courts in recent cases.

(a)   The courts have examined the question of whether the illegality is directly associated with the cause of action or merely tangential to it. *Saunders* v. *Edwards* illustrates this point as does a dictum of Asquith L.J. in *N.C.B.* v. *England* (1954). Postulating the case of two burglars on their way to blow up a safe, he said that no action lay by either burglar for negligence in relation to the blowing-up of the safe, but that he did not doubt that if one picked the pocket of the other on the way to the scene of the crime, an action would lie.

(b)   A second approach proceeds on the basis of determining whether or not in an action for negligence, the illegal conduct makes it impossible for the court to determine the standard of care owed to the plaintiff. This derives from a decision of the Australian High Court in *Jackson* v. *Harrison* (1977) and was adopted by Dillon and Balcombe L.JJ. as their reason for the decision in *Pitts* v. *Hunt* (1989)—plaintiff pillion-passenger who had been urging the defendant motor-cyclist to drive recklessly and break the speed limit could not recover damages from the defendant for injuries suffered in an accident caused by his negligence. This approach also explains the non-liability of the driver of a getaway car to his accompanying criminal occupant and also the non-liability of the police to a passenger in a car which was involved in a police chase (*Marshall* v. *Osmond* (1983)—decision based on no duty of care rather than illegality, but the latter seems to be the true basis of the defence since it is clear that the police in a similar case owe the normal standard of care to lawful users of the highway (*Gaynor* v. *Allen* (1959)).

(c)   Evaluating the seriousness of the illegal conduct is an approach that has commended itself to some judges. For example, the comparative triviality of the plaintiff's misconduct was part of the reason for the decision in

Saunders v. *Edwards* and the potentially serious criminal consequences of the plaintiff's behaviour in *Pitts* v. *Hunt* was relied on by Beldam L.J., though Dillon L.J. in the same case disagreed on the ground that a "graph of illegality" was unworkable.

The courts have still not provided a satisfactory solution to the seemingly simple problem of the availability of the defence against a person who starts a fight and then gets the worse of it. The illegality of the consent given by participants in an illegal prize-fight for the purposes of criminal prosecution (*R.* v. *Coney* (1882) would not prevent the defence of consent being available to either party in civil proceedings (*cf.* also *Madalena* v. *Kuun* (1987)—consent of girl under 16 to intercourse was valid consent in civil action brought by her). Lord Denning in *Murphy* v. *Culhane* (1977) was prepared to allow the defence against one who had participated in an affray. But mere provocative behaviour does not give rise to the defence (*Lane* v. *Holloway* (1968)), even though the provocation is of an extreme nature (*Barnes* v. *Nayer* (1986)), though it now seems possible for a reduction of damages for contributory negligence by the plaintiff to be made here (*supra*, p. 83).

SELF-HELP

Self-help is present in other defences such as self-defence or defence of property. The four defences to be considered here go further in that the self-help which they recognise as a defence may also be an alternative remedy to the bringing of an action in tort by the person executing the self-help.

1. Recaption of chattels

In certain circumstances an owner or one entitled to the immediate possession of a chattel is entitled to recapt it, *i.e.* to take it back from another person, or to enter land and retrieve it from the land. In the former case, recaption may operate as a defence to trespass to the person, in the latter to trespass to land.

In the case of recaption from the person, *Blades* v. *Higgs* (1861) appears to establish that the privilege is available against any person found to be in possession and not merely against the original taker, though in the case itself the plaintiff was found to have been the wrongful taker of the chattel. There is no conclusive authority on what amount of force is legitimate in effecting recaption but it is suggested that it must be no more than reasonably necessary to effect the retaking, and that the recaptor would have the same privilege to overcome resistance as one acting in self-defence or effecting a lawful arrest. Recaption is not available to a bailor against his bailee, since here the commencement of possession is lawful as against the bailor (*Devoe* v. *Long* (1951)).

In the case of recaption from land, it is clear that this remedy is available where the chattel came on to the land by the act of its occupier (*Patrick* v. *Colerick* (1838)). In addition, according to Tindal C.J., speaking *obiter*, in *Anthony* v. *Haney* (1832) it is available where the chattel came on to the land:

(a) accidentally (the example normally given is that of fruit falling on the land from a tree—the *Thorns* case (1466). Whether it would extend to negligent actions of human beings is uncertain—probably not);

(b) by the felonious act of a third party (with the abolition of the distinction between felonies and misdemeanours by the Criminal Law Act 1967, it may be that any criminal act would suffice, though theft is the main probability);

(c) where the occupier refuses a request for redelivery of the chattel (this case might apply on the facts of *British Economical Lamp Co.* v. *Empire Mile End Theatre* (1913) (*supra*, p. 50) which held that the occupier committed no tort in refusing a request for return of the plaintiff's chattel that had been left upon the premises by a third party). This is the difficult case since on the one hand Tindal C.J. in *Anthony* v. *Haney* justified a right of recaption on the ground that the defendant's refusal to return the chattel or allow the plaintiff to retake it is evidence of a conversion, whereas the *British Economical Lamp* case rules out conversion. Legislation seems needed to make an unreasonable refusal to return the chattel, or allow entry to enable it to be removed, conversion.

The list in *Anthony* v. *Haney* clearly excludes the case where the chattel arrived on the land by the intended act of its owner, or under his bailment to the occupier of the land.

2. Re-entry on land

At common law a person entitled to the immediate possession of land could enter it and eject, using only reasonable force, the person in possession. This right operated as a defence to an action for trespass to land. Section 6 of the Criminal Law Act 1977 makes it an offence for anyone other than a "displaced residential occupier" to use or threaten violence for the purpose of securing entry into the premises, provided there is someone on the premises opposed to the entry. It seems likely that this section, like the Forcible Entry Act 1381 which it replaced, will not be interpreted as taking away the entrant's defence to an action of trespass by the occupier (*Hemmings* v. *Stoke Poges Golf Club* (1920)). Under section 3 of the Protection from Eviction Act 1977 it is unlawful for an owner of premises, which have been let under a tenancy which is not a statutorily protected tenancy, to enforce against the occupier of the premises upon the termination of the tenancy his right to recover possession of them except by court proceedings. This section appears to take away the owner's defence to an action of trespass by the occupier (*obiter dicta* of Ormrod L.J. in *McCall* v. *Abelesz* (1976)).

3. Abatement of nuisance

The right of abatement of a nuisance enables one affected by the nuisance to take steps of his own in order to remove the nuisance. Where the abatement is effected by an entry on the land on which the nuisance exists, it affords a defence to the owner's action of trespass.

Abatement as a remedy has an archaic flavour. It is still possible legitimately to abate a nuisance but the privilege is subject to a number of limitations. There are also a number of doubtful points surrounding it. It is settled that the abater must choose the least mischievous or damaging method of abatement if more than one exists. He must give notice to the occupier except where entry on the land on which the nuisance exists is not necessary in order to abate it (*Lemmon* v. *Webb* (1894)) or the case is one of emergency, *i.e.* where there is danger to life or property. None of the cases allow the abater to use force and it is therefore possible that the remedy exists only where it can be effected peaceably. It is also possible, though unsettled, that the nuisance must be one which the court would restrain by injunction, mandatory or prohibitory, though this appears to create a difficult decision for the abater. It is unlikely to be allowed where the damage caused by abatement is disproportionate to the harm inflicted by the nuisance, even though only one method of abatement is possible. This is illustrated by *Perry* v. *Fitzhowe* (1846)—abatement was no defence where the defendant demolished the plaintiff's inhabited house which interfered with the defendant's easement of pasture over the plaintiff's land. Resort to abatement does not, on the better view, take away the option to pursue a remedy in damages for the nuisance (*Smith* v. *Giddy* (1904)).

4. Distress damage feasant

If the plaintiff's chattel is unlawfully on the defendant's land, and has caused or is causing damage there, the defendant may seize the chattel and retain it until the plaintiff compensates him for the damage. This form of distress operates as a defence to the plaintiff's action for conversion or detinue. The defence now applies only to the seizure of inanimate chattels, and of animals not forming "livestock" within section 7 of the Animals Act 1971 (*infra*, p. 296). For example, in *Ambergate Ry. Co.* v. *Midland Ry. Co.* (1853) the defendants lawfully distrained damage feasant the plaintiff's railway engine which was encumbering the lines of the defendant. Under the common law right, the chattel must have come on to the land in circumstances amounting to a tort, commonly trespass or nuisance, it must not be in use at the time of seizure, and the right to seize is available only as long as the chattel remains on the land.

6. NEGLIGENCE

Negligence is a universal concept in legal systems. But as a ground of liability in itself for causing damage it is not so common. The evolution of negligence as a tort separate from trespass has already been considered (pp. 13–17, *supra*). It is now time to look at the tort of negligence itself.

At one time, although there were numerous instances of liability in negligence, there was no connecting principle formulated which could be regarded as the basis of all of them. In 1932, the House of Lords in *Donoghue* v. *Stevenson*, had to decide whether a cause of action in tort existed where the plaintiff alleged that, owing to the negligence of the defendant, a manufacturer of soft drinks, a bottle of ginger beer manufactured by the defendant and purchased for the plaintiff by a friend, contained a snail, which appeared in decomposed form when the plaintiff poured the contents of the bottle into a glass from which she was drinking, and as a result of which the plaintiff suffered personal injury in the form of gastro-enteritis and nervous shock. While the manufacturer was in contractual relationship with retailers of his products, he had no contract with the plaintiff and it had been supposed till then that a person in a contractual relationship with another person could owe no duty of care in the performance of that contract to persons not parties to the contract. This the majority in the House of Lords held not to be the law. They laid down the important rule that a manufacturer of products owes a duty of care in their manufacture to all persons who are foreseeably likely to be affected by lack of care in the preparation of those products. The "privity of contract" objection was therefore disposed of, and the so-called narrow rule in *Donoghue* v. *Stevenson* was established (for the effect of this rule *infra*, p. 229 *et seq.*).

90

The case owes its chief importance, however, to the fact that it contains an attempt by the chief appellate court to provide a general formulation of liability in negligence. Lord Atkin's judgment is most important in this respect. He said that negligence depends upon proof that one person has committed a breach of duty of care binding upon himself and owed to another and has thereby caused injury to that other. Whether a duty of care is owed to another depends upon whether that other is in law a neighbour and Lord Atkin described a neighbour as a person "so closely and directly affected by [my] act that I ought reasonably to have [him] in contemplation as being so affected when I am directing my mind to the acts or omissions which are called in question." This statement is often described, for convenience's sake, as "the neighbour principle." It is clear that Lord Atkin considered that a person was under a duty of care in respect of his acts or omissions whenever it was foreseeable that lack of care either in acting or omitting to act would produce injury or damage to another human being.

The existence of a separate tort of negligence was thus conclusively established. In the years since 1932, the tort has developed to such an extent that it is clearly now the most important tort. Quantitatively, actions in negligence far exceed those brought for any other tort. Besides this, negligence is in the process of absorbing other areas of tortious liability. Thus liability for defective premises and chattels is now governed almost exclusively by negligence. Negligence has taken over much of the area of liability formerly occupied by trespass, and appears at the moment to be in the process of doing the same thing to nuisance. On the other hand, the breadth of Lord Atkin's statement in *Donoghue* v. *Stevenson* has not received acceptance. It is not universally true that whenever there is foreseeability of harm the defendant is under a duty to so regulate his conduct that such harm is not produced. A number of so-called exceptions to the neighbour principle, the extent of which will be discussed in this chapter, were recognised by the courts. In *Home Office* v. *Dorset Yacht Co.* (1970), the House of Lords gave its consideration to the question of the basis upon which such exceptions rest. In that case it was held by a majority of four to one that the Home Office owed a duty of care to the plaintiffs in respect of the detention of certain borstal trainees who had escaped from a borstal institution and had caused damage to the plaintiffs' yacht. Of those in the majority, Lords Reid, Morris and Pearson clearly thought that the neighbour principle of Lord Atkin had the status of a rule of law, subject only to exceptions based upon a "justification or valid explanation," or upon grounds of policy. Lord Diplock thought, however, that foreseeability was only one element in determining the existence of a duty of care. In deciding whether to recognise a new duty, the court must also look at previous decisions by way of analogy and at the policy aspects of the case. Applying this to the facts of the case before him, Lord Diplock was prepared to extend the duty that already existed in respect of actions of prisoners committed inside the prison (*Ellis* v. *Home Office* (1953)) to actions committed by the prisoner on escape in the vicinity of the prison.

Anns v. London Borough of Merton (1977)

The Dorset Yacht case left the law relating to duty of care unsettled. There were minor differences in the formulation of the duty among those judges in general agreement with each other (Lords Reid, Morris and Pearson) and Lord Diplock had a different conception of it. *Anns* provided an attempt at synthesis. In *Anns* the question was whether a local authority owed a duty of care in relation to the exercise or non-exercise of its statutory powers of inspection of the foundations of houses under construction in its area to future purchasers of those houses. The House of Lords held that a duty of care might under certain conditions come into existence (the precise basis of the decision is considered later in this chapter). The importance of *Anns* for present purposes is that it provided a general test for duty of care in the judgment of Lord Wilberforce with which three other members of the House of Lords including Lord Diplock agreed. According to this test the court must decide two questions: first, whether there is a sufficient relationship of proximity or neighbourhood between defendant and plaintiff so that the former reasonably contemplates that carelessness on his part may damage the latter; secondly, granted that such proximity exists, whether there are any grounds on which the law should negative, reduce or limit the scope of the prima facie duty that is owed.

The *Anns* two-tier test provided at first sight a reasonably convincing solution to the problem of defining the conditions for determining the existence of a duty of care. By "reasonable contemplation" it is apparent that Lord Wilberforce referred to foreseeability, but it is also clear that the foreseeability of harm must be reasonable and would not extend to mere fanciful possibilities. The prima facie duty identified at the first stage did not of course transfer any burden of proof to the defendant since the question was one of law. And the second-tier stage gave the court the widest possible choice amounting to a discretion, including the factors of both policy and justice, as to whether or not to uphold the prima facie duty established at the first stage.

Retreat from the Anns two-tier test

The earliest signs of retreat from the two-tier test came in cases concerning the same (or similar to) factual situation as that in *Anns* (*i.e.* the duty of care owed by local authorities as regards the inspection of the foundations of houses). In *Peabody Donation Fund* v. *Parkinson* (1984) the House of Lords held that no duty of care was owed by a local authority where the plaintiff owner of the house was not its occupier since the loss as far as the owner was concerned was pure economic loss; nor was any duty owed to an owner where, as in the *Peabody* case, the owner's agent was jointly responsible for the defectiveness of the foundations. Both points were justified by the argument that the first tier stage of *Anns* was not solely concerned with foreseeability—it also must be found to be just and reasonable that a duty should exist. Next in *Leigh & Sillavan* v. *Aliakmon Shipping Co.* (1986) the House of Lords held that the *Anns* test was concerned only with novel duty situations (*i.e.* those which had not been previously considered by the courts), so that the basic rule that an action in negligence for an act of the defendant causing pure economic loss was not available, applied. Then in *Yuen Kun Yew* v. *A.-G. of Hong Kong* (1987) the Privy Council held that the Commissioner of Deposit-taking Companies in Hong Kong owed no duty of care to depositors in the company, who had lost money through the fraud of those running it, in relation to the Commissioner's powers of refusal of registration to or deregistration of the company, since there was no sufficiently "close and direct relationship" between the Commissioner and the depositors, bearing in mind that the Commissioner had no control over the day-to-day running of the company. The words "close and direct" were taken from Lord

Atkin's judgment in *Donoghue* v. *Stevenson*. It is doubtful whether he meant any more by them than that foreseeability must be reasonable, but the Privy Council found them to create an additional test.

These qualifications on *Anns* were put together in the decision of the House of Lords in *Caparo Industries plc* v. *Dickman* (1990). In *Caparo* the House of Lords was concerned with the question whether accountants in preparing the annual audited accounts of a company owed a duty of care to a shareholder in the company which had on the strength of the accounts increased its shareholding in the company and had lost money when it was found that the accounts overstated the company's assets. The leading judgments of Lords Bridge and Oliver establish that there are three requirements in determining the existence of a duty of care in a novel fact situation (which this was as far as the House of Lords was concerned). There must be reasonable foreseeability of the relevant loss, it must be just and reasonable that a duty should exist and there must exist a sufficient relationship of proximity between defendant and plaintiff (the *Yuen Kun Yew* requirement). Clearly the first requirement was satisfied, but the House held that no duty of care existed by reference to the second and third requirements. Lords Bridge and Oliver emphasised, however the lack of clear indication that these additional tests gave. According to Lord Oliver: "The three requirements of proximity, justice and reasonableness and degree of foreseeability might be regarded as facets of the same thing." Proximity was a convenient expression but was not a definable concept but a "description of circumstances from which pragmatically the law concludes that a duty of care exists." This seems to mean that proximity can only express a result—it cannot indicate what that result should be. Lords Bridge, Oliver and Roskill all approved a statement of Brennan J. in the Australian case of *Sutherland S.C.* v. *Heyman* (1985): "The law should develop novel categories of negligence incrementally and by analogy with existing categories rather than by a massive extension of a prima facie duty of care restrained only by indefinable 'considerations.' " (*i.e.* the *Anns* test). Lord Keith in the *Yuen Kun Yew* case expressly recognised that the second tier of Lord Wilberforce's test would now seldom be relied on by a court to solve a duty problem. It now seems reserved for pure issues of policy (for example, it was to some extent used in *Hill* v. *Chief Constable of W. Yorkshire Police* (1988) to produce a conclusion that the police owed no duty of care to citizens in relation to the apprehension of criminals). It is also thought to explain the decision in *Rondel* v. *Worsley* (1967) that a barrister owes no duty of care to his client as regards the conduct of litigation).

It is too early to assess the impact of the present approach of the House of Lords to the duty of care. Three points seem, however, to be readily apparent. First, in refusing to recognise reasonable foreseeability as even a prima facie indicator of duty the law has regressed to a pre-*Donoghue* v. *Stevenson* position (though of course the duties of care established under that case continue to stand). Secondly, the difficulty of establishing a "novel" duty of care is greater under the present approach than under any of the previous approaches. Thirdly, the element of discretion in the decision whether to establish a new duty is more frankly recognised than it has been in the past.

The demise of Anns—Murphy v. Brentwood D.C. (1990)

The collapse of the two-tier test was achieved before *Murphy* under the cases just considered. In *Murphy* the House of Lords overruled *Anns* as far as its own duty situation was concerned, *i.e.* the duty of care owed by local authorities as regards the statutory powers of inspection of buildings under construction in their area to future purchasers. The case is considered under liability for pure economic loss in this chapter.

Novel duties, notional duty; duty on the facts

The law has generally drawn a distinction between two aspects of the duty of care in the tort of negligence, the notional duty and the duty on the facts. The notional duty is the duty of care that arises as a matter of law in the generalised factual situation before the court (for example motorist towards road-users, occupier towards visitors, employer towards employees); the duty on the facts is concerned with the particular factual situation before the court (for example, should the particular motorist have foreseen harm to the particular road-user as the result of his negligent driving). It should be noted that duties of care in negligence are owed to particular persons—there is no general duty of care, no "negligence in the air." The plaintiff must therefore show a duty of care owed to him, or to a class including him.

The notional duty device is a convenient one, allowing duties of care to be stated in prospective terms (whereas duty on the facts can only be determined retrospectively), but has the limitation that it can only be made use of where the existence of a duty situation has previously been determined by a court. When under Lord Atkin's neighbour principle foreseeability was arguably the sole determinant of duty, in a novel fact situation the determination of duty on the facts fulfilled the function of determining the existence of a notional duty at the same time (and even on Lord Wilberforce's two-tier test it could establish a prima facie duty). Now that under *Caparo* foreseeability has become a mere necessary condition of duty, this is no longer possible. The concept of duty on the facts is likely to disappear, being subsumed into that of breach of duty of care.

CONSTITUENT REQUIREMENTS OF NEGLIGENCE

The tort of negligence is not merely carelessness causing damage. There must be a duty of care recognised by law in the situation in which the defendant finds himself. There must be a breach of that duty. There must be damage resulting from that breach. The damage that results must not be too remote a consequence of the breach. These constituent requirements of the tort will be examined in this and the succeeding chapters beginning with the examination of the requirement of duty of care.

Duty of care in law
In the remainder of this chapter will be considered a number of well-known cases where for reasons relating to the factors considered relevant by *Caparo* courts have been reluctant to recognise a duty of care. In some cases this is expressed by an outright refusal to impose a duty; in others, by the recognition of a duty less extensive than that which would apply if foreseeability alone were the test.

1. Negligent statements
The courts have been reluctant to establish a rule that a defendant who negligently makes a false statement is always liable

if the plaintiff foreseeably suffers loss as the result of the statement. This has been because it was thought that to some extent different considerations applied to words than to acts. A plaintiff suing in tort would be likely to be relying on a statement by the defendant for which the latter had not been paid, and this led to the view that it would be unfair to hold the defendant liable. Also, "words travel faster than deeds." The problem of indeterminacy arises, *i.e.* of excessive liability because the defendant may be liable to an "indeterminate class, for an indeterminate time and in an indeterminate amount" (*Ultramares Corp.* v. *Touche* (1931)). The problem of indeterminancy is particularly apparent where liability exists for pure economic loss. Thus until 1964 the courts refused to award damages for negligent statements causing financial loss to the plaintiff unless the false statement constituted a breach of contract made between plaintiff and defendant, or the defendant was in a fiduciary position towards the plaintiff. Where the defendant's statement did not amount to a breach of contract but had induced the plaintiff to contract with the defendant (called a misrepresentation) the plaintiff could not recover damages from the defendant but was allowed the equitable remedy of rescission of the contract. The position differed if the false statement was made fraudulently by the defendant. Then the plaintiff could get damages for the amount of his loss in the tortious action of deceit.

The position thus summarised has been altered by two important changes in the law, by means of which it is now possible for the courts to make an award of damages for a negligent statement. The first change was brought about by the decision of the House of Lords in *Hedley Byrne & Co. Ltd.* v. *Heller and Partners Ltd.* (1964). The second change was the enactment of the Misrepresentation Act 1967.

The Hedley Byrne case

In this case the plaintiffs, Hedley Byrne & Co. who were advertising agents, asked their bank to inquire into the financial position of one of their clients, a company on behalf of which they wished to undertake certain advertising orders. The bank made inquiries of the defendants, the company's bank, which gave favourable references about the company, stating that these were made "without responsibility." As a result of relying on this advice, the plaintiffs lost money when the company went into liquidation. The plaintiffs' action in negligence against the defendants failed because of the defendants express disclaimer of responsibility for their reference.

The importance of the decision lies in the fact that all the members of the House of Lords thought that in appropriate circumstances an action for a negligent statement would lie, disagreeing with the contrary decision of the Court of Appeal in *Candler* v. *Crane, Christmas & Co.* (1951). The principle that negligent statements may be actionable in tort may be taken to be established, since the *Hedley Byrne* reasoning has been followed on a number of occasions both here and in Commonwealth jurisdictions.

It is a more difficult matter to deduce from the speeches of the House of Lords what circumstances are necessary in order to make the statement actionable. All the members of the House were agreed that mere foreseeability of harm by the maker of the statement was not enough; that a special relationship between plaintiff and defendant was necessary. There were differences in the explanations of what gives rise to this relationship. Lord Reid thought it arose where the "party seeking the information or advice was trusting the other to exercise such a degree of care as the circumstances required, where it was reasonable for him to do that, and where the other gave the information or advice when he knew or ought to have known that the inquirer was relying on him." Lord Morris, with whom Lords Hodson and Pearson were in agreement, said that a voluntary undertaking to apply a special skill possessed by the defendant for the assistance of the plaintiff would give rise to a duty of care "quite irrespective of contract." That liability included the giving of gratuitous information or advice by the defendant to the plaintiff who is known or should be known to be relying on it. Lord Devlin went no further than to say that a relationship "equivalent to contract" must exist between plaintiff and defendant. The varying formulations of the special relationship in the speeches of the House of Lords in *Hedley Byrne* may give rise to different results in their application to particular situations. Lord Reid's rubric is close to the facts of the *Hedley Byrne* case itself in requiring the giving of information or advice by the defendant to the plaintiff and a reliance on that advice by the plaintiff. It may be assumed that the reliance would have to be detrimental, *i.e.* that the plaintiff should have to act on the advice to his loss. Lord Morris's ratio, though it includes within itself Lord Reid's, is wider since it extends to voluntary undertakings to use skill in general, so that liability would arise for failure to perform the undertaking, and that liability could arise whether the failure consisted in words or deeds. It is now clear that *Hedley Byrne* liability is not limited to the simple case of words spoken by the defendant to the plaintiff and acted on by the latter to his loss, but the limits of liability for undertakings are by no means clear. Under Lord Morris's ratio, for example, a detrimental reliance does not seem necessary if we accept his example of the liability of a doctor who voluntarily undertakes to treat a sick man and negligently fails to cure him. According to Lord Morris the doctor would there be liable even if the patient was unconscious at the time of the treatment. The matter remains untested. Common to the judgments of the members of the House of Lords is the requirement that the defendant should voluntarily assume responsibility for the giving of careful advice or the exercise of care in the undertaking. Clearly this assumption of responsibility may be implied rather than expressed. Also, it can be expressly negatived, as indeed was the case in *Hedley Byrne* itself. The precise function of the concept of voluntary assumption of responsibility has never been clear. The mere voluntary making of a statement is clearly not enough to bring it into play. It is more a question of volunteering to be liable for the statement, but as Lord Griffiths points out in *Smith* v. *Bush* (1989) that sort of position is never expressly taken by the defendant and is therefore merely an inference of the court drawn from the circumstances in which the statement is made. The expression is now generally used by courts to refer to one of two things: (i) a voluntary undertaking to act or make a statement in the future (as in the Court of Appeal decisions in *Banque Keyser Ullman S.A.* v. *Skandia Insurance Ltd.* (1988) and *Reid* v. *Rush & Tompkins Group plc* (1989); (ii) a shorthand way of expressing the requirement of proximity between defendant and plaintiff insisted on by the House of Lords in *Caparo Inds. plc* v. *Dickman* (1990)—the defendant must "assume responsibility" towards the plaintiff or a class including the plaintiff.

The *Hedley Byrne* case was an action for purely economic loss. Hitherto it had been thought to be the case that actions for negligence did not lie in relation to such loss. Certain statements in the judgments of Lord Devlin to the effect that no distinction should be drawn according to whether the loss is physical damage or economic only, have not been accepted by later decisions (*infra*, p. 116), and the *Hedley Byrne* decision must continue to be regarded as an exception to the basic rule.

An attempt to whittle down the generality of the *Hedley Byrne* principle was made in the Privy Council decision of *Mutual Life and Citizens' Assurance* v. *Evatt* (1971). In that case the Privy Council suggested a limitation upon *Hedley Byrne* to the effect that it applied only to advice given in the ordinary course of the business or profession of the adviser, or to advice given where there was an express undertaking by the adviser to exercise business or professional skill, or possibly where the adviser had a financial interest in the advice being taken. The Privy Council therefore held by a majority that a pleading which alleged that an insurance company had negligently misrepresented to the plaintiff the financial condition of one of its related companies, in which as a result the plaintiff invested his money and lost it, disclosed no cause of action, since the case fell outside the three categories. As a Privy Council case, *Mutual Citizens* does not bind English courts, and had the peculiarity also that two of the leading judges in the *Hedley Byrne* case (Lords Reid and Morris) were the dissenting minority in it. It was open to the objection that it applied the need for business or professional skill to the mere giving of information, whereas that sort of skill might not be needed to produce the information concerned. In this it ran contrary to an earlier first instance decision (*Anderson* (*W.B.*) v. *Rhodes* (*Liverpool*) (1967)) and was soon not followed by the Court of Appeal in *Esso Petroleum Co.* v. *Mardon* (1976)—defendants held liable for a statement as to the annual throughput of petrol sold at their garage.

As regards advice, the position is more difficult. In Australia, the majority of the High Court refused to accept the *Mutual Citizens* limitations whether the statement was one of information or advice, taking the view that no absolute distinction could be drawn between them, though the case itself concerning a statement by the defendant Council as to whether a road-widening scheme existed affecting land the plaintiffs were intending to buy was a clear case of mere misinformation (*L. Shaddock* v. *Parramatta C.C.* (1981)). The reason given by the Privy Council in *Mutual Citizens* for not imposing a duty of care on a defendant not professing business or professional skill, *i.e.* the impossibility of fixing a standard of care for such a person has some cogency in relation to advice of a business or professional nature but could be answered (as it was by the minority in *Mutual Citizens*) by applying a lower standard of care to the defendant. Even if the possibility of a duty is recognised in these circumstances, the section could fail for standard *Hedley Byrne* reasons, for example the defendant could establish that he ought not to have realised reliance was being placed on him, or that the plaintiff's reliance was unreasonable.

Effect of the Hedley Byrne decision

The effect of the *Hedley Byrne* decision will now be considered in the light of the case law that has arisen in the years after it was decided.

(a) *Hedley Byrne and contract.* There is a clear possibility of overlap between negligent breach of contract and liability for negligence under the *Hedley Byrne* case. In particular, Lord Morris's ratio in *Hedley Byrne* based on liability for a voluntary undertaking to use skill for the benefit of the plaintiff creates possibilities of overlap with contractual liability of professionally skilled persons, though the undertaking these persons give is not voluntary in the sense of being gratuitous. *Midland Bank Trust* v. *Hett, Stubbs and Kemp* (1978) accepted that there could be overlapping duties of care in contract and tort owed by a solicitor to his client. In that case it was held that the defendants' negligent failure to register an estate contract in time to prevent its being unenforceable through conveyance of the land to a third party gave rise to liability both in contract and in tort under the *Hedley Byrne* case. The liability was here truly concurrent, *i.e.* the same facts gave rise to both causes of action. The courts, however, have shown resistance to allowing the tort action based on the *Hedley Byrne* case to intrude into contractual situations in such a way as to extend contractual liability or to defeat contractual arrangements deliberately entered into. In *Tai Hing Cotton Mill* v. *Liu*

Chang Hing Bank (1986) the Privy Council held that a bank customer's duty of care towards his bank arising under the implied terms of his contract was limited to not drawing cheques in such a way as to facilitate fraud or forgery and to informing the bank of unauthorised drawing of cheques on the account, and that no higher duty of care could be established by relying on tort. So also in *Greater Nottingham Co-operative Society* v. *Cementation Piling Ltd.* (1988) the court refused to find a voluntary assumption of responsibility by the defendant going beyond the specific provisions of the contract itself. An example of refusal by the courts to allow the tort action to interfere with contractual arrangements deliberately entered into by the parties is the case of *Pacific Associates Ltd.* v. *Baxter* (1989). The plaintiffs had entered into an oceanic construction contract with the employers on the terms that the question whether delays in the work were unforeseeable was to be referred to the defendant engineer who was employed under contract with the employers. The plaintiffs' contract contained an arbitration clause for the resolution of disputes on this matter and a clause exempting the defendant from liability to the plaintiffs for the performance of his work. Dissatisfaction with the defendant's refusal to certify that difficulties in the work were unforeseeable and with the results of an arbitration led the plaintiffs to sue the defendants for negligence. The Court of Appeal held that quite apart from the arbitration and exclusion of liability clauses, the defendant was not liable to the plaintiffs because the contractual arrangements entailed that he assumed responsibility to the employers alone. The two clauses merely confirmed that position.

As regards negligent statements which induce the making of a contract the Court of Appeal decided in *Esso Petroleum Co.* v. *Mardon* that *Hedley Byrne* liability might exist in relation to such statements. There is here the possibility of overlap with the remedy under section 2(1) of the Misrepresentation Act 1967. The remedy under the Misrepresentation Act is in some respects more advantageous to the plaintiff than the action under *Hedley Byrne* (*infra*, p. 114 *et seq.*).

(b) *Legal advisers.* The *Midland Bank Trust* case held that the solicitor may be liable for his professional negligence in tort as well as contract. The barrister who is not in contractual relation with his clients, can only be sued in tort. The courts have accepted in principle that barristers may be sued in negligence as a result of the *Hedley Byrne* decision (thus tending to confirm the "undertaking" ratio of Lords Morris and Hodson). However, a major exemption from liability exists, applying to both barristers and solicitors but peculiarly available to barristers. This is that an immunity from liability in negligence exists in relation to the conduct of litigation; this immunity extends to some pre-trial work (*Rondel* v. *Worsley* (1967); *Saif Ali* v. *Sydney Mitchell & Co.* (1977)). On the other hand, in relation to non-litigious work such as the drafting of wills and settlements and the giving of opinions, barristers, as well as solicitors, may be liable for negligence.

There are two questions arising concerning the immunity. First, why should it exist at all? Secondly, what is its extent? Among the reasons given by the courts in the *Rondel* and *Saif Ali* cases are the advocate's public duty to the court as well as to his client, the necessity to protect him while carrying out his task from the anxiety of a threatened law-suit, the public interest requiring that the decision of one court should not be questioned by another court (except through the appeal process), and the immunity from suit extended to other participants in the judicial process.

One of the main problems in deciding on the liability of a legal adviser for professional negligence was that it might require the trial court to consider whether, apart from that negligence, the decision of the court in which that negligence played a part would have been differently decided. The Court of Appeal has now decided in *Somosundaram* v. *M. Julius Melchior & Co.* (1989) that this inquiry will not be entertained, that in so far as the claim requires the court to decide whether the decision of another court has been properly made, it will not be allowed to succeed. The case makes clear that the rule applies whether the other decision is that of a criminal or civil court. This, therefore, is now no longer a mere factor in determining whether an action for professional negligence against the legal adviser will be allowed, but an absolute bar applicable to actions against both barrister and solicitor. There are of course limits to the bar—the plaintiff may have suffered loss through negligence even though the eventual result of a case is in his favour, and this would apply even where he succeeded on a technicality. As regards the extent of the advocate's immunity, the test laid down in the New Zealand case of *Rees* v. *Sinclair* (1974) was approved by the majority of the House of Lords in the *Saif Ali* case:

> "Each piece of pre-trial work should be tested against the one rule—that the protection exists only where the particular work is so intimately connected with the conduct of the case in court that it can fairly be said to be a preliminary decision affecting the way that the cause is conducted when it comes to a hearing."

(c) *Judges, arbitrators etc.* A judge is not liable for negligence in the performance of his duties, part of the general judicial immunity from suit. That immunity applies only to acts done in performance of his judicial office and at least in the case of the judge of an inferior court does not extend to acts done in excess of jurisdiction (*cf. Sirros* v. *Moore* (1975); *McC.* v. *Mullan* (1984)). Arbitrators, also, are not liable in negligence to the parties to the arbitration (an appeal may lie to the courts on fact or law from the arbitrator's decision—Arbitration Act 1979). The mere fact, however, that a person is to decide a question, rather than resolve a dispute, as between two parties does not give him the status of an arbitrator (*Arenson* v. *Casson, Beckman Rutley* (1975)). Thus a person who agrees to value shares owes a duty of care in respect of the valuation to both seller and prospective buyer (*Arenson* case). So also the House of Lords held in *Sutcliffe* v. *Thackrah* (1974) that an architect, employed to certify to his client that building work undertaken for his client by a building contractor had been properly completed, owed a duty of care to the client in respect of the certification. The distinction between the function of the arbitrator and cases of the latter sort is that the arbitrator must act in accordance with the submissions and evidence of the parties to the arbitration whereas in the latter type of case the expert appointed is entitled to rely in addition on his own expert opinion (see *Palacath* v. *Flanagan* (1985)).

In *Sutcliffe* v. *Thackrah* there were dicta of the court (especially of Lord Salmon) to the effect that a duty of care would also have been owed by the architect to the building contractor who was not in contract with him. This received disapproval from Purchas L.J. in *Pacific Associates Ltd.* v. *Baxter* (*supra*) on the ground that the architect's only assumption of responsibility was to the building owner under his contract with him, even though in performing that contract he had to maintain an even hand between owner and contractor. The *Arenson* and *Palacath* cases seem to be free of this problem since in both cases the services of the defendants were jointly requested by the parties to the issue.

(d) *Nature of statement.* It is now clear that the rules of equity which placed limits upon the notion of misrepresentation for the purpose of equitable rescission do not apply to misstatements for the purpose of *Hedley Byrne* liability. Thus misstatements of law, of opinion and of intention are actionable under that case (for a case imposing liability for a negligent misstatement as to a third party's intention, see *Cherry* v. *Allied Insurance Brokers* (1978)). Liability clearly may exist in relation to opinions, although these are particularly, though not exclusively, subject to Lord Pearce's qualification in *Hedley Byrne* that the circumstances in which they are given must emphasise the gravity of the inquiry. It would clearly be inappropriate, for example, to expect a considered diagnosis of a certain company's shares from a financial adviser at a cocktail party. This merely follows from the rule laid down in Lord Reid's speech in *Hedley Byrne* that reliance on the statement must be reasonable. Opinions may differ on the question whether the circumstances emphasise the gravity of the inquiry on particular facts. In *Howard Marine Dredging Co.* v. *Ogden* (1978) Lord Denning held that an oral statement concerning the carrying capacity of barges which the defendants were thinking of hiring from the plaintiffs made by the plaintiffs' representatives during pre-contractual negotiations was made off-the-cuff since the speaker had not purported to look the matter up. Shaw L.J., however, thought, more persuasively, that the speaker should be liable, since the defendants had travelled from the south of England to the north east to discuss the matter, and the carrying capacity of the barges was vital to their decision whether to hire them. The defendant is of course able to put the matter beyond doubt by pointing out that he is not purporting to make a considered statement. There is no authority at present on the position where the defendant invites reliance upon the statement by the plaintiff, who is unduly credulous and acts on the statement where a reasonable person would have concluded that a considered statement had not been made and would not have so acted.

Liability would here exist if there was deceit on the defendant's part, but probably not if he merely should have foreseen that the plaintiff would act on the statement.

(e) *Voluntary undertaking by the defendant producing detrimental reliance by the plaintiff.* Where the plaintiff has actually acted to his loss on the undertaking, there is no problem with the nonfeasance rule (*infra*, this chapter) so that the case is a form of *Hedley Byrne* liability, though liability is for failure to carry out the undertaking rather than for misstatement. There are numerous pointers to liability existing in this case though generally of a fairly weak nature. There are dicta to this effect of Slade L.J. in *Banque Keyser Ullman S.A.* v. *Skandia Insurance Co. Ltd.* (1988) and of Ralph Gibson L.J. in *Reid* v. *Rush & Tompkins Ltd.* (1989) though both speak of assumption of responsibility rather than undertaking. There are the first instance decisions in *Chaudhury* v. *Prabhakar* (1989) (defendant undertook to find accident-free car for the plaintiff and selected one which had been in an accident— but the duty was conceded and the case could anyway be regarded as an implied statement rather than an undertaking case); and *Balsamo* v. *Medici* (1984) (defendant had assumed responsibility but not to the plaintiff of whose identity he was unaware and therefore was not liable to him). The troublesome case of *Junior Books* v. *Veitchi* (1982), in which a sub-contractor was held liable to the plaintiffs for laying a defective floor in a factory bought by the plaintiffs although it was not in contractual relationship with them, tends to be explained by the present judiciary in terms of assumption of responsibility and reliance, the sub-contractor being nominated under the terms of the main contract by the plaintiffs (see, for example Lord Bridge in *Caparo Industries plc* v. *Dickman*). The clearest example of this form of liability being imposed is the New Zealand decision in *Meates* v. *A.-G.* (1983). The New Zealand government was there held liable for certain non-contractual promises of financial support which it gave to a company and its shareholders in reliance on which the shareholders had refrained from liquidating the company at a time when there was some money left for shareholders. The financial support not being forthcoming from the defendant, the company was forced into liquidation and the shareholders suffered a total loss for which in part the defendant was held liable. *Meates* indicates that this form of liability, though related to *Hedley Byrne*, is quite far removed from it. The liability was not for negligently promising but for negligently failing to carry out the promise, which is more like contract than tort.

(f) *Duty to speak.* Where the defendant has offered to explain a point to the plaintiff, he must provide a full explanation which does not give only half the truth. In *Cornish* v. *Midland Bank* (1985) the defendants undertook to explain to a wife the nature of a mortgage which the bank had taken over her house, but omitted to inform her of the unusual nature of the mortgage in question in that it covered not just the initial loan but also all further advances made by the bank to her husband. The defendants were held to be unable to enforce the mortgage in respect of those further advances. *Cornish* rests on the existence of an assumption of responsibility (or voluntary undertaking) to speak by the defendant.

The next problem arises where the defendant becomes aware of the falsity of the statement after it was made, not being negligent at the time of making it. Here there are two conflicting cases. In *Argy Trading Development Co.* v. *Lapid Development Co.* (1977) the defendant landlords had informed the plaintiff tenants that the demised premises were insured against fire with the result that the plaintiffs took out no insurance of their own on the premises. This statement was true. The policy was renewed once by the landlords, but was then allowed to expire with the result that when fire destroyed the premises they were uninsured. The defendants were held not liable in negligence to the plaintiffs. *Argy* was based upon the finding that the defendant's statement was one of fact which was true when made. However, the behaviour of the defendants here could surely have given rise to an inference by the plaintiffs that the defendants intended to keep the building insured, and in these circumstances it would not seem unreasonable to hold that the defendants should have corrected the impression in the plaintiffs' mind when they decided not to renew the insurance. In other words the law should here impose a duty of care to make a statement, rather than the normal duty to make a careful statement. That this type of duty might be imposed is recognised by the New Zealand case of *Abrams* v. *Ancliffe* (1978)—a builder of a house was held to owe a duty of care to correct a building estimate given to the purchaser when he found that it had become incorrect.

The third problem is the case where there is no voluntary undertaking or previous statement by the defendant, but it is arguable that the relationship between the parties should impose a duty to speak. Here it seems that this question has nothing to do with *Hedley Byrne* liability but is a straight question of whether the nonfeasance rule is to operate. Two Court of Appeal decisions have refused to impose a duty to speak in circumstances in which a moral obligation to speak might have been thought to arise (*Banque Keyser Ullman S.A.* v. *Skandia Insurance* (1988)— insurance company had no legal obligation to inform plaintiffs of the fraud of the plaintiffs' insurance broker which would have avoided the insurance transaction. It should be noted that the House of Lords (1990) found that it did not have this effect); the *Good Luck* (1989)—insurance company had no duty to inform the insured shipowners that the insurance was being imperilled by the ship being sailed in excluded war zones. In both cases the Court of Appeal admitted the possibility of a duty to speak arising independently of an assumption of responsibility by the defendant, but clearly that case would be an unusual one.

(g) *Statements to third parties who act on them to the plaintiff's loss.* If A makes a negligent misstatement to B who acts on it to C's loss, can C successfully sue A? Clearly there is no reliance by C on A—equally there is no relationship equivalent to contract. In certain cases, however, it seems that C will succeed. In *Ministry of Housing* v. *Sharp* (1970) a local authority was held liable for the negligence of its clerk who issued a "clear" certificate to an intending purchaser of land, the result of which was that the purchaser bought the land, and the Ministry's development charge over the land was destroyed. Lord Denning M.R. expressly based his judgment on *Hedley Byrne*; Salmon L.J. expressly thought it did not fall within the principle; Cross L.J. thought it unnecessary to decide the matter. However, the question fell for resolution before Megarry V.C. in *Ross* v. *Caunters* (1980). He had to decide whether a solicitor, who had negligently advised a testator in the drawing up of his will with the result that a gift to the testator's intended beneficiary failed, was liable in negligence to that beneficiary. Holding the defendant liable, he did so on the basis that this was not *Hedley Byrne* liability but liability under general principles of negligence; that liability existed only if there was a sufficient degree of proximity between plaintiff and defendant; that this was present in the instant case because the defendant actually had the plaintiff in mind when advising the testator. *Ross* v. *Caunters* was a first instance decision which rested on an application of the *Anns* two-tier test. In view of the virtual abandonment of that test by the House of Lords, and the emphasis in connection with the *Hedley Byrne* rule of the need for reliance *by the plaintiff* (*cf.* the speeches in *Smith* v. *Bush* (1989) and *Caparo Inds. plc* v. *Dickman*), the continuing authority of the case is uncertain. It derives support from another first instance in *Lawton* v. *B.O.C. Ltd.* (1987) (defendant employer owed his employee a duty of care in relation to a reference given to a third party) but *Lawton* also is a dubious case since the occasion was one of qualified privilege and the rule is that that is defeated only by malice on the defendant's part (*infra*, p. 349).

Extent of the Hedley Byrne special relationship

The emphasis in the speeches in *Hedley Byrne* upon the need for a special relationship between defendant and plaintiff and the limited formulation of that special relationship in the speech of Lord Reid together with the emphasis placed by all the members of the House of Lords on the need for an assumption of responsibility by the defendant make clear the fact that liability will not be imposed where there is mere foreseeability of reliance by the plaintiff and the plaintiff has so relied. The need to avoid an indeterminately great liability also produces that conclusion, although the problem of indeterminacy was not expressly referred to in *Hedley Byrne*. The rule about the extent of liability has nevertheless taken a long time to be settled, and there was in the interim a brief flirtation with a test of mere foreseeability which now is seen to have been clearly misguided (*J.E.B. Fasteners* v. *Marks & Bloom* (1981)—not necessary to decide the matter on appeal in 1983). In *Smith* v. *Bush* (1989) the House of Lords, in deciding on the liability of valuers who had valued a house for a building society knowing that the valuation would be relied on by the plaintiff purchasers, emphasised the need for close proximity between defendant and plaintiff, but this was clearly satisfied on the facts of the case. The question concerning extent of liability was affirmatively raised, however, in *Caparo Inds. plc* v. *Dickman* (1990). In that case the question before the House of Lords was whether a firm of accountants which had prepared the annual audited accounts of a company owed a duty of care to the plaintiff shareholders in the company which had increased its shareholding in the company in reliance on the accounts and had lost money because the accounts overstated the company's assets. The annual accounts of the company are prepared under contract with the company itself and are sent to each shareholder for the purpose of being considered in the general meeting of the company. Clearly they are not prepared with any person or set of persons other than the shareholders as a whole in mind; nor are they prepared for the purpose of any particular transaction. The House of Lords held that in these circumstances the defendants owed the plaintiffs no duty of care. Lord Bridge rested his judgment principally on the fact that the plaintiffs could not establish a duty of care based merely on reasonable foreseeability to themselves, which they were attempting to do. He relied on these words of Woodhouse P. in his dissenting judgment in the New Zealand case of *Scott Group* v. *McFarlane* (1978): "I do not think that such a relationship should be found to exist unless, at least, the maker of the statement was, or ought to have been, aware that his advice or information would be made available to and be relied on by a particular person or class of persons for the purposes of a particular transaction or type of transaction." Lord Oliver laid particular emphasis on the statutory provisions of the various Companies Acts affecting auditors, the effect of these being in his opinion to make clear that the sole purpose of the provision of the accounts was to enable the shareholders as a body to exercise their controlling functions over the company. Lord Bridge's approach seems preferable. It is difficult to see the relevance of the legislative intention to an action for common law negligence as opposed to breach of statutory duty. However, Lord Oliver was in agreement with Lord Bridge on the effect of the common law principles.

Caparo thus confirms the original thinking of the House of Lords in the *Hedley Byrne* case about the need for close proximity between defendant and plaintiff. It has not solved all the problems that may arise. For example, Lord Bridge in the case itself left open the question that arises where the accounts negligently *understate* the amount of the assets with a consequent depressing effect on the value of the shares of all shareholders. Can a shareholder who sells at a loss recover this loss from the accountants? Following *Caparo*, *Al-Nakib* (*Jersey*) *Ltd.* v. *Longcroft* (1990) held that where a prospectus had been issued to existing shareholders in order to consider a rights offer of shares, no liability existed in relation to market transactions engaged in by shareholders in reliance on the prospectus, since its purpose was not related to market transactions. In *James McNaughton* v. *Hicks Anderson* (1991) it was held to be not just and reasonable that accountants should owe a duty of care to a prospective bidder for a company where they had merely prepared draft accounts and made an off-the-cuff statement which only partially misrepresented the target company's known bad financial condition. But in *Morgan Crucible Co. plc* v. *Hill Samuel Bank* (1991) the Court of Appeal refused to strike out a cause of action alleging negligence against the board of the target company in relation to statements about the financial condition of the company made to the plaintiff take-over bidder in a defended bid. Clearly the bidder was an identified person who might be influenced by the statements to offer a higher price for the company.

Exclusion of liability

The *Hedley Byrne* case itself decided that the defendant may exclude his liability to the plaintiff by a suitable disclaimer, a so-called "without responsibility" clause. This is rationalised in the judgments on the ground that liability under the case rests on a voluntary assumption of responsibility for the statement which the disclaimer will negative. Nevertheless this ability to exclude liability in tort by notice is unusual. Perhaps it is justifiable on the ground that the plaintiff who accepts and acts upon advice which is given without responsibility consents to the exclusion of liability (similar reasoning justifies the other main tort example, the ability of the occupier to exclude liability to his visitors by notice, *infra*, p. 215 *et seq.*).

The ability to exclude liability in tort for negligent statements has been curtailed by the provisions of the Unfair Contract Terms Act 1977. Liability for common law negligence falls within the ambit of the Act (s.1(1)(b)). Section 2(2) requires a contract term or notice excluding or restricting liability in negligence for loss or damage other than personal injury to be reasonable. Section 2(2) is extended by section 13 to include terms or notices which exclude or restrict the duty to act carefully. In one way or the other, the "without responsibility" clause seems clearly to be caught. It should be noted that the Act applies only where "business liability" is in question (s.1(3)); that it applies to non-contractual notices which would be the normal class in which the "without responsibility" clause is likely to fall.

The provisions of the Act will not, it seems, affect the validity of a warning by the maker of the statement that care has not been taken in its preparation. The defendant is here not negligent in any way—the statement invites non-reliance, which is not so in the case of a statement that purports to be carefully made, but contains an exclusion clause. A problem that has not yet arisen for solution is whether the defendant may rely on an exclusion clause which has not been communicated to the person who relies on the statement. After *Caparo* this is unlikely to be a problem because the insistence on proximity between defendant and plaintiff in that case makes it also likely that the disclaimer will be communicated.

Liability for misstatement causing physical injury

Although no case seems directly to confirm this point, it seems clear that there may be liability in negligence when the statement causes personal injury or damage to property. A case such as *Clay* v. *A. J. Crump* (1964) comes close to confirming such liability. The defendant architect was held liable for leaving a wall on a demolition site standing without making a proper inspection of it, and thereby causing injury to the plaintiff, a workman on the site, when the wall fell. The defendant's conduct was clearly interpretable as a statement that the wall was safe. The *Hedley Byrne* judgments were considered in *Clay's* case but the requirement of special relationship was not applied, although it would have been simple enough to find such a relationship on the facts. It may well be the law, however, that the requirement of special relationship applies only in cases of purely financial loss, the justification for this being the need to control the extent of the right to sue in negligence for such loss. If that is so, where the statement has caused personal injury or damage to property, the ordinary rule of foreseeability would determine the extent of the duty of care.

This receives support from the judgment of Lord Oliver in *Caparo Inds. plc* v. *Dickman* (1990). He postulates the case of the mislabelling of a dangerous chemical causing personal injury and indicates his opinion that liability would be determined by ordinary foreseeability and not by the need for a special relationship. Liability could no doubt be extensive but because of the nature of personal injury would not be indeterminate.

Reliance on the statement

The plaintiff under *Hedley Byrne* must prove his reliance on the statement. Normally he will do this by showing that he acted on the statement to his loss, though it was pointed out earlier in this chapter that the speech of Lord Morris in the *Hedley Byrne* case may indicate that a detrimental reliance is not necessary. Reliance is a causal concept—the plaintiff must establish that but for his reliance on the defendant he would not have suffered the loss that he did. In *J.E.B. Fasteners* v. *Marks & Bloom* (1983) the defendants were held not liable to the plaintiffs who had purchased the shares of another company after studying the accounts of that company which had been prepared by the defendants and which presented a false picture of the size of its assets. The plaintiffs could not establish reliance since it was found as a fact that even had they known the true position, they would still, because of other motivating factors, have purchased the shares. Reliance causes problems where there are, for example, two statements upon which the plaintiff has relied. If neither statement is enough by itself to have induced him to act, there is no problem. If either by itself would have been sufficient to induce him to act there is a difficulty, since the "but for" test might seem to produce the result that but for either statement he would still have acted as he did because of the existence of the other statement. The correct test, however, should be not what the plaintiff would have done independently of the making of any statement by the defendant, but what he would have done had that statement been a careful one. Only if it is proved that the plaintiff would have acted as he did despite the making of a careful statement to him is reliance negatived. That was in fact the case in the *J.E.B. Fasteners* case since the court found that even had a careful statement been made showing the true picture of the company's assets, the plaintiffs would still have bought the company.

Damages

It is assumed that the tort measure of damages applies to *Hedley Byrne* liability as it now appears to do in cases of liability for negligent misrepresentations (*infra*). This means putting the plaintiff into the position he would have been in had the tort not been committed, which means asking what he would have done had a careful statement been made. He is of course entitled to out-of-pocket loss but is also entitled to a reasonable profit on money lost if it is proved that he would have otherwise invested it. *Swingcastle Ltd.* v. *Gibson* (1991), a recent decision of the House of Lords, has confirmed that the measure of damages is the tortious rather than the contractual measure (under which the plaintiff would be entitled to be compensated for loss of the "expectation" engendered by the contract).

Misrepresentation Act 1967

The common law did not allow an action for damages for an innocent misrepresentation, even where it was made negligently. Any contract entered into by the representee with the representor as a result of the misrepresentation could be rescinded in equity, subject to the various limitations upon that right. But rescission remained the only remedy until the *Hedley Byrne* decision allowed an action for damages where the misrepresentation was negligent. Further changes have been made by the Misrepresentation Act 1967. Section 2(1) of the Act provides as follows:

Where a person has entered into a contract after a misrepresentation has been made to him by another party thereto, and as a result thereof he has suffered loss, then if the person making the misrepresentation would be liable to damages in respect thereof had the misrepresentation been made fraudulently, that person shall be so liable notwithstanding that the misrepresentation was not made fraudulently, unless he proves that he had reasonable ground to believe and did believe up to the time that the contract was made that the facts represented were true.

The effect of this section is to prove an additional remedy by way of an action for damages where the misrepresentation is negligent. The following points may be noted about it:

    (a)   The subsection only applies where the defendant has made a misrepresentation. As has already been mentioned the term "misrepresentation" had limitations under equitable principles. Representations of law, of opinion and of intention were excluded. Representations of this sort are, however, actionable if they are made fraudulently under the tort of deceit. Further, section 2(1) provides that there is liability for the misrepresentation provided that the defendant would have been liable had the misrepresentation been made fraudulently. This means that the equitable limits upon the notion of an actionable misrepresentation will not apply to an action under section 2(1).

(b) Liability under section 2(1) is wider than under *Hedley Byrne* in that the plaintiff does not need to show the existence of a special relationship between the defendant and himself, merely a false statement inducing the making of a contract between them. It was common ground among the members of the Court of Appeal in *Howard Marine Co.* v. *Ogden* (1978) that liability would arise under section 2(1) in relation to an off-the-cuff statement in relation to which a common law duty of care did not exist.

(c) The plaintiff under section 2(1) has the advantage that, having proved the misrepresentation, the burden of proving that he has reasonable grounds for making the statement rests on the defendant.

(d) Although not finally settled, it seems likely that the measure of damages under section 2(1) is the tortious rather than the contractual measure. The plaintiff is therefore to be placed in the position that he would have been in had there been no misrepresentation, rather than had it proved to be true (see *Sharneyford Supplies* v. *Edge and Barrington Black & Co.* (1985) throwing doubt on some earlier authority applying the contractual measure—see especially *Watts* v. *Spence* (1976)). However, it is still not clear whether the deceit measure of damages, under which the defendant is liable for all damage flowing directly from the misrepresentation whether foreseeable or not, applies (the deceit measure was applied in *McNally* v. *Welltrade International Ltd.* (1978)—this appears to take the fiction of fraud in section 2(1) too literally—but the fraud measure was upheld by one judge in the Court of Appeal, Balcombe L.J. in *Royscot Trust Ltd.* v. *Rogerson* (1991)).

Esso Petroleum v. *Mardon* (1975) held that where a negligent misrepresentation by the defendant induces the making of a contract between defendant and plaintiff, the plaintiff may base his action upon *Hedley Byrne*, so that in this situation he has the alternative of suing in tort or basing his action on section 2(1) of the Misrepresentation Act.

The 1967 Act made a further change in that section 2(2) allows damages to be awarded in the discretion of the court and in lieu of rescission for a non-negligent misrepresentation.

2. Pure economic loss caused by negligent acts

(i) The basic rule

It has long been regarded as the law that negligent acts causing pure economic loss are not actionable, on the ground that no duty of care exists in relation to such loss. Pure economic loss may be defined as economic loss to the plaintiff which is not caused by injury to his person or damage to property in which he has a proprietary or possessory interest. A bailee, for example, who has a possessory interest in a chattel, may recover for his economic loss arising from damage to it. So also may the charterer of a ship under a voyage charterparty recover for economic loss arising from damage to the ship since he has possession of it—it is otherwise if it is a time charterparty. The basic rule has come under question twice in recent times but in both cases has survived it. There were dicta in the judgment of Lord Devlin in the *Hedley Byrne* case that the exclusion of liability in negligence for pure economic loss should no longer apply in the case of acts as well as statements. The Court of Appeal, however, applied the usual rule in *Spartan Steel Alloys* v. *Martin* (1972). The defendants negligently caused damage to an electricity cable, the property of the local electricity board, and thereby cut off the supply of electricity to the plaintiffs' factory for several hours. As a result a "melt" in the plaintiffs' furnace was damaged and four other melts were incapable of being performed during the period of cut-off. The plaintiffs recovered damages for loss of the existing melt since that was damage to property but not for the loss of production involving the four other melts since that was pure economic loss.

The rule also came under question after the introduction of Lord Wilberforce's two-tier test in *Anns* v. *London Borough of Merton* (1977). The question arose whether it was necessary to examine the rule in terms of "considerations" which might negative or reduce the prima facie duty of care which reasonable contemplation (foreseeability) of harm produced. In *Leigh & Sillavan* v. *Aliakmon Shipping* (1986) sellers of steel had shipped it under a contract with the shipowners which limited the liability of the latter for damage to the goods in transit in accordance with the Hague Rules. Property in the steel remained in the sellers until it was paid for by the buyers, but the risk passed to the buyers under the contract. The steel was badly stored through the negligence of stevedores for which the shipowners were vicariously liable, and was found to be damaged on inspection after arrival. The buyers were unable to pay for the steel on arrival in port, and this had unfortunate consequences for them since it meant that the bill of lading was not indorsed to them so that they obtained no assignment of the rights of action of the sellers against the shipowners. The buyers took delivery of the steel, at first as agents for the sellers, but then they paid for it and acquired property in it. They then sued the shipowners for the damage to the steel. This action had to be brought in tort rather than under the contractual action that would have existed under the bill of lading and the buyers faced the problem that the damage was, *vis-à-vis* themselves, pure economic loss. Nevertheless the Court of Appeal examined the question in the light of the two-tier test propounded by *Anns*. The majority held that the prima facie duty identified at the first stage was negatived at the second stage by the need to preserve the protection afforded by the limitation on liability in the Hague Rules which did not bind the buyers who were not parties to the contract between sellers and shipowners (though Goff L.J. thought that the rules of privity of contract would not have operated here). The House of Lords affirmed the decision of the Court of Appeal but merely by an application of the basic rule. The *Anns* two-tier test was not intended to apply to existing situations of no duty. The House agreed with the Court of Appeal that it would be unfortunate if the action in tort were to be allowed to override contractual arrangements deliberately entered into by the parties. They rejected Lord Goff's view that the shipowners could have relied on the limitation clause against the buyers, since there was no privity of contract between them.

After the *Leigh & Sillavan* case the basic rule has gone unquestioned by the courts and has been applied several times (see *Candlewood Navigation Corp.* v. *Mitsui O.S.K. Lines* (1985)—time charterer could not sue for damage to ship; *Muirhead* v. *Industrial Tank* (1985)—purchaser of defective electrical pumps for supplying oxygen to live lobsters in tank succeeded against manufacturer for loss of lobsters but not for loss of future production through fresh lobsters not being introduced; *Reid* v. *Rush & Tompkins Group plc* (1989)—employer owed no duty of care to employee to insure him against personal injury while on service in foreign country which did not provide compensation for personal injury; *Van Oppen* v. *Bedford School* (1989)—school had no duty to insure pupil against football injury sustained in school sport). The next question is what policy justifies a refusal by courts to compensate persons who have suffered economic loss as the result of another person's negligence? It is suggested that there are two main grounds of policy. In the first place the indeterminacy problem posed by the famous dictum in *Ultramares Corp.* v. *Touche* (1931) (liability "in an indeterminate amount for an indeterminate time to an indeterminate class") is at its most acute in the area of purely economic loss. The economic repercussions of any major accident are likely to be vast. They are quite literally endless—there is no built-in limit such as applies in the case of personal injury or property damage. Much of this economic loss will be foreseeable so that the remoteness of damage test supplies no means of limiting the defendant's liability. This ground for refusing to impose liability was expressly relied on by Blackburn J. in *Cattle* v. *Stockton Waterworks* (1875). The second policy factor is generally not articulated by the courts but is nevertheless of some importance. Economic loss is seldom irreparable, forming a sharp contrast with personal injury which very often is. Many of the persons who suffer large financial losses through negligence are businessmen who are in a position to absorb the loss or to transfer it to the public by increasing their charges. This is hollow comfort to the small person who has suffered a devastating financial loss, and that factor may underly the willingness by the courts to vary the rule to compensate the purchasers of a defective house.

In a number of exceptional cases the courts have allowed recovery in negligence for purely economic loss. The *Hedley Byrne* principle is one clear area in which the basic rule does not operate. This is justified by reason of the need for close proximity between the plaintiff and defendant which the House of Lords in *Caparo Inds. plc.* v. *Dickman* (1990) has recently affirmed. The defendant must assume responsibility towards the plaintiff or a class including him and in respect of the particular transaction or type of transaction engaged in by the plaintiff. The plaintiff must act in reliance on that assumption of responsibility. The relationship thus becomes in the words of Lord Devlin "equivalent to contract" and there is no difficulty about the recovery of pure economic loss in contract. As mentioned earlier in the chapter, the notion of voluntary assumption of responsibility (or undertaking) together with reliance are applicable to acts as well as statements, and this now constitutes the only credible explanation of the House of Lords' own decision in *Junior Books* v. *Veitchi* (1982) in which a sub-contractor was held liable in negligence for laying a defective floor in a factory. Although there was no contract between the plaintiff purchasers of the factory and the sub-contractor the relationship was as close as it could be short of actual privity because the sub-contractor was nominated by the plaintiffs under the terms of the main contract. This explanation of *Junior Books* was accepted but found inapplicable to the facts of two later Court of Appeal decisions (*Simaan General Contracting Co.* v. *Pilkington Glass* (1988); *Greater Nottingham Co-op.* v. *Cementation Piling Ltd.* (1989)). It was also advanced as the explanation for the decision in *Junior Books* by Lord Bridge in the *Caparo* case. More difficult is the fate after *Caparo* of the cases such as *Ross* v. *Caunters* where there is no reliance by the plaintiff, but by a third party who acts on the statement to the plaintiff's loss.

(ii) The building of defective houses; Anns overruled by Murphy v. Brentwood D.C. (1990)

The main features of the *Anns* case have already been considered. It concerned the question of whether a duty of care was owed by local authorities in relation to the exercise or non-exercise of their powers of inspection of the foundations of houses under the Public Health Act 1936 to future purchasers of those houses. *Anns* raised difficult questions relating to nonfeasance and liability for the exercise of statutory powers. But the overruling of *Anns* which took place in *Murphy* was achieved without reference to these difficulties, which will therefore be considered in the next sections of this chapter. *Murphy* was able to achieve this because *Anns* itself was based on the premise that only if the builder owed a duty of care as regards the building of the defective house would it be proper to impose a duty of care on the local authority. The House of Lords in *Murphy* was therefore able to focus the entire attention of the court on the question whether the builder did in fact owe such a duty. It should be pointed out that *Murphy* in no way cast doubt on the ruling in *Anns* that a builder of houses owes a duty of care in relation to personal injury or property damage caused by the house. The departure from *Anns* taken by *Murphy* is to deny a duty of care in the builder not to build a house that is merely defective.

Before considering the decision in *Murphy* it is necessary to consider some further features of *Anns*. *Anns* reached the conclusion that the Public Health Act provisions were aimed at protecting the health or safety of occupiers of houses against dangers arising from defectively constructed houses. Where a house became dangerous through defects in its construction, that was damage to property and the cause of action arose only at the time when the house was a present or imminent danger to health or safety. Further, the measure of damages was limited to the cost of repair needed to render the house safe. It was these particular aspects of *Anns* that the House of Lords in *Murphy* fastened on in its criticism of the decision. The facts in *Murphy* bore a number of non-essential differences from those in *Anns*. In particular the case concerned statutory duty rather than power; the authority had in breach of duty approved of a raft foundation for the houses concerned which infringed the building by-laws. But the action was clearly for negligence rather than breach of statutory duty so that nothing turned on this. Also Murphy had sold the house at the time of the action, but again this made no difference because his loss on the sale was less than the repair costs and was clearly recoverable provided a duty of care existed. As in *Anns*, Murphy was the occupier of the house and was in no way responsible for the defective raft foundation which had been designed by consultant engineers employed by the builders.

In deciding that the builder of the house and therefore the defendant local authority owed no duty of care to Murphy, the House of Lords relied on certain grounds which are in effect common to all or the great majority of the members of the court, except Lord Mackay L.C. These common grounds were: that the loss in question was purely economic since a house cannot damage itself—that being so it fell within the rule that no duty of care in tort exists as regards pure economic loss; that the complex structure theory put forward in *D. & F. Estates* v. *Church Commissioners* (1989) under which one part of a house may be regarded as damaging another part must be abandoned, although it may according to Lords Keith and Bridge be applicable to parts of houses such as wiring or central heating installed by contractors which damage the rest of the house; that it is illogical to distinguish between defectively constructed houses and defectively manufactured chattels and the law does not impose liability in relation to the latter (relying on the decision of the U.S. Supreme Court in *E. River S.S. Corp.* v. *Transamerica Delaval Inc.* (1986) and the decision of the majority of the Canadian Supreme Court in *Rivtow Marine Ltd.* v. *Washington Iron Works* (1973)); that it is illogical to regard the cause of action as arising only when the house becomes a present or imminent danger to its occupants—in particular why distinguish the case where a structural survey revealed the defect before it became a danger and the house was then repaired, or the case (Lord Bridge) where the defect was never discovered but the house collapsed injuring no one?; that the legislature had provided its own remedy in section 1 of the Defective Premises Act 1972 so that judicial intervention in this area was unnecessary (common to all members of the House of Lords). In *Dept. of the Environment* v. *Thomas Bates* (1990) the House applied its own decision in *Murphy* to hold a builder of a defectively constructed office block not liable in negligence to the plaintiff lessees. The building concerned was not a danger to its occupants, but after *Murphy* it would have made no difference if it had been.

Critique

First, the decision in *Murphy* that the loss is pure economic loss seems unquestionably correct; also the criticism of the illogicality in *Anns* of regarding the damage in question as property damage

which may occur some time even later than the house shows
the first signs of it. Nevertheless, the decision in *Anns* might
still be supported as creating a limited duty situation, *i.e.* a
duty of care owed to the occupier of a dangerous house in
respect of the pure economic loss sustained by him in repairing
the house and removing the danger. Houses are unlike chattels
in that their occupier may have no choice about whether to
live in them. Since the House of Lords is clearly of the opinion
that the occupier would recover damages for personal injuries
caused by the house (at least from its builder—the local authority's
position is considered under nonfeasance in this chapter), it
may seem not unreasonable to allow the occupier to recover
as damages the amount of money he needs to spend to avoid
the payment of damages by the defendant for personal injury
which may far exceed the repair costs. To recognise a limited
exception to the basic rule about negligent acts causing pure
economic loss would be in line with the emphasis on "incremental-
ism" in the judgments of the House of Lords in *Caparo Inds.
plc.* v. *Dickman.* The rule about the non-liability of the
manufacturer of a chattel for defects in it which have not caused
further damage or injury has never been fully argued in an
English case and the House of Lords' unquestioning acceptance
of the decision of the Supreme Court of the United States
in the *E. River* case has aroused criticism on the ground that
it reads too much into that decision (Cooke, 106 L.Q.R.; Fleming,
105 L.Q.R. It is doubtful whether the imposition of a duty of care
as regards the merely defective chattel would add greatly to the
insurance burdens of manufacturers—they are already strictly
liable for defects at the end of the chain of warranties (which
direct action by the consumer would short-cut). Finally, the
House's conclusion that the existence of the statutory remedy
under the Defective Premises Act 1972 should preclude a
common law duty of care causes some difficulty. The legislature
clearly does not make the same assumption since legislation
is constantly adding to existing common law duties. In any case,
judges are in theory at least discovering the common law rather
than creating it. Whatever the merits of the third argument, it is
reasonably clear that section 1(1) of the Act has no application to
local authorities exercising their statutory powers under the Public
Health Act.

Anns and *Murphy* have been considered at this point because the main point at issue was whether the loss in question was pure economic and whether liability should exist for it. The details of liability for the construction of defective buildings are considered in Chapter 11.

3. The nonfeasance rule

The problem of liability for an omission to act is not necessarily connected with the tort of negligence. The conduct of the person who, seeing a drowning man and being capable of saving him, makes no effort to do so, is deliberate rather than negligent. But since most of the problems concerning omission arise in connection with negligence, the topic will be treated here. The rule of English law is that pure omissions to act are not actionable in tort. The reason for this reluctance to impose liability for omissions (shared by other legal systems) is that legal obligations to take affirmative action ought not to be imposed upon people without their consent.

It must be emphasised that the omission must be a pure omission. When a person by some positive action has incurred a duty of care towards other persons, he may be liable for omissions in the performance of that duty. Thus a motorist by the act of driving incurs a duty of care towards other road-users and the fact that his negligence consists in an omission to give a signal will not prevent his being liable. Similarly the act of employing other persons puts the employer under a duty of care towards those persons; his obligation to provide proper machinery is not discharged by the provision of initially proper machinery which becomes defective through his failure to have it serviced. Setting up a casualty outpatients ward in a hospital puts the defendant under a positive duty to treat persons who attend there for that purpose (*Barnett* v. *Chelsea Hospital Management Committee* (1969)). The occupation of land carries with it positive duties to protect the safety of visitors on that land, and also to remedy natural conditions arising on that land without the act or default of the occupier and which threaten persons outside the land (*Goldman* v. *Hargrave* (1967); *Leakey* v. *National Trust* (1980)).

The above cases could be explained on the basis that the defendant has voluntarily assumed a status to which the law sees fit to attach positive duties. That explanation is not adequate, however, for the case of *Mercer* v. *S.E. Ry.* (1922). The defendant railway company had made a practice of closing the gates of a level crossing on the approach of trains. The plaintiff, who knew of and relied on this practice, was struck by a train and injured when using the level crossing, the gates of which had been carelessly left open by the defendant's servant. The defendant's liability to the plaintiff for failing to close the gates was based upon their previous practice of so doing and the plaintiff's reliance on that practice. Clearly the reliance here was of a detrimental nature. In fact the situation in *Mercer* is not a case of nonfeasance at all—the defendant by his conduct *caused* the plaintiff to act to his own loss. This makes the case one of misfeasance. This element of detrimental reliance is also present in those cases of liability for voluntary undertakings considered under the *Hedley Byrne* rule.

Where there is no detrimental reliance by the plaintiff induced by the defendant's act or undertaking, we are in the area of nonfeasance and it makes no difference whether the defendant has been guilty of total inaction, beginning to act and not completing it, or negligence in the performance of the act or undertaking, provided this merely fails to improve matters, and does not make them worse. An example illustrating the latter point is the case of *East Suffolk Rivers Catchment Board* v. *Kent* (1941). The defendants were empowered by statute to repair, *inter alia*, sea walls. The plaintiff's land had become flooded by the bursting of a sea wall. The defendants commenced repair of the wall but carried this out so negligently that, whereas a competent repair would have taken 14 days, it in fact took the defendants 164. The plaintiff's action in negligence for the extra period of delay in removing the flood water from his land failed. The defendants did not cause the flooding and, since they had a mere power rather than a duty to act, their negligence when acting was not actionable unless it caused a deterioration in the situation. Of course it would have made a difference if the plaintiff had in some way detrimentally relied on the defendants' exercise of its powers, and Lord Atkin in his dissenting judgment seemed to think that that may have existed in the form of his refraining to call in his own assistance, but that point does not appear in the judgments of the majority.

The *East Suffolk* reasoning that if there is no duty to act, there is no duty when acting except not to make matters worse was answered in *Anns* v. *London Borough of Merton* (1977) as far as statutory powers were concerned by finding a positive duty, not to act, but to give due consideration to acting. Where a person is not exercising a statutory power, however, it still appears to be the law that where no duty to act exists, the only duty where action is taken is to take care not to make matters worse. A rescuer, for example, is not bound to exercise care so as to effect a rescue—he is required only not to aggravate the situation. However, there are two qualifications to this. Where a special relationship exists between plaintiff and defendant, the defendant is required to take care to improve matters. So in the *Hedley Byrne* case Lords Morris and Hodson thought that where a doctor gratuitously undertakes to treat an accident victim knowing that his professional skill is being relied on (which might even be the case where the victim was unconscious), he is liable for failure to take reasonable care, even though the victim's condition is no worse as a result. These dicta are open to the objection that they tend to discourage "good Samaritan" acts by professional persons. The other qualification is that where an antecedent duty of care exists, on principles explained above, the defendant is liable if his lack of care fails to improve matters. So in the Canadian case of *The Ogopogo* (1971) it was held that an occupier of a boat owed a duty to his invitee on that boat to attempt to rescue him when he fell overboard; that care must be taken in order to achieve the rescue; but that the standard of care required must take into account the emergency situation, and that in the circumstances the defendant's failure to achieve the rescue was not negligent. There is as yet no authority on whether a positive duty of care to save life exists in the case of persons such as lifeguards, firemen or policemen (see *infra*, this chapter, for the nonfeasance rule as it applies to damage caused by third parties).

4. Negligence in the exercise of statutory powers and duties

It has long been accepted that a person who negligently carries out a statutory power or duty thereby inflicting damage is not immune from an action in tort (*Geddis* v. *Bann Reservoir* (1878)). *Geddis*, however, was merely taken to mean that the statutory power in the case afforded no defence to an action brought in nuisance or negligence were the defendant had been negligent. Not until the case of *Home Office* v. *Dorset Yacht* (1970) was it accepted that a negligent failure to perform a statutory duty or carry out a power might itself give rise to an action for ordinary negligence. In that case the House of Lords held that the defendant owed a duty of care to persons in the vicinity of the prison whose property might be damaged by escaping prisoners to properly exercise their statutory power and duty to keep prisoners inside the prison. The allegation in the *Dorset Yacht* case was of an operational failure to keep the prisoners under detention. All the members of the House of Lords were in agreement that ordinary principles of negligence were not applicable to discretionary decisions such as the decision to keep an open prison, where the defendant would have to weigh the increased danger to the public against the better prospect of rehabilitation which an open prison might afford. Lord Diplock went so far as to say that liability for the exercise of that sort of discretion would only exist if the defendant had acted *ultra vires* the power, for example, by acting in bad faith, for an improper purpose or for irrelevant reasons (and provided the other requirements of negligence were satisfied). The distinction between operational negligence and the exercise of discretionary powers was accepted by Lord Wilberforce in the *Anns* case.

Dorset Yacht may be regarded as a case of misfeasance—the defendants had created the risk by establishing the prison (quite lawfully of course) and then had (allegedly) failed to exercise their statutory powers to eliminate the risk that created. Operationally negligent misfeasance in the exercise of statutory powers also gave rise to liability in *Levine* v. *Morris* (1972)—siting of concrete traffic sign near highway increased the danger to persons in cars which had left the highway; *Bird* v. *Pearce* (1979)—defendants had obliterated existing road signs without replacing them or otherwise warning motorists of an approaching road junction and were held liable to the plaintiff who was in a car crash which occurred as a result.

Anns on the other hand was clearly a case of nonfeasance. The allegations against the authority in that case were of a negligent failure to exercise its statutory powers of ensuring that the foundations of the maisonettes in question were taken down to a sufficient depth to conform with the plans and specifications that had been approved by the authority as conforming to its by-laws, whether this occurred through negligent inspection or a negligent failure to inspect at all, the result being subsidence and the appearance of cracks in the walls of the maisonettes. The builder of the maisonettes was guilty of misfeasance in building in breach of the relevant by-laws. The defendants had merely failed to prevent him from doing so, a case of nonfeasance. We have already seen that Lord Wilberforce's judgment was able to avoid the nonfeasance problem by finding that a positive duty to give due consideration to the exercise of the power of inspection existed. That being so, the authority if it decided to inspect had a positive duty of careful inspection. That solved the causal problem raised by the *East Suffolk* case, since if there is a duty to inspect carefully, then there is no difficulty in finding that the defendant has caused defects which the inspection should have revealed (though there is still a problem with the duty to give due consideration to the exercise of the power, since this being discretionary the court will not substitute its own discretion for that of the authority—an unresolved problem).

The principles established in *Dorset Yacht* and *Anns* apply to public bodies in general and the overruling of *Anns* has not affected this. In the period referred to earlier as the "retreat from *Anns*" a number of cases came before the courts in which allegations of negligence in the exercise of statutory powers were made against public bodies. All these actions failed, but the failure in every case arose because the plaintiffs were unable to satisfy the court that the situation was one warranting the imposition of a duty of care under the modifications to the *Anns* test introduced by *Peabody* v. *Parkinson* and *Yuen Kun Yew* v. *A.-G. of Hong Kong*. Mention may be made of *Jones* v. *Dept of Employment* (1988)—no duty of care owed by the Department to an applicant for unemployment benefit because an appeal existed from a refusal; *Calveley* v. *Chief Constable* (1989) (Court of Appeal)—no duty of care owed to policemen who were the subject of a police disciplinary inquiry, since the inquiry ought not to be constrained by the possibility of a negligence action being brought against those holding it; *Yuen Kun Yew* v. *A.-G. of Hong Kong* (1987)— no duty of care owed by Commissioner of Deposit-taking Companies to depositors in relation to the exercise of its powers of refusal of registration or deregistration of companies (followed in *Davis* v. *Radcliffe* (1990)); *Minories Finance Ltd.* v. *A. Young* (1989)—no duty owed by Bank of England to commercial bank to exercise its powers of supervision to prevent the commercial bank making imprudent investments.

All these cases except *Yuen Kun Yew* and *Davis* were decided under the *Peabody* "just and reasonable" test. The courts made no attempt to distinguish them according to whether they raised issues of misfeasance or nonfeasance and it may be that that part of *Anns* which finds the nonfeasance rule irrelevant in the case of statutory powers survives the overruling of the decision. In *Murphy* v. *Brentwood D.C.* Lords Mackay, Keith and Bridge reserved their positions on the liability of the local authority if the house causes personal injury or damage to property. On the other hand all the above cases involved pure economic loss though this was not the ground given for the non-recognition of a duty of care in them (except by the House of Lords in *Calveley*). It does seem, however, that it will be extremely difficult to establish a duty of care in relation to the alleged failure by a public body to exercise its statutory powers in such a way as to prevent pure economic loss.

The courts in the cases of *Davis* v. *Radcliffe* (1990) (especially) and to some extent *Yuen Kun Yew* regarded the fact that discretionary powers were vested in the defendant as a reason for denying a duty of care. This goes one stage further than *Dorset Yacht* and *Anns* which only afford immunity when the defendant is actually exercising the discretion and subject to a requirement that the defendant be acting *intra vires*. It is arguable that this provides the public defendant ample protection. It is hard to see the justification for a decision such as *Clough* v. *Bussan* (1990) which held that no duty of care was owed by police to a motorist on being informed that traffic lights are not working in respect of personal injury to the motorist. It is hard to see why a wholly unreasonable failure to respond to the danger should receive immunity in a case of this sort.

The fundamental question raised by these cases is whether public bodies should be subjected to the sanction of a negligence suit for misuse of their powers, a question that spills over into constitutional and administrative law. Under the present state of the law, there is virtually no sanction against the public body except the force of public opinion.

R.S.C. Order 53; section 31 Supreme Court 1981

The procedure set up in 1977 by this Order confirmed by section 31 allows a claim for damages to be combined with an action for judicial review of the decision of a public body. The House of Lords has indicated that where the plaintiff's claim in tort is based upon the need to review the decision of a public body, the Order 53 procedure is the appropriate one and action begun by private writ will be struck out as an abuse of the process of the court (*Cocks* v. *Thanet U.D.C.* (1982)).

5. Nervous shock

The reasons for the courts' restrictions upon the right to recover damages for nervous shock are different from those denying a claim for purely financial loss. For a long time the courts doubted the genuineness of nervous shock as a form of damage. When finally the force of medical opinion could admit of no further doubt as to the genuineness of physical symptoms produced by nervous shock, the courts' recognition of this was still somewhat gradual with the result that inconsistencies still exist in the law. Even now, the courts refuse to recognise extreme distress or grief as compensable damage. The term "nervous shock" means actual illness, in the form of genuine psychiatric disease whether or not accompanied by physical symptons (as in *Hinz* v. *Berry* (1970)— morbid depression produced by plaintiff witnessing death of her husband and simultaneous injury to her children).

Actions for nervous shock were first allowed:

1. When it accompanied actual physical injury, where the courts were less inclined to doubt the genuineness of the symptoms of shock.
2. Where the plaintiff was put in fear of physical injury through the defendant's negligence and suffered nervous shock though not physical injury as a result (*Dulieu* v. *White and Sons* (1901)).
3. Where the defendant had intentionally done an act calculated to cause nervous shock to the plaintiff (*Wilkinson* v. *Downton* (1897)).

Whether the law should go further than this and compensate victims of shock who have neither suffered injury nor been in fear of such injury has been disputed (for a medical opinion to the contrary, see Havard, 19 M.L.R. 478) but actions in negligence have succeeded on a number of occasions where the plaintiff witnessed an accident caused by the defendant's negligence and he

and the victim were in a sufficiently close relationship. Thus close
relatives of the victim have been allowed to recover damages
(*Hambrook* v. *Stokes Bros.* (1925); *Boardman* v. *Sanderson* (1964);
a fellow employee (*Dooley* v. *Cammell, Laird Ltd.* (1951); and a
rescuer (*Chadwick* v. *British Transport Commission* (1967)).
Hambrook v. *Stokes* is difficult to reconcile with another Court of
Appeal decision in *King* v. *Phillips* (1953). The ratio of neither
case is easy to determine, but it is suggested that there is no real
basis for distinguishing them in point of fact and that *Hambrook* v.
Stokes allowing damages to the relative is the preferable decision.
Difficulties experienced by the court in *King* v. *Phillips* in deciding
whether the relative's presence near the victim was foreseeable
should not really cause problems in view of the extensiveness of
foresight expected of defendants today (*infra*, Chapters 7 and 8).
Equally it seems absurd that the relative should be in a worse
position than the employee or rescuer. The plaintiff does not have
to see the victim being injured, provided such injury is reasonably
apprehended (*Hambrook* v. *Stokes*); nor does any injury actually
have to occur, again if it is reasonably apprehended (*Dooley* v.
Cammel, Laird). In the above cases some of the plaintiffs had
conditions which may have predisposed them towards suffering
nervous shock. For example, Mrs. Hambrook's claim was brought
by her estate, she herself being pregnant and, having suffered a
miscarriage brought on by the shock, having died. Both Dooley
and Chadwick had a history of nervous disorder. In none of these
cases was the issue of the hypersensitivity of the plaintiff faced.
Recently in *Brice* v. *Brown* (1984), however, Stuart-Smith J. held
that the test for duty was that of foreseeability of shock to a
person of ordinary phlegm and normal disposition. If the
defendant was liable under that test, he was liable for any
aggravation of the shock suffered by the plaintiff that was caused
by the plaintiff's own greater susceptibility to shock since he took
the victim as he found him. This seems to ignore the possibility
that numerous predisposing conditions may well be foreseeable,
granted the level of neurosis in the community at large.

   The law now, therefore, has accepted that persons who have a
sufficiently close relationship to accident victims may recover
damages for nervous shock if they are present at the accident and
suffer shock because of their reasonable apprehension of injury to
the victim. More difficulty arises where the plaintiff satisfies the

requirements of "relationship" but is not present at the accident, or where the plaintiff has no relationship to the victim but witnesses the accident that injures him. These difficulties arise because it is still not clear whether in cases of nervous shock the courts are applying a rule of policy to restrict the right of recovery, or whether the test of recovery is entirely based on foreseeability. The first type of case was considered by the House of Lords in *McLoughlin* v. *O'Brian* (1982) and presented the House with an opportunity to clarify the law. Unfortunately the reasoning of the members of the House is inconclusive. The case concerned a wife whose husband and three children were injured in a road accident caused by the defendant's negligence. The plaintiff was not at the scene of the accident but was told about it soon after it occurred. On visiting the hospital, she saw her husband and injured children, witnessed the extent of their injuries and was told that her daughter had been killed. As a result she suffered severe nervous shock. The House of Lords unanimously held that in these circumstances the plaintiff's shock was foreseeable and damages were recoverable for it in negligence. Upon the important issue of principle concerning the right to recover damages for nervous shock there was division among the members of the House. Lord Wilberforce and Lord Edmund-Davies both thought there to be reasons of policy which might deny recovery of damages for nervous shock even in a case where nervous shock was foreseeable. Lord Wilberforce stressed the possible proliferation of claims including fraudulent claims if foreseeability were to be the only requirement, and the evidentiary difficulties that might arise if recovery were to be extended beyond the plainest cases. He was in favour of a limitation whereby only those persons would receive compensation who witnessed the accident or its immediate aftermath (that included the present case) and who bore a sufficiently close relationship to the accident victim. Lord Bridge of Harwich with whom Lord Scarman was in basic agreement, denied altogether the element of policy as a reason in itself for denying recovery of damages for nervous shock. He was not impressed by the possibility of excessive claims being made for nervous shock. The evidentiary problem was merely one which the court would in some cases have to resolve. There should be no arbitrary limits based on "contemporaneity" or of "relationship." Shock to the person who heard or read about the accident, or to the casual spectator of an accident might in appropriate circumstances be reasonably foreseeable and, if so, damages should be recoverable. Lord Russell merely indicated that no consideration of policy impelled him to decide otherwise than for the plaintiff in the present case. *Jones* v. *Wright* (1991) was a case arising out of the Hillsborough soccer disaster in which the question of the degree of proximity that needed to exist between the plaintiff, the accident victim and the accident itself was considered. At first instance, Hidden J. held that only the immediate blood relations and spouse of the victim could claim for shock, but that this class included brothers and sisters; also that persons within the requisite degree of relationship could claim for shock caused by witnessing of the accident on television. On both points he was reversed by the Court of Appeal. Brothers and sisters fell outside the permitted classes; the witnessing of the accident through the medium of television was quite different from actually being present and seeing it. The finding on the latter point makes it appear that *Ravenscroft* v. *Rederiaktiebolaget Transatlantic* (1991) is wrongly decided (mother awarded damages for nervous shock arising from the death of her son in an industrial accident, even though she saw neither the accident nor the son's body afterwards). But the Court of Appeal recognised the divergences of opinion in the judgments of the House of Lords in *McLoughlin* and leave of appeal to the House of Lords was given. Perhaps the difficulties over nervous shock will soon be resolved.

The division in the House of Lords in *McLoughlin* also entails that three other problems continue to exist. In *Bourhill* v. *Young* (1945) the House of Lords held that the plaintiff who bore no relationship to the accident victim and who suffered shock not by witnessing the accident but by hearing its noise and later by seeing blood on the road could not recover damages in negligence from the person who caused the accident. This case has often been explained on the ground that it decided that in no circumstances could a casual spectator recover damages for nervous shock (a policy limitation). An alternative reason for it, and one certainly bearing more relation to the actual reasoning in the case, is that shock to the plaintiff was not reasonably foreseeable on the facts since the plaintiff saw neither the accident nor the injured person. The second difficult area is that of words causing shock. If "contemporaneity" is essential so that the plaintiff can never recover damages for shock experienced through being told later about the accident, it appears to follow that no action would lie for negligently being misinformed that an accident had occurred, the result of that misinformation being the suffering of nervous shock. *Wilkinson* v. *Downton* (1897), however, though a case concerning the intentional giving of misinformation to the plaintiff, seems to accept that shock arising from that sort of information may be reasonably foreseeable. If that is correct, and there seems to be no reason to doubt it, the only reason for denying recovery for negligently misinforming the plaintiff about, for example, an injury to a loved one, can be policy. Authority though sparse is divided on the issue (*Guay* v. *Sun Publishing Co.* (1952)—a Canadian case—no liability; *Furniss* v. *Fitchett* (1958); *Barnes* v. *C'th* (1937)—liability. The *Ravenscroft* case (*supra*) tends to support liability). A third problem, that of nervous shock caused by damage to the plaintiff's property, concerned the Court of Appeal in *Attia* v. *British Gas Corp.* (1987). The defendants' negligence in installing a central heating boiler in the plaintiff's house caused a fire which she returned home in time to witness and the house burned down. The Court of Appeal held that she could recover damages for her shock provided it was reasonably foreseeable and ordered a new trial on this point (in which the plaintiff later succeeded). Dillon and Bingham L.JJ. felt able to avoid having to answer the question of whether policy should exclude recovery of damages in this case, since a breach of duty to the plaintiff was established so that the question was one of remoteness of damage and therefore foreseeability alone. This is not satisfactory because where different interests of the plaintiff are threatened by the same negligence, it is generally accepted that separate duty questions arise in relation to each interest—certainly that is the case with pure economic loss. Bingham and Woolf L.JJ. thought that in any case no policy bar to recovery existed on the facts of the case itself. But it is difficult to know how far the case extends, and whether it was the sight of the house burning down that was important or whether the mere loss of property would have been enough (nervous shock caused by loss of money could well be thought to be reasonably foreseeable, or as Bingham L.J. speculated, by a scholar's loss of his manuscript).

Duty in relation to human conduct

In this section will be considered the question whether a duty of care may arise to anticipate and take steps to prevent the deliberate or negligent action of another human being which causes damage to himself or to other human beings. As stated the question is one of duty of care, though there may seem also to be difficulties over causation. How can the defendant be regarded as having caused damage that another human being has deliberately inflicted? The answer to that is that if a duty is recognised to prevent the human action in question, it would be stultifying for the law to hold that a failure in that duty was not the cause of damage caused by the human action. The causal problems that may arise in relation to human conduct are considered in Chapter 8. Different considerations may affect the issue of duty according to whether the conduct is deliberate or negligent and whether the human action is that of the plaintiff or a third party.

(i) *Deliberate human action*

(a) *The rescue principle.* Where a person deliberately faces a risk created by the defendant and is injured, an action brought by that person will fail either on the ground that he caused his own injury or that he consented to the risk (sometimes expressed by saying that he was a volunteer). Quite early in the present century an exceptional case was recognised in which the plaintiff could recover. This was the case of the rescuer. In attempting to rescue another person endangered as a result of the defendant's negligence, the courts have determined that the act of rescue does not operate as the cause of any injuries suffered by the rescuer— nor does he consent to the risk of those injuries. In the earliest case, *Haynes* v. *Harwood* (1935), a policeman was injured when he attempted to stop the defendant's runaway horses from injuring other persons. He recovered damages in negligence from the defendants who had been negligent in the circumstances leading to the horses' bolting. The original decisions on rescue were founded on the breach of a duty of care to the person who was the object of rescue. That created problems where no duty of care was owed by the defendant to the person in need of rescue, or when the defendant had created by his negligence a need for his own rescue. The law has now accommodated the problem by finding that the rescue principle is based upon the breach of an independent duty of care owed by the defendant to the rescuer himself, that duty being not to create a condition in which a rescue attempt is necessary. This was the basis of the decision of the Court of Appeal in *Videan* v. *British Transport Board* (1964) (duty owed to plaintiff rescuer though not to person being rescued who was a trespasser) and of the decisions in *Harrison* v. *British Railways Board* (1981) and of the court at first instance in *Baker* v. *Hopkins* (1959) (defendant created need for his own rescue).

The justification of the rescue principle is that the feeling of moral compulsion under which the plaintiff acts renders his act of rescue in law not voluntary. The rescuer is, nevertheless, equally able to recover damages where he has acted under legal compulsion, for example, that deriving from the terms of his employment (for example, firemen—*Hartley* v. *British Railways Board* (1981); *Salmon* v. *Seafarer Restaurant* (1983); *Ogwo* v. *Taylor* (1987)). The plaintiff must show that his rescue attempt was reasonably necessary, the force of the word "reasonably" being that the necessity must be one which a reasonable man would apprehend to exist on the facts known to him—it does not matter that the course of events proves that the rescuer need not have acted. In *Cutler* v. *United Dairies* (1935) the plaintiff went to the assistance of the defendant's servant in attempting to pacify the defendant's unruly horse in circumstances for which the defendants were accountable in negligence. The plaintiff was injured when the horse bolted. His action failed because since no one was endangered by the horse, he was not acting as a rescuer but as a volunteer. Since the action of the plaintiff was clearly reasonable, the case shows that the condition for recovery is the involuntariness of the plaintiff's action rather than its reasonableness (for the position as to contributory negligence by rescuers, see *infra*, p. 190). It needs to be stressed that the liability of the defendant towards the rescuer in the cases under consideration is based on negligence, and that that tort requires the circumstances of the rescuer's injury to be foreseeable. *Crossley* v. *Rawlinson* (1981) illustrates the point, although the application of the rule to the facts of that case is disputable. The plaintiff rescuer in that case was an A.A. patrolman who, on seeing the defendant's car on fire some 100 yards from the patrol post, ran towards it with a fire extinguisher and in doing so tripped in a hole near the path and injured his leg. The court dismissed his action on the ground that his injury was not reasonably foreseeable.

(b) *Other cases*. Where the basis of the rescue principle was the commission by the defendant of an incipient tort towards other persons, it did not seem to stretch the existing rules of tort too far. Where the basis of the principle is, as it is now recognised to be, that the defendant has by negligence created a condition in which the plaintiff may foreseeably by his deliberate act injure himself, that being a breach of a duty of care owed independently to the plaintiff, it is clear that the rescue cases form part of the much wider question of to what extent the defendant may be found to owe a duty of care in relation to the deliberate actions of other persons including the plaintiff. Where the other person is the plaintiff, the rescue principle allows recovery of damages when the plaintiff's act is in law involuntary, creating the possibility of other cases in which a duty of care may exist to prevent the plaintiff injuring himself by his own deliberate though in law involuntary action. In *Kirkham* v. *Chief Constable of Greater Manchester Police* (1989) it was held that the police owed a duty of care to a prisoner when transferring him to a remand centre to inform the centre of the prisoner's known suicidal tendencies, and were consequently liable for the prisoner's death through suicide when they failed to pass on the information.

Where the case concerns the question of whether the defendant owes any duty of care in relation to the deliberate infliction of damage by third parties upon the plaintiff, the issue becomes more difficult since the avenue of potential liability in tort is greatly widened. In this part of the law it is apparent that mere foreseeability of the third party's action is not enough and that as a matter of policy the courts will place limitations upon the right of recovery. It is now settled law that a duty of care may be found to exist in keepers of prison in relation to the acts of prisoners in their charge both in relation to acts committed inside the prison (*Ellis* v. *Home Office* (1953)) and those committed outside the prison, at least when they are committed in the vicinity of the prison and immediately after escape (*Home Office* v. *Dorset Yacht* (1970)). In the latest decided case on this difficult question the prison cases were explained on the basis of the special relationship of legal control existing between keeper and prisoner justifying the imposition of a duty of care to control the actions of the prisoners. (*Perl* v. *Camden L.B.C.* (*per* Oliver and Goff L.JJ.)). An alternative test favoured by Lord Reid in the *Dorset Yacht* case and by Waller L.J. in the *Perl* case is that a higher degree of foreseeability is required in relation to these cases. The act of the human being must be not merely foreseeable but likely. The trend of decisions in English cases has been to deny the existence of a duty of care. Employers have been found to owe no duty of care to their employees to prevent theft of their property (*Deyong* v. *Sherburn* (1946)); nor does an occupier owe a duty of care to his visitors to prevent theft of their property committed on his premises (*Tinsley* v. *Dudley* (1951)). In *Perl* v. *Camden L.B.C.* (1983) the Court of Appeal held that an owner of a house owed no duty of care to secure it against entry by thieves who entered the house and thereby gained entry into the plaintiff's adjoining property in the absence of a special relationship under which the owner could control the acts of the thieves. *Perl* is not difficult to reconcile with *Stansbie* v. *Troman* (1948) in which a painter/ decorator employed by the plaintiff left the house unattended and unlocked for two hours contrary to the plaintiff's instructions during which time a theft of the plaintiff's jewelry occurred. The defendant was held liable for the loss of the jewelry. Unlike the *Perl* case, there was here a relationship of proximity arising from assumption of responsibility and reliance. The assumption of responsibility related to the very risk which had occurred, however unlikely its occurrence. A more difficult case is that where there is no control by the defendant over the acts of the third party nor any relationship based on assumption of responsibility and reliance. In *Smith* v. *Littlewoods Ltd.* (1987) the House of Lords was concerned with whether the defendants who owned a cinema which was not being used or occupied were liable to the plaintiffs when a youth entered the cinema and started a fire there which spread to and damaged the plaintiff's neighbouring premises. The House of Lords, with the exception of Lord Goff, found that a general (notional) duty of care existed on the facts of the case, but that on the facts known to the defendant there was no reasonable foreseeability of the third party's action. Lord Mackay L.C. thought that the test in such cases was always one of reasonable foreseeability though in the case of damage caused by a human being, liability depended on a finding that the act was likely to happen rather than merely foreseeable. The position taken by the majority of the House of Lords in this case appears to ignore the nonfeasance problem. If the only question is one of fact, *i.e.* reasonable foreseeability, it might be appropriate to adopt Weir's suggestion (*Casebook on Tort* (6th ed), p. 103) that the question be treated as one of breach rather than duty. In *Smith*, for example, where the only way of deterring entry was thought to be the mounting of a 24 hour guard, not to have done so would have been reasonable and therefore no breach of duty. *Perl* is less easy to defend on those lines, because it seems to have been accepted in that case that the defendants could easily have deterred entry by placing a lock on the door. Lord Goff, though concurring in the result in *Smith* v. *Littlewoods*, did so on the ground that the case was one of nonfeasance and that in such cases the occupier of land owes a duty of care to his neighbours as regards the acts of trespassing third parties only where either he negligently caused or permitted the creation of a source of danger on his land where it was foreseeable that third parties might trespass and activate the danger, or where he has the knowledge or means of knowledge that a third party is creating or has created a fire risk on his land (the latter point derived by inference from *Goldman* v. *Hargrave* (1967)). The decision of the House of Lords in *Smith* v. *Littlewoods Ltd.* illustrates the difficulty of ascertaining the present status of the nonfeasance "rule." Is it still, to some extent, a rule of law, or now, as seems more likely, merely a factor in the determination of a duty of care?

Knightley v. *Johns* (1982) is an earlier decision of the Court of Appeal which supports the conclusion of Lord Mackay in *Smith* that a higher degree of probability than mere foreseeability applies in deciding on liability for the deliberate acts of human beings. In that case the defendant motorist had by his negligence caused an accident at the end of a tunnel carrying motor traffic. A police inspector ordered the plaintiff, a constable, to ride his motor-cycle the wrong way down the tunnel in order to close it, a breach of the inspector's instructions which required him to use the telephone for this purpose. The plaintiff was hit and injured by an oncoming car. Finding the defendant not liable for the plaintiff's injury, the Court of Appeal did so on the ground that the inspector's act in sending the plaintiff down the tunnel was not the natural and probable consequence of the defendant's negligence. The court looked at the case as one of remoteness of damage but it is difficult to see what breach of duty had been committed by the defendant towards the plaintiff unless it was the causing of him to be sent down the tunnel. Looked at in terms of duty, consideration might have been given to the issue as a matter of policy whether a motorist who causes an accident should bear any responsibility for the deliberate actions of police who have taken charge of the accident scene, whether these are foreseeable or not.

The recent case of *Cunningham* v. *Reading Football Club Ltd.* (1991) is relevant here, though it is distinguishable in that it concerns the liability of an occupier to a lawful visitor so that there was no difficulty in establishing a notional duty of care. In that case the club was held liable both at common law and under the Occupiers' Liability Act 1957 to the plaintiff police constable for a serious injury he received when hit by a piece of concrete thrown by a visiting football supporter. The basis of liability was the known likelihood of acts of violence committed by the visiting supporters and the failure by the club to maintain the concrete structure of the ground, thus giving easy access to lumps of concrete.

The cases just considered concern actions by third parties who are in law responsible for their actions. There is less difficulty in finding a duty of care to exist in relation to the acts of irresponsible persons which should have been foreseen and guarded against. Thus a parent may be liable for entrusting a dangerous implement or weapon to its infant child (*Smith* v. *Leurs* (1945); *Donaldson* v. *McNiven* (1952); *Newton* v. *Edgerley* (1959)); a school authority for allowing a very young child to escape on to the highway and cause an accident (*Carmarthenshire County Council* v. *Lewis* (1955); an occupier in relation to the acts of mischievous children committed on his property (*Shiffman* v. *Order of St. John* (1936)).

(ii) *Negligent conduct*

Negligence is it seems always foreseeable and there is abundance of authority that the defendant may be under a duty of care in relation to the negligent actions of the plaintiff which injure himself, or of third parties which injure the plaintiff. An example of the former type of case is *Levine* v. *Morris* (1970). The defendants were held liable for siting a concrete road-sign adjacent to a main highway to the plaintiff who lost control of his car and drove into the sign. The only way in which the sign could have caused injury of this sort was by reason of negligence of one sort or another. Clearly a substantial reduction of damages for contributory negligence will occur in cases of this sort.

An example of the second type of case is *Hale* v. *Hants & Dorset Motor Services* (1947). The defendants allowed branches of their trees to overhang the highway, negligently and in breach of their statutory duty. The second defendant's servant drove their bus too near to the roadside and the plaintiff was injured when a branch caused the shattering of a window. Both defendants were held liable in negligence to the plaintiff. Neither the conduct of the first nor that of the second defendant was by itself enough to have caused this injury. Each defendant was in effect held liable for failing to foresee the negligent conduct of the other.

Conclusion

The last few years have seen a concerted attempt by the courts to keep the tort of negligence within reasonable bounds, evidenced by the overruling of *Anns* and the more stringent attitude taken towards the *Hedley Byrne* rule. The courts have also indicated that duties of care will not be recognised in situations where there already exist settled rules of law which the recognition of a duty of care would subvert. In *Moorgate Mercantile Co.* v. *Twitchings* (1977) the refusal to impose a duty of care on the members of an association of car dealers, formed to pass on information about hire-purchase contracts affecting their cars to other members, to actually pass on that information is best explained on the ground that the recognition of a duty would outflank the established rule that the owner of property cannot be held to be contributorily negligent if he negligently allows it to be lost. In *Parker-Tweedale* v. *Dunbar Bank* (1990) the Court of Appeal held that a mortgagee when exercising a power of sale in the mortgage owed no duty of care to a person holding a beneficial interest in the mortgaged property, since the mortgagee owed equitable duties to the mortgagor and its surety and it would not be useful to add further duties in tort to the existing framework. In *Business Computers Ltd.* v. *Registrar of Companies* (1987) the court held that no action lay at the suit of one litigant against another in respect of the negligent mis-serving of legal process, by analogy with the rule concerning the immunity of witnesses from liability for evidence given in trials and because the legal process itself was designed for the rectification of such matters. In *C.B.S. Songs Ltd.* v. *Amstrad* (1988) the House of Lords refused to allow an action in negligence by a producer against a manufacturer of machines which allowed the transfer of the contents of those tapes on to other tapes— existing copyright law did not cover this situation but it was for the legislature to close the gap. In some cases, however, new duties of care have been recognised. For example, it has been held recently that a duty of care exists towards the child at the foetus stage (*B.* v. *Islington Health Authority* (1991)). Also, going contrary to the South Australian decision in *Robertson* v. *Swincer* (1989), it was held that a parent owes a duty of care to its very young child to protect it from injury, though the standard of care to be required must take into account the infinite number of circumstances in which injury could be caused and the policy factors against legal interference in family relationships (*Surtees* v. *Hughes*, also called *Surtees* v. *Royal Borough of Kingston* (1991)).

7. BREACH OF DUTY OF CARE IN NEGLIGENCE

Introduction

In the case of some torts, of which battery may be given as an example, the definition of the tort allows us to form a clear mental picture of the defendant's conduct in committing it. Negligence is not like this. To say that a person has acted negligently tells us nothing about the type of conduct involved. It merely evaluates that conduct as against some ideal standard. The standard against which the defendant's actions are judged is that of *reasonableness*; to be more precise, the question is asked whether the defendant has acted as a reasonable man would have acted in the situation in which he found himself. If the defendant's conduct fails to pass this test, he is said to be in breach of his duty of care. The phrase, "standard of care," which is often used to indicate the standard of reasonable conduct by which the defendant's conduct is measured is misleading in that it suggests that a pre-existing standard is available to determine whether or not the defendant is negligent. In fact, the court always reaches its decision by an *ex post facto* adjudication that on the actual facts of the case the defendant acted reasonably or unreasonably. Previous decisions on similar facts, though they are evidence of what has in the past been regarded as reasonable or unreasonable conduct will not bind the court in its decision in the instant case.

How breach of duty is established

The vagueness of the rule that the judge has to apply in deciding whether a person was negligent and the lack of binding force in

142

previous judicial determinations of the same question inevitably create a measure of judicial discretion and therefore of uncertainty in the law. Negligence is not alone in this respect. Unreasonableness (though not necessarily the unreasonableness of the defendant's conduct) is the central requirement of the tort of nuisance. Furthermore, the uncertainty is mitigated by the existence of certain guiding principles of law which control the exercise of the judicial discretion. Thus, in arriving at his decision, the judge must take into account:

1. The degree of risk to the plaintiff created by the defendant's conduct. In this matter, the question of the foreseeability of the plaintiff's injury by the defendant is important.
2. The seriousness of the harm that the plaintiff may suffer.
3. The social utility of the defendant's action.
4. The expense and practicability of taking precautions against the risk.

These criteria for deciding the reasonableness of the defendant's conduct are interrelated, and cannot therefore be separately assessed. Thus, it is impossible to decide the question whether the degree of risk created by the defendant is sufficient to involve him in liability without also examining the seriousness of the harm that may result from the risk materialising. Equally the social importance of the defendant's conduct may justify the creation of a higher degree of risk than is normally permissible. Essentially the court's decision is an attempt to strike a balance between these various factors.

(1) *Degree of risk*

In order to decide whether the defendant has created a sufficient risk of the harm which the plaintiff suffers, it is not enough to ask whether this harm was a foreseeable result of the defendant's conduct. The harm must be *reasonably* foreseeable: it must therefore result from a risk which a reasonable man would regard as one against which precautions ought to be taken. Clearly the inquiry involved in deciding whether a certain danger was so sufficiently likely that the defendant ought to have taken care to prevent it happening is similar to the question of whether a "duty in fact" exists. It is not quite the same, however. Foreseeability is here not the sole determinant. The court must decide whether the degree of foreseeable risk of danger is sufficiently great that, bearing in mind factors 2, 3 and 4, the defendant acted unreasonably in failing to regulate his conduct to avert it.

For example, in *Bolton* v. *Stone* (1951), the defendants were occupiers of a cricket ground. The plaintiff who was standing on the highway outside the ground was struck by a cricket ball hit during the course of a match on the ground. The plaintiff's action of negligence against the defendants was unsuccessful. The House of Lords took the view that in view of the distance from the wicket to the fence which marked the perimeter of the ground, the upward slope from the wicket to the fence, the infrequency with which balls had been hit into the road (estimated at six times in the previous 30 years), the plaintiff had not established that the defendant had created a sufficient risk of the injury she suffered happening. It may be noted that in this case the defendants took no precautions whatsoever to prevent balls being struck into the road. This shows again that the expression "standard of care" may be misleading since the defendant may have acted reasonably although he has taken no precautions whatsoever against the risk. If the risk is sufficiently slight he is justified in ignoring it altogether.

In later cases the courts have taken a more stringent attitude where the defendant has created only a slight risk of harm.

In *The Wagon Mound* (No. 2) (1967) the defendants' servants carelessly allowed furnace oil to spill into Sydney harbour. The oil drifted towards a wharf (owned by the plaintiffs in *The Wagon Mound* (No. 1) and on which oxyacetylene welding was being carried out by their servants, in the course of repairing a ship belonging to the present plaintiff). The oil was ignited by the fall of pieces of hot metal from the welding operations. The plaintiff's ship was damaged in the resulting fire. The defendants were held liable to the plaintiff for this damage in negligence. The finding of fact by the trial judge in Australia was that a reasonable man in the position of the defendants' servant would have regarded the ignition of furnace oil on water as a possibility but one which could become an actuality only in very exceptional circumstances. This did not excuse the defendants. In the words of Lord Reid, delivering the judgment of the Privy Council:

"If a real risk is one which would occur to the mind of a reasonable man in the position of the defendants' servant, and which he would not brush aside as far-fetched, and if the criteria is to be what that reasonable man would have done in the circumstances, then surely he would not neglect such risk if action to eliminate it presented no difficulty, involved no disadvantage and required no expense."

This raises the problem of distinguishing this case from *Bolton* v. *Stone*. It seems impossible to separate the two cases on the question of the degree of likelihood of the harm occurring. Equally it seems wrong to regard the damage in *The Wagon Mound* (No. 2) as more serious than that in *Bolton* v. *Stone*—the cricket ball could have caused serious injury. The difference seems to be that in *Bolton* the defendants were carrying on a lawful activity, arguably of social benefit, and would have been put to expense in providing precautions against the risks of the activity. The discharging of oil by the servants of the *Wagon Mound* was on the other hand anti-social, unnecessary and unlawful (as a public nuisance). In the circumstances the defendants were not entitled to ignore any risk involved provided they should have foreseen it. This comparison shows how factors 3 and 4 (*supra*) can impinge on the question whether the degree of risk created by the defendant was sufficient (*Miller* v. *Jackson* (*infra*, p. 251)) shows that the social benefit in playing cricket will not prevail where there is a more significant risk of injury or damage to a person outside the ground.

Another case which shows that a court may be prepared to find negligence though the risk of injury is slight is *Haley* v. *London Electricity Board* (1965). In that case a blind person recovered damages in negligence from the defendants for personal injuries received through falling into an excavation made by the defendants' servants in the pavement. The House of Lords found that the defendants' duty of care was not discharged by safeguarding, as they had, normal persons from falling into the excavation; they must also take into account the use of the pavement by blind persons, for whom the excavation was not reasonably safe.

Foresight or hindsight? Some of the cases already dealt with in this book indicate that the reasonable man is expected to foresee some quite improbable events. The presence of a relative near an accident victim, the presence of a blind man near a hole in the ground, the action of a rescuer in throwing himself into the path of a runaway horse are all within the range of his foresight. The element of foresight is that which determines the necessity to use care on the part of the defendant. But it is not a simple notion to apply. Take the case of the car driver. The reasonable driver, if asked why he should drive with care, would reply that otherwise he might hit somebody or something on the road. To ask whether he should also take into account as a reason for driving carefully the possibility that he may cause nervous shock to the relative of a person he hits (or narrowly misses), or that his bad driving may cause a fire which burns down a shop three hundred yards from the scene of the accident, is to ask a meaningless question of him. Yet because of the rule of English law that duties of care cannot exist in the abstract but must be owed to the particular person who suffers harm, such questions will often need to be answered. The real test here seems to be not whether a reasonable driver would actually have borne the unlikely risk in mind, but whether, assuming the injury or damage that occurred were the only possible result of bad driving, the reasonable driver if asked at the time of his driving would have said that the existence of such a risk was sufficient to impose an obligation on his part to exercise care. A complicated question of this sort looks much more like a test of hindsight rather than foresight and this seems to be the truth of the matter in a number of cases. The advantage of this approach is that persons who by carelessness have created obvious risks should not escape on the ground that the result of their carelessness is unusual rather than obvious. In some cases the only risk created by the defendant is an unusual one, and in such cases it seems the defendant is only liable if a reasonable person in his position would actually have borne that risk in mind. *Haley* v. *London Electricity Board* is a good example of this.

(2) *The seriousness of the injury*

It is an obvious proposition that the defendant's obligations become greater with the greater seriousness of the injury his actions may threaten. The more serious the injury or damage, the less the defendant will be entitled to argue that the degree of risk involved in his actions was insufficiently large, or that he would have needed to incur considerable expense in order to avoid the risk.

In *Paris* v. *Stepney Borough Council* (1951) the House of Lords held that the defendants' omission to provide protective eye goggles for their servants while possibly not negligent in the case of a two-eyed man was negligent in the case of the plaintiff who had only one eye. Such omission clearly did not increase the risk of injury to the plaintiff but only the risk that if he did suffer injury it would be more serious. After the cases of *The Wagon Mound* (No. 2) and *Haley*, the *Paris* reasoning is only likely to be applied in rare circumstances.

(3) *The social utility of the defendant's action*

It has become apparent in the present century that certain inventions, such as the train, the motor-car and various forms of industrial machinery, though by and large regarded as beneficial to humanity, inevitably by their operation involve danger to human life and limb. When the first cases of train and motor-car accidents came before the court, it would have been possible for them to have laid down a rule that the mere operation of the train or motor-car involved so great a risk of injury that it was in itself negligent. Instead the courts decided that there was no negligence provided the vehicle was operated with proper care. The courts reached this result by balancing the social utility of the inventions against the risk of injury where they were operated with due care. Cases in which the defendant is excused on the ground of the usefulness of the activity he is carrying on are therefore somewhat rare, because it will be unusual for such a consideration to excuse what would otherwise be negligence in the activity itself. The only English case in which a plea of utility has been unequivocally recognised is *Daborn* v. *Bath Tramways* (1946) (and even this is a decision on contributory negligence rather than negligence itself). In that case the driver of a left-hand drive ambulance in wartime was held not contributorily negligent in failing to signal a right turn prior to a collision with a bus driven by the defendants' servant, because the shortage of ambulances in wartime conditions justified the use of a vehicle in which it was impossible to give such a signal. In *Watt* v. *Hertfordshire Corporation* (1954) the plaintiff, a fireman, was injured when a heavy jack in a lorry belonging to his employers, the defendants, and in which he was travelling, moved on to him. Although the jack was insecurely tied on, the court held that there was no negligence because the jack was urgently needed in order to save a person trapped under a lorry, and the emergency justified the risk of travelling with the jack insecurely tied. The most acceptable explanation for the case appears to be that given in the judgment of Singleton L.J. to the effect that firemen are deemed to accept the risks incidental to dealing with such an emergency as part of their employment. It seems doubtful whether the emergency would have justified the defendants' action had the jack injured a member of the public.

That it may be necessary to make this distinction is apparent from two cases involving the use of police vehicles. In *Gaynor* v. *Allen* (1959) the defendant police motor-cyclist while exceeding the speed limit in conditions of twilight struck and injured the plaintiff, a pedestrian, who was crossing the road. The defendant was engaged on his police duties at the time but the court in finding him liable found that it made no difference and that he must be judged by the same standards as other motorists. In *Marshall* v. *Osmond* (1982) the plaintiff was a passenger in a stolen vehicle that was being chased by the police and was injured by being struck by the police car on alighting from the stolen vehicle. The court found the driver of the police car not liable on the ground that the same duty as that owed to law-abiding citizens was not owed to occupants of a vehicle believed to be stolen and of which the police were in hot pursuit. The duty here is a reduced one and may be limited to abstaining from deliberately injuring the plaintiff.

(4) *The expense and practicability of taking precautions*

From the dearth of decisions where the relevance of the practicability and expense of taking precautions against the risk has been discussed, it appears that the courts do not look with favour upon an argument by the defendant along these lines. In *Latimer* v. *A.E.C.* (1952) it was argued on behalf of the plaintiff that the defendants should have shut down their factory, the floor of which had been flooded in a thunderstorm, rather than subject the night-shift workers, who included the plaintiff, to the risks caused by the resulting slipperiness of the floor, on which the plaintiff slipped and suffered injury. The House of Lords accepted this argument in principle, though finding that insufficient evidence had been presented by the plaintiff to show that such a step was necessary.

Where the defendant is being sued in negligence for failing to remedy the state of affairs on his land where that state of affairs arose without his default, the expense of remedying the state of affairs and the means and resources of the particular defendant are relevant factors in deciding whether a defendant is negligent. Thus, in *Goldman* v. *Hargrave* (1967) since the fire could have been extinguished at nominal expense, the defendant was held liable for allowing it to spread from his land to that of the plaintiff. It seems reasonable to apply a subjective test of this sort where the defendant has done nothing to create the risk, but is liable merely because of his occupation of land upon which the risk spontaneously arises.

The objective standard: the reasonable man

In imposing a requirement on a defendant that he should have acted reasonably, the law is judging him by a standard external to himself. The standard by which the defendant's conduct is assessed is that of a reasonable man in the same situation as that in which the defendant finds himself. It is sometimes said that the standard is an objective rather than a subjective one; but the defendant could hardly be judged by his own standards; this would not be a standard at all. It is important to note that the standard by which the defendant is judged though objective is also hypothetical; the court must imagine what a non-existent reasonable person in the position of the defendant would have done. In effect the court must make up its own mind as to what is reasonable in the light of the evidence.

Difficulty arises where the defendant has some defect, whether physical or mental, which makes it impossible for him to show the same standard of care as a normal person. Are these defects engrafted upon the reasonable man, so that the question is what is it reasonable to expect of a person with those defects? On this matter it seems there are two competing viewpoints. The first is that, unless the defect is taken into account, the "fault" basis of negligence will be ignored, and it will operate as a tort of strict liability. Against this it is argued that unless the test is largely objective, liability in negligence will be hard to establish because all sorts of trifling defects might be put forward in excuse for what is in fact a careless act. To a great extent the problem may be solved by application of the principle that one who, with knowledge of his own defects puts himself into a position where those defects made it impossible to display a proper standard of care, is negligent. So a car-driver with slow reactions cannot plead that in an accident caused by his slowness of reaction he was not negligent. On these matters there is a dearth of English authority, and a paucity of discussion of principle in those authorities that exist. The cases, such as they are, tend to support those who argue for a subjective interpretation of negligence. Many of the decisions are, however, on contributory negligence rather than negligence itself and it may be that different considerations apply (a court may excuse a child for failure to look after itself—but what of a failure to look after the safety of other people?). There is also the problem of fixing the standard of care in cases where specialised knowledge or skill may be required of the defendant.

Defects caused by immaturity

Clearly very young children have a different standard of care from adults both in matters of negligence and of contributory negligence. But the courts have also applied a different standard of care, at least in contributory negligence cases, to older children. In *Gough* v. *Thorne* (1966) a 13-year-old child was held to be not contributorily negligent in crossing the road on a signal from a lorry driver without checking that the way was clear beyond the lorry. Where the child is nearing adulthood, however, the same leniency will not be shown to him. In *Gorely* v. *Codd* (1967) the court held a boy of 16½ liable for his negligence in "larking about" with an air-rifle as a result of which he shot the plaintiff.

Defects caused by age

There is little authority about the effect of old age on the standard of care. Old people are not expected to show the same agility as the young (*Daly* v. *Liverpool Corporation* (1939) in which an old person who was struck by a bus while crossing a street was held to be not contributorily negligent where a younger person would have succeeded in crossing). Clearly, however, an old person must not put himself in a position which calls for the reactions or agility of a younger person; also he must make allowances for the slowing-up processes of age (for example, when driving a car).

Illness

In *Ryan* v. *Youngs* (1938) a driver who had a heart attack and lost consciousness at the wheel prior to an accident was held not negligent in causing the accident. Although it has been argued that even in such a case the defendant should bear the loss because he is insured against it, there does not seem any sense in which the defendant's conduct could be described as negligent. There is a difference, however, if the driver of the car retains consciousness. In *Roberts* v. *Ramsbottom* (1980), the defendant driver suffered a cerebral haemorrhage which caused a clouding of consciousness with the result that he was, through no fault of his own, unable to drive properly but also incapable of realising this. He was held liable in negligence for a collision with another car. The decision reflects a tendency to impose what is virtually strict liability on car drivers (*cf. Nettleship* v. *Weston, infra*, p. 153). There is of course no difficulty in imposing liability in negligence if the defendant knows of his illness or its likelihood in advance.

Intelligence and character

It seems certain, although there is no authority, that a defendant is not excused by such defects as stupidity, absentmindedness, accident-proneness, inability to learn from experience, and the like. This is not surprising because if these were regarded as excusing factors few actions in negligence would succeed.

Knowledge

Every adult is expected to possess a certain quantum of knowledge. That petrol is highly inflammable, that dynamite explodes, that acid burns, that toadstools are dangerous, are matters of common knowledge. Apart from this a person may be expected to acquire knowledge by observation from his surrounding circumstances. Expert knowledge is not required of a defendant unless he has acted on the footing that he is an expert. A landowner who has trees growing on his estate is not expected to possess scientific knowledge of diseases that may affect the trees—the knowledge required of him is "somewhere between that of an urban observer and a scientific arboriculturist" (*Caminer* v. *Northern and London Investment Trust* (1951)). But such a landowner also owes a duty to call in experts to inspect the trees from time to time to assess their safety, especially where, as in that case, one of the trees is an elm, which a reasonable landowner ought to know possesses special hazards and the elm in question overhangs or adjoins the public highway. Equally, although expert knowledge is not required of a ship's engineer, he is expected to know that furnace oil might in exceptional circumstances be ignited on water (*The Wagon Mound* (No. 2)) (1967), knowledge that clearly would not be expected of the average person. In *Luxmoore-May* v. *Messenger, May, Baverstock* (1990) the Court of Appeal held that provincial auctioneers who undertook to "research" the value of a painting owed a duty merely to act honestly and with due diligence and were not to be assessed by the standard of care required of a city auction house.

Skill

Skill is very often interrelated with knowledge, although of course a skill may exist which does not require a body of knowledge. Sometimes the skill and knowledge of an expert is required of a person, for example, a surgeon in performing an operation. In other cases only ordinary skill or knowledge is required, for example, that required of a motorist in driving a car. In general it may be said that the person who holds himself out as possessing the skill and knowledge required for performing a certain task must show that skill and knowledge in the exercise of the task.

The courts have not been too ready to decide that a person must show more than ordinary skill. In *Philips* v. *Whiteley* (1938) it was held that a jeweller who pierced the plaintiff's ears at her request was not bound to show proper medical skill in performing the operation—he need only show the standard of care of a reasonably competent jeweller. In *Wells* v. *Cooper* (1958) the defendant was held not negligent in fitting a new door-handle, the plaintiff suffering injury because it came away when he pulled on it and he fell down some steps. The defendant had shown the standard of care of a reasonably competent amateur carpenter, and professional expertise was not required of him. Both cases seem open to the objection that they encourage the doing by amateurs of tasks which involve danger to others. In *Nettleship* v. *Weston* (1971), on the other hand, the Court of Appeal held that a learner-driver must show the standard of driving skill of a reasonably competent qualified driver and was therefore liable to a passenger for injuries the passenger received through his failure to do so. The case is a strong pointer towards "objectifying" the fault element in negligence, although the fact that the defendant was insured against liability clearly influenced the decision (there can be no real objection towards this decision now that insurance against liability towards passengers is compulsory). But in *Cook* v. *Cook* (1986) the Australian High Court refused to follow *Nettleship*, on the ground that a reduced standard of care applies between learner-driver and instructor because of their special relationship.

A confusing concept of recent origin seemingly applicable mainly to professional negligence, that of "error of judgment," has now been put firmly into its place by the House of Lords in *Whitehouse* v. *Jordan* (1981). In that case the Court of Appeal had found against negligence by the defendant hospital registrar in the manner in which he performed a Caesarian operation since even if he did use excessive force in the use of forceps, he had committed a mere error of clinical judgment. The concept was tentatively adopted as a basis by Mocatta J. for his decision that a commodity investment broker was not liable for investment advice given in relation to the commodities market (*Stafford* v. *Conti Commodity Services* (1981)). None of the members of the House of Lords in *Whitehouse* v. *Jordan*, however, relied on the concept of "error of judgment" and three of them expressly rejected it as unhelpful. Some errors of clinical judgment may be completely consistent with the due exercise of professional skill, others may be not. The test to be applied was the usual one whether the defendant acted reasonably in the circumstances.

Superior qualities

There is little English authority on the question of whether the person of superior intelligence or skill is liable for failing to use those qualities in a situation where such person is not holding himself out as possessing these qualities. Is a racing driver liable for causing an accident in ordinary traffic in which he showed the skill of an ordinary motorist, but had he driven with the skill to be expected of a racing driver the accident would have been averted?

In *Stokes* v. *G.K.N. (Bolts and Nuts)* (1968), Swanwick J. observed in relation to the standard of care of an employer of workmen that "where he has in fact greater than average knowledge of the risks, he may be thereby obliged to take more than the average or standard precautions." The passage in which this was contained was quoted with approval by Mustill J. in *Thompson* v. *Smith Shiprepairers* (1984). On the other hand, the standard of care relating to a member of a skilled profession is that of an ordinary member of that profession and it appears that a member of the profession with specially high skill is not liable for failing to use that skill unless he has in some way undertaken to use it for the particular task in hand (*George Wimpey Ltd.* v. *Poole* (1984)).

Sporting contests

Clearly there are dangers incidental to the playing of sport which are not present in everyday life. This could be represented by the law of tort in one of two ways. The first is by application of the *maxim volenti non fit injuria* to the case of those who play or otherwise participate in sport. The second is by regulating the standard of care of those involved in the sport to reflect the incidental risks. English law has adopted the second approach for good reasons. In particular the defence of *volenti* requires an individual consent to the risk in order to be effective and would need to be separately applied to each participant, whereas the regulation of standard of care can be applied to all participants. In *Wooldridge* v. *Sumner* (1963) Diplock L.J. said, "if the participant does so concentrate his attention and consequently does exercise his judgment and attempt to exert his skill in circumstances of this kind which are inherent in the game or competition in which he is taking part, the question whether any mistake he makes amounts to a breach of duty must take account of those circumstances." The reduced standard of care will apply as between all who are privy to the risks of the game including players (see *Condon* v. *Basi* (1985)) and spectators. In *Wooldridge* v. *Sumner* itself the defendant who was riding a horse in a competition was held not liable to the plaintiff, a photographer who was standing inside the competition area and who was injured when the horse took a wrong turn as a result of an error of judgment on the part of the rider. The reduction in the standard of care also protects the organiser of sporting contests (see *Murray* v. *Harringay Arena* (1951)—a six-year-old spectator at an ice-hockey match was struck by an ice-puck struck from the rink—no liability in negligence). But the danger must be one that is reasonably incidental to the playing of the sport in question. So in *Harrison* v. *Vincent* (1982) the plaintiff was a passenger in a sidecar on a motor-cycle which was taking part in a competition. The brakes of the motor-cycle failed and the plaintiff was injured when the sidecar combination struck a parked recovery vehicle. The plaintiff succeeded in negligence against the rider of the combination who had failed to align properly the brake calipers of the vehicle and against the organisers of the contest who had improperly positioned the parked vehicle. Neither act of negligence was incidental to the contest since both took place before it began.

If the standard of care is a reduced one, by how much is it reduced? *Wooldridge* v. *Sumner* in excusing the participant for an error of judgment seemed to create a liability only for causing injury intentionally or recklessly. In *Wilks* v. *Cheltenham Car Club* (1971) Edmund Davies L.J., speaking *obiter*, specifically disapproved the exemption from liability for errors of judgment. There should be liability if the error was one that "a reasonable competitor being a reasonable man of the sporting world would not have made." That the standard of care is objectively determined, though taking account of the risks of the sport, was accepted by the Court of Appeal in *Condon* v. *Basi* (1985) in which the defendant soccer player was held liable for an injury caused by his foul tackle on the plaintiff. But it was found as a fact that the tackle was reckless. There are likely to be few examples of conduct which is adjudged careless though not reckless when committed in the heat of the sporting contest.

General practice of those engaged in the activity

It may be relevant evidence of the fact that the defendant acted reasonably to show that he acted in accordance with the general practice of those who carry on the activity. The standards of a profession, for example, are presumed by the law to be reasonable standards. Such evidence is not by itself conclusive. It is not enough to act in accordance with a general practice if it ought to be apparent to a reasonable man that it is a negligent practice. In *Thompson* v. *Smith Shiprepairers* (1984) the plaintiffs who were employed as labourers or fitters in the defendant's shipyards brought action in negligence on the ground that for a period of time stretching from the 1940s to the 1970s they had been subjected without protection to excessive noise in their employment which had damaged their hearing. The court found that though the presence of the risk to hearing was known to the defendant employers their indifference to it in line with prevailing practices in the industry did not constitute negligence until 1963 when expert advice on the noise problem and adequate and reasonable protective devices became available to employers generally.

In the case of one profession at least, the medical profession, the prevailing standard within that profession is regarded by the court as conclusive on the issue of negligence. The test laid down in questions of medical negligence by *Bolam* v. *Friern Hospital Management Committee* (1957) that the defendant must be judged by the standard of skill or knowledge regarded as necessary by the medical profession as a whole or by a substantial body of opinion within (*Gold* v. *Haringey Health Authority* (1987) has recently been accepted by a majority of the House of Lords in *Sidaway* v. *Bethlem Royal Hospital Governors* (1985)—by Lords Diplock, Keith and Bridge, Lord Templeman expressing no opinion and Lord Scarman dissenting on this point). Where on the other hand the defendant has departed from approved medical practice, the onus rests on him to show that it was reasonable to do so (*Clark* v. *McLennan* (1983)). The *Bolam* test in effect places the standards of one profession beyond the reach of criticism by courts. *Gold* v. *Haringey Health Authority* (1987) held that the *Bolam* test was indivisible and that no distinction could be drawn between medical advice to a wife given in a therapeutic and a contraceptive context.

The *Sidaway* case itself concerned a problem that has caused considerable difficulty in court decisions over recent years, that of the amount of information that must be supplied to a patient before the doctor may legitimately expose him to the risks of an operation. It has been pointed out earlier in the book that provided the patient is correctly informed as to the general nature of the operation and he consents to have it, no action of trespass is available to him (*supra*, p. 74). Is it possible, however, for a patient to establish a cause of action in negligence based on the fact that a risk of a certain operation about which he has not been informed actually materialises because of the operation and in the absence of negligence in the conduct of the operation by the doctor? The answer given by *Sidaway* is that such an action is possible if the risk is one that current standards within the medical profession would have required to be disclosed to the patient (*i.e.* the *Bolam* test—though the House of Lords thought *obiter* that specific questions about particular risks by the patient to the practitioner must be answered, even though these related to risks of which medical practice would not require the patient to be informed). The House of Lords in *Sidaway* rejected the doctrine of "informed consent" which prevails in the District of Columbia and certain other American States and also Canada (*Reibl* v. *Hughes* (1980)) under which the patient is to be informed about those risks about which a "reasonable" patient would expect to be informed even if some of those risks would not be disclosed under current medical practice. The House of Lords felt that the task of defining those risks would be beyond the power of the courts and would give rise to unacceptable uncertainty (for other examples of the English position see *Hills* v. *Potter* (1983); *Freeman* v. *Home Office* (1984)).

8. Causation and Remoteness of Damage in Negligence

The question of whether damage suffered by the plaintiff is too remote to be actionable arises, in the case of torts other than negligence, only when it has been established that the defendant has committed the tort. In negligence, however, the question arises as soon as it has been established that the defendant was in breach of his duty of care to the plaintiff. In order to show that the damage he suffered was not too remote, the plaintiff under the present law must prove both that the damage was caused by the defendant's breach of duty to him, and that this was foreseeable. The two issues of causation and foreseeability will be examined in this chapter. Remoteness of damage must be distinguished from measure of damages. The former concept is concerned with what damage suffered by the plaintiff the defendant must compensate the plaintiff for; the latter with the amount of money the defendant must pay in order to produce that compensation. Since negligence does not, generally speaking, lie for purely pecuniary loss, the question of remoteness of damage in negligence is normally concerned with for what physical consequences of the defendant's breach of duty the plaintiff can recover damages.

LEGAL CAUSE—CAUSATION IN FACT AND IN LAW

(1) *Causation in fact*

The plaintiff must prove that the defendant caused the damage. He must first of all show that the defendant's conduct was a cause in fact of his damage. This he satisfies by showing that but for the defendant's negligence the damage would not have occurred. In *Barnett* v. *Chelsea Hospital Management Committee* (1969) the defendants' servant carelessly failed to examine the plaintiff who attended their hospital for treatment complaining of vomiting. The plaintiff was suffering from arsenical poisoning and later died. The action of his estate against the defendant failed because it could not establish that proper treatment would have diagnosed the plaintiff's condition in time to save him. In *McWilliams* v. *Arrol Ltd.* (1962) the plaintiff had been injured in an accident at work. The defendants, his employers, had in breach of their duty to him, failed to supply him with a safety-belt which would have prevented his injury. The plaintiff's action failed because he could not prove that on the balance of probabilities he would have worn the belt. Finally, in *Cutler* v. *Vauxhall Motors* (1971), the plaintiff, an employee of the defendants, grazed his ankle in an accident at work for which the defendants were liable in negligence. The graze caused ulceration of the leg necessitating an immediate operation for the removal of varicose veins in it. The plaintiff could not recover damages in respect of this operation because the court found as a fact that he would in any case have needed the operation within five years.

The last case illustrates that the tortfeasor takes the benefit of his victim's condition. It is cheaper to injure a person who has only weeks to live than a healthy person. This caused a problem in *Baker* v. *Willoughby* (1970). The plaintiff had received an injury to his leg through the defendant's negligence, and the leg was partially disabled as a result. Later the plaintiff was shot in the leg by another person and the leg was in consequence amputated. The need for amputation did not arise because of the existing disability in the leg. Nevertheless the House of Lords held that the plaintiff should recover compensation from the defendant on the basis of a continuing disability in the leg arising from the earlier injury. Lord Reid's explanation of the decision was that the later event merely operated as a concurrent cause of the plaintiff's disability along with the earlier injury. It did not "obliterate" the effects of that injury. There were two causes of the plaintiff's disability. Only if it improved the plaintiff's condition, therefore, would the later event be causally relevant. Lord Pearson based his judgment on the injustice that would arise if the plaintiff received less than full compensation from the first defendant for his injury. The first defendant would have to pay damages only up to the time of the second injury; the second defendant would have to pay damages only for causing the loss of an already damaged leg. Though injured by two torts, the plaintiff would receive less in compensation than the value of the leg to him.

This explanation of Lord Pearson entails that a difference might exist where the later event was not a tort. There was indeed authority for this point prior to *Baker* v. *Willoughby* in *The Carslogie* (1952) and this case has been confirmed by the House of Lords decision in *Jobling* v. *Associated Dairies* (1981). The plaintiff had sustained an injury to his back at work which had reduced his working capacity by 50 per cent. and for which his employer, the defendant, was liable to compensate him. Before trial he developed a condition of his back (called spondylotic myelopathy) quite independently of the first injury. This condition destroyed his working capacity altogether. The House of Lords unanimously upheld the verdict of the Court of Appeal that the later natural event must be taken into account in awarding damages, the effect being that no damages were awarded for the loss of working capacity after the onset of the myelopathy. A number of points emerge from the judgments in the case. All the members of the House of Lords were in agreement that Lord Reid's explanation of *Baker* v. *Willoughby* based upon the idea of successive concurrent causes was not generally supportable. Later detrimental events were relevant to causation because in general the courts in awarding damages make some deduction for the so-called "vicissitudes of life," these being thought to work on the whole adversely to the plaintiff. If one such vicissitude has actually occurred at the date of trial, it would therefore be wrong to ignore it. This reasoning throws considerable doubt upon the decision in *Baker* v. *Willoughby* itself but no member of the House actually stated that that case was wrongly decided and there was some support for Lord Pearson's view that the case turned on the fact that the plaintiff's injuries had been caused by successive torts. The distinction between a later tort and a later natural event seems therefore to have won the guarded approval of the House of Lords. It is justifiable on the ground that where the defendant by his tort has caused a reduction in the amount of damages that the plaintiff will receive from a later tortfeasor (who takes the plaintiff as he finds him), the defendant should not receive a benefit through the actual occurrence of that tort. It should be noticed that the *Baker* v. *Willoughby/Jobling* problem only arises in the case where each event is by itself a sufficient cause of the damage which the plaintiff suffers. Where the defendant's negligence needs to act in combination with a later act of negligence in order to produce the relevant damage, there is no difficulty in finding factual causation established in regard to both acts of negligence.

A slightly different problem in relation to factual causation is that in which the evidence makes it impossible to say whether or not the defendant's act caused the plaintiff's damage. Normally this means that the action will fail. But in the Canadian decision of *Cook* v. *Lewis* (1952), the plaintiff was shot by one of two members of a hunting party both of whom had fired their rifles in the plaintiff's direction at the same time. The Canadian Supreme Court held that if it could be established that both persons were in breach of their duty of care to the plaintiff in firing their rifles, the plaintiff's action would succeed against both, unless either could show it was not his shot which hit the plaintiff. This was explained on the ground that where the plaintiff has been injured as the result of a tort committed by someone, and all possible tortfeasors have been careless towards the plaintiff, and the result of that carelessness is to prevent the plaintiff proving which person committed the tort, the plaintiff should succeed against all (subject to apportionment of liability among the tortfeasors—*infra*, this chapter). The decision works a certain rough justice—perhaps it may be justified on the ground that the plaintiff's action is for negligence causing him pecuniary loss, *i.e.* his inability to establish his cause of action for personal injuries. But in view of the attitude taken by the House of Lords in the *Wilsher* case (*infra*), it is doubtful whether the case would be followed in this country.

A similarly intractable problem arises where there are other possible causes of the plaintiff's damage which are non-tortious in character. In *Bonnington Castings Ltd.* v. *Wardlaw* (1956) the plaintiff had contracted a lung disease through exposure to noxious fumes for some of which his employers were liable and for some not. The plaintiff was found to have discharged his burden of establishing causal connection between his disease and the culpable fumes. It is true as Lord Salmon observed that the plaintiff need not show that the defendant's negligence was *the* cause, merely a cause of the injury. But clearly the House of Lords here dispensed the plaintiff from having to prove that the non-tortious fumes were probably not a sufficient cause of the disease (in *Bonnington* the damage due to the non-tortious fumes was not regarded as severable from that caused by the tortious—a different result was reached in *Thompson* v. *Smith* (*Ship Repairers*) (1984) in which the court, distinguishing *Bonnington*, was able to apportion damage where an earlier non-tortious exposure to noise causing hearing problems was succeeded by a later tortious exposure to noise). In *McGhee* v. *National Coal Board* (1973) the House of Lords went a stage further than *Bonnington*. In that case the plaintiff contracted dermatitis allegedly as a result of the defendants' admitted negligence in failing to provide showering facilities at work and the consequent prolonged contact with the plaintiff's skin of brick dust. The plaintiff's problem was that dermatitis may have a number of causes quite unconnected with brick dust, although it was accepted that that may have been a cause, whereas in *Bonnington* it was clear that the fumes whether or not tortiously emitted were the cause of the disease. Nevertheless the House of Lords held that the plaintiff had established the necessary causal connection. Some of the judgments in the House, in particular that of Lord Wilberforce, proceeded on the basis that the plaintiff need establish only a breach of duty by creating a risk of a certain harm occurring and the occurrence of that harm. The defendant then had the burden of proving that the harm has another cause. This judicial reversal of the burden of proof on causation has itself been reversed by the decision of the House of Lords in *Wilsher* v. *Essex Area Health Authority* (1988). The plaintiff in that case had been born prematurely and had then been given, negligently by the defendants, a surplus of oxygen. Later he went blind. Blindness can occur in babies born prematurely from a number of causes, including a surplus of oxygen. The Court of Appeal held in favour of the plaintiff, adopting the Wilberforce reasoning in *McGhee*. On this they were reversed by the House of Lords which ordered a new trial. The burden of proof on the issue of causation remains throughout with the plaintiff. The cases of *Bonnington* and *McGhee* were not inconsistent with this because in both cases the House of Lords had drawn inferences of fact as to the probability of causal connection favourable to the plaintiff.

The problem that arises, especially in medical cases, is that the court may be operating in the dark as to the real causes and is therefore able to work only by inference. In certain cases the inference is more easily drawn than in *McGhee*—thus in *Kay* v. *Ayrshire Health Board* (1990) the plaintiff contracted meningitis and was then negligently given penicillin after which he became deaf. The court found that the likely cause of the deafness was not the penicillin but the meningitis, since the latter commonly causes deafness whereas this was unknown in the case of penicillin. Where inferences are difficult to draw, it might be suggested that as a matter of rough justice there should be an apportionment of damage as between plaintiff and defendant. This, however, is impossible under the present system of torts law, a fact recently confirmed by the decision of the House of Lords in *Hotson* v. *East Berkshire Health Authority* (1987). The plaintiff had suffered an injury from which he had had a one in four chance of complete recovery if diagnosed in time, but the injury was incorrectly diagnosed by the defendants and the plaintiff suffered the full consequences of the injury. The Court of Appeal awarded the plaintiff 25 per cent. of the later consequential damage for being denied the chance of a full recovery. The House of Lords reversed this on the ground that the plaintiff had not established his cause of action on the balance of probabilities. Where, however, a cause of action has been established, so that the only question is one of quantification or measure of damages, the plaintiff is entitled to be compensated for contingencies which are less than 50 per cent. likely to occur. (Therefore if Hotson had proved a 51 per cent. chance of his full recovery he would have succeeded against the defendants in full; whereas a more than 50 per cent. contingency on a question of measure of damages is assessed at that and no more.)

(2) *Causation in law: remoteness of damage*

The "but for" test merely serves to eliminate certain factors as causes of the plaintiff's damage. It does not identify those causes in respect of which legal liability exists. A test for determining what causes in fact are also causes in law of the plaintiff's damage is therefore required. Under the decision of the Court of Appeal in *Re Polemis* (1921) the defendant was liable for damage which was the direct or immediate consequence of his negligence to the plaintiff. This test gave way in certain cases to allow the defendant to be held liable for indirect consequences provided they were foreseeable. The decision in *The Wagon Mound* (No. 1) (1961) replaced the *Polemis* rule with the rule that the defendant was liable only for the foreseeable consequences of his breach of duty to the plaintiff. The decision at the time it was made appeared to introduce a more restrictive test for remoteness of damage than *Re Polemis*. Whether it has done so is for consideration in this chapter. It may be pointed out here, however, that the *Wagon Mound* (No. 1) appears to allow the defendant to be held liable for all the foreseeable consequences, direct or indirect, to the plaintiff of which the defendant's breach of duty is a cause in fact whereas, generally speaking, under *Polemis* liability existed only for damage arising directly.

The present law and its evolution

The *Wagon Mound* (No. 1) was a decision of the Privy Council on appeal from the courts of New South Wales. Such a decision is not in theory binding on any English court, though it has undoubted persuasive force. Decisions of the Court of Appeal bind all English courts apart from the House of Lords, including the Court of Appeal itself. Despite this, and as support for those who argue that there are no binding rules of precedent in English law, the cases subsequent to the Privy Council decision have applied the rule for remoteness it laid down rather than the rule in *Re Polemis*. This has happened in a number of first instance decisions and at Court of Appeal level in *Doughty* v. *Turner Manufacturing Co.* (1964). The House of Lords has not yet had to consider the correctness of the decision in *The Wagon Mound* (No. 1) (*Hughes* v. *Lord Advocate* (*infra*, p. 168) was a decision on Scots law which never accepted *Re Polemis*). It is assumed that the decision in *The Wagon Mound* (No. 1) now represents English law.

A comparison between the two cases remains of interest. In *Re Polemis* the defendants were charterers of a ship belonging to the plaintiffs. The defendants' servants carelessly allowed a plank to fall into the hold of the ship. The hold contained petrol vapour which was present because of leakage of petrol from tins in the hold. The fall of the plank caused a spark which ignited the vapour, and in the ensuing conflagration the ship was totally destroyed. The defendants were admittedly responsible for the breach of duty of care by their servant since some damage to the ship was foreseeable. But the presence of the petrol vapour was found as a fact to be unforeseeable. Nevertheless the defendants were liable to the plaintiffs for the loss of the ship. The fire was the direct result of their breach of duty of care. Foreseeability was irrelevant once a breach of duty had been established.

It is significant that 40 years elapsed before a case came before the courts in which the correctness of the decision in *Re Polemis* had to be examined. The facts of *The Wagon Mound* (No. 1) were similarly extraordinary. The defendants were charterers of the ship "The Wagon Mound." By the carelessness of their servants, who were ship engineers, a spillage of a quantity of furnace oil into Sydney harbour occurred. The oil spread to a wharf owned by the plaintiffs and on which the plaintiffs were carrying out welding operations. After taking advice that the oil was not ignitable, the plaintiffs' servant continued to carry on these operations. The oil was ignited by the fall of hot metal from the wharf, and extensive damage by fire occurred to the plaintiffs' wharf. The trial judge found that the defendants were in breach of a duty of care to the plaintiffs since damage to the wharf through the fouling of its slipways by oil was foreseeable, and had actually occurred. Damage by fire was, however, unforeseeable, because furnace oil has a high ignition point, and it was unforeseeable that it would ignite on water. The presence of the oil was nevertheless found to be a cause of the fire damage. On these findings the Privy Council refused to apply the *Polemis* rule and held the defendants not liable for the damage by fire since it was not a foreseeable consequence of their breach of duty to the plaintiffs.

The plaintiffs in *The Wagon Mound* (No. 1) were reluctant to argue that the defendants should have foreseen the possibility of the oil being ignited, because if that had been found, it would have been arguable that their own servant should have foreseen this possibility, and that therefore the welding operations should have been discontinued. The failure to do so would therefore have operated as a cause, and possibly the sole cause of the damage. No such problem confronted the owners of the ship, the *Corrimal*, which was moored at the plaintiffs' wharf and which was extensively damaged in the fire. In a later action (*The Wagon Mound* (No. 2) (*supra*, p. 144)), brought by the owners of that ship against the defendants in the earlier case, the court made a different finding as to foreseeability and the defendants were held liable.

The concept of foreseeability

Foreseeability is a more flexible notion than that of causation. It will be easier for the courts to take into account matters of policy in their decisions than before, and on the whole this seems desirable. But the flexibility of foreseeability is both its strength and its weakness. With foreseeability now the test both of breach of duty and of remoteness of damage there is a real danger of uncertainty in the law producing lack of confidence in the courts' decisions.

It has been suggested that, now that the test both of the defendant's breach of duty and of remoteness of damage is one of foreseeability, there is no longer any need to answer the two questions, "Should the defendant have foreseen any damage to the plaintiff?" and to decide whether he was in breach of duty, and "Was the damage the plaintiff suffered a foreseeable consequence of that breach?" A single question such as "Was the plaintiff's damage a foreseeable consequence of the defendant's act?" should be sufficient. But in deciding whether there has been a breach, the court does not simply ask the question whether the defendant's conduct created a foreseeable risk to the plaintiff. The degree of risk to the plaintiff must be sufficiently great that the defendant should have to take steps to prevent its occurrence, bearing in mind also that the defendant's conduct may have social value, or that the elimination of the risk may present great difficulty. The balancing operation that courts perform in deciding whether there has been a breach may, it seems, be performed only once. Once the defendant's conduct has been adjudged negligent as against the plaintiff in respect of a certain risk, it is not possible to weigh its utility or the difficulty of its removal against the degree of likelihood of other risks occurring, even though those other risks are less likely. It may be therefore that in deciding what is foreseeable for the purposes of remoteness of damage factors that are relevant to the question of breach, such as degree of risk, the knowledge and circumstances of the defendant, the utility of his conduct and the difficulty and expense of averting the risk are irrelevant. The court must merely ask itself whether the damage was foreseeable within the confines of universal human knowledge. The courts have not yet had to consider this point, but at the moment there is nothing to indicate that different tests of foreseeability exist. A decision such as that in *Tremain* v. *Pike*

(1969) seems directly contrary to such a view. In that case, in considering a question of remoteness of damage, the court had to consider the foreseeability of a disease called Weil's disease which is caught by contact with rat's urine. There was evidence that the disease was known to medical officers of health and public health inspectors, but that it was very rare and would not be known about by the ordinary, reasonable farmer. The defendant was a farmer. The court found that Weil's disease was not reasonably foreseeable.

It is relevant to remind the reader here that if two different tests of foreseeability are to be applied, one in deciding the issue of breach, and the other the issue of remoteness of damage, the plaintiff must, in order to raise the question of remoteness at all, establish a breach of duty of care to himself by the defendant. He cannot rely on any breach of a duty of care which the defendant may have committed towards other persons.

Foreseeability and risk

If the defendant is liable for the foreseeable consequences of his breach of duty, how precise does this foreseeability have to be? Clearly exact foreseeability is not required. In the words of Lord Denning M.R. in *Stewart* v. *West African Air Terminals* (1964):

> "It is not necessary that the precise concatenation of circumstances should be envisaged. If the consequence was one within the general range which any reasonable person might foresee (and was not of an entirely different kind which no one would anticipate) then it is within the rule that a person who is guilty of negligence is liable for the consequences."

Lord Denning's statement may be taken to refer to the case where a number of events in themselves foreseeable combine together to produce damage in a way that is not foreseeable. The so-called "risk principle," which as far as English law is concerned is more an academic theory than something deriving from established authority, would take matters a little further. The theory would hold the defendant liable for any *type* of harm, which was a foreseeable result of his conduct, even though the *manner* in which the harm occurred was unforeseeable. Risks would, therefore, be classified broadly and in terms of their effects rather than their causes. Some risks lend themselves easily enough to differentiation in this way. The foreseeable risk of impact damage to property is distinguishable from the risk of fire (as in *Polemis*); the risk of oil fouling slipways from the risk of fire through its ignition on water (as in *The Wagon Mound* (No. 1)). It should not be difficult to convince the reader, however, that it is impossible to draw an absolute distinction between type of harm and manner of occurrence of harm. What about disease, for example? Are all bodily diseases to be aggregated as one type of harm? That would certainly be to take the risk principle a long way, bearing in mind that diseases with broadly similar effects may have quite distinct origins. All that can be concluded in terms of principle from the existing case law is that the courts have not thrown aside as irrelevant the manner of occurrence of the harm, though they have not required that it should be precisely foreseen. The cases of *Hughes* v. *Lord Advocate* (1963) and *Doughty* v. *Turner Manufacturing* (1964) show the sort of difficulties the courts face. In the former case workmen employed by the defendant left a manhole shelter unattended during their tea-break. Four lighted paraffin lamps were placed at the corners of the shelter. The plaintiff, a boy aged eight, took one of the lamps into the shelter to explore the manhole. He tripped over the lamp which fell into the hole. An explosion occurred in which the plaintiff suffered severe burns. The trial judge held that though the workmen were negligent in leaving the shelter unattended, in that they had created a risk of the plaintiff being burned by the lamp, injury by explosion which occurred through vaporisation of the paraffin in the lamp and its subsequent ignition was not foreseeable. Nevertheless the House of Lords held the defendants liable in negligence. They had created a foreseeable risk of injury by burning, and this risk included burning by explosion, which though itself unforeseeable was sufficiently similar to the foreseeable risk created to count as part of it. In *Doughty's* case, the defendants kept on their premises a large bath containing sulphuric acid heated to a temperature of 800 degrees centigrade. The bath had a loose cover made of a compound of asbestos and cement. This cover was knocked into the bath by the plaintiff's fellow workman. A chemical reaction took place between the acid and the cover and an eruption of acid followed in which the plaintiff received burns.

This was found to be unforeseeable. The Court of Appeal held the defendants not liable in negligence. Even if there had been a breach of duty when the cover was knocked into the acid because of the risk of splashing (which was not determined), it was unrealistic to regard the eruption which occurred as a mere variant of the perils of splashing. The court described the eruption in the words of Lord Reid in *Hughes* v. *Lord Advocate* as "the intrusion of a new and unexpected factor." *Hughes* v. *Lord Advocate* was applied in *Bradford* v. *Robinson Rentals* (1967) (frostbite unforeseeable but part of the risks attached to undue exposure to cold); and *Parsons* v. *Uttley, Ingham & Co.* (1978) (E-coli infection in pigs unforeseeable but part of the general risk of gastro-intestinal upset caused by eating mouldy food); but was not applied in *Tremain* v. *Pike* (1969) (unforeseeable Weil's disease caused by contact with rat's urine was not part of the general risk of disease associated with rat infestation, for example rat-bite or contaminated food). The last case is unsatisfactory and has in any case been overtaken by time—Weil's disease (or leptospirosis) is now well known in the agricultural community.

Cases where the damage is aggravated by physical peculiarities of the victim

While *Polemis* was law it was never doubted that the principle was that the tortfeasor took the victim as he found him, so that the greater amount of damage suffered by the haemophiliac or the man with an egg-shell skull was recoverable. After *The Wagon Mound*, it was arguable whether the peculiarities of the victim which were probably unforeseeable could be allowed to affect the extent of the defendant's liability. But the courts have made it clear that the rule remains unchanged.

In *Smith* v. *Leech, Brain & Co.* (1962) the Court of Appeal allowed the deceased's estate to recover damages from the defendants for his death from cancer of the lip. The lip had been in a pre-malignant condition and cancer broke out when the deceased received a burn from molten metal owing to negligence by the defendants. The egg-shell skull rule was applied. The egg-shell skull principle is not limited to physical conditions. It extends also to acceleration or exacerbation of nervous disorders of the personality (*Malcolm* v. *Broadhurst* (1970)—a wife recovered damages for nervous shock in relation to the exacerbation of a previously-held nervous condition caused by her own physical injury, and the effect upon that disorder of her husband's injury, foreseeably caused in the same accident by the defendant; *Meah* v. *McCreamer* (1985)—a petty, largely non-violent criminal became a rapist after receiving brain injury. The defendant did not even argue that this damage was too remote, accepting that he was liable if his infliction of the brain injury caused his change in personality—but he was not allowed to recover compensation for the damages he had had to pay to the victims of the rapes, seemingly on grounds of policy (*Meah* v. *McCreamer* (No. 2) (1986)).

It is not necessary that the extra damage suffered by the plaintiff should arise through an aggravation of his condition. It is enough if there is causal connection between the plaintiff's thin skull condition, and the effect of injury on it, and a later event inflicting another injury. In *Wieland* v. *Cyril Lord Carpets* (1969), the plaintiff received personal injuries in a car accident through the defendant's negligence. Because of the shakiness induced by the accident, she could not adjust to the wearing of bi-focal glasses and suffered further injury in a fall soon after the first injury. She recovered damages for the second injury as well. In *Robinson* v. *Post Office* (1974), the plaintiff suffered minor injuries to his leg through the defendant's negligence. He was given an anti-tetanus injection but suffered an unusual adverse reaction to it and suffered brain damage. He recovered damages for the resulting condition from the defendant (but in *Alston* v. *Marine Ins. Co.* (1964) the plaintiff, who had been given the drug Parstellin after receiving brain damage in a traffic accident, died as a result of eating cheese, the fatal consequences of this combination not then being known to medical science. It was held that death was too remote, not being reasonably foreseeable. But why should the egg-shell skull plaintiff be favoured over the *Alston* plaintiff?)

The thin-skull rule probably has as its justification the analogous though distinct rule concerning measure of damages. In assessing measure of damages, the tortfeasor must take the victim as he finds him, paying, *ceteris paribus*, more to the millionaire than to the bank clerk. So also in evaluating the extent of the injury suffered by the plaintiff the courts do not make any reduction for the fact that the plaintiff's injury has been aggravated by his own condition. So explained it seems essential that the plaintiff should have suffered an injury for which the defendant is liable in negligence. It does not seem enough that the defendant has committed a breach of duty of care to the plaintiff, and the plaintiff's pre-existent condition has caused the injury to happen. But in *Bradford* v. *Robinson* Rees J. thought *obiter* that if the plaintiff had caught frostbite only through his abnormal susceptibility to that condition, he would still have recovered damages because a tortfeasor takes his victim as he finds him. This suggests that there is no need for any foreseeable damage to occur. If this is so, the basis of the rule is far less clear and it is more difficult to reconcile with the principles laid down in *The Wagon Mound* (No. 1). Mention must be made here of *Brice* v. *Brown* (1984) in which the court held that where the defendant's action is such that it is foreseeable that it will cause nervous shock to a person of normal disposition and phlegm, but the shock that it produces in the plaintiff constitutes the activation or aggravation of a mental disorder previously held by the plaintiff, the defendant is liable here under the egg-shell skull rule regardless of whether the condition from which the plaintiff suffered from previously is foreseeable. This seems defensible if only on the ground of the impossibility of determining whether the plaintiff had suffered any "normal" nervous shock apart from that produced by her condition.

Two further points about the rule may be made. The "condition" of the victim does not include his surrounding circumstances. Otherwise the decision in *Re Polemis* would be decided in the same way despite *The Wagon Mound* (No. 1). Where, on the other hand, the damage that was foreseeable occurs in the manner that was foreseeable, an increase in the extent of that damage caused by the victim's surrounding circumstances is not too remote. The extent of foreseeable damage does not itself need to be foreseeable (*Vacwell Engineering Co.* v. *B. D. H. Chemicals* (1971)). So in *Great Lakes S.S. Co.* v. *Maple Leaf Milling Co. Ltd.* (1923) as a result of the defendants' negligent failure to lighten the plaintiffs' ship, the ship ran aground. The damage was increased by the fact that the ship came to rest on a submerged anchor, the presence of which was unforeseeable by the defendants. The plaintiffs recovered the full extent of their damage from the defendants. On the other hand, and perhaps illogically, though neurosis is a foreseeable result of an injury, the fact that it is perpetuated by the victim's family circumstances does not enable the victim to claim for the increased amount. (*McLaren* v. *Bradstreet* (1969)). (*Nader* v. *Urban Transport Authority* (1985), a New South Wales case, allowed recovery for nervous shock exacerbated by family conditions).

Liability for intervening human conduct

Cases where the only negligence alleged against the defendant is his failure to anticipate and prevent the act of another human being raise questions of duty rather than remoteness of damage, *Stansbie* v. *Troman* (*supra*, p. 137) is an example of this type of case. Where the breach of duty threatens other damage to the plaintiff, a question arises whether the intervening act of a human being excuses the defendant. This raises a true question of remoteness of damage and will be discussed in this chapter. Where the defendant is excused by the later human act, it is referred to as a *nova causa* (or *novus actus*) *interveniens*, and it is commonly said to "break the chain of causation" between the defendant's negligence and the plaintiff's damage.

The chief difficulty in relation to *nova causa interveniens* centres around the question of whether the later deliberate or negligent act of a human being interrupts causation. Where the later act is neither deliberate nor negligent there is no legal problem since the solution turns entirely on the foreseeability of the act. The same applies to the intervening acts of irresponsible persons such as children. On the other hand, the problems caused by the deliberate or negligent acts of responsible human beings are acute (*cf.* the admission of defeat on this point by Tasker Watkins L.J. in *Lamb* v. *London Borough of Camden* (1981)). There have been a number of different approaches by the courts to the problem, so that at the moment the law may be presented only in the form of guidelines providing possible solutions to the problem. The question of causation that arises here is that of causation in law—causation in fact is inevitably established by a finding that but for the defendant's negligence the third party would not have caused the harm.

Deliberate conduct whether of the plaintiff or a third party

The law draws a distinction between deliberate conduct and negligent conduct. The former is more likely to interrupt the chain of causation than the latter because it is not reasonably foreseeable. So in *Philco Radio* v. *Spurling* (1949), the defendants who had negligently and by mistake delivered some highly inflammable material to the plaintiff's premises were held liable for a fire started by the plaintiffs' typist on the ground that her act in starting the fire was negligent rather than deliberate.

Deliberate human action does not, however, always operate as a *nova causa interveniens*. Such action may operate not to do so where it is reasonable or is not reasonably foreseeable. The test of reasonableness was adopted by Lord Reid as the ground for his decision in *McKew* v. *Hannen, Holland and Cubitts Ltd.* (1969). In that case, the plaintiff, having received an earlier injury to his leg for which the defendants were liable, fell while attempting to descend some steps, which had no handrail, without assistance which was at hand. The House of Lords held that the defendants were not liable for the further injury caused by the fall, since the plaintiff had deliberately ignored the risk brought on by his earlier injury and had therefore acted unreasonably. Lord Reid stressed that a test of reasonable foreseeability would produce an unsatisfactory result here, because unreasonable actions of the sort in question might well be foreseeable. Again, reasonableness of the intervening act rather than its foreseeability was the test applied in *The Oropesa* (1943) in which the plaintiff was successful. In that case, the defendants' ship negligently collided with another ship, the *Manchester Regiment*. The captain of the *Manchester Regiment* decided to put to sea in a lifeboat along with others including the plaintiff in order to discuss the possibility of salving the *Manchester Regiment* with the defendants' crew. The lifeboat capsized in heavy seas and the plaintiff was drowned. His estate recovered damages for his death from the defendants. The captain's decision was a reasonable reaction to a situation of peril created by the defendants and could not be likened to the deliberate infliction of harm by a third party. Again, where the plaintiff's action, though unreasonable, is not truly voluntary, and is foreseeable, it does not break the chain of causation. In *Pigney* v. *Pointer's Transport Services* (1957), the plaintiff committed suicide less than two years after receiving a head injury through the defendants' negligence. The suicide was found to be the result of an acute anxiety neurosis and depression produced by the head injury. The defendants were held liable to the plaintiff's estate for his death, which was found to have been caused by the earlier injury. Unlike McKew, Pigney was not fully responsible for his later deliberate act—its unreasonableness was therefore not relevant.

The test of unreasonableness in relation to the deliberate acts of human beings seems particularly applicable where it is the plaintiff who claims that the deliberate act does not constitute a *nova causa interveniens*. That test when applied to the deliberate acts of third parties who have inflicted harm on the plaintiff would produce too narrow a field of compensation. In such cases the courts have applied a test of the reasonable foreseeability of the third party's action, though it is apparent that this is not the ordinary test of foreseeability. Here the courts require that the third party's act be something more than a mere possibility (*cf. The Wagon Mound* (No. 2) test) and therefore a probable consequence of the original negligence. In *Lamb* v. *London Borough of Camden* (1981) the defendants had negligently caused damage to the plaintiff's house, necessitating its vacation by the plaintiff's tenant. During its vacancy it received damage through successive invasions of squatters. The Court of Appeal held unanimously that this damage was too remote. Oliver L.J. found that the Official Referee's finding that the damage was reasonably foreseeable did not suffice to render the defendants liable since the requirement of foreseeability in these cases was of probability of the later human action. This was adopted as the basis of his judgment by Scott J. in *Ward* v. *Cannock Chase D.C.* (1985) in which, however, the *Lamb* case was distinguished on the ground that the entry by vandals on the property in the case in question was likely to occur given the particular circumstances of that property (*i.e.* it was a council estate rather than residential property in Hampstead as in *Lamb*). There was also an important difference between the two cases as regards the time at which the test of foreseeability was to be applied. This must be judged at time of the negligent act, so that while it was difficult to argue that the workman while damaging the water main which caused the flooding of Mrs. Lamb's house should have foreseen as likely its invasion by squatters, Ward's case was different in that the council had after the collapse of the wall undertaken a duty to repair it, so that the time for testing foreseeability was at the later time of when they should have carried out the duty to repair.

Negligent conduct (whether of the plaintiff or a third party)

Different considerations apply to later negligent conduct. Negligence is *ex hypothesi* unreasonable, so to apply the unreasonableness test would be inappropriate. Equally it is inappropriate to apply a test of reasonable foreseeability, which would create too generous a test for establishing liability, since negligence is almost universally foreseeable (not helped by asking whether it is probable, a meaningless question). Clearly later negligence does not necessarily interrupt the chain of causation, and we have the contribution between tortfeasors and the contributory negligence legislation to recognise that fact and deal with it. There are nevertheless cases in which later negligence will be regarded as a *nova causa interveniens*. In general, if the defendant's negligence merely places the plaintiff in the position in time and place in which he suffers the consequences of the later negligence, that later negligence will operate as a *nova causa*. In order that it should not, the earlier negligence must have put the plaintiff or third party into a situation of heightened risk, which may be defined as a situation of peril exceeding that encountered as part of everyday life but one which may nevertheless be avoided by the exercise of due care. Two cases illustrate this distinction. In *S.S. Singleton Abbey* v. *S.S. Paludina* (1927) the *Paludina* was in collision with the *Singleton Abbey* due to the negligent navigation of the *Paludina*. The *Singleton Abbey*, having been cast adrift, caused another collision in which another ship, the *Sara* was cast adrift. Later the *Sara* again collided with the *Singleton Abbey* and was sunk. The *Sara* was found to be negligent in respect of the last collision. The House of Lords held the owners of the *Paludina* not liable for the sinking of the *Sara*. There was no more reason for the last collision to have occurred than if the *Sara* had been on a normal voyage—the effects of the earlier negligence were spent. In the *Calliope* (1970), on the other hand, a collision occurred between a ship called the *Calliope* and another called the *Carlsholm*, for which the negligence of the latter was 45 per cent. to blame. The *Calliope* was grounded and suffered damage but was refloated. On the following day, while executing an "exceptionally difficult" turning manoeuvre in fog, which was necessary for it to resume the original voyage, it grounded twice and collided with its tug, thus suffering further damage. The *Calliope* was found to be negligent in the execution of this turn. Nevertheless the owners of the *Carlsholm* were held to be partially legally liable for the later damage. The *Calliope* had not acted unreasonably in attempting the manoeuvre despite its difficult nature. The defendants' earlier negligence was clearly still operative in producing the later damage, even though by proper skill the plaintiffs could have surmounted the difficulty presented them by the defendants. Similar principles to those applied in these cases will no doubt determine the thorny question of the defendant's liability for an injury that is aggravated by later medical negligence. To be placed on the operating table through the negligence of the defendants seems clearly to be a situation of heightened risk; whatever goes wrong in the course of at least a normally conducted operation, the defendant should, it seems, bear some responsibility for it. But English courts have to date never squarely faced the question. (In *Mahoney* v. *J. Kruschich* (1985) the High Court of Australia held that medical negligence only interrupted causation if it was "inexcusable"—the reverse side of the coin from the heightened risk position).

The two rules of remoteness of damage compared

At the time of the decision in *The Wagon Mound* (No. 1), its correctness divided academic opinion, and it was the subject of a voluminous literature. Supporters of *Re Polemis* argued that where the question arose as between innocent plaintiff and negligent defendant who should bear the loss caused by that negligence, the defendant should be chosen. They were fortified in their stance by the consideration that defendants in tort suits generally had the means to satisfy liability; most plaintiffs were impecunious. Supporters of *The Wagon Mound* (No. 1) founded themselves on a moralistic argument that a defendant should not be held liable in negligence to an extent greater than the foreseeable amount of the damage. They also disliked the "mechanical" test of causation laid down by *Polemis*. Foreseeability was a more flexible notion in which the requirements of justice and policy could be taken into account. Some of the cases decided since *The Wagon Mound* (No. 1) have indicated that this flexibility is bought at a price, and that there is now more uncertainty in the law than formerly. The cases deriving from *Hughes* v. *Lord Advocate* are not easily reconcilable with each other. The extent of the thin-skull rule and its harmonisation with principles of foreseeability remain doubtful.

The overriding impression, however, is how little change has actually resulted from the Privy Council decision. The thin-skull rule has survived it. *Hughes* v. *Lord Advocate* shows that the courts do not insist that the manner in which the plaintiff's accident occurred should be precisely foreseeable. Nor does the extent of harm inflicted by the defendant need to be foreseeable. The cases on intervening human conduct are unaffected by the change in the law since the *Polemis* rule was not applied in relation to them. No case decided since 1961, with the possible exception of *Doughty* v. *Turner Manufacturing Co.*, would have produced a different result under *Polemis* principles. It is interesting to note that the finding on foreseeability which led to the decision in *The Wagon Mound* (No. 1) was reversed on the same facts (but as between different parties) in *The Wagon Mound* (No. 2).

MULTIPLE CAUSES AND THE APPORTIONMENT OF DAMAGE

The cases on liability for intervening causes show that the law recognises that an event may have more than one cause. Where two tortfeasors have combined to produce the same damage to the plaintiff, each is liable for the full amount. A further question then arises whether a tortfeasor held liable in full for that damage is entitled to recover a contribution from another tortfeasor also liable for the same damage. This question will be examined in this chapter. It is felt that to deal with the law's handling of multiple causation in tort in the chapter on causation in negligence, the tort which most commonly produces the problem, should be an aid to understanding. It must be remembered, however, that the principles governing this question are applicable to all torts, not just negligence. The present law is laid down in the Civil Liability (Contribution) Act 1978, which replaces and extends the Law Reform (Married Women and Tortfeasors) Act 1935.

Although cases of multiple causation appear to demand a mechanism for apportioning responsibility among tortfeasors, the recognition of this has been slow to occur in England. There are two reasons for this. First, tortfeasors were thought to be immoral persons to whom the courts should not lend their aid in enforcing claims against each other. This reasoning has lost most of its validity with the expansion in the tort of negligence and the recognition of torts of strict liability. It is no doubt still true that a tortfeasor who was malicious or fraudulent would be unable to claim contribution from other tortfeasors because of the *ex turpi causa* rule. Secondly, the phenomenon of multiple causation is generally found in cases where the various parties have been negligent, and only in the present century has negligence become established as a tort.

Before discussing the introduction of the rule allowing apportionment of damage, it may be said that the problem only arises where two or more have tortiously contributed to the *same* damage, and it is impossible to allocate different parts of that damage to different persons. Where the plaintiff's damage can be separately allocated, there is no problem of apportionment. Thus if A and B simultaneously commit battery against C, it may be possible to show that A caused one injury and B another (but the harm will not be divisible if A and B have acted in the furtherance of a common design—see *infra*).

The damage may, however, not be readily divisible among the tortfeasors responsible. In a motor accident caused by the negligent driving of X and Y and in which Z, a pedestrian, suffers personal injuries, it would obviously be impossible to attribute any particular part of Z's injuries to X or Y. In such a situation X and Y are said to be separate concurrent tortfeasors (they will be referred to hereafter as concurrent tortfeasors). Each is liable for the whole of Z's injuries and Z may choose to sue either of them for his damages. (Nevertheless in *Thompson* v. *Smith* (*Shiprepairers*) (1984) Mustill J. found himself able to apportion damage in relation to deafness which had arisen from original non-tortious noise succeeded by tortious noise).

In English law a distinction is drawn between concurrent tortfeasors and joint tortfeasors. The distinction may be explained as follows. Concurrent tortfeasors are responsible for different torts producing the same damage, whereas joint tortfeasors in law commit the same tort. The most important examples of joint tortfeasors are:

(i)   In cases of vicarious liability, the person vicariously liable is a joint tortfeasor with his servant, an employer with his independent contractor.

(ii) In cases where there has been concerted action in the furtherance of a common design, those participating are

joint tortfeasors. Thus conspirators are joint tortfeasors. So
are the author, publisher, and printer of a defamatory
work. *Brooke* v. *Bool* (1928) furnishes another illustration:
the defendant landlord invited his lodger to help him look
for an escape of gas by striking a match in the vicinity of
the escape. The landlord and the lodger were held to be
joint tortfeasors in respect of the damage caused by the
ensuing explosion.

(iii) Where one person has instigated or authorised another to
commit a tort, the two are joint tortfeasors. Thus the
landlord who authorises his tenant to commit a nuisance is
a joint tortfeasor with the tenant.

The distinction between joint and concurrent tortfeasors must
still be drawn, although it has lost much of its importance. The
rule in *Brinsmead* v. *Harrison* (1872) that judgment obtained
against one or more of several joint tortfeasors released all of them
was abolished by the 1935 Act (see now Section 3 of the Civil
Liability (Contribution) Act 1978). The common law rule about
the effect of judgment did not apply in the case of concurrent
tortfeasors.

The common law rule that release of one joint tortfeasor
released all the rest remains unchanged, so that it is still
necessary to distinguish joint from concurrent tortfeasors.
But the courts have lessened the effect of the rule by distinguishing a release from a covenant not to sue, the latter
having no effect on the continuance of liability of other joint
tortfeasors.

Contribution

Section 1(1) of the 1978 Act provides: subject to the following
provisions of this section, any person liable in respect of any
damage suffered by another person may recover contribution from
any other person liable in respect of the same damage (whether
jointly or otherwise).

Who may recover contribution?

Any "person liable" may recover contribution. In this context
"liable" will normally mean held liable. But section 1(2) says that
this includes a person who has ceased to be liable, provided that

he was so liable immediately before he made or was ordered or agreed to make the payment in respect of which contribution is sought. Section 1(4) removes a problem that existed under the former law by providing that a person who makes a bona fide settlement or compromise of a claim against him in respect of any damage may recover contribution without the need for proving his own liability for that damage, provided that "he would have been liable assuming the factual basis of the claim against him could be established."

From whom may contribution be claimed?

The person from whom contribution may be claimed is defined by section 1(2) of the Act to be any other person liable in respect of the same damage (whether jointly or otherwise). Section 6(1) expands this by providing that the requirement of liability is satisfied whatever the legal basis of liability, whether tort, breach of contract, breach of trust or otherwise. The 1935 Act only allowed contribution between tortfeasors so that this is a considerable extension. A tortfeasor, for example, liable in respect of certain damage may now recover contribution from one liable in breach of contract for the same damage. A further extension is section 1(3) which provides that contribution may be claimed from one who has ceased to be liable, unless this was through the expiry of a limitation period which extinguishes the right on which the plaintiff's claim is based. One example of that sort of limitation period is that applying to actions for conversion, but most limitation periods merely operate to make the plaintiff's right unenforceable rather than to extinguish it. Under the former law, where the tortfeasor had the defence of limitation he was immune to liability to make contribution, so here again the Act effects an important change. Contribution proceedings themselves must be brought within two years of the date on which the right to recover contribution accrues (*infra*, pp. 442–444). Section 1(3) also extends to allowing contribution to be claimed from one who has reached an out-of-court settlement with the plaintiff, or from one against whom the plaintiff's action has been dismissed for want of prosecution. Section 1(3) also affects the case where an action against the first tortfeasor has actually been brought and has failed because of procedural reasons such as limitation or want of prosecution (*Nottingham Health Authority* v. *Nottingham C.C.*

(1988); *R. A. Lister & Co.* v. *E. G. Thomson Ltd.* (1987)). This does not prevent a claim for contribution being made against that tortfeasor. However, no contribution may be claimed from a person who in earlier proceedings has been found not liable on the merits of the case (section 1(5)).

Amount of contribution

Section 2(1) and (2) of the 1978 Act provide: (1) subject to section 2(3), in any proceedings for contribution under section 1, the amount of the contribution recoverable from any person shall be such as may be found just and equitable having regard to the extent of that person's responsibility for the damage in question: (2) subject to section 2(3), the court shall have power in any such proceedings to exempt any person from liability to make contribution, or to direct that the contribution to be recovered shall amount to an absolute indemnity.

It is now established that in exercising its discretion under these subsections, the court must take into account both the causative potency of the defendant's act and its degree of blameworthiness. The test is the same as that established for assessing the reduction for the plaintiff's contributory negligence under the Law Reform (Contributory Negligence) Act 1945 (*infra*, p. 187 *et seq.*).

Section 2(3) provides for certain limitations upon the court's discretion under section 2(1) and (2). Section 2(3)(*a*) provides that where the liability of any person is "subject to any limit imposed by or under any enactment or by any agreement made before the damage occurred," the right to recover contribution is limited in the same way. It may be noted that, although the case may not be a suitable one for ordering an indemnity under section 2(2), the provisions of a contract may produce this effect under section 2(3)(*a*). (Thus in *Sims* v. *Foster, Wheeler* (1966), an employer and his sub-contractor were adjudged to be at fault to the extent of 25 per cent. and 75 per cent. respectively on the claim of the plaintiff employee. Nevertheless the employer obtained under the terms of his contract with the sub-contractor a complete indemnity). Section 2(3)(*b*) provides, in effect, that where the amount of damages recoverable from a tortfeasor is subject to a reduction for the plaintiff's contributory negligence, the amount recoverable in contribution proceedings from that tortfeasor shall not exceed the reduced amount. Normally all the defendants will get the benefit of such a reduction. If one of the defendants is liable in breach of contract alone, however, it now seems settled that in his case there can be no reduction of damages under the 1945 Act for the plaintiff's contributory negligence (see *infra*, p. 187). If so, the following result would emerge from the 1978 Act's provisions. Suppose that D1, by his breach of contract, and D2 by his tort have caused the same damage amounting to £1000 to the plaintiff and the plaintiff is 75 per cent. contributorily negligent. Assume that D1 and D2 are equally at fault. D1 is liable to the plaintiff for the whole amount, but can recover only £250 contribution from D2 (*i.e.* the contribution is limited to the maximum amount D2 would have had to pay the plaintiff if sued alone——£1000 reduced by 75 per cent).

Nature and machinery of contribution proceedings

The right to claim contribution is an independent, statutory right, having its own period of limitation. It is, however, uncommon for separate proceedings to be brought for enforcement of the right. Where the plaintiff has not joined all possible tortfeasors as defendants to his action, the defendant actually sued may issue a third-party notice against anyone from whom he is claiming relief whether by way of contribution or indemnity, under Order 16, Rule 1 of the Rules of the Supreme Court (a similar right exists in the county court). The effect of this is to make the third party a defendant to the plaintiff's action, so that the court may apportion responsibility for the damage among him (if found liable) and all other defendants similarly liable. The plaintiff is provided with an incentive to join all possible tortfeasors as defendants to his action by section 4 of the 1978 Act which allows the court a discretion to deprive the plaintiff of the costs of any actions brought by him subsequent to the first.

9. DEFENCES TO NEGLIGENCE

The two defences to be dealt with in this chapter may operate as defences to negligence as such, as well as in situations where negligence is the gist of the action, such as employers' liability, occupiers' liability and liability for chattels. Their applicability to other torts is considered in the relevant sections of the book.

CONTRIBUTORY NEGLIGENCE

It should be noted that the term refers to negligence *of the plaintiff.*

Introduction

The rules of contributory negligence deal with the situation where the plaintiff has suffered damage through the negligence of the defendant, but has also contributed to that damage through his own negligence. The law on this seemingly straightforward situation was formerly full of complications, but now, because of the courts' power to apportion responsibility for the damage as between the plaintiff and defendant, generally works satisfactorily.

Before the Law Reform (Contributory Negligence) Act 1945, where the defendant successfully established contributory negligence on the part of the plaintiff, this was a complete defence to the plaintiff's action. The basis of the defence appeared to be that the plaintiff's negligence destroyed the causal link between the defendant's negligence and the damage, rather than that, where both the parties had been negligent, in the absence of a power to apportion the damage, the loss should lie where it fell. So where the defendant's negligence post-dated that of the plaintiff it could be seen effectively as the cause of the damage; in the reverse situation the plaintiff was regarded as having caused his own downfall (*cf.* the old cases *Davies* v. *Mann* (1842) with *Butterfield* v. *Forrester* (1809)). The courts therefore applied, more or less mechanically, a rule of letting the loss fall on whichever of the plaintiff or defendant had the last opportunity of avoiding the accident.

The decisions on this so-called rule of last opportunity are no great credit to our jurisprudence. But the courts were faced with the difficulty that, in the absence of a power to apportion the damage, they were forced to take the negligence of one party as the only cause of the damage. Even so, there was no reason why the later negligence should always have been chosen. The problem was recognised in *Swadling* v. *Cooper* (1930) in which a trial judge's direction to a jury in a negligence action that the question was, if both plaintiff and defendant were negligent whose negligence substantially caused the accident, was upheld by the House of Lords.

The Court of Admiralty, which had to deal with similar problems of dual responsibility in connection with collisions at sea, was not so hamstrung in its approach to the problem, because of its power to apportion damages under the Maritime Conventions Act 1911. In a famous judgment in *The Volute* (1922) Viscount Birkenhead made it clear that there was no rule of admiralty law corresponding to the rule of last opportunity. It was therefore to be expected that with the provision in 1945 of a general statutory power to apportion damages in all cases of contributory negligence, the last opportunity rule would disappear. Cases decided since then have borne out this expectation.

LAW REFORM (CONTRIBUTORY NEGLIGENCE ACT) 1945

Section 1(1) provides as follows:

> "Where any person suffers damage as the result partly of his own fault and partly of the fault of any other person or persons, a claim in respect of that damage shall not be defeated by reason of the fault of the person suffering the damage, but the damages recoverable in respect thereof shall

be reduced to such extent as the court thinks just and equitable having regard to the claimant's share in the responsibility for the damage."

FAULT OF THE PLAINTIFF

In order that the power of apportionment be exercised in his favour, the defendant must show both that the plaintiff was at fault and that this fault contributed to his damage. "Fault" is defined by section 4 of the Act to mean negligence, breach of statutory duty or other act or omission which gives rise to a liability in tort, or which would, apart from the Act, give rise to the defence of contributory negligence. Although, therefore, it is possible that the plaintiff's contributory negligence may consist in a tort or breach of a duty of care owed to someone else, it is clear that this is not necessary, and that it may consist simply in a failure to look after his own safety. For example, in *Davies* v. *Swan Motor Co. Ltd.* (1949) the plaintiff was held to be contributorily negligent in that he rode on the back of a dust lorry contrary to his employer's instruction and thus unnecessarily exposing himself to danger.

The defendant must also show that the plaintiff's fault contributed to the damage he suffered. In the first place, *dicta* in *Jones* v. *Livox Quarries* (1952) show that the present rule of remoteness of damage in tort, that the plaintiff's damage must be a foreseeable consequence of the defendant's negligence, applies also in determining whether the plaintiff's damage is contributed to by his own fault. For example, Singleton L.J. thought that there would be no reduction of damages where the plaintiff negligently sat on an unsafe wall, and the defendant negligently drove into the wall and injured the plaintiff. Denning L.J. thought that the same would apply if the plaintiff were to be hit by a shot fired by a negligent sportsman.

Apart from being within the risk of the plaintiff's negligence, the defendant must also show that the plaintiff's damage is *caused* by that negligence. With the court's power to apportion damages, there has been a great deal of simplification of the causal problems connected with contributory negligence. The courts are now able to recognise that an event may have more than one cause, and by their apportionment to reflect the comparative importance of each cause. Thus in *Davies* v. *Swan Motor Co.* (*supra*) the plaintiff was injured while riding on the back of a dust lorry in an accident caused by the combined negligence of the driver of the lorry and the driver of a bus. Liability was apportioned between the two defendants, the employers of the bus driver and the lorry driver and the plaintiff was found to be contributorily negligent to his own damage.

Several cases have made it plain that, because the negligence of one party occurred later than that of the other, this does not excuse the earlier negligent person. The definition section must be interpreted to mean "the kind of fault" that would, apart from the Act, give rise to the defence of contributory negligence, not fault that actually did so. Otherwise the last opportunity rule would still operate. Thus in *Henley* v. *Cameron* (1949), the defendant left his car without lights on the highway at night. The plaintiff's husband carelessly drove his motor-cycle into the car and was killed. The plaintiff recovered damages on behalf of the estate subject to a reduction for contributory negligence. It is now clear, therefore, that there is no such thing as a rule of last opportunity. Of course it is still possible for a court to regard the negligence of one party as so pre-eminently the cause of the damage that the other, despite being negligent, is totally excused. Furthermore, this situation seems most likely to arise where a clear margin of time exists between the two acts of negligence. But whether this is so depends upon the normal principles of causation and remoteness of damage, already outlined, not on a rule which always takes the last act of negligence as the sole cause.

Thus, in *Rushton* v. *Turner Bros. Asbestos Co.* (1960), the defendants, in breach of their statutory duty under section 14(1) of the Factories Act 1937, failed to fence a dangerous part of their machinery. The plaintiff attempted to clean the machine while it was in motion by inserting his hand into it despite instructions by the defendants never to clean the machine while it was in motion. It was held that the plaintiff was solely responsible for his own injuries.

Fault of the defendant

Section 4 of the Act of 1945, in so far as it refers to the fault of the defendant, requires him to have committed negligence, breach of statutory duty, or other act or omission which gives rise to a liability in tort. The latter words clearly permit the power of apportionment in the case of all torts. So far, however, contributory negligence as a defence has had virtually no application outside negligence, the torts deriving from it, and breach of statutory duty.

Until recently it was not clear whether the statutory provisions allowing an apportionment of damage apply where the defendant has committed a breach of contract rather than a tort. The wording of the Act, "negligence ... or other act or omission which gives rise to a liability in tort," suggests strongly that the negligence must give rise to a liability in tort and that a negligent breach of contract by itself is not enough. If that is so, the action in contract will succeed in full unless the defendant is able to establish another defence, for example, that the plaintiff caused his own loss. The matter of the availability of the defence seems now to be authoritatively settled by *Forsikrings Vesta* v. *Butcher* (1988). Where the action in contract is based on the breach of a contractual term not requiring negligence for its breach, the apportionment provisions are inapplicable (as in *Basildon D.C.* v. *J. E. Lesser* (1985)), and even though as in that case the breach was negligent. The same is true where the action is brought for breach of a contractual term requiring negligence for its breach, provided the negligence does not also constitute a tort. Where, however, the same act is both the breach of a contractual duty of care and of a duty of care in tort (*i.e.* concurrent liability), the apportionment provisions are applicable whether the action is brought in contract or tort.

Basis of apportionment

The plaintiff's damages will be reduced "to such extent as the court thinks just and equitable, having regard to the plaintiff's share in the responsibility for the damage." It is now settled that the courts apply two tests in deciding the extent of the reduction of damages the plaintiff must suffer. They must assess (i) the causative potency of the acts of the plaintiff and defendant; (ii) the degree of blameworthiness to be attached to these acts (*per* Lord Reid in *Stapley* v. *Gypsum Mines* (1953)). Degree of blameworthiness appears to mean, at least as far as negligence is concerned, degree of departure from the requisite standard of care rather than degree of moral blameworthiness. Although the two tests have been criticised (the causative potency test was criticised by

Glanville Williams (1954) 17 M.L.R. 66 at p. 69, on the ground that causation itself was difficult enough, and that degrees of causation would be a nightmare), they seem justifiable on the ground that in some torts there is no element of blameworthiness so that no other basis of assessment than causative potency exists. An example of this is *Jerred* v. *Roddam, Dent & Son* (1948). In that case the two defendants were held liable for the same failure to act. In the case of one defendant, liability was for breach of statutory duty and was strict, the defendant not being at fault. In the case of the other defendant, liability was for common law negligence. The apportionment was 10 per cent. to the former defendant and 90 per cent. to the latter. Another possible argument in favour of assessing causative potency separately from blameworthiness is that this enables the court to express in its apportionment the weight to be attached to the use of, for example, dangerous machinery, independently of the degree of blameworthiness in the operation of such machinery. Very few cases have produced a difference in the result produced by the two tests but one such was *Cavanagh* v. *London Transport Executive* (1956). In this case the plaintiff was injured by a bus negligently driven by the defendants' employee. The plaintiff was contributorily negligent. Devlin J. found that on the causative potency test the plaintiff should recover half his damages, but found the bus driver only 20 per cent. blameworthy on the second test. He therefore compromised by holding the defendants 33 and one-third per cent. responsible for the plaintiff's damages.

The mathematics of apportionment are by no means difficult, typical reductions being one-fifth, one-third, one-half and three-quarters. It is unusual for a court to find a plaintiff less than 10 per cent. responsible for his damage, nor more than 90 per cent. But in *Laszczyk* v. *National Coal Board* (1954) where the plaintiff's contributory negligence consisted in a breach of statutory duty binding on himself and committed under instructions from a superior, his damages were reduced by 5 per cent. A finding of 100 per cent. contributory negligence should not be made, because it is inconsistent with the 1945 Act. (*Pitts* v. *Hunt* (1989)).

The problem of how to handle a case in which the plaintiff is found to be contributorily negligent, and there also needs to be made an apportionment of liability between concurrent tortfeasors caused the courts unusual difficulties in *Fitzgerald* v. *Lane* (1988) and these eventually had to be resolved by the House of Lords. The plaintiff in that case negligently crossed a pedestrian crossing on a red light and was hit and injured by two cars, the drivers of which were both found to be negligent. The trial judge found all three to be equally at fault, and held the plaintiff to be one-third contributorily negligent. This approach was erroneous in that it conflated the issues of contributory negligence and apportionment of liability, whereas they are separate issues. The Court of Appeal correctly disentangled them, but then incorrectly assessed the fault of the plaintiff against that of each individual driver in deciding the issue of contributory negligence. This produced a different result— the plaintiff was held responsible for 50 per cent. of his own damage as against each driver. The House of Lords pointed out that the incorrectness of the Court of Appeal's approach was because the liability of concurrent tortfeasors was in solidum for the whole of the damage, and it was against this figure that the plaintiff's contributory negligence needed to be assessed. Only when that is done is it permissible to apportion liability between tortfeasors. The trial judge had therefore come to the right result by the wrong reasoning, but the House of Lords left undisturbed the Court of Appeal's assessment on the basis that the plaintiff was significantly more at fault than the trial judge had decided (but if causative potency is still of importance, should the plaintiff have had to bear 50 per cent. of his loss?).

PARTICULAR CASES OF CONTRIBUTORY NEGLIGENCE

(1) *Workmen*

In *Staveley Iron and Chemical Co.* v. *Jones* (1956) it was suggested by Lord Tucker that in cases of liability for breach of statutory duty not every "risky act due to familiarity with the work or some inattention due to noise or strain" amounted to contributory negligence. The suggestion was concurred in by Lord Reid. Lord Tucker thought that this applied even if the particular risky act might involve the employer in liability to third parties. It is difficult to say whether the same doctrine applies in the case of actions for common law negligence by the workman. There appears no reason to differentiate such actions and some of the statements in the *Staveley* case appear to support the application of the doctrine.

(2) *Children*

It has already been pointed out (*supra*, p. 150) that a lower standard of care is expected of children than adults and that this applies to both negligence and contributory negligence.

(3) *Agony of the moment*

Where the plaintiff has been put into a position of peril by the defendant's negligence, compelling him to choose one of two or more risky alternatives, he is not guilty of contributory negligence if his choice turns out to be a mistaken one.

Thus, in *Jones* v. *Boyce* (1816), the plaintiff, a passenger in a coach owned and driven by the defendant, reasonably believed that the coach was about to overturn through the defendant's negligent driving. The plaintiff jumped off the coach, breaking his leg. The coach did not overturn, but the plaintiff was found not to be contributorily negligent. The requirement for the operation of this principle is often stated to be that the plaintiff must have acted in the agony of the moment. But it may be that the principle applies in all cases where the defendant has by his negligence caused the plaintiff a difficult dilemma, even where the plaintiff has time to stop and think. The basic question is whether the plaintiff's choice was reasonable in the circumstances. A person who has made a reasonable decision on being faced with a difficult dilemma may nevertheless be held contributorily negligent in the execution of that decision. The plaintiff in *Sayers* v. *Harlow U.D.C.* (1958) (*supra*, p. 24) acted reasonably in trying to climb out of the toilet but was contributorily negligent as to 25 per cent. in stepping on the toilet-roll which caused her to fall.

(4) *Contributory negligence by rescuer*

Sayers v. *Harlow U.D.C.* is clear authority that a deduction for contributory negligence may be made where the rescuer has injured himself through his negligent performance of the rescue attempt. But the standard of care required of rescuers must take account of the emergency in which they act. "It is well established that the court, recognising the need to encourage salvors, should take a lenient view where negligence or lack of skill is alleged against salvors." (*per* Willmer L.J. in the *Tojo Maru* (1970); see also *The Ogopogo* (1971)). It is also clear that the dilemma principle will apply to rescuers. If a rescuer is presented with a choice between two or more risky modes of rescue and makes what turns out to be a mistaken decision, this will not be regarded as contributory negligence. It is also clear that a rescuer who chooses to incur the virtual certainty of injury will not have his damages reduced for contributory negligence if he reasonably considered this to be the only effective means of rescue (see, for example, *Haynes* v. *Harwood* (1935) where the plaintiff who dived in front of the defendant's runaway horses pulling a van was found not to be contributorily negligent). Even where only damage to property is foreseeable, the rescuer who chooses to incur a considerable risk of injury may recover the whole of his loss (see, for example *Hyett* v. *G. W. Ry* (1948).

Earlier authority suggested that a rescuer who chose a dangerous method of rescue in preference to a safe one would recover no damages at all (*Sylvester* v. *Chapman* (1935)). *Harrison* v. *British Railways Board* (1981) shows however that the appropriate solution is a reduction of damages for contributory negligence by the plaintiff, at least where the choice is not a deliberate and considered one. In that case, the plaintiff train guard attempted to pull a passenger on board a moving train, ignoring his employer's instructions that the proper course in this situation was to first apply the emergency brake. The plaintiff received a 20 per cent. reduction in his damages. Where there is no necessity for rescue, a person who chooses to face a risk is a volunteer and will recover no damages at all. In *Cutler* v. *Utd. Dairies* (1933) the plaintiff went to the assistance of the defendants' servant in attempting to pacify the defendants' unruly horse and was injured by the horse. His action for damages failed because no one was endangered by the horse and he could therefore not argue that he had assumed the role of rescuer. Clearly the need for a rescue must be objectively assessed. But what if Cutler had mistakenly thought a rescue attempt to be necessary? Perhaps a reduction for contributory negligence rather than complete failure of the action would be the appropriate answer here (there was no possibility of this in *Cutler* itself which was decided before the power of apportionment became available under the 1945 Act).

(5) *Seat belts, crash helmets*

Where the negligence of the plaintiff had the effect merely of failing to mitigate damage, some of which would in any case have occurred to him, there is considerable doubt whether the defence of contributory negligence would have been available to the defendant at common law. Furthermore, section 4 of the 1945 Act does not increase the range of contributory negligence beyond what would have been regarded as giving rise to the defence at common law. This difficulty has been ignored by the courts in deciding whether failure to wear a crash helmet or a seat belt justifies an apportionment of damage under the Act. *Froom* v. *Butcher* (1976) in holding that failure to wear a seat belt was contributory negligence under the Act, indicated that the appropriate deduction was 25 per cent. if wearing the belt would have prevented the injury altogether, and 15 per cent. if it would have reduced its extent. The defendant who has the burden on this issue, fails unless he shows that some injury would have been avoided by wearing the belt (*Owens* v. *Brimmells* (1977)). The principles as to apportionment laid down in *Froom* v. *Butcher* apply also to failure to wear a crash helmet (held to be contributory negligence in *O'Connell* v. *Jackson* (1971)—see *Capps* v. *Miller* (1989)—insecurely fastened crash helmet led to reduction of 10 per cent. rather than the full 15 per cent. under *Froom*).

(6) *Drunken drivers*
Volenti non fit injuria is excluded as a defence to an action by a drunken driver against his passenger (section 149(3) of the Road Traffic Act; *Pitts* v. *Hunt* (1989)). Contributory negligence remains an applicable defence (*Owens* v. *Brimmells* (1977)).

IMPUTED CONTRIBUTORY NEGLIGENCE

Under a largely discredited common law doctrine, the contributory negligence of one person might be imputed to another so as to constitute contributory negligence on the part of that other. Several decisions have whittled away the doctrine, so that now the only importance case of it is that the negligence of a servant acting in the course of his employment is imputed to his master. But the negligence of a carrier is not imputed to his passenger, that of an adult is not imputed to a child of whom he is in charge, and that of an independent contractor is not imputed to his employer.

It is not easy to see why the rule should survive in the case of master and servant. It cannot be explained on the ground of the master's vicarious liability for the negligence of his servant committed in the course of his employment, since the basis of policy underlying the doctrine of vicarious liability is that the servant's liability is transferred to a financially solvent defendant, whereas imputed negligence affects the case where the employer is the injured party, and there is no reason of policy requiring financially solvent plaintiffs to meet part of their own loss out of their own pockets. By an unwarranted extension of the doctrine, it applies also in those cases where the owner of a car is vicariously liable for the negligence of the person driving the car (*infra*, pp. 321–323). Thus, in *Lampert* v. *Eastern National Omnibus Co.* (1954), it was held that the plaintiff who had delegated the driving of a car which she owned to her husband was contributorily negligent as to the amount of his negligence in an accident caused also by the negligent driving of the defendant. This is less serious now that the liability of the person driving the car towards passengers is required to be covered by insurance under section 145(3)(*a*) of the Road Traffic Act 1988. Clearly Mrs. Lampert would not have been defeated by contributory negligence if she had sued her husband.

VOLENTI NON FIT INJURIA

The defence of *volenti non fit injuria* was of importance during the nineteenth century, when it was confined within less narrow limits than it is today. In particular it was used to defeat actions by workmen who had suffered injuries in the course of their employment as the result of their employer's negligence; it was enough to establish the defence that the workmen knew of the negligence and had remained in his employment. This doctrine was removed by *Smith* v. *Baker* (1891) which held that an employee who chose to stay in his job, knowing of a dangerous situation created by his employer's negligence was not *volens* to that negligence. The present century has seen a further narrowing down of the defence. Clearly behaviour which might give rise to the defence of *volenti* may also amount to contributory negligence, and it now seems correct to say that the courts look with disfavour on the former defence, which operates as a complete defence, preferring to apply the apportionment provisions of the 1945 Act. This tendency may receive a further impetus from the Unfair

Contract Terms Act 1977, which considerably limits the right to contract out of liability for negligence.

Volenti applies to the unintentional torts

The basis of the defences of consent and of *volenti non fit injuria* is the same—the plaintiff has in effect consented to his own injury. But the defence is normally called consent where the plaintiff has consented to the commission of what would otherwise be a tort against himself, for example, consent to the commission of a battery by one who has a haircut. The defence is called *volenti non fit injuria* where the plaintiff consents to the risk of tortious behaviour injuring him in the future. This means that the defence of consent applies to the intentional torts, since only in their case is there a certainty of the torts being committed. *Volenti* applies to the torts of negligence and strict liability, the relevant consent being to behaviour which may or may not produce a tort. Both defences require an actual subjective consent, although in both it is possible to infer that consent from the plaintiff's conduct. The rules of capacity to consent and reality of consent are the same in *volenti* as in the defence of consent itself (*supra*, pp. 72–74).

Extent of defence

Volenti may arise from express agreement between plaintiff and defendant under which the defendant is exempted from liability or his duty is excluded; or it may arise from an inference of consent drawn from the plaintiff's conduct. The latter case will be looked at first.

(1) *Volenti based on inference from plaintiff's conduct*

It has already been mentioned that the courts nowadays seem to disfavour the defence of *volenti*. The most extreme expressions of this judicial approach are the judgments of Diplock L.J. in *Wooldridge* v. *Sumner* (1963) and of Lord Denning M.R. in *Nettleship* v. *Weston* (1971). Diplock L.J. observed: "the maxim (*volenti non fit injuria*) in the absence of express contract, has no application to negligence simpliciter where the duty of care is based solely on proximity or neighbourship in the Atkinian sense." *Wooldridge* v. *Sumner*, as pointed out earlier (pp. 154–155) was a case in which the court chose to adopt a reduced standard of care approach rather than one based on *volenti non fit injuria* to the issue of liability of sportsmen who are engaged in sporting contests and it is possible that Diplock L.J.'s statement should be limited to that context. Nevertheless Lord Denning M.R. in *Nettleship* v. *Weston* also held in a different context (liability of learner driver to instructor/passenger) that *volenti* could arise only from express agreement and could not be inferentially established. The other members of the Court of Appeal in these two cases did not go so far.

There is nevertheless clear support for the survival of the *volenti* defence outside the area of express agreement in the House of Lords decision in *I.C.I.* v. *Shatwell* (1965). In that case the plaintiff and his brother in disregard of the instructions of their employer and in breach of statutory regulations binding themselves chose to test certain detonators without taking the necessary precautions. The plaintiff was injured in the ensuing explosion. The plaintiff's action against his employers based upon their vicarious liability for the negligence and breach of statutory duty of his brother failed because of *volenti non fit injuria*. A stronger case for its application could hardly be imagined. The plaintiff not only willingly ran the risk of his brother's negligence at the very time it was happening but also participated in it.

Despite *Shatwell* there continued to be doubts as to how valid were the earlier statements of opinion of Lord Denning and Diplock L.J. and these doubts centred on the issue of whether *volenti* could ever operate as a defence, in the absence of express agreement between defendant and plaintiff, where the alleged consent preceded the act of negligence. These doubts were fuelled by the early decision in *Dann* v. *Hamilton* (1939) in which Asquith J. expressed doubt as to the availability of *volenti* in a case of a passenger travelling with a drunken driver on the ground that the plaintiff could not know in advance the nature and extent of the risk he ran (this doubt was endorsed by Diplock L.J. in *Wooldridge* v. *Sumner*). *Volenti* cannot in any case operate as a defence as between driver and passenger whatever the nature of the driving because of section 149(3) of the Road Traffic Act 1988. In *Morris* v. *Murray* (1991) the Court of Appeal upheld a defence of *volenti* where the plaintiff and defendant had shared a prolonged drinking bout prior to taking a flight in a plane piloted by the defendant and in which the negligence of the defendant caused the death of himself and the serious injury of the plaintiff.

The court distinguished *Dann* v. *Hamilton* on the ground that in that case the defendant became drunk only during the course of a journey in which the plaintiff joined him at the start and on the ground that Asquith J. left open the possibility of exceptional circumstances operating in which the defence would apply. Diplock L.J.'s remarks in *Wooldridge* v. *Sumner* were thought by the Court of Appeal to be specifically related to sporting contests, in which players and spectators were deemed to accept to risks incidental to the ordinary playing of the sport, not because of *volenti* but because of the special relationship that existed between them. *Volenti* could not be established against a plaintiff in these circumstances because whatever actionable negligence occurred was outside the ordinary risks and therefore unforeseeable. The facts of *Morris* v. *Murray* on the other hand established a clear case where later negligence was likely to occur.

Whatever the common law status of the defence, it is retained in section 2(5) of the Occupiers' Liability Act which provides the occupier with the defence that the visitor willingly accepted the risk and section 5(2) of the Animals Act 1971 which preserves the defence in the case of liability for animals under the Act.

(2) *Consent to express exclusions of liability*

Before considering the provisions of the Unfair Contract Terms Act 1977, the common law position must be set out. Subject to certain specific statutory exceptions it has until 1977 been generally possible to exclude liability in negligence by a provision in a contract or other agreement. In the case of a contractual provision, this could become a term of the contract either because the plaintiff had expressly agreed to it, or because the defendant had taken reasonable steps to bring it to the plaintiff's attention as the basis on which he was contracting. Whether the agreement is contractual or not, the basis of the defence to the plaintiff's action is *volenti non fit injuria*. The ability to establish *volenti* by non-contractual agreement may be of advantage where the plaintiff lacks contractual capacity. Thus exclusionary notices displayed in cars have in certain cases been held to be binding upon infant passengers, where the defendant had taken proper steps prior to commencement of the journey to draw the attention of the passenger to them (*Buckpitt* v. *Oakes* (1968); *Bennett* v. *Tugwell* (1971); *Birch* v. *Thomas* (1972)). The power of exclusion of liability by notice available to occupiers of premises also seems to be based upon non-contractual agreement. The notice of exclusion must be displayed with suitable prominence at the entry to the premises, and, if so, the entrant is deemed to have entered subject to this term.

Unfair Contract Terms Act 1977. Under this Act certain exclusions of liability in negligence are either rendered wholly inoperative or subjected to a test of reasonableness. Negligence is defined by section 1(1) as the breach: (a) of any obligation arising from the express or implied terms of a contract to take reasonable care or exercise reasonable skill in the performance of a contract; or (b) of any common law duty to take reasonable care or exercise reasonable skill, or (c) of the common duty of care imposed by the Occupiers' Liability Act 1957. The ambit of the Act's provisions is restricted to "business liability" which is defined by section 1(3) as liability for breach of obligations or duties arising from things done or to be done by a person in the course of his own business or another's; or from the occupation of premises used for business purposes of the occupier. Section 2(1) prevents a person excluding, by reference to any contract term or to a notice given to persons generally or to particular persons, liability in negligence for causing death or personal injury. In the case of negligence causing other loss or damage, section 2(2) requires that the contract term or notice must satisfy the requirement of reasonableness. Section 2(3) abolishes the defence of *volenti non fit injuria* in cases covered by section 2(1) and (2). A person's agreement to or awareness of the contract term or notice does not give rise to that defence. Section 13 extends the notion of excluding or restricting liability contained in section 2. In particular exclusion or restriction of liability extends to terms or notices making the liability or its enforcement subject to restrictive conditions, excluding the remedy for enforcement of the liability, or excluding or restricting the duty breach of which gives rise to the liability.

Other statutory restrictions upon the power to exclude. A number of specific restrictions upon the power to exclude liability in tort continue to exist outside the 1977 Act. Two examples may be given. Section 1(3) of the Law Reform (Personal Injuries) Act 1948 prevents an employer from contracting out of his vicarious liability for the torts of employees committed in the course of their employment against their fellow employees. Under section 149(3) of the Road Traffic Act 1988, a car driver cannot by any agreement exclude or restrict his liability towards his passengers. Furthermore the fact that the passenger has "willingly accepted as his the risk of negligence on the part of the driver" is not to be treated as negativing the driver's liability. The defence of *volenti non fit injuria*, whether based on agreement or on the conduct of the passenger is therefore excluded altogether (*Pitts* v *Hunt* (1989)).

10. PROOF OF NEGLIGENCE

Judge and Jury

It was at one time important to differentiate between the functions of judge and jury in the trial of civil actions for negligence. Appellate courts, while willing to overrule the judges' decisions on points of law would seldom disturb the findings of the jury unless they were completely unreasonable having regard to the evidence in the case. This was a quite serious limitation upon the function of the appellate court, since juries were not confined to determining the actual facts of the case, but also had to perform the evaluation of the defendant's conduct (in the light of the judge's direction to them about what standard was demanded of the defendant) required in order to decide whether he was negligent. But with the virtual disappearance of the jury in actions of negligence, it is no longer of much importance to attempt to distinguish "jury questions" from those which the judge has to decide. The judge sitting alone will decide all the issues in the case, the actual facts, the inferences to be drawn from those facts, and matters of law, such as the existence of a duty of care, the standard of care required by the defendant in discharging that duty, and questions of remoteness of damage. Furthermore, the appellate court will not regard itself as precluded from reviewing decisions of the trial judge on matters which were formerly left exclusively to the jury, for example, the decision whether the defendant has acted negligently, and the award of damages in the action, though the appellate court will invariably accept the judge's findings on the actual facts of the case rather than inferences to be drawn from those facts. The differentiation in function between judge and jury remains in those cases where the action is heard before a jury. In this case the appellate court will accept the jury's findings both of fact and of the inferences to be drawn from them unless satisfied that the latter are wholly unreasonable. It should be pointed out finally, that despite the virtual disappearance of juries in tort actions, it is still common to refer to the fact-finding process at the trial as a "jury question" and to define a prima facie case of negligence as one where there is sufficient evidence of negligence to be left to a jury.

Evidence of negligence; burden of proof

The legal burden of proving negligence rests on the plaintiff. He must establish at the trial that on the balance of probabilities the defendant was negligent. If his proof falls short of probability, for example, if he shows an equal likelihood of negligence as of absence of negligence on the defendant's part, the action will fail. An exception to the normal rule as to burden of proof is section 11(1) of the Civil Evidence Act 1968 which allows a conviction to be used as evidence of the facts which constitute the offence. So a conviction for careless driving may be used as evidence of negligence in a civil court. The defendant is of course allowed to rebut that evidence by evidence of his own but the legal burden of rebutting the facts for which the conviction forms evidence rests on him (*Stupple* v. *Royal Insurance Co.* (1971)). But a convicted person is not allowed to raise the issue of his guilt for the offence in subsequent civil proceedings even though that issue is raised only collaterally—such an action will be struck out as an abuse of process of the court (*Hunter* v. *Chief Constable of the West Midlands Police* (1982)). The Court of Appeal has subsequently qualified this principle by allowing a civil action in tort to proceed where the finding of fact in the criminal proceedings was inferential rather than the express finding made in *Hunter* (*Simpson* v. *Chief Constable of South Yorks. Police* (1991)).

The plaintiff's evidence may seek to establish negligence by the defendant in one of two ways. He may either give direct evidence of negligence, *i.e.* of facts which themselves show negligence; or he may give evidence of facts from which negligence may be inferred. The case of *res ipsa loquitur* is a special example of the latter type. The plaintiff under this rule of evidence is allowed in certain circumstances merely to rely on the actual occurrence of the event in question to show negligence by the defendant—the "facts themselves speak."

When civil actions for negligence were tried before juries, it was an important function of the trial judge to rule on a submission of no case to answer, *i.e.* that there was no evidence of negligence sufficient to be left to the jury. The ruling was one of law and could be upset on appeal. With the virtual disappearance of jury trial in negligence actions this part of the trial judge's function has lost most of its importance. It is still possible for the defendant to submit that there is no case to answer at the conclusion of the plaintiff's evidence. However, the likelihood of his doing so is remote, granted that a submission of no case to answer constitutes an election to call no evidence if that submission fails; also, with the virtual disappearance of juries in negligence trials, a failure in that submission inevitably means defeat in the action itself, since it is no longer possible to leave the plaintiff's uncontradicted case to the jury, and a judge is unlikely to rule in the plaintiff's favour that there is a case to answer and yet conclude that it does not amount to proof on the balance of probabilities, even though theoretically it would be possible for him to do so.

Res ipsa loquitur

The effect of this rule of evidence is to allow the plaintiff to treat the actual facts of the case as evidence of the defendant's negligence—the facts speak for themselves. The rule is an important concession to plaintiffs since it recognises the difficulty that exists in the case of many accidents of furnishing direct evidence that they were the result of negligence. In order that the rule should operate three conditions are necessary: (1) the plaintiff's damage must be such as does not in the ordinary course of things happen in the absence of negligence; (2) the facts proved must point to negligence by the defendant; (3) the court must not have facts before it which enable it to make up its mind on the issue of negligence independently of *res ipsa loquitur*. Whether the rule applies to the case before it is a question of law for the judge to decide.

(1) *The plaintiff's damage is such that it would not in the ordinary course of things have happened without negligence*

The rule has been applied to the case of objects falling from upper storeys of buildings on to the highway below (for example, in *Byrne* v. *Boadle* (1863), flour bags falling from the upper window of the defendant's building). Numerous cases have established the applicability of the rule to motor vehicles going out of control (for example, *Laurie* v. *Raglan Building Co. Ltd.* (1942)—a lorry driven at 10 m.p.h. skidded and mounted the pavement, killing the plaintiff's husband) and it has been applied to stones found in buns (*Chaproniere* v. *Mason* (1905)), to sulphites found in underpants (*Grant* v. *Australian Knitting Mills Ltd.* (1936)) and to the effects of a surgical operation upon the plaintiff (*Cassidy* v. *Minister of Health* (1951)), disposing of doubts whether *res ipsa loquitur* applied in medical cases, though not every medical operation which goes wrong raises a case of *res ipsa loquitur*.

(2) *Facts proved must point to negligence by the defendant*

If the facts proved merely point to negligence by one of a number of persons of whom the defendant is one, this is insufficient (for qualifications upon this when negligence is proved to be committed by one of the defendant's servants or independent contractors, see *infra*, Chapter 20). The second requirement is sometimes stated to be that the "*res*" must be under the defendant's control. So in *Easson* v. *L. & N. E. Ry. Co.* (1944) the fact that a door of the defendants' train fell open when the train, an express, was in between stations, did not raise a presumption that the defendants' servants had failed to close it on leaving its last stop. But in *Gee* v. *Metropolitan Ry. Co.* (1873) when the train door fell open shortly after the train had left a station, it was held that *res ipsa loquitur* applied. In *Lloyde* v. *West Midlands Gas Board* (1971) the members of the Court of Appeal appeared to agree that exclusive control by the defendant is not necessary to establish *res ipsa loquitur*. The plaintiff would, however, have to establish the improbability of outside inter-ference in order that the doctrine should apply. Further in *Ward* v. *Tesco Stores* (1976) the majority in the Court of Appeal held that *res ipsa loquitur* applied merely on proof of the presence of a slippery substance (yoghurt in this case) on a supermarket floor and even in the absence of evidence as to how long the substance had been there. There is force in the dissenting judgment of Ormerod L.J. who refused to apply *res ipsa loquitur* in the absence of evidence on the latter point.

The rule is qualified to some extent in the case of collisions between motor vehicles. Where a collision occurs between two such vehicles and there is nothing in the evidence on which the court can make up its mind as to which driver was to blame, or as to the proportions in which each driver was to blame, then the court will hold each driver equally responsible. This result was arrived at in *Bray* v. *Palmer* (1953) (head-on collision near centre of road) and *France* v. *Parkinson* (1954) (collision on cross-roads of equal status). This is in fact a case of *res ipsa loquitur* where the facts establish a balance of probability of two people sharing equally in the responsibility for the damage.

(3) *Facts must not be present before the court which enable it to make up its mind on the issue of negligence independently of res ipsa loquitur*

Where the court is able to determine the cause of the accident on the balance of probabilities, there is no room for the application of *res ipsa loquitur* and the plaintiff must adduce evidence showing that the defendant was negligent in relation to that cause. In *Barkway* v. *South Wales Transport* (1950) it was determined by the court that the defendants' lorry had gone out of control solely because of a burst tyre. The plaintiff therefore had to prove that the defendants were at fault in relation to the defect in the tyre, and succeeded in doing this by showing a negligent system of tyre inspection at the defendants' garage. There is no real hardship to the plaintiff in this—the defendants had to lead evidence showing the nature of their system of tyre inspection, although the legal burden of proving that this was negligent was on the plaintiff. It now seems clear that the plaintiff has the legal burden of proving fault, whether he is relying on direct evidence of negligence or *res ipsa loquitur* (*infra*).

Burden on the defendant

In order to rebut a prima facie case of negligence that may exist on the facts proved by the plaintiff, the defendant clearly must provide evidence of facts which show the contrary. He may attempt directly to controvert the plaintiff's allegations of fact; he may resort to proof that he took all reasonable care, leaving the court to infer that the occurrence of the damage to the plaintiff was entirely accidental or had some other cause; or he may provide evidence of another cause. What is the nature of the burden resting on him in this regard? Clearly his evidence must have some degree of cogency. It is not enough to point to the possibility of another cause of the damage to rebut a prima facie case that his negligence was the cause of the damage. The nature of the burden on the defendant is such that he is entitled to succeed if the totality of the evidence leaves the balance of probabilities evenly poised as between negligence and no negligence on his part. The legal burden of proof remains with the plaintiff throughout the trial. The nature of this so-called evidential burden of proof resting on the defendant differs from case to case. One instructive example of a failure by the defendant to discharge his evidential burden is the decision of the House of Lords in *Henderson* v. *H. E. Jenkins* (1969). The brakes of the defendants' lorry failed and it caused the death of the plaintiff's husband on its descent down a steep hill. The plaintiff was able to show that the brake failure was due to corrosion of a brake pipe situated under the lorry and only detectable by inspection after the pipe's removal. The defendants were able to prove a system of visual inspection of the brake pipe which was in accordance with Ministry of Transport recommendations. The likelihood was that the degree of corrosion was due to some unusual treatment of the lorry, for example, its prolonged exposure to chemicals. The defendants chose to call no evidence as to the use to which the lorry had been put. The plaintiff succeeded in the House of Lords by a three to two majority. Her evidence showing the corrosion of the pipe raised a prima facie inference of negligence by the defendants, and in order to rebut that inference it was incumbent upon the defendants to provide evidence to show that the lorry had been put to no unusual use requiring a system of inspection based on removal of the brake pipe rather than mere visual inspection.

It is sometimes suggested that where a case of *res ipsa loquitur* applies, the defendant must disprove the inference of negligence on the balance of probabilities, *i.e.* that he assumes the legal burden of proof. This suggestion rests upon a statement of Asquith L.J. in *Barkway* v. *South Wales Transport* (1948) to the effect that the defendant in a case where *res ipsa loquitur* applies must prove either a specific cause of the accident which does not connote negligence on his part but points to its absence as more probable, or that he used all reasonable care. This was unnecessary for the eventual decision in the case since it was decided by the House of Lords on another point. There followed inconclusive Court of Appeal decisions (*Moore* v. *Fox* (1956); *Ward* v. *Tesco Stores* (1976) both of which contained suggestions that the legal burden of proof once *res ipsa loquitur* applied was with the defendant. The recent decision of the Privy Council in *Ng* v. *Lee* (1988) is, however, quite clear that in a case of *res ipsa loquitur* the legal burden of proof remains with the plaintiff. The effect of its operation is therefore that the defendant succeeds if he shows at least that the probabilities are equally balanced as between negligence or no negligence on his part.

Since *res ipsa loquitur* applies only where the cause of the accident is not known, the defendant will very often seek to prove the operation of a careful system by himself or persons in his employ which would have eliminated the possibility that his negligence could have been responsible. Such evidence may well establish that the defendant himself has not been personally at fault, but it may leave open to the court the inference that the fault is that of someone in the operation of the system for whose acts the defendant is vicariously liable. So in *Grant* v. *Australian Knitting Mills* (1936) the plaintiff contracted dermatitis because of the presence in his underwear manufactured by the defendants of excess sulphites. The defendants' evidence showed that they had manufactured 4,737,600 pairs of underpants previously without complaint. Nevertheless they were held liable because the likelihood was of lack of care by someone in their employment. *Daniels* v. *R. White* (1938) was an unsatisfactory decision which appeared to run contrary to these principles. It held that when the defendant chose to show that he had taken reasonable care to establish a safe system of manufacture, if he succeeded in showing this, the plaintiff failed even though the likelihood was of negligence in the operation of that system by someone employed by the defendant. The case was expressly not followed by another court at first instance in *Hill* v. *James Crowe* (*Cases*) *Ltd.* (1978) and is also inconsistent with the Privy Council's decision in *Grant's* case.

Proof of causation

The plaintiff also has the legal burden of proof on the issue of causation—he must establish on the balance of probabilities that the defendant's negligence caused his damage (*Bonnington Castings* v. *Wardlaw* (1956))—for the difficulties involved in proving causation, see Chapter 8).

11. LIABILITY FOR PREMISES

Liability for defective premises (the term includes land itself) is in the process of being assimilated to liability in negligence. But it justifies separate treatment because to some extent special rules still apply to it. In particular the common law distinguished the liability of the occupier towards those injured when on his premises from those who were injured when outside the premises. The latter could, if they could prove injury from a dangerous condition in the premises, sue in nuisance or negligence. The former made use of the special rules of occupiers' liability. Whatever the logic of the distinction, it has been preserved because the Occupiers' Liability Act of 1957 has rendered the obligations of the occupier towards his visitors statutory while leaving untouched his obligations to those outside his premises. But as the Act has gone a long way towards making the liability of the occupier turn entirely on his negligence the divergence is now no longer very marked. It is clear that the rules relating to occupiers' liability place positive duties of care on the occupier and therefore create a major exception to the nonfeasance rule.

In this chapter there will be considered the rules concerning the liability of occupiers and other persons towards those who suffer personal injury or damage to property while they or their property are on premises.

OCCUPIERS' LIABILITY

Classes of entrant

The old law recognised five different classes of entrant: (1) the invitee; (2) the licensee; (3) the person entering under a contract with the occupier; (4) the person entering as of right; (5) trespassers and others. The duties owed to the first three are now governed by the Occupiers' Liability Act of 1957; to the last two by that of 1984.

The invitee was a person who was both permitted to enter and whose entry was in the material interest of the occupier, for example, a customer entering a shop. The licensee was one merely permitted to be on the land, for example, a person permitted to take a short-cut over the occupier's land. The importance of the distinction was that more onerous obligations were owed to the invitee than to the licensee, to whom the occupier's only obligation was to warn of concealed dangers of which the occupier was aware. Criticism of the distinction between invitee and licensee, and the injustices it led to, in particular by the Law Reform Committee in 1954, was the chief reason for the passing of the Occupiers' Liability Act in 1957.

The person entering under contract with the occupier might himself be in contractual relationship with the occupier, or might be permitted to enter under the terms of the occupier's contract with another. In the former case the occupier's duties depended on the terms of the contract, and in the absence of an express term, the courts would imply a term that the premises were to be reasonably safe for the purposes for which entry was made. The latter type of entrant was treated as a licensee of the occupier.

Various persons have a right to enter premises, without obtaining the permission of the occupier. Persons such as Gas and Electricity Board officials or factory inspectors enjoy statutory rights of entry. Police officers have rights to enter premises, for example, in the execution of a search warrant or in order to make an arrest. Private individuals may also in some situations enter land without committing trespass, for example, in order to recap a chattel on that land, or to abate a nuisance. A private individual may also enter land in the exercise of a public or private right of way... There is also the person who enters under an access agreement or order made under the National Parks and Access to the Countryside Act 1949. The duty owed to the entrant as of right varied according to the status of the entrant (*infra*, this chapter).

The fifth type of entrant is the person who enters without permission of the occupier and not in exercise of a right conferred by law. The trespasser is by far the most important case, but there are others. For example, a person thrown on to the land by another person is not a trespasser but comes within this category.

OCCUPIERS' LIABILITY ACT 1957; THE COMMON DUTY OF CARE

The distinction between invitees and licensees has now been abolished by the Occupiers' Liability Act 1957. The occupier now owes the same duty, the "common duty of care," to all his lawful visitors, defined by the Act as comprising those persons who would at common law be treated as his licensees or invitees (this result is achieved by sections 1(1), 1(2) and 2(1) in combination). The common duty of care is defined by section 2(2) as a duty to take such care as in all the circumstances of the case is reasonable to see that the visitor will be reasonably safe in using the premises for the purposes for which he is invited or permitted by the occupier to be there. The Act has therefore created a common duty of care to replace the special duties which an occupier owed to his invitees and licensees at common law. The common duty of care under the Act applies only to those persons who prior to the Act were regarded as invitees or licensees of the occupier. The liability of the occupier towards persons who fell outside these classes, including trespassers and certain entrants as of right is now expressly regulated by the Occupiers' Liability Act 1984 which is dealt with later in this chapter.

Section 1(3)(b) provides that the rules of the Act apply to regulate the obligations of an occupier of premises in respect of "damage to property, including the property of persons who are not themselves his visitors," but only "in like manner and to the like extent as the principles applicable at common law to an occupier of premises and his invitees or licensees." The intention seems to be that if a duty of care would exist at common law in respect of property on the premises, this is replaced by the common duty of care under the Act. The result seems to be that a case such as *Tinsley* v. *Dudley* (1951) would be decided in the same way under the Act. In that case the Court of Appeal held that no duty of care bound the occupier of premises to safeguard from theft the property of an invitee, left with the occupier's permission on those premises, in the absence of any delivery of the property into the occupier's possession under a bailment. On the other hand, it seems clear that the occupier will be liable for damage to the visitor's property if it arises from a hazardous condition on the premises (*A.M.F. International Ltd.* v. *Magnet Bowling Ltd.* (1968)).

Activity duty

The pre-1957 law distinguished between the occupier's duty in respect of the static condition of his premises (occupancy duty) and his duty in respect of his activities carried out on those premises (activity duty). In particular, the distinction between invitee and licensee was not relevant in the case of the latter, the occupier's liability being governed by principles of ordinary negligence (*Slater* v. *Clay, Cross & Co.* (1956)). With the removal of the distinction between invitees and licensees by the Act of 1957, it is now hardly necessary to distinguish the two duties. The Act, however, unfortunately fails to make the fate of the activity duty clear. It may continue to exist at common law, unaffected by the Act's provisions; or it may have become statutory. The answer depends upon the interpretation given to section 1(1) and (2) of the Act. Subsection (1) states that the rules made by the two following subsections shall have effect in place of the common law duties of the occupier regarding the state of his premises *or things done or omitted to be done on them.* Subsection (2) states that the rules so enacted shall regulate the nature of the duty imposed by law in consequence of a person's occupation or control of premises. Since the activity duty is hardly imposed in consequence of a person's occupation or control of premises, the bizarre result of the Act might be that it has abolished the activity duty without replacing it. For this reason, it seems better to confine the ambit of section 1(1) to "things done" on the premises which affect their static condition, thus allowing the activity duty to survive outside the Act. (The courts appear to assume that the activity duty remains a common law duty—*cf.* the Court of Appeal decision in *Ogwo* v. *Taylor* (1987) and dicta of Lords Oliver and Goff in *Ferguson* v. *Welsh* (1987)).

Conditions for the application of the Act: "occupier"; "premises"

The defendant must under section 1(2) be in occupation or control of the premises in order that the statutory obligation be demanded of him. As it is clear that no legal or equitable interest in the premises is necessary to satisfy the requirements of the statute, the circumstances of each case will have to be considered to decide whether such occupation or control exists.

In *Wheat* v. *Lacon & Co.* (1966) the plaintiff, a guest staying in a public house owned by the defendants, was killed in a fall from a defective staircase, the staircase being in the part of the public house which was occupied as his private living-quarters by the defendants' manager. The court decided that the defendants retained sufficient control over the premises to be in occupation within the meaning of section 1(2), although it was held that the manager, also a defendant, was also an occupier.

The case makes it clear that exclusive occupation of the premises such as is necessary to maintain an action of trespass is not required. The manager, for example, could not have forbidden entry to the agents of the defendants. It shows also that a continuing physical presence on the premises is not necessary to constitute occupation. This is borne out also by *Harris* v. *Birkenhead Corporation* (1976). The defendant local authority which had served a notice to quit on the tenant of a house acting under a compulsory purchase order, was found to be the occupier of the house on its vacation by the tenant, even though it had exercised no acts of physical occupation or control in relation to it. In both *Wheat* and *Harris*, occupation clearly was founded on the right to enter and exercise control at any time. It seems probable, however, that a mere contractual right of entry to do repairs reserved by a landlord under a lease would not constitute the landlord an occupier, although precise authority is absent on the point. *Wheat* v. *Lacon* shows also that a case of joint occupation is possible. This is demonstrated also by *Hartwell* v. *Grayson Docks* (1947). In that case it was found that a contractor who was converting a ship into a troopship in dry dock was an occupier of the ship. This finding was clearly not inconsistent with occupation by its owner.

The common law rules applied not only to land and buildings on the land, but also other erections and structures on the land, such as electricity pylons, diving-boards and grandstands. Movables such as ladders, ships and aeroplanes were also included provided they were occupied by the defendant, and provided the plaintiff's injury resulted from some structural defect in them. If, for example, a ladder is lent by A to B, and B suffers injury because of a defect in the ladder, A's liability is governed by the principles of liability for chattels, since he no longer occupies the ladder (*Wheeler* v. *Copas* (1981)). And negligent operation of any locomotive was governed by ordinary negligence, not occupier's liability. These rules are preserved by section 1(3)(*a*) of the Act—the rules of the Act regulate the obligations of a person occupying or having control of any "fixed or movable structure, including any vessel, vehicle or aircraft," "in like manner and to the like extent" as the common law rules of occupiers' liability regulated the liability of persons occupying such structures.

SPECIAL PROVISIONS ABOUT THE COMMON DUTY OF CARE

It is clear that most cases on occupiers' liability will turn on questions of negligence indistinguishable from negligence at common law. There are, however, certain provisions in the Occupiers' Liability Act about the nature of the common duty of care, its discharge, and the defences available to an action for breach of it, which need to be specially considered. Section 2(3) provides that the circumstances relevant for the purpose of deciding whether the occupier has committed a breach of his duty of care, include the degree of care, and of want of care, which would ordinarily be looked for in a visitor, so that in proper cases (a) an occupier must be prepared for children to be less careful than adults; and (b) an occupier may expect that a person, in the exercise of his calling, will appreciate and guard against any special risks ordinarily incidental to it, so far as the occupier leaves him free to do so.

Duty towards children

The first problem concerns the occupier's liability towards children who are lawfully present on his land. He must not have on his land objects that are dangerous but are also an allurement or invitation to them. Thus, in *Glasgow Corporation* v. *Taylor*

(1922), the plaintiff, a child aged seven, died through eating some poisonous berries which he picked from a tree in the defendants' public gardens. The defendants were held liable despite the commission by the plaintiff of an otherwise trespassory act in picking the berries. The allurement therefore both negatived the trespass and established liability on the defendants' part. The concept of an allurement involves the idea of "concealment and surprise, of an appearance of safety under circumstances cloaking a reality of danger" (*per* Hamilton L.J. in *Latham* v. *Johnson and Nephew Ltd.* (1913)). Thus in that case a child who was injured while playing with a heap of stones on the defendants' land was held to have no remedy against the defendants. Equally, in *Perry* v. *Wrigley Ltd.* (1955), a hole in the ground into which a child fell was held to be no allurement to a child who was injured by falling into the hole. It is perhaps questionable whether this emphasis on the concealment of the danger is desirable. The obviousness of the danger may increase its attractions to a child. This seems to be recognised by *Gough* v. *National Coal Board* in which slow-moving railway trucks were held to be an allurement and also in *Holdman* v. *Hamlyn* (1943) in which the same was held of a threshing machine.

The question whether there is an allurement on the land is also relevant to the question whether the child is a trespasser or licensee on the land. This is discussed below in this chapter.

Very young children

To the very young child, almost anything can be dangerous. Furthermore, the obviousness of the danger will not prevent the child from encountering it. It might be expected therefore that the law would differentiate between the occupier's duty to the young and to the very young child. This was confirmed in *Phipps* v. *Rochester Corpn.* (1955). The plaintiff, aged five, and his sister, aged seven, were licensees on the defendants' land. There was a trench on the land, nine feet deep by two-and-a-half feet wide. The plaintiff fell into this and broke his leg. The defendants were held not liable because they could not anticipate that a child of this age would not be accompanied by a responsible person and so had not broken their duty of care.

Though often expressed in terms of duty, the decision in *Phipps* is clearly one of standard of care, *i.e.* the occupier had behaved reasonably in taking no precautions against the event of very young unaccompanied children being present on his land and being injured by an obvious danger such as the trench. The decision on the question of reasonableness turns on matters of fact and degree. Devlin J. himself suggested that the decision might go against the occupier where the "social habits" of the neigbourhood decreed the likely presence of very young unaccompanied children or the children were in a recognised playground where a parent would reasonably expect the child to be safe though unaccompanied.

Where the danger on the land is one that is not apparent to an adult, Devlin J. in *Phipps* contemplated that the duty would be discharged by the giving of a suitable warning. Suppose that a very young child is unaccompanied and is injured by a danger on the land of which no warning has been given. The occupier would here be liable to the child for its injury, and would not be able to claim contribution from its parent, because even if the latter was negligent in allowing the child to roam unaccompanied that negligence is not causally relevant to the child's injury since the parent's presence would not have avoided it.

Risks incidental to calling

Section 2(3)(b) was judicially considered in *Roles* v. *Nathan* (1963). In that case, the plaintiffs, two chimney-sweeps, were employed by the defendants to block up holes in the flues of a heating-system which employed coke. They attempted to block up one of the holes while the coke-fire was lit, despite a warning against this by their employer's agent. Both were killed by the escape of carbon monoxide gas. One of the grounds for the Court of Appeal's decision in favour of the defendants was that this was a risk incidental to their calling which they appreciated and should have guarded against.

Volenti non fit injuria; contributory negligence; warning

The defence of *volenti non fit injuria* is expressly provided for by section 2(5) of the Act of 1957. Mere knowledge of the danger on the visitor's part does not establish by itself a willingness to assume the risk within section 2(5) of the Occupiers' Liability Act 1957. However, section 2(4) provides that a warning of the danger given by the occupier to the visitor has the effect of discharging the occupier's duty of care if in all the circumstances it is enough for the visitor to be reasonably safe. This changes the common law rule in *London Graving Dock Co.* v. *Horton* (1951) which held that mere knowledge of the danger by an invitee absolved the occupier even though it was not enough to render the invitee reasonably safe. The subsection was applied in *Roles* v. *Nathan* as an additional ground for the decision in that case.

Knowledge of the danger on the part of the visitor may of course be a factor in establishing the statutory defence of a willing assumption of the risk or in enabling the court to conclude that the visitor's act in facing the danger was a *nova causa interveniens*. But neither of these is of necessity established by reason of the mere fact that the visitor has faced a known danger. In *Bunker* v. *Charles Brand* (1969), for example, it was held that a workman who chose in the course of his employment to attempt a walk along rollers which he knew to be dangerous without making use of the handhold was merely 50 per cent. contributorily negligent in his action for damages brought against the occupier. (The Act itself does not provide for the defence of contributory negligence, but the courts invariably assume that the defence applies). *Bunker's* case was one in which the visitor's knowledge of the danger did not enable him to be reasonably safe. What is the position where the visitor's knowledge of the danger gained without the giving of a warning by the occupier is nevertheless sufficient to enable the visitor to be resonably safe? The court might here wish to preserve parity with section 2(4) of the Act and allow the visitor no compensation but there are difficulties. The occupier is clearly in breach of his duty of care to the visitor and it has been held recently that a finding of 100 per cent contributory negligence against a plaintiff is inappropriate (*Pitts* v. *Hunt* (1989)). The matter remains unsettled.

EXCLUSION OF LIABILITY BY THE OCCUPIER

Section 2(1) of the Occupiers' Liability Act provides that the occupier owes the common duty of care to all his visitors, "except in so far as he is free to and does extend, restrict, modify or exclude his duty . . . by agreement or otherwise."

The power to exclude liability is thus made subject to any legislative or judicial restrictions that may be imposed on it. A major restriction has now been imposed by the provisions of the Unfair Contract Terms Act 1977 which expressly regulate exclusion of the common duty of care. The Act is limited to "business liability" which in the case of occupiers means liability arising from the occupation of premises used for business purposes of the occupier. Liability to trespassers is also outside the Act since it is not based on common law negligence or breach of the common duty of care.

It is clear that at common law the occupier could exclude his liability for breach of both occupancy and activity duties, and as regards both licensees and invitees (see *Ashdown* v. *Samuel Williams* (1957); *White* v. *Blackmore* (1973)). Exclusion could be based on express agreement between occupier and entrant, but it could also be achieved by the display of a suitably prominent notice at the entry to the premises. The words "by agreement or otherwise" in section 2(1) of the Occupiers' Liability Act preserve the common law position. This common law power to exclude liability continues to exist except where "business liability" of the occupier applies. The juridical basis of the power of exclusion by notice causes some problems. Courts have generally regarded the exclusion clause as a term of the licence under which the visitor enters. This causes difficulties with trespassers and entrants as of right who do not enter under licence. An alternative basis is that the defence of *volenti non fit injuria* is available to the occupier against one who enters with knowledge, or presumed knowledge of the notice. Again the trespasser presents a problem since the method of his entry may make it impossible for him to have read the notice. But he can hardly be in a better position than the lawful entrant. If *volenti* is the basis, the consent must be a real one. A prisoner, for example, could hardly be held bound by an exclusionary notice displayed outside the prison. This is supported by *Burnett* v. *British Waterways Board* (1972). The plaintiff was not bound by an exclusionary notice displayed outside the defendants' dock since he had an obligation under his contract of employment to enter the dock. Under section 2 of the Occupiers' Liability Act 1984, business liability on the part of the occupier is not incurred where admission to the premises is for recreational or educational purposes unless that admission falls within the business of the occupier. The payment of a fee for admission is likely to distinguish the cases where business liability exists from those where it does not.

Liability for independent contractor

Section 2(4)(*b*) has settled a question which caused uncertainty at common law, by allowing, subject to certain conditions, the occupier to discharge his duty of care by delegating its performance to an independent contractor. The section provides that the occupier is not to be treated without more as answerable for the danger if in all the circumstances he has acted reasonably in entrusting the work to an independent contractor and has taken such steps (if any) as he reasonably ought in order to satisfy himself that the contractor was competent and that the work had been properly done.

The subsection has confirmed the decision in *Haseldine* v. *Daw and Sons Ltd.* (1941) in which the defendant occupier was held not liable to the plaintiff, his licensee, who had been injured through the fall of a lift negligently repaired by a third party, the occupier's independent contractor. It appears not to have affected *Woodward* v. *Mayor of Hastings* (1945) which held that the clearing of snow from a school steps was not a task which involved technical knowledge and the occupier was therefore liable for the contractor's failure to carry it out properly. It is not altogether clear why an occupier who has acted reasonably in delegating some non-technical task to an independent contractor and who is not personally at fault by, for example, failing to inspect properly the contractor's work, should be held liable for the contractor's negligence. But the distinction between the technical and the non-technical task has been approved (*Green* v. *Fibreglass* (1958)).

Section 2(4)(*b*) of the 1957 Act seems open to the interpretation that the occupier in order to escape liability need only carefully select the contractor and take resonable steps to ensure that the work on its completion was properly done. However, the House of Lords in *Ferguson* v. *Welsh* (1987) thought that special circumstances might arise in which an occupier owed a duty of care to supervise the contractor during the actual performance of the work, for example, to point out to the contractor that he was adopting an unsafe system of work. It is suggested that these circumstances would indeed need to be exceptional for them to operate in this way—Lord Goff suggested they would never apply to the ordinary householder.

Liability to contractual visitor

Section 5(1) regulates the occupier's duty to one who enters under his own contract with the occupier. Section 3(1) regulates the liability of the occupier to those whom he is bound by contract to permit to enter, but who are not under contract with him.

Liability to contracting party

Clearly if there is an express term in the contract regulating the occupier's liability to the other party, this will be conclusive. In the absence of such a term, section 5(1) implies a term that the occupier's duty is to be the common duty of care. Liability whether under an express or implied term is contractual rather than tortious, and can therefore be excluded only by subsequent variation of the contract with the agreement of the other contracting party—unilateral notice of exclusion of liability given by one contracting party to the other is not sufficient. Equally the implied term that arises under section 5(1) in the absence of an express term cannot be excluded by express provision in the contract where the occupier's business liability is concerned and the effect of the provision is to exclude liability of the occupier for death of or personal injury to the contracting party who is an entrant on the premises (sections 1(1)(*a*) and 2(1) of the Unfair Contract Terms Act 1977). In the case of other loss or damage the term or notice must satisfy a test of reasonableness (section 2(2)).

Liability to persons permitted to enter under third party's contract with occupier

Since persons entering under the terms of a contract with the occupier formerly came within the class of licensees, they are now his visitors within the meaning of the Act of 1957, and are therefore owed the statutory common duty of care by the occupier. But section 3(1) reinforces this by providing that the occupier cannot restrict the duty of care he owes to such visitors by a provision in the contract, and also that if in the contract he has undertaken obligations going beyond the common duty of care, the duty of care he owes to them "shall include the duty to perform his obligations under the contract." Section 3(4) makes it clear that a lease is within the provisions of section 3(1). This means that a landlord, who will normally retain occupation and control of common staircases, passage-ways and lifts in such demised premises as a block of flats, owes the visitor of his tenant the common duty of care and cannot contract out of this by provision in the lease. This is a twofold improvement on the former law, since the duty he formerly owed was that towards licensees, and he could expressly exclude this by provision in the lease. Section 3(2) provides in effect that the occupier is not liable under section 3 for the defective execution of any work of "construction, maintenance, repair or other like operation" by an independent contractor, where he, the occupier, has taken all reasonable care, unless the contract expressly so provides.

A further question remains, whether the occupier can exclude his liability to persons entering the premises under the contract by exhibiting a notice to this effect on the premises. Clearly the policy arguments which found the exclusion of the visitor's rights by provision in the contract undesirable, on the ground that the visitor would lose his rights without his knowledge, do not apply to an exclusionary notice. Further there seems no reason why the entrant under contract should be in a better position than other visitors. The law is not yet settled but the better view is that the occupier is entitled to exclude his liability to visitors who enter under contract by means of a properly displayed notice. The provisions of the Unfair Contracts Terms Act (*supra*) will, however, apply in this situation also.

OCCUPIERS LIABILITY TO PERSONS OTHER THAN VISITORS

The occupier's liability to persons other than his lawful visitors—the position prior to the Occupiers' Liability Act 1984

There are two main classes of such persons, trespassers and entrants as of right, though there is also the case of the person whose entry on the land is entirely involuntary. In the case of the trespasser, there was originally no duty of care owed to him at all—the occupier's only duty was not to wilfully or recklessly injure him. The House of Lords then introduced a hybrid duty of "common humanity," owed by the occupier to the trespasser, in *British Railways Board* v. *Herrington* (1972). The workings of the humanity test had not been completely formulated prior to 1984, but its main features were that it required on the part of the occupier something more than mere reasonable foreseeability of the danger and of the trespasser's presence on the land, and in deciding on the measures needed by the occupier to discharge the duty the occupier's own means and resources were relevant (comparable on the latter point, therefore, to the test laid down for the occupier's liability for natural nuisances in *Goldman* v. *Hargrave* (1967)). The courts had also, in order to curb the severity of the common law principles concerning liability towards trespassers, made considerable use of what can now be regarded as a fiction, *i.e.* that of the implied licence. Narrow distinctions of fact were taken by the courts in determining whether the entrant was an implied licensee or a trespasser (*cf. Cooke* v. *Midland Great Western Ry. of Ireland* (1909) with *Edwards* v. *Railway Executive* (1953)). With the introduction of a duty of care owed by the occupier of land to trespassers in the Occupiers' Liability Act of 1984 it is certain that the largely fictitious implication of licences will disappear, although the implication of a licence to enter remains of course theoretically possible.

The duty of care owed to entrants as of right varied from the high duty (*i.e.* standard of care) owed to entrants such as firemen who were classed as invitees (*Hartley* v. *Mayoh & Co.* (1954)) to the low duty owed to entrants under an access agreement (who under section 1(4) of the Occupiers' Liability Act 1957 were equated with trespassers).

The Occupiers' Liability Act 1984 has now largely assimilated the duties of care owed by an occupier to trespassers and to entrants as of right, making it in each case one of reasonable care, and abolishing the "humanity" test as far as personal injury is concerned. Of course the standard of care required to pass the test of reasonableness will vary from case to case.

The Occupiers' Liability Act 1984

The main provision is section 1(3). Under this subsection the occupier owes a duty to an entrant on his premises who is not his visitor if:

(a) He is aware of the danger or has reasonable grounds to believe that it exists;

(b) He knows or has reasonable grounds to believe that the (entrant) is in the vicinity of the danger concerned or that he may come into the vicinity of the danger (in either case whether the entrant has lawful authority for being in that vicinity or not); and

(c) The risk is one against which, in all the circumstances of the case, he may reasonably be expected to offer the (entrant) some protection.

Section 1(4) defines the duty under section 1(3) as one to take such care, as is reasonable in all the circumstances of the case, to see that the entrant does not suffer injury on the premises by reason of the danger concerned. The duty under the Act applies to trespassers, to involuntary entrants, to persons entering as of right, including entrants under a private right of way, and to entrants under an access agreement with the occupier. Liability of the occupier towards an entrant on the highway (*i.e.* any sort of public right of way) is, however, expressly excluded from the Act's provisions by section 1(7) and continues to be governed by the common law. This is not a very serious gap since most highways are maintained at the public expense by a designated highway authority and such authority is now liable in tort for both its negligent misfeasance and non-feasance under the provisions of the Highways Acts 1961 and 1980. (Where the highway is not under a highway authority, the only possible liability is that of the occupier for acts of misfeasance causing the highway to become more dangerous—*Greenhalgh* v. *British Rys. Board* (1969)).

The important case of liability to the trespasser has clearly undergone a change under the Act. The requirements that the defendant occupier should merely have "reasonable grounds" to believe in the danger, and "reasonable grounds" to believe in the presence of the trespasser in the vicinity of the danger seem to weigh the balance of the law more heavily against the occupier than does the humanity test under *Herrington*. However, the court retains a large amount of discretion to excuse the occupier on the ground that he could not "reasonably be expected" to offer protection against the risk (no liability, probably, towards burglars as the Law Commission itself suggested in its Report leading to the passing of the Act (Law Commission Report No. 75)). It will also be the case that (c) is far more likely to be satisfied in the case of child rather than adult trespassers). Also it may be decided that the amount of care shown by the occupier is "reasonable in all the circumstances of the case," even though it falls below the normal standard of care requirement in negligence (in particular allowing the court to base the required standard on the occupier's own means and resources). Section 1(8) of the Act excludes from the Act's provisions the case of loss of or damage to property. In *Tutton* v. *A. D. Walter* (1985) the court applied the test of humanity in deciding whether the occupier was liable for spraying his crops with insecticide at a time when such spraying was likely to kill bees, and a colony of the plaintiff's bees was destroyed. The court found the defendant in breach of his duty of humanity; alternatively on the assumption that the bees could not be regarded as trespassing chattels, he was liable under ordinary principles of negligence for causing foreseeable damage to the property of his neighbour.

LIABILITY OF NON-OCCUPIER IN RESPECT OF PREMISES

The law on this topic previously was complex and to some extent remains so. The only way it can be understood is to set out the common law position first, dealing separately with three cases, the vendor, the lessor and the builder; then to examine the Defective Premises Act 1972.

Common law position

(1) *Vendor*
The vendor of premises had complete immunity from an action in tort for defects in the premises. He was not liable in tort for injuries to the buyer, other persons in the premises, or to persons injured outside the premises.

(2) *Lessor*
He had the same immunity as the vendor from actions in tort for injuries to his lessee or other persons injured inside the demised premises. He might be held liable in nuisance or negligence to

persons injured outside the premises by reason of their defective condition. He might incur contractual liability to the lessee in the case of furnished premises for breach of an implied warranty that the premises and furniture were fit for occupation at the commencement of the tenancy. Also, if he undertook the duty of repair, the lessee might sue him in contract for injuries suffered by reason of his failure to perform it. This, however, gave no remedy to any person other than the lessee (*Cavalier* v. *Pope* (1906)). The lessor had the normal duty of care in respect of the condition of his own premises. Thus in *Cunard* v. *Antifyre* (1953) some defective roofing and guttering forming part of the premises retained by the defendant lessor fell on to premises let by him to the plaintiff's husband. The plaintiff suffered personal injuries and recovered damages in negligence from the defendant.

(3) *Builder*

The decision in *Anns* establishing a duty of care binding local authorities as regards the inspection of houses under construction in their area rested in part on a conclusion that the common law immunity from a common law duty of care of a vendor/ or lessor/ builder should no longer apply. According to *Anns* this was so not only in the case where the building caused damage in the form of personal injury or damage to property but also where the building had defects in its construction through the negligence of the builder without causing any further damage. Whether the same limitation applied to the builder's liability as it did to that of the local authority, *i.e.*, that the defects in the house must threaten the health or safety of its occupier, was never finally determined. In any case the matter is now of academic interest because that part of *Anns* which holds the builder liable in the absence of the house damaging person or property has been overruled by *Murphy* v. *Brentwood D.C.* (1990) and *Dept. of the Environment* v. *Thomas Bates* (1990), and it matters not that the house as constructed threatens the safety of its occupants. There is still the possibility of liability on the part of the builder on the basis of *Junior Books* v. *Veitchi* (1982) (*i.e.* voluntary assumption of responsibility to build properly on the part of the builder and reliance on that by the plaintiff) which was not removed from the law by the decision in *Murphy* v. *Brentwood D.C.* (1990) overruling the *Anns* case. A vendor/builder owes a contractual duty to the buyer of a house which consists of a three-fold warranty that the builder will do his work in a good and workmanlike manner with proper materials and that the house when finished will be fit for human habitation (*Hancock* v. *B. W. Brazier* (1966)).

Defective Premises Act 1972

(1) *Vendor*

It should be noted that the position of a vendor, who is not a builder, and who has done no work on or in relation to premises, is not affected by the statute.

(2) *Lessor*

In the case of the lessor of premises, the combined effect of section 4(1), (2) and (4) of the Defective Premises Act is to make the lessor liable in respect of defects in the state of the premises to "persons who might reasonably be expected to be affected by" such defects, for personal injury or damage to their property, provided the lessor has an obligation under the tenancy agreement to keep the premises in repair, or has under the tenancy agreement an express or implied right to enter and do repairs, and provided the lessor knows or ought to know of the defect needing repair. Section 4(1) of the Occupiers' Liability Act 1957 is expressly repealed. The new obligation goes further than section 4(1) of the 1957 Act in that it may be owed to trespassers, it covers cases where a lessor has a mere right to enter and do repairs, and notice of the need for repair by the lessee to the lessor is unnecessary. Under section 4(5) of the Defective Premises Act 1972, statutory obligations to repair premises imposed upon lessors (for example, that arising under Housing Act 1985) are to be treated as being imposed by the tenancy agreement. Where the lessor has a mere right to enter and do repairs, and the obligation to repair is imposed on the lessee by the tenancy agreement, the lessor will not be liable to the lessee if the latter is injured because of defects in the premises due to want of repair.

There is still no liability for the mere letting of a "tumbledown" house in the absence of express terms in the contract creating that liability. And in the absence of a duty in the lessor to repair or a reservation of the right to enter and do repairs in the lease, there is still no liability for injury or damage caused by such a house to persons entering it, although where the house has caused injury or damage to persons outside the premises, liability exists in nuisance or negligence (*Brew Bros.* (*Ltd.*) v. *Snax* (*Ross*) *Ltd.* (1970).

(3) *Builder*

Section 1(1) of the Defective Premises Act 1972 provides that a person taking on work for or in connection with the provision of a dwelling (whether the dwelling is provided by the erection or by the conversion or enlargement of a building) owes a duty—to every person who acquires an interest (whether legal or equitable) in the dwelling to see that the work which he takes on is done in a workmanlike or, as the case may be, professional manner, with proper materials and so that as regards that work the dwelling will be fit for habitation when completed.

Section 1 has become of increased importance now that the House of Lords has held in *Murhphy* v. *Brentwood D.C.* and *Dept. of the Environment* v. *Thomas Bates* that there is no liability in tortious negligence for the mere building of a defective house. The following points may be noted about section 1 as a whole. The liability applies only to work on "dwellings." The liability extends beyond builders to persons such as architects, surveyors and sub-contractors (including, arguably, the installer of ancillary services such as central heating). Under section 1(4)(*a*) the liability is made to apply to developers and under section 1(4)(*b*) to statutory housing providers such as local authorities. The duty under section 1(1)(*b*) extends to all persons who acquire an interest, legal or equitable, in the dwelling, clearly a class which includes non-occupiers. The duty as expressed looks like one of care only, with the exception of the duty to provide proper materials, on which there is authority that it is not discharged merely by purchasing them from a reputable source (*Young & Marten* v. *McManus Childs* (1969)). The concept of unfitness for human habitation may be wider than that of an unsafe house. The cause of action for all persons is complete at the time the dwelling is completed (section 1(5)—not, it should be noted, the date of first purchase). This limitation period is unaffected by the more generous periods of limitation set up by the Latent Damage Act 1986. Section 2 of the Act provides an important exception to liability under section 1 in that it does not apply to dwellings protected by the National House-Building Council scheme. That scheme applies to most new houses and requires that the builder warrant to the purchaser that the house is soundly constructed and that he will remedy any defects in it during the "Initial Guarantee" period of two years from initial purchase and also that he will obtain N.H.B.C. insurance cover against structural defects for a further eight years. The benefit of the scheme is available to both initial and subsequent purchaser.

Section 3(1) of the Act was designed to remove the immunity that vendors and lessors of premises, which they had built or done work on prior to the sale or lease, enjoyed at common law. With the courts' own removal of that immunity, the subsection seems to be on the whole redundant, though it is worth mentioning that it applies to anyone who does work on premises, not merely the vendor or lessor of those premises. It is also clear that the subsection applies only where the building work causes personal injury or damage to property.

Building Act 1984

Under this Act, the Secretary of State for the Environment is empowered by section 1 to make building regulations with respect to the design or construction of buildings and the provision of services, fittings or equipment to buildings for the purpose *inter alia* of securing the health, safety, welfare and convenience of persons in or about the buildings. Section 38(1)(a) provides that breach of a duty imposed by the regulations so far as it causes damage is actionable. "Damage" is defined to include death or personal injury. Liability under section 38(1)(a) is for breach of statutory duty and clearly may be strict. Section 38(3) provides in effect that the section does not affect the bringing of actions for common law negligence in relation to the construction etc. of buildings. Section 38 is one of those sections of the Act which have not yet been brought into force.

Liability of the non-occupier towards the trespasser

The non-occupier did not enjoy the same immunity from liability in negligence towards the trespasser as did the occupier (*cf. Buckland* v. *Guildford Gas, Light & Coke Co.* (1949)). His liability appears to be governed by ordinary principles of negligence.

12. LIABILITY FOR CHATTELS

It is now probably true to say that the law relating to liability for chattels is governed by ordinary principles of negligence. Nevertheless, it requires separate consideration because of the preciseness of the formulation of the manufacturer's duty in *Donoghue* v. *Stevenson* (matched by an equal degree of imprecision about the standard of care required of some other transmitters of chattels) and because a distinction between dangerous and non-dangerous chattels which at one time received some judicial support had never been formally removed from the law, although it is unlikely that it survives. It should be appreciated that liability for chattels is generally concerned with the liability of the person who has put into circulation a dangerous or defective chattel which has caused injury or damage. It is not concerned with the negligent operation of chattels, for example, the negligent driving of a motor car. Where the chattel is capable of being occupied, liability of the occupier of the chattel to an entrant on the chattel who suffers injury because of a defect in the chattel is governed by the rules of occupiers' liability. Some cases might be regarded as turning on ordinary negligence or liability for chattels without any significant difference in the result, for example, the liability of a car owner who allows his vehicle through defective maintenance to become dangerous and who as a result causes injury when driving it.

In considering the liability of those who have put into circulation a dangerous or defective chattel, a useful division may be made between the case of those persons who have manufactured or otherwise done work on the chattel and those who have merely transmitted it. The chief difference between the two lies not in relation to the existence of a duty of care, which will apply in all cases, but in the standard of care required to discharge that duty. The standard required of the mere transmitter of a chattel is less onerous than that of the manufacturer or one who has done professional work on the chattel.

CHATTELS DANGEROUS IN THEMSELVES

The law at one time drew a distinction between the chattel which was dangerous in itself and the chattel which was dangerous by reason of defective construction or maintenance. The dangerous qualities of the former the defendant was assumed to know, and his liability was assessed accordingly. In the case of the latter, however, he was liable only if he had actual knowledge of the dangerous condition of the chattel. The distinction drew judicial criticism, for example, by Scrutton L.J. who did not "understand the difference between a thing dangerous in itself, as poison, and a thing not dangerous as a class but by negligent construction dangerous as a particular thing. The latter if anything seems the more dangerous of the two: it is a wolf in sheep's clothing rather than an obvious wolf." (*Hodge and Sons* v. *Anglo-American Oil Co.* (1922)).

The distinction clearly no longer applies to manufactured articles or those which have been subject to repair, as far as liability of the manufacturer or repairer is concerned. The last case in which it was applied in the case of a mere transmitter of a chattel was *Ball* v. *London County Council* (1949) in which the defendant landlords were held not liable for the installation in the plaintiff's flat of a defective boiler, which exploded and injured the plaintiff, on the ground that the boiler was not known by the defendant to be defective. The likelihood is that the distinction no longer has any force. It is clear, for example, that transmitters of chattels are in certain circumstances required to take care to ascertain defects in those chattels even though the chattel is not dangerous in itself and the defect is not apparent on visual inspection (see, for example, the cases cited under "mere transmitters," especially *Griffith* v. *Arch Engineering* (1968) in which the distinction was rejected).

LIABILITY OF THE MANUFACTURER OF A CHATTEL

Lord Atkin expressed the narrow ratio of *Donoghue* v. *Stevenson* as follows:

> "A manufacturer of products, which he sells in such a form that he intends them to reach the ultimate consumer in the form in which they left him with no reasonable possibility of intermediate examination and with the knowledge that the absence of reasonable care in the preparation or putting up of the products will result in injury to the consumer's life or property, owes a duty to the consumer to take that reasonable care."

The liability of the manufacturer is best treated by considering this formulation in sections.

"Manufacturer"

A similar liability has been applied to the repairer of a motor car (*Stennett* v. *Hancock* (1939)); the person who reconditions the engine of a motor car (*Herschtal* v. *Stewart and Arden* (1940)) and the repairer of a lift (*Haseldine* v. *Daw* (1941)).

"Products which he sells in such a form, etc."

The words "in such a form" do not mean that the goods must reach the consumer in the same container in which they left the manufacturer. They mean that the manufacturer contemplates nothing of substance being done to the goods after they leave him.

"Possibility of intermediate examination"

It is now clear that the mere possibility of intermediate examination of the goods after they have left the manufacturer is not enough; it must also be a reasonable expectation of the manufacturer. Thus, in *Grant* v. *Australian Knitting Mills Ltd.* (1936) the manufacturers argued that their underpants should have been washed before use. Lord Wright dismissed this by saying: "It was not contemplated that they should first be washed." The effect

of failure by the plaintiff consumer to prove compliance with the
second and third requirements of Lord Atkin's formulation seems
to be that there is no liability on the defendant's part at all on the
basis that the absence of these requirements entails there is no
duty of care. This is unsatisfactory. The duty should be regarded as
established merely by showing that the manufacturer has put into
circulation a product involving a foreseeable risk to consumers.
The factors relating to whether the goods remain in the same form
as they left the manufacturer and whether there was a possibility of
intermediate examination raise issues not of duty but of breach,
causation or contributory negligence. This is all the more so now
that in relation to the latter two issues an apportionment of
liability as between the manufacturer and third party or
manufacturer and plaintiff may take place (this was not possible at
the time of *Donoghue* v. *Stevenson* itself). *Kubach* v. *Hollands*
(1937) is a case in which an apportionment of liability between
defendants would have been appropriate whereas the manufacturer
escaped liability. In that case the manufacturer had supplied a
highly dangerous chemical to a distributor who had sold it to a
school. The chemical was mislabelled by the manufacturer as being
a relatively harmless one but the manufacturer had indicated to the
distributor that it should be tested before use. This test was not
carried out and the chemical exploded on use in a chemical
experiment in school and injured the plaintiff. The distributor was
held liable to the plaintiff; the manufacturer was not. The
manufacturer's lack of indication of a dangerous chemical seems on
these facts causally relevant to the plaintiff's injury. The mere
possibility of intermediate examination is, however, clearly not
enough to exonerate the manufacturer—it must be reasonably
contemplated by him (*Griffiths* v. *Arch Engineering*).

A different problem arises where the examination has been
successful in revealing the defect in the goods. Here it seems clear
that, on causal principles, the manufacturer ought to be excused
since to use the goods (or to pass them on) after discovering the
defect seems a clear *novus actus*. So in *Taylor* v. *Rover Car Co.*
(1966), where the plaintiff's foreman discovered a defect in a
hammer manufactured by the defendants but continued to allow it
to be used, the plaintiff's employers were liable to him but the
defendants were not. (To similar effect is *Farr* v. *Butters Bros. &
Co.* (1932) in which the plaintiff himself discovered defects in the

parts of a crane manufactured by the defendants, but nevertheless attempted to assemble it and was killed as a result.) But knowledge of the defect by the plaintiff does not help the manufacturer where there is no safe way of dealing with the chattel, but it is necessary to do so (as in *Denny* v. *Supplies & Transport Co.* (1950)—the plaintiff had to unload badly stowed timber as part of his employment. Although he realised the danger, he recovered in full for the injuries he suffered from the defendants who had stowed the timber because no safe way of unloading the timber existed).

"Ultimate consumer"

These words received an extremely liberal interpretation by the court in *Stennett* v. *Hancock and Peters* (1939) in which it was held that a pedestrian could recover damages from the defendants who were repairers of a lorry. Due to the defendants' negligence in the course of repair the flange of the lorry came apart from the lorry while it was being driven, and struck and injured the plaintiff. In view of this decision, it may be that anyone foreseeably injured because of the defect in the chattel is a consumer within the meaning of the rule.

Standard of care

The standard of care required by the manufacturer is a stringent one. The work of manufacture must be carried out with the care and skill to be expected of a reasonable manufacturer of the product in question. Inspection of the chattel for safety purposes before it leaves the manufacturer's possession is also a normal requirement. The strictness of the law regulating the manufacturer is emphasised by the fact that the existence of a defect in the chattel within a relatively short time of the chattel leaving the manufacturer's possession (*cf. Evans* v. *Triplex Safety Glass Co.* (1936)) raises a case of negligence against the manufacturer based on *res ipsa loquitur*; that the manufacturer does not succeed in rebutting this case by showing a reasonably careful system of manufacture if the likelihood is of negligence by one of his employees in the operation of that system; that if this is so, the plaintiff does not need to identify the negligent employee nor the particular act of negligence involved (*Grant* v. *Australian Knitting Mills* (1936)).

MERE TRANSMITTERS OF THE CHATTEL

The question to be faced is what standard of care applies to the person who merely transmits a chattel without undertaking any sort of work on it. The chief cases to be considered are distributors, retailers, donors, lenders and other bailors of the chattel. A duty of care will exist in every case. The essential question is what is the standard of care required to discharge that duty. Fixing the standard of care is a matter of law but it is not a matter of legal rule and will take into account all the circumstances of the case. So, as in standard of care questions generally, actual decisions do not create binding precedents as to the standard to be applied to a particular class of transmitter of a chattel. Nevertheless there has been a tendency for the courts to speak here in terms of rules of law rather than of application of the standard of reasonableness to particular facts. A line was drawn between gratuitous transfer of the chattel and transfer for reward. In the case of gift, for example, there is nineteenth century authority to the effect that the only liability is for failure to give warning of defects actually known to the donor (*Gautret* v. *Egerton* (1867). This unusually low standard would probably today be rejected. There should at least be liability for failure to notice patent defects in the chattel and for negligence in its safekeeping allowing defects to arise (for example, storage of perishable commodities in such a way as to allow them to perish). Where the transmission of the chattel is for a consideration, the standard required of the transmitter is clearly more onerous. It would clearly comprehend the latter two requirements just mentioned. The chief question is whether the transmitter is also required to undertake careful inspection or testing of the chattel sufficient to establish the existence of defects that are not patent before the chattel leaves his possession. That duty has been imposed upon the seller of a second-hand motor-vehicle (*Andrews* v. *Hopkinson* (1957)), the seller of a chemical to a school (*Kubach* v. *Hollands* (1937)—duty to undertake a test stipulated by the manufacturer), and the distributor of a hair-dye (*Watson* v. *Buckley, Osborne, Garnett & Co.* (1940)—duty to test strength of solution which had been bought from a manufacturer not known to be reputable by the defendant). All three cases present special circumstances and would no doubt be distinguishable from the ordinary case of the seller of new products. (The commercial seller of goods is strictly liable for their condition under warranties as to the quality and fitness for purpose of the goods under section 14 of the Sale of Goods Act 1979. See also, for similar warranties as to the condition of goods in contractual transfers apart from sale of goods, the Supply of Goods and Services Act 1982). In the case of loan of a chattel for a consideration, the courts again have imposed a positive duty to take care to ensure the safety of the chattel before its use by the borrower (*Griffith* v. *Arch Engineering* (1968)—a grinding machine used by plaintiff workman of the sub-contractor; *Wheeler* v. *Copas* (1981)—a ladder used by plaintiff who was a building contractor employed by the defendant).

Generally speaking, an adequate warning of a known danger will be sufficient to discharge the defendant's duty of care even in the case of the manufacturer. Otherwise commercial dealings in substances such as poisons or explosives would be impossible. The rule about warning underlies the case of *Hurley* v. *Dyke* (1979). A second-hand car had been sold in an auction sale on the terms stipulated by the defendant seller that the car was sold "as seen and with all its faults and without warranty." The car was soon resold by the purchaser and then caused a serious injury to the later purchaser because of a defect in its chassis. Plaintiff's counsel conceded that the notice constituted an adequate warning sufficient to cause a reasonable purchaser to carry out his own safety inspection of the car, but argued that this did not apply where the defendant knew of the defect in the car. This argument failed on the facts, since the defendant knew only of a defective carburettor, but two members of the House of Lords (Viscount Dilhorne and Lord Scarman) warned against the assumption that even if the defendant knew of the defect the warning would not have protected him.

NATURE OF DAMAGE RECOVERABLE

Liability for chattels clearly will cover personal injury or damage to property caused by the chattel. It will not normally extend to purely economic loss whether in the form of loss of profit, out-of-pocket expenses or an excessive amount paid for a defective chattel (*Lambert* v. *Lewis* (1982); *Muirhead* v. *Industrial Tank* (1985)), although *Junior Books* v. *Veitchi* (1982) shows that under certain conditions an action may lie, *i.e.* where there is a voluntary assumption of responsibility by the defendant and reliance on it by the plaintiff. (See also *Chaudhury* v. *Prabhakar* (1988) and Chapter 6, under *Hedley Byrne* liability).

The Consumer Protection Act 1987

The Act was passed in order that the United Kingdom should perform its treaty obligations to make English law accord with a Directive on liability for defective products adopted by the E.C. (The Pearson Commission had made a recommendation on similar lines to the Directive, based on the view that the introduction of strict tort liability for defective products would produce little change since the manufacturer who sells his products is already subject to strict liability in contract.

The Act of 1987 on its face introduces strict liability but the defence in section 4(1)(*e*) in relation to design defects seems likely to be interpreted in such a way as to enable the defendant to succeed by showing that reasonable care was taken in the design of the product. As regards production defects where clearly liability is strict, the manufacturer is already subject at common law to what it tantamount to strict liability by the operation of *res ipsa loquitur*.

The gist of the Act is that producers of products are liable for personal injury, or property damage over a certain amount, caused by a defect in the product. The liability is stated in absolute terms but is subject to a number of defences. The producer is defined in section 2(2) as: (a) the manufacturer; or (b) the person who has won or abstracted materials (for example oil, minerals, gravel); or (c) the person who has carried out an "industrial or other process" in relation to a product which has not been manufactured, won or abstracted (for example, agricultural produce—strengthened by section 2(4) which excludes liability in relation to agricultural produce and game where no industrial process have been applied to them). There is plenty of room for argument about the application of (c) to, in particular, farmers. For example, is the production of eggs by battery farming covered? Section 2(2) also imposes liability on the "own brander" of the product and on the importer of the product from outside the E.C. into the E.C. A supplier of the product not within the latter two classes is not liable under the Act, except under section 2(3) for a non-compliance with a request by the injured person to identify the producer as defined in section 2(2) or his own supplier.

Product is defined in section 1(2) as any goods or electricity including property comprised in another product whether as component or raw material. "Goods" under section 45(1) include "substances, growing crops and things comprised in land by being attached to it and any ship, aircraft or vehicle." Components of houses or vehicles are therefore covered, but not in all probability the completed house, though the completed vehicle is covered. Information is not within the definition, but it seems likely that chattels which mechanically provide information such as clocks, speedometers, oil warning-lights and computers would be covered. Live animals are not included.

Damage is defined in section 5 of the Act to include death or personal injury (which presumably would cover nervous shock) and property damage exceeding £275 in amount. The product must be one intended for private use (section 5(3)). Property damage is defined to exclude damage to the product itself or the whole or any part of any product which has been supplied with the product in question comprised in it (section 5(2)).

Defect is defined in section 3 as being present where "the safety of the product is not such as persons generally are entitled to expect". The difficulties invoked by this definition are obvious. In particular, a question arises how far manufacturers are entitled to effect price reductions on the product by eliminating or reducing safety measures or devices. Section 3 specifies criteria for determining the main question, and in particular it may be noted that in (c) the fact that a product has become superseded in terms of safety by a later model is not to be taken as indicative of a defect in it at the time it was produced (different, therefore, where the original is kept in production). This does not cover the case of a drug such as Thalidomide which was clearly unacceptably dangerous at any time, but whose dangers were not appreciated at the time. A defence under section 4(1)(e) would need to be established here by the producer.

The following alternative defences to liability under the Act are recognised by section 4(1): (a) defect attributable to compliance with requirement of law; (b) defendant did not supply the product to another; (c) the supply was non-commercial (as regards (b) and

(c) it must be remembered that mere suppliers are not caught by the Act); (d) defect did not exist when product was put into circulation; (e) the state of scientific and technical knowledge at the relevant time was not such that a producer of products of that sort might be expected to have discovered the defect; (f) defect was wholly attributable to the incorporation of the product into a subsequent product which is defective either because of its design or because the producer of the original product complied with instructions given to him by the producer of the subsequent product.

Section 4(1)(e) is a controversial defence because it is doubtful how far it properly implements the E.C. Directive and because its interpretation could lead to the conclusion that a large part of the "introduced" strict liability arising under the Act is in fact fault-based. Clearly the test for establishing the defence is an objective one, and much will depend upon the meaning given to the words, "might be expected." But it seems quite likely that the defence will be interpreted to allow the producer to escape liability if it proves that the product was produced in accordance with currently accepted scientific, industrial or medical technology. Liability would thus be fault-based, though the legal burden of proof rests on the producer. Under section 6(4) "fault" is deemed to exist on the part of persons liable under the Act even though that liability exists in the absence of fault, the result being that the Law Reform (Contributory Negligence) Act 1945 provisions allowing reduction of damages for contributory negligence are applicable. Apportionment in cases of strict liability on the defendant's part has caused no undue difficulty under that Act.

Any exclusion of liability under the Act by the defendant, contractual or otherwise and whatever the nature of the damage, is rendered void by section 7. The limitation period on liability is dealt with in Chapter 29.

13. EMPLOYERS' LIABILITY

Introduction

It is now necessary to consider the duties which the employer owes at common law towards the persons he employs. The employer's common law duties are now considerably supplemented by the vast number of statutory duties which are imposed upon employers for the protection of employees, particularly in the industrial field. A detailed account of these duties is beyond the scope of this book, and the general topic of breach of statutory duty is postponed to a later chapter.

The common law duties of the employer towards his employees combine with the employer's vicarious liability for the torts of his employees committed in the course of their employment against their fellow employees in such a way that the employer is normally liable where an employee has been injured through negligence at the place of work. At one time this was not so, because under the doctrine of common employment an employer was not vicariously liable for the negligence of one employee committed in the course of his employment and injuring his fellow. The rule of common employment was abolished in 1948, but it has left its traces in the law. Thus, it could be by-passed if the employer was shown to be in breach of a personal duty owed to the employee. So, an employee injured by the negligence of another employee might succeed against an employer for the latter's negligence in choosing that employee. The necessity of placing emphasis upon the employer's personal duties rather than on his vicarious liability no doubt explains the completeness of formulation of such duties and the tendency to regard them as a separate branch of negligence

237

rather than as an example of a duty of care based upon Atkinian proximity. The absence of vicarious liability no doubt also accounts for the personal duties of the employer being construed as non-delegable—they could not be discharged through the medium of his employees or independent contractors, no matter how reasonable such delegation might be. This attribute of non-delegability has survived the abolition of the doctrine of common employment.

As far as his personal duties are concerned, the employer's duty is only to take reasonable care for the safety of his employees. There is no question of his being subject to strict liability at common law, although he may be subject to strict duties imposed by statute. Although the employer clearly has a general duty to take reasonable care for the safety of his employees, it is customary both in decided cases and in works of reference to make a tripartite division of such duty. On the basis of this division the employer must provide (1) competent staff; (2) proper plant, premises and equipment; (3) a safe system of work. These individual duties must now be examined. The employer's duties of care as regards the safety of his workmen while at work include positive duties—they thus represent a further exception to the nonfeasance rule.

Competent staff

The importance of this duty has considerably lessened with the abolition of the doctrine of common employment, since it will normally be possible to rely on the vicarious rather than the personal liability of the employer where the plaintiff has been injured by the negligence of a fellow employee. The duty, however, came to the assistance of the plaintiff in *Hudson* v. *Ridge Manufacturing Co.* (1957). The plaintiff was injured in the course of horseplay committed against him by a fellow worker. The latter was known to be addicted to such behaviour and had several times been reprimanded for it. The employer was held to be in breach of his personal duty to the plaintiff to provide competent staff. In *Hudson* no reliance was placed by the plaintiff on the employer's vicarious liability for the act of the fellow worker and it was generally assumed that on those facts there would have been no vicarious liability, on the ground that the horseplay would have been regarded as being committed outside the course of the fellow worker's employment. The general assumption that horseplay is outside the course of employment was negatived, however, in *Harrison* v. *Michelin Tyre* (1985) in which the employer was held vicariously liable where the worker's action was a piece of horseplay but was nevertheless committed in relation to an act the worker was employed to carry out, *i.e.* the pushing of a truck.

Proper plant, premises and equipment

The employer's common law duty is to take reasonable care to provide proper tools, machinery, working places and premises generally, and to maintain them as such. The duty in respect of equipment has now been statutorily strengthened. *Davie* v. *New Merton Board Mills Ltd.* (1959) had held that the employer's duty to provide proper equipment is satisfied by the purchase of such equipment from a reputable source. So in that case where the plaintiff suffered injury through the use of a tool which had a defect in it because of the negligence of its manufacturer, it was held that the plaintiff's employer was not liable to him since he had purchased the tool from reputable suppliers who themselves had purchased from reputable manufacturers. The law as a consequence of this decision was hard for the employee who received injury in this way and was unable to discover the manufacturer's identity or found the manufacturer not worth suing. Accordingly the Employers' Liability (Defective Equipment) Act 1969 makes the employer liable to the employee where the latter has suffered personal injury in the course of his employment in consequence of a defect in equipment provided by the employer for the purposes of his business, provided that the fault is attributable wholly or partly to the fault of a third party whether the latter is identified or not. The Act thus imposes strict liability upon the employer but only if the employee can prove the defect was due to the fault of a third party. In view of the acceptance in principle of strict liability and the difficulty often involved in establishing fault, it is hard to see why the Act did not go further and make the employer liable for all defects in equipment which cause injury to his employees.

Safe system of work

The distinction between an unsafe system and dangers caused by "isolated and day-to-day acts of the servant of which the master is not presumed to be aware and which he cannot guard against" appears to be one of degree, and is today of vastly reduced importance now that the master is liable for casual acts of negligence committed by an employee against another employee in the course of operating an otherwise safe system of work. It is established that an unsafe system of work may exist in an operation which is to be performed once and for all and may never again arise. *General Cleaning Contractors* v. *Christmas* (1953) is an example of an employer's liability for an unsafe system of work. The defendants required their workmen, who were window cleaners, to work on a narrow sill 27 feet above the ground without instructing them to keep one section of a window open or providing any appliance to enable this to be done. They were held liable to the plaintiff who fell and was injured when the sash of the window fell on his fingers compelling him to release his hold on the other sash. The argument was put to the House of Lords in that case that the plaintiff as an experienced workman knew of the risk of sashes slipping and should have devised a system of work to eliminate the risk. This argument was rejected by Lord Reid in the following words: "Where a practice of ignoring an obvious risk has grown up, I do not think that it is reasonable to expect an individual workman to take the initiative in devising and using precautions." It is the duty of the employer to consider the situation and to devise a suitable system. (The duty extends to ensuring that a safe system of work is safely operated—*McDermid* v. *Nash Dredging Ltd.* (1987)).

Delegability of the duty

The personal nature of the employer's duties means that they are incapable of being discharged through the medium of a third party such as an employee or independent contractor. The duty to provide a safe system of work, for example, is a duty to provide a system that is as safe as reasonable care and skill can make it. That duty cannot be discharged by the mere appointment of a competent employee or contractor to provide the system (*Wilsons and Clyde Coal Co.* v. *English* (1938) confirmed in *McDermid*, *supra*), although it will of course be discharged if the system provided by the employee or contractor is one that is reasonably safe. The duty of the employer here is sometimes described as a duty to see that care is taken, but this conceals the fact that the case may operate as one of strict liability. In the case of delegation to an independent contractor, particularly, the employer's circumstances may dictate that delegation of the duty to the contractor is not only reasonable but necessary, yet the employer is liable for the contractor's negligence. *Davie* v. *New Merton Board Mills* (*supra*) threw doubt on the proposition that in no case could the employer's personal duties be discharged through the medium of an independent contractor. The reasons for the decision of the House of Lords in that case were two: (1) purchase of the tool from a third party was not delegation to an independent contractor; (2) the employer's duty was to provide, not to manufacture, proper equipment and this duty was satisfied by purchasing the equipment from a reputable source. The latter reason opens up the possibility of vicarious performance of certain of the employer's duties through a competent contractor being permissible but it is difficult to say whether this would extend from cases of purchase of equipment (now in any case covered by the 1969 Act) to other contracts, for example, the building of factory premises on the employer's land. In *Sumner* v. *William Henderson & Sons* (1964) it was held that an employer was liable for the negligence of any of a number of independent contractors employed to install an electric cable, purchased by the employer, in his factory, but not liable if the negligence was in the manufacture of the cable.

Duty one of reasonable care

The employer's duty in respect of his employee's safety is, apart from the non-delegability of the duty, one of reasonable care only and not a strict duty. The question whether the employer has committed a breach of duty is decided in exactly the same way as it is in actions of negligence generally. Again, decisions on standard of care in particular situations are not to be taken as binding precedents. Thus there is no automatic obligation on the employer as a matter of law to exhort and urge the wearing of safety clothing and equipment by his employees, though such a duty might be found to exist on the facts of a particular case (*Qualcast* v. *Haynes* (1959)).

Extent of employer's duties

Some of the employer's duties are self-limiting, for example, the duty to provide proper plant and premises and the duty to provide a safe system of work. But it may be doubted how far the duty to provide proper equipment extends. If the workman takes home a defective tool and is injured in using it, can he sue the employer? There may be a limitation that the plaintiff must be acting in the course of his employment, but this is not so in the analogous tort of breach of statutory duty (*infra*). No doubt a line must be drawn which would probably rule out liability in the above example, but it seems difficult to formulate a test other than that the injury must have some reasonable connection with the performance of the plaintiff's duties.

Employees are not the only persons who may be present on the premises of an employer. There may, for example, be persons present employed by the employer's independent contractor or self-employed persons. The nature of the employer's duty to such persons is by no means clear. There is clearly no liability *qua* employer, but there may be liability *qua* occupier or under ordinary principles of negligence. What is not clear is to what extent the employer must take positive action to ensure the safety of such persons, as he must in the case of his own employees. In the analogous tort of breach of statutory duty, persons other than employees have generally been held to be unable to sue the employer for breach of factory safety legislation (see Chapter 19). The Health and Safety at Work Act 1974, has introduced a duty (section 3(1)) on the employer to take reasonable care for the health or safety of such persons, but civil liability for breach of this duty is expressly excluded.

Pearson Commission Report

The Commission recommended no change in the basis of employers' liability to employees. In particular they were against the introduction of strict liability because the present action for breach of statutory duty goes far enough in this direction. This is hard to follow. If strict liability is desirable, it is not sufficiently achieved by the action for breach of statutory duty, which is a hybrid, sometimes involving strict liability but more often operating as a form of statutory negligence. Very similar arguments as to the cost of introducing strict liability apply in the case of employers' liability as exist in the case of products liability. The employer is required under the present law (Employers' Liability (Compulsory Insurance) Act 1969)) to be insured against liability to his employees; any increase in the cost of insurance brought about by introducing strict liability could no doubt be transferred to the consumer at a very low cost per head.

14. TORTS OF STRICT LIABILITY— INTRODUCTION

Strict liability is liability which arises without the necessity for fault on the defendant's part in the form of intentional or negligent wrongdoing. The instances of strict liability in the English law of tort are of a somewhat unconnected nature. Although it might be possible to deduce a principle of strict liability for carrying on an extra-hazardous activity under the rule in *Rylands* v. *Fletcher* (1868) and liability for animals, the courts have refused to recognise any such general principle (*cf. Read* v. *Lyons & Co.*, *infra*, p. 277). The strict liability involved in breach of statutory duty depends upon interpretation of the relevant statute. Vicarious liability for the acts of servants is justified mainly by reason of the fact that the employer is a financially responsible person, whereas the servants who commit the torts while carrying on his business are generally speaking not worth suing. In nuisance and liability for fire there appear now to be only vestigial traces of original strict liability. It must be remembered that other torts, though requiring an intentional act on the defendant's part, may operate as torts of strict liability. Conversion, trespass and defamation are examples.

The Pearson Commission Report disappointingly made little attempt to analyse the merits of introducing strict liability into areas of personal injury traditionally requiring proof of fault. The Commission rejected its introduction for road accidents, chiefly for the reason that strict liability together with the recommended no fault social security-type scheme would place an unfair burden of cost on the motorist. Surely, however, the two should have been considered as alternatives to each other? In the previous chapter of this book it was pointed out that the reason given by the Report for rejecting strict liability in the case of industrial accidents also seems unsatisfactory. Once these two areas of tort are excluded, there was clearly no scope for a general proposal concerning strict liability. The nearest the Report gets to making such a proposal is its recommendation concerning exceptional risks. The Report recommended that liability should be strict in respect of those things or operations which either, by reason of their unusually hazardous nature require close, careful and skilled supervision, the failure of which may cause death or personal injury; or, although normally by their nature perfectly safe, are likely if they do go wrong to cause serious and extensive casualties. In view of the considerable scope for argument about what falls into these categories, the Report wisely recommended a system of listing of dangerous things or activities falling within the two categories by means of statutory instruments under the authority of a parent statute. This form of liability would also co-exist with the existing cases where strict liability exists at common law. It seems safe to conclude that the law would not change greatly if this proposal were implemented. The Commission also favoured the introduction of strict liability into three additional areas: products liability; the liability of an authority to a volunteer for medical research or clinical trial who has suffered severe damage as a result; the liability of the Government or local authority concerned in relation to severe damage suffered by anyone as the result of vaccination which has been recommended in the interests of the community (under the Vaccine Damage Payments Act 1979, the Government is liable to make payment of £10,000 to anyone who is severely disabled as a result of vaccination against certain prescribed diseases. This is, however, not a form of tortious liability). It may be noted that statutory forms of strict liability in tort already exist, for example, section 76 of the Civil Aviation Act 1982, the Nuclear Installations Act 1965, the Merchant Shipping (Oil Pollution) Act 1971, and the Control of Pollution Act 1974. Details of these are beyond the scope of this book.

15. NUISANCE

Much of the confusion that centres round the word "nuisance" in the law of tort is caused by the fact that the term covers two concepts, those of private and public nuisance, which, while not totally dissimilar, are not too closely related. In private nuisance the central idea is that of interference with the enjoyment of the plaintiff's land, generally speaking by the defendant's causing some sort of deleterious invasion of it, for example, by noise, smell, vibrations, water, or chattels. (In *British Celanese* v. *A. H. Hunt* (*Capacitators*) (1969), however, nuisance was found to be established by reason of a *withdrawal* of electric power from the plaintiffs' factory causing a solidification of molten metal in their machinery). Private nuisance derives in the words of Lord MacMillan in *Read* v. *Lyons & Co* (1947), "from a conception of mutual duties of adjoining or neighbouring landowners" (the words were actually spoken in relation to *Rylands* v. *Fletcher* but there is no question they also apply to nuisance). Nevertheless, the tort is not limited to the case of adjacent landowners, although it still requires the plaintiff to be in occupation of land. Private nuisance clearly can be committed from the highway. So it may be private nuisance to picket premises on the highway, actionable at the instance of the occupier (*Lyons & Sons* v. *Wilkins* (1899); *contra*, *Ward Lock* v. *Operative Printers' Society* (1906)—the question is unresolved—(*Hubbard* v. *Pitt* (1976)). So also, private nuisance was found to be committed by the defendant's allowing the use of his premises for prostitution

246

causing the parading of prostitutes in the street opposite the plaintiff's house (*Thompson-Schwab* v. *Costaki* (1956)). Private nuisance may also be committed from the airspace above the plaintiff's land (*Bernstein* v. *Skyviews* (1977)).

Public nuisance derives from the criminal law, its place in the law of tort depending upon the fact that a member of the public who can prove that he has suffered special damage from the defendant's commission of the common law crime of public nuisance may sue the defendant in tort. It does not require the invasion of private land, but the annoyance of the public by such acts as the obstruction of the highway, the pollution of the public water supply, and the keeping of a common gaming-house. The generic concept underlying both forms of nuisance, which may be expressed by saying that the defendant must have acted to the annoyance of another person or persons, is so broad as to be valueless.

The difference in origin of the two torts explains certain differences between them. For instance, the inability to sue in private nuisance for personal injury is explained because that tort protects exclusively the plaintiff's interest in his land; the same limitation does not exist in public nuisance. Generally speaking, however, the courts appear to assume that the two forms of nuisance are governed by similar rules.

PRIVATE NUISANCE

The plaintiff in private nuisance will not succeed merely by proving an interference with the enjoyment of his land by the defendant. He must show that the interference is unreasonable. Private nuisance as a tort has the following attributes. Since it is derived from the action on the case, it lies in general only for indirect, non-trespassory interference with the plaintiff's land. The type of interference required by the tort of private nuisance may be either actual damage to the plaintiff's land or property thereon, or an interference with the enjoyment of such land not accompanied by any actual damage, or both.

The use interfered with by private nuisance may be the normal one of residing on the land and putting it to domestic use, but it is possible for other types of use to be protected, for example, agricultural, commercial or industrial use. The interference may be caused by a variety of different types of invasion: by vibrations, flooding, electricity, fire, smell, noise, dust, sewage, or offensive sights (the basis of the claim in *Thompson-Schwab* v. *Costaki* (1956)).

There is, however, no right to a particular view from one's house, provided that the defendant does not replace this with such an eye-sore that this is in itself a nuisance. Equally, nuisance does not protect a monopoly of view of what takes place within one's land. Thus, in *Victoria Park Racing Co.* v. *Taylor* (1937), the defendant, by broadcasting commentaries of racing held on the plaintiff's premises, which he was able to view from an adjoining building, did not commit nuisance. In *Home Brewery* v. *William Davis* (1987) the court thought that the defendants would have been liable in nuisance for the filling in of their waterlogged land thereby impairing the flow of water from the plaintiffs' through that of the defendants and thereby causing it to be waterlogged, but for the fact that the defendants' action was in the circumstances reasonable. In the absence of an easement, it is difficult to see that the plaintiffs should have been able to establish a nuisance here even if the defendants had acted unreasonably (*Elston* v. *Dore* (1982), an Australian High Court decision, supports the view that this would not be a nuisance).

Private nuisance and other torts

Nuisance has to be distinguished from other torts, with some of which it may overlap. The difference between nuisance and trespass to land is the difference between indirect and direct interference with the plaintiff's land: in theory there can be no overlap between the two torts. But it is arguable that in the case of repeated trespasses of a trivial nature, the plaintiff ought to be able to sue in nuisance, in which case he might recover substantial damages, whereas each particular trespass would support a claim only for small or nominal damages. In *Bernstein* v. *Skyviews* (1977), the court thought that repeated invasions by airflight of the plaintiff's airspace might support a claim for private nuisance, even though each flight was not a trespass.

The differences between nuisance and *Rylands* v. *Fletcher*, which often overlap on the same facts, are dealt with in Chapter 16.

The greatest difficulty is experienced in distinguishing between the torts of nuisance and negligence. Clearly negligence is much wider than nuisance, in the sense that the interests which it protects are not limited to the use and enjoyment of land. Apart from this the following differences exist between the two torts:

(i) In negligence, the plaintiff must establish that the defendant was under a legal duty to take care. In nuisance, there is generally no requirement of a duty of care, though where the nuisance arises by omission to act, the plaintiff must normally show that the defendant has a positive duty of care (*infra*, p. 258).

(ii) Nuisance may be committed intentionally, or, perhaps, without negligence (*infra*, pp. 256–258). It is certain that in nuisance, negligence does not have to be *proved* by the plaintiff, though it may be relevant to show the unreasonableness of the interference.

(iii) It seems unlikely that mere interference with the enjoyment of land would be sufficient to constitute damage for the purpose of an action in negligence.

(iv) In nuisance, the question whether there has been an unreasonable interference must be determined both in the light of the defendant's conduct and of the seriousness of the interference suffered by the plaintiff. In negligence, any damage, however small, is always sufficient to support the action, although the triviality of the anticipated damage may be a factor in the court's decision that the defendant did not need to take precautions against the risk of its occurrence.

Unreasonableness

Interference with the enjoyment by the plaintiff of his land is not, as such, actionable. The plaintiff must show that such interference is unreasonable. The question of unreasonableness in nuisance is Janus-like: the court must consider *both* the conduct of the defendant in creating the interference *and* the effect that such interference has upon the victim, the plaintiff. These factors are not considered in isolation from each other. Thus the fact that the defendant has acted carelessly or maliciously may tip the scales in favour of showing an unreasonable interference, even though the degree of interference may be small. Equally, however carefully the defendant may have acted, if it is proved that the interference is sufficiently unreasonable, he will be liable in nuisance. Besides this, the court may take into account factors external to the parties, such as the locality in which the alleged nuisance takes place. In the light of these factors, the court must then ask itself the question that is central in all nuisance actions, "Is it reasonable that the plaintiff should have to put up with this interference?"

Conduct of defendant

In some cases, the mental state of the defendant may make his conduct nuisance, although, had that mental state been different, nuisance would not have been committed. Where, for example, he is actuated by spite or malice toward the plaintiff, nuisance may be committed for that reason. Thus, in *Christie* v. *Davey* (1893), the plaintiff was a music teacher who held lessons in her house. The defendant, a neighbour, made a variety of noises during these lessons, solely, as the court found, for the purpose of annoying the plaintiff and in retribution for the annoyance which he felt the piano lessons of the plaintiff had inflicted upon him. He was held liable in nuisance. Again in *Hollywood Silver Fox Farm* v. *Emmett* (1936) the defendant was found liable for causing the discharging of guns on his land for the vindictive purpose of interfering with the breeding of the plaintiff's silver foxes, a purpose which he achieved. His argument that the noise he created was only that which a reasonable landowner might create on his land during the course of shooting failed, since his malice defeated that privilege.

It may be that the court would have found, in each case, that the interference was unreasonable also by reason of the annoyance to which it subjected the plaintiff. The nature of the defendant's conduct, however, made it possible to regard his action as unreasonable without reference to the degree to which it interfered with the plaintiff's enjoyment of his land. The two cases are not inconsistent with the earlier decision in *Bradford Corpn.* v. *Pickles* (1895). The right to appropriate water from water percolating in undefined channels beneath the defendant's pond is not, like the right to make a noise on one's land, a right limited by the requirements of reasonableness. It is an absolute right, and the fact that it is exercised maliciously does not make it a nuisance. This has recently been re-emphasised in *Stephens* v. *Anglian Water Authority* (1987) in which it was held that the right could be exercised even though it led to the subsidence of the plaintiff's neighbouring house.

Another factor which may go towards rendering the defendant's conduct unreasonable is that he has not taken reasonable care to prevent the interference of which the plaintiff complains. If a factory emits smell or noise which could be circumvented by some reasonable outlay or trifling precaution by the defendant, this might well determine the court's mind that the interference caused by the smell or noise is unreasonable. On the other hand, the fact that the defendant has taken all reasonable care to prevent the nuisance arising does not necessarily exclude liability. Whether this makes private nuisance a tort of strict liability is discussed below.

Where the defendant is carrying out an activity which has public utility and has taken all reasonable care to prevent a nuisance arising, it is a moot point whether the utility of his activity may have relevance in deciding whether there is liability in nuisance. On the whole the courts have looked with disfavour on an argument based on the public interest. There is no reason, short of legislative authority to that effect, why the public in general should be entitled to draw benefit from an activity which damages one or more private persons. Nor have the courts accepted the lesser option of refusing an injunction against the perpetrator of the nuisance, but awarding damages in lieu of the injunction for anticipated future interference under Lord Cairns' Act (see *Shelfer* v. *London Electric Co* (1895) which lays down restrictive conditions under which damages may be awarded in lieu of an injunction). The clearest expression of the courts' attitude is the Irish case of *Bellew* v. *Cement Co* (1948). The court there issued an injunction against the defendants even though it meant the closing down of the only cement factory in Ireland at a time when the building of houses was of considerable public importance. In *Miller* v. *Jackson* (1977) Lord Denning M.R. held that the public interest in the playing of cricket in the only possible place within the village where it could be played ruled out liability in nuisance created by the repeated hitting of balls into the plaintiff's garden. The majority of the Court of Appeal, however, found private nuisance committed on the facts, but Cumming-Bruce L.J. gave public interest as one of his two reasons for refusing an injunction. In *Kennaway* v. *Thompson* (1980), however, an argument based on the public interest in the continuance of a recreational facility (water-skiing) as a ground for refusing an injunction against the commission of a nuisance was emphatically rejected by a differently constituted Court of Appeal.

There is the authority of Bramwell B. in *Bamford* v. *Turnley* (1862) that "those acts necessary for the common and ordinary use and occupation of land and houses may be done, if conveniently done (*i.e.* reasonably), without subjecting those who do them to an action." He gave as examples, the burning of weeds, the emptying of cesspools and the making of noises during repairs. The principle undoubtedly remains in force but rather as a facet of reasonableness than as an independent rule of law. *Sampson* v. *Hodgson-Pressinger* (1981) illustrates the unusual case of normal, domestic use of property giving rise to liability in nuisance. The first defendant occupied an upper storey flat above that of the plaintiff, which had a roof terrace on which the first defendant was accustomed to walk and to entertain guests. The terrace as constructed was inadequate to stifle the noise of treading feet and conversation. Its use for these purposes was assumed to be an actionable nuisance on the part of the first defendant. The liability in this case of the second defendant landlord is discussed later in this chapter.

Another factor which may influence the court is the temporary nature of the disturbance. In the case, for example, of demolition or construction work on buildings, what might appear an intolerable interference with the plaintiff's enjoyment of his land if committed in perpetuity may be justifiable on the ground that the plaintiff need only suffer it for a short time. The defendant must not however abuse the position and must take reasonable steps to safeguard the plaintiff from unnecessary interference. Thus in *Andreae* v. *Selfridge & Co. Ltd.* (1938), the plaintiff, a hotel owner, recovered damages from the defendants who in the course of demolition operations carried out by them had subjected the plaintiff's premises to an unnecessary amount of noise and dust.

Seriousness of the interference

In *Walter* v. *Selfe* (1851) Knight Bruce V.C. stated the test to be whether the interference was an "inconvenience materially interfering with the ordinary comfort physically of human existence, not merely according to elegant or dainty modes and habits of living, but according to plain and sober and simple notions among the English people." Thus stated it is clear that questions of degree must be resolved in order to decide whether the interference was sufficiently serious. The reports are full of examples of courts' decisions on the seriousness of the interference but as in each case the question is one of fact and degree, these cases will not be catalogued here (a good example is *Halsey* v. *Esso Petroleum* (1961) in which Veale J. found private nuisance established by the defendants in respect of the use of their oil depot, creating an undue degree of noise, smell and the entry into the plaintiff's land of acid smuts).

An unresolved question is whether the degree of interference is taken into account where the plaintiff has suffered damage to his property (*contra*, *Clerk & Lindsell on Torts*, para. 24.04; *pro*, *Street on Torts*, p. 326). Such slight authority as there is supports Street (in *Halsey's* case Veale J. appeared to assess degree in the case of the damage caused by acid smuts; and in the Scottish case of *Watt* v. *Jamieson* (1954) the court found an insufficient interference where the defendant had, by discharging a considerable amount of water periodically from his house through a gable common to his property and to that of the pursuer caused damage to the walls of the pursuer's house). Against this the exclusion of locality as a factor where the interference consists in damage to property justifies the opinion that degree is far less important where actual damage occurs. The justification for its having to be assessed at all may be that in every case of nuisance interference with the *enjoyment* of land must be established. Trivial damage not sufficient to support an action in nuisance is no doubt recoverable in negligence, in which as we have seen the degree of damage is irrelevant.

Locality of nuisance

In *St. Helens Smelting Co.* v. *Tipping* (1865) the plaintiff complained of a nuisance by fumes from the defendants' factory which had caused damage to his shrubs. The defendants argued that, since the locality in question was an industrial one, the plaintiff must put up with the invasion of industrial fumes into his land. The court held, however, that though locality was an important consideration where the alleged nuisance took the form of interference with the occupier's comfort and enjoyment of his land, it was irrelevant where physical damage to property had been occasioned. In the case of this factor, therefore, the distinction between physical damage to property and mere interference with the enjoyment of property is vital. An example of locality influencing the decision that the defendant's act was a nuisance is *Sturges* v. *Bridgman* (1879). In this case the plaintiff was a physician whose use of his consulting room at the foot of his garden was interfered with by noise from the defendant's machinery which he used in his business of confectioner. The court found that the interference was unreasonable in view of the fact that the area was one in which numerous medical practitioners had their consulting rooms. Again in *Halsey* v. *Esso Petroleum Co* (1961) the court based its conclusion that a nuisance existed in part on the fact that the plaintiff's house was in an area that had been zoned residential under planning legislation.

The distinction between physical damage to property and interference with enjoyment

As we saw above, where the plaintiff can establish actual damage to his land or other property, he is seldom required to do more in order to show a sufficient degree of interference for nuisance. It is certain, also, that the locality of the alleged nuisance is then irrelevant. It therefore becomes important to distinguish between what is actual damage for the purposes of the tort and what is a mere interference with the enjoyment of land. This distinction, though easy to state and to appreciate, is not without difficulty. In the first place, the courts insist on visible change in the property and require such change to be palpable to the ordinary observer. Scientific evidence of the damage is therefore excluded, presumably on the ground that if the plaintiff's damage can only be detected by scientists the damage is not sufficiently substantial. But may not such serious damage as the undermining of the foundations of the plaintiff's house be only capable of being established by scientific evidence?

Damage to property includes damage to the land itself, to buildings on the land, to plants and shrubs and to chattels on the land (*Halsey* v. *Esso Petroleum Co. Ltd.* (1961)). It appears to exclude financial damage such as loss of the plaintiff's business profits, or depreciation in the value of his land. In the case of the latter this is not surprising. If this were allowed to rank as damage to property, for the purpose of the rule, the distinction would lose most of its foundation, since in few cases in which there is a substantial interference with the comforts of the occupier will his property retain its value.

Unusually sensitive plaintiffs

Where the plaintiff has put his land to some special use, nuisance will not lie for interference with such use if it is shown that the amount of protection required goes beyond that required by persons generally. So, in *Robinson* v. *Kilvert* (1889) it was held that nuisance was not available where heat rising from the defendant's flat damaged brown paper manufactured by the plaintiff on his premises. There was no allegation that the heat was excessive, and the process of manufacture was exceptionally sensitive to heat. Opinions clearly may differ as to what is a special use. In *Bridlington Relay Ltd.* v. *Yorkshire Electricity Board* (1965) the court said *obiter* that the reception of television by the private householder was a special use of land. In the same case it was doubted *obiter* whether nuisance would ever lie for interference with a purely recreational use of land. Both opinions are clearly debatable, and on the reception of television, a Canadian case has reached a contrary conclusion (*Nor-Video Services* v. *Ontario Hydro* (1978)). The rule as to extra-sensitivity again is a facet of reasonableness rather than an absolute rule. It has already been pointed out how malice by the defendant alters the picture in the plaintiff's favour.

Once nuisance has been established, the plaintiff can recover for interference with a special use. For example in *McKinnon Industries* v. *Walker* (1951) the plaintiff's injunction against the emission of sulphur dioxide from the defendants' premises which entered his own extended to the damage caused to the plaintiff's orchids even though it was accepted that they were hypersensitive. It is not clear, however, whether the special use needs to be foreseeable under the normal rule for remoteness of damage or whether the tortfeasor takes the victim as he finds him and is liable for all the damage stemming from the nuisance.

Damage

The generally-held view that nuisance is actionable only on proof of damage must be understood in the sense that the plaintiff does not have to show physical damage to his property to succeed—any

substantial interference with his enjoyment of his land will suffice.
Even where the requirement of damage is stated in this way, it is
difficult to reconcile certain cases on projections with it. In *Fay* v.
Prentice (1845) the court held that nuisance was established in
relation to a cornice on the defendant's building which projected
over the plaintiff's land. The plaintiff attempted to prove actual
damage to his land through rain-water dripping from the cornice
but failed to do so. Nevertheless the defendant was held liable
since damage was to be presumed from the mere overhanging of
the cornice. This looks very like saying that in cases of this sort
nuisance is actionable *per se*.

The plaintiff in private nuisance does not appear to be able to
recover for his personal injuries. The explanation generally given
for this, that private nuisance protects only the plaintiff's interest
in the enjoyment of his land, does not seem adequate in a case
where there is an interference with enjoyment leading to personal
injury (where, for example, fumes cause physical illness). Certainly
damage to chattels is recoverable in private nuisance, not only
where there is a sufficient degree of interference to constitute
nuisance apart from the damage to chattels (*Halsey* v. *Esso
Petroleum Co.* (1961)), but also where there is an isolated escape
producing damage to chattels (*British Celanese* v. *A. H. Hunt*
(1969)). It is not clear why this distinction should be drawn
between personal injury and damage to chattels. The rule is in any
case not well settled, resting largely on dicta of Lord MacMillan in
the House of Lords in *Read* v. *Lyons* (1947) which were *obiter* and
spoke about liability under *Rylands* v. *Fletcher* (Chapter 16).

Strict liability in nuisance

Differences between the torts of nuisance and negligence have
already been noted. In this section, the question will be examined
when, if ever, private nuisance operates as a tort of strict liability.
Nuisance differs from negligence in that most nuisances are of a
continuing nature whereas the damage complained of in negligence
generally occurs once and for all. This fact means that in the
majority of nuisance actions the defendant either knows of the
nuisance (in which case he may be regarded as intending it) or
should be aware of it (in which case he is negligent). *Davey* v.
Harrow Corporation (1958) suggested the possibility of liability
arising for a continuing nuisance even before the defendant knows

or should know of it, but the Court of Appeal in *Solloway* v. *Hampshire C.C.* (1981) in dealing with a similar nuisance, *i.e.* the entry into the plaintiff's land of roots from the defendant's trees, insisted upon proof of fault on the defendant's part by showing that he either knew or ought to have known of the possibility of the entry of the roots.

Two other situations may give rise to the possibility of strict liability. The first is the case of the non-continuing nuisance, or nuisance created by the isolated escape. It is settled that an action in nuisance will lie for such an escape provided the escape is the result of a state of affairs of some permanency on the defendant's land (for example, defective electric wiring causing an escape of fire (*Spicer* v. *Smee* (1946); defective insulation in electric cables causing volatised gas to escape and explode (*Midwood* v. *Manchester Corporation* (1905)). If an isolated escape of this sort is actionable in nuisance in the absence of negligence by the defendant, there is no difficulty in regarding private nuisance as a tort of strict liability. The case law, however, does not point firmly in that direction. In *Midwood* the defendants were found to be negligent, but the court thought that a nuisance would have existed apart from negligence. In *Spicer* v. *Smee* the court found the defendant liable either on the ground that the defect in the wiring was caused by the negligence of an independent contractor for whose acts the defendant was responsible, or, if not, it was a defect of which the defendant ought to have known. In *British Celanese* v. *A. H. Hunt (Capacitators)* (1969), Lawton J. held the defendants liable in nuisance for an escape of strips of metal foil from their factory premises which by settling on bus-bars in a nearby power station caused a power failure and a consequential solidification of metal in the plaintiffs' machines. The defendants were also held liable in negligence but Lawton J. did not rely on that in holding the defendants liable also in nuisance. In strict theory the present position seems to be governed by the ruling of the Court of Appeal in *Midwood*, but that authority is a slender one and out of line with the present current of authority in nuisance cases (including the latest decision *Home Brewery* v. *William Davis* (1987)—see earlier this chapter). The second case is that of the nuisance which arises initially without fault on the part of the occupier and is allowed to continue. It now seems clearly settled that whether the nuisance arises from the act of a third party or from a natural condition, the defendant is only liable if he can be shown to be at fault in failing to remove the nuisance. The matter is dealt with in the next section.

One clear instance of strict liability in nuisance is provided by the rule in *Wringe* v. *Cohen* (1940) discussed below, at p. 271. It seems likely, however, that this form of liability is in public nuisance only, and is based on the necessity of protecting users of the highway from the dangers that arise from unsafe constructions on the highway.

The fact that the defendant has been held liable in nuisance even though he has taken reasonable care to prevent it arising does not render nuisance a tort of strict liability, although this is probably one of the main reasons for its being regarded as such. This is because the defendant has the option of avoiding liability merely by desisting from the nuisance-producing activity. If he continues with it knowing of its effects, his liability can hardly be regarded as strict. In *Rapier* v. *London Tramways* (1893), for example, the plaintiff complained of a nuisance by smell created by the overcrowding of horses in the defendant's stables. The court refused to accept the defendant's argument that he had taken all possible precautions to prevent the nuisance. "If they cannot have 200 horses together, even where they take proper precautions, without committing a nuisance, all I can say is, they cannot have so many horses together" (*per* Lindley L.C.J.). (It is of interest to note that in *R.H.M. Bakeries* (*Northern*) v. *Customs and Excise Commissioners* (1985) the House of Lords decided that *culpa* (*i.e.* fault) is necessary for the creation of a private nuisance under Scots law.)

Failure to remedy a nuisance

The liability of the occupier on whose land a nuisance has arisen without any fault on his part has caused problems. Does he have to take steps to remove the nuisance, and, if so, what is the extent of his obligation? Although once complicated, the law on this point seems now relatively easy to state as the result of three decisions of the higher courts. In *Sedleigh-Denfield* v. *O'Callaghan* (1940) the House of Lords held that an occupier of land who had knowledge of a nuisance created there by a trespasser had a duty, in so far as he was able, to remove it. If he failed to do so, he was liable for continuing or adopting the nuisance. It should be noted that removal of the nuisance involved the simple task of placing a grid over a culvert-pipe to prevent the accumulation of refuse, and the judgments of the House do not explore the extent of the occupier's obligations. In *Goldman* v. *Hargrave* (1967) the defendant, a landowner in Western Australia, discovered that a redgum tree on his land had caught fire. He decided to fell the tree and let the fire burn itself out, but a sudden change of wind caused the fire to spread to the plaintiff's neighbouring land and cause damage there. The fire could have been extinguished at minimal expense to the defendant by the use of water. Holding the defendant liable in nuisance, the Privy Council did so on the basis that liability in nuisance was in this situation indistinguishable from liability in negligence. A duty to take careful action to remove the nuisance had to exist. There was no rule that such duty could not exist in the case of conditions arising naturally on land. But whether the duty existed and the extent of it should take into account the means and resources of the particular occupier on whose land the nuisance has arisen. If, for example, the only way of removing the nuisance was through expensive works, no duty might exist at all, except to invite the assistance of neighbours in dealing with the problem. *Goldman* v. *Hargrave* has been followed by the Court of Appeal in *Leakey* v. *National Trust* (1980). The defendants owned and occupied land on which existed a hill known as the Burrow Mump. Because of its soil base, it was "peculiarly liable to cracking and slipping as a result of weather." The defendants knew of this but had refused to undertake repairs, with the result that the plaintiff's land suffered damage on a number of occasions. The defendants were held liable in nuisance, their means being more than sufficient to undertake the necessary protective work.

It may now be assumed that the same principles determine liability whether the nuisance arises naturally or through the act of a third party. All three cases have concerned occupiers with actual knowledge of the nuisance, but dicta in the *Sedleigh-Denfield* case suggested that the occupier is liable if he ought to have known of the nuisance.

It should be mentioned here that the former doubt that existed about whether there was any obligation to remedy nuisances arising naturally did not affect structural premises. The occupier of such premises has a duty of care to persons outside the premises to keep them in good repair (see *Payne* v. *Rogers* (1794); *St. Anne's Well Brewery* v. *Roberts* (1929); *Bradburn* v. *Lindsay* (1983)). His liability for failure to do so lies in nuisance or negligence.

Who can sue in nuisance?

The plaintiff in nuisance must, with rare exceptions (*cf. Newcastle-under-Lyme Corporation* v. *Wolstanton Ltd.* (1947)), show that he was in occupation of land affected by the nuisances under some legal or equitable title. So the tenant of land may sue in nuisance, but his wife and children resident with him are excluded. Similar considerations no doubt will determine the ability of a licensee with exclusive occupation to sue as were indicated in connection with trespass to land. A reversioner may sue if he can show that his interest in the land has been affected (where, for example, the nuisance has caused permanent damage to the land).

Who can be sued in nuisance?

(1) *Creation; authorisation of nuisance*

The person who creates a nuisance on land is liable although he may have given up occupation of the land, and cannot enter it in order to remove the nuisance. It is, however, an unsettled question whether the creator must have been in occupation or control of the land at the time of the creation. A dictum of Devlin J. in *Southport Corporation* v. *Esso Petroleum Co. Ltd.* (1953) supports the view that a nuisance can be created by a licensee or even a trespasser. In principle this seems correct.

The person who authorises the commission of a nuisance by another is also liable for creating that nuisance. Where a landlord let a field, knowing it was to be used as a lime quarry, he was held liable for authorising the nuisance created by working the quarry, since it was clear that such working would almost inevitably create a nuisance (*Harris* v. *James* (1876)). Also in *Sampson* v. *Hodgson-Pressinger* (1981) the second defendant had taken an assignment of the reversion of a lease of a flat knowing that the mode of construction of the roof terrace which had been built by the assignor of the reversion was causing the commission of a nuisance by the tenant. He was held liable in nuisance on the basis that he had authorised it, since he occupied in relation to the tenant precisely the same position as his predecessor in title, whose actions clearly amounted to an authorisation of the nuisance. In *Tetley* v. *Chitty* (1986) a landlord was held liable for authorising a nuisance by the tenant in permitting "Go Kart" racing on the premises. This was particularly likely to cause a nuisance but the court indicated the possibility that mere reasonable forseeability of the nuisance would be enough. That the authorisation cases mainly concern landlord and tenant is because the landlord surrenders control of the premises at the commencement of the lease, so that he cannot be regarded as "continuing" a nuisance begun by the tenant (though a right of re-entry in the lease where the tenant has created a nuisance might influence a different result). In general, however, the landlord's liability must be assessed at the start of the lease, and it must therefore be shown that he expressly or impliedly authorised the nuisance. Express prohibition against committing a nuisance contained in the lease was enough to excuse the landlords in *Smith* v. *Scott* (1973)—a local authority which had let a property to a problem family was held not liable for nuisances arising from general harassment of the plaintiffs, their neighbours, since the tenancy agreement prohibited the creation of a nuisance by the tenant. It is tempting to explain the decision on grounds not contained in the judgment, *i.e.* that the authority had a statutory obligation of housing persons, and that provided it exercised its powers in good faith it would be immune from an action in negligence on the principles laid down in *Anns* v. *London Borough of Merton* (1977). But, as we shall see later in the chapter, that immunity does not seem to apply in cases of nuisance.

(2) *Continuation, adoption of nuisance*

There is liability for continuing a nuisance created by another person if the defendant merely allows it to continue; for adopting it if he uses the condition causing the nuisance for his own purposes. The principle is similar to that considered in relation to failing to remedy a nuisance arising naturally on land with the difference that here a liability in nuisance already exists in another person, whereas in the case of failure to remedy a natural condition there is no such original liability. *Sedleigh-Denfield* v. *O'Callaghan* (1940) was a case of adopting a nuisance. The nuisance had been created by a trespassing third party by laying a culvert-pipe on the defendants' land, which had become blocked by leaves, causing a flood on the plaintiff's land. The defendants made use of this pipe for drainage, and were therefore found to have adopted the nuisance. As in the case of failure to remedy a natural condition, the defendant is not liable in the absence of fault on his part. *Page Motors* v. *Epsom and Ewell B.C.* (1981) is an example of liability for continuing a nuisance. The defendant council had for five years permitted gypsies to trespass on their land and create a nuisance to the adjoining occupiers, the plaintiffs. The council was held liable for the nuisance, their responsibility for it and the damages payable to be assessed from a point in time a year after the original entry of the gypsies. Liability for continuing a nuisance may also be established in relation to nuisances created by a predecessor-in-title of the defendant, though here again there is the requirement that the defendant either knows or ought to know of the nuisance. (*St. Anne's Well Brewery* v. *Roberts* (1929)).

(3) *Vicarious liability*

There is of course liability on the part of a master whose servant has created a nuisance in the course of his employment. Whether there is liability for a nuisance created by an independent contractor is to some extent bound up with the question whether nuisance is a tort of strict liability and is not completely settled. The courts rely on the principle that the employer is liable if the work commissioned created a particular risk of the creation of a nuisance (*Bower* v. *Peate* (1876)—risk of loss of support to plaintiff's land through excavations carried out on the defendant's land; *Matania* v. *National Provincial Bank* (1906)—risk of nuisance by noise and dust arising from building work). What is not clear is whether the contractor must be at fault in creating the nuisance.

(4) *Landlord and tenant*

Special rules govern the respective liabilities of the landlord and tenant for nuisances created by the condition of the demised premises. The rules have become complex, largely because liability may exist under three separate heads, for failure to repair arising from negligence, under section 4 of the Defective Premises Act 1972, and under the strict liability imposed by the case of *Wringe* v. *Cohen* (1940). The latter case imposes strict liability in respect of defects arising through want of repair in premises situated on the highway. Its substance will be considered under public nuisance of which it appears to be an example, but something must be said about it in this connection.

The tenant as occupier must take reasonable care to keep the premises in good repair. He is liable to persons outside the premises in negligence if they are injured through his failure to maintain the premises in good repair, and in negligence or private nuisance if they receive damage to property as a result of the failure. He is also strictly liable for defects arising from want of repair under the rule in *Wringe* v. *Cohen*. The fact that the landlord has covenanted to repair does not relieve the tenant of liability to third parties who are not bound by the contract. On the other hand, this would be a good case for a full indemnity of the tenant by the landlord.

There are clearly many reasons of policy and equity for also holding landlords liable in respect of nuisances on the premises even though they do not occupy them. The landlord is liable in the following circumstances:

(i) He is liable in nuisance or negligence to a third party injured, or whose property is damaged, outside the premises if he knew or ought to have known of the nuisance at the commencement of the lease (*Brew Brothers Ltd.* v. *Snax* (*Ross*) *Ltd.* (1970). In such a case he is not excused where he has taken a repairing covenant from the tenant—otherwise he could defeat his obligations by letting to a man of straw.

(ii) He has a duty of care to "all persons who might reasonably be expected to be affected by defects in the state of the premises" (which, of course, includes persons outside the premises) under section 4 of the Defective Premises Act, provided two conditions are fulfilled. The defect must be one of which he knows or ought to know. He must have an obligation under the lease to carry out repairs. This requirement is satisfied by express or implied provision in the lease itself, by obligations to repair arising under statute (for example, under the consolidating Housing Act 1985), or even where the lease gives the landlord an express or implied right to enter and do repairs.

(iii) He is strictly liable in nuisance under the rule in *Wringe* v. *Cohen* for defects arising from want of repair in premises situated on the highway, if he has covenanted to repair (*Wringe* v. *Cohen*), or if he has reserved, expressly (*Wilchick* v. *Marks and Silverstone* (1943)) or impliedly (*Mint* v. *Good* (1951)), the right to enter and do repairs. The rule in *Wringe* v. *Cohen* probably extends, also, to breach of the obligation to repair imposed by the Housing Act 1985.

Defences to private nuisance

Prescription

The right to commit a nuisance may be acquired by prescription, that is, by 20 years' exercise of the acts constituting the nuisance, provided that this exercise is *nec vi, nec clam, nec precario* the owner of the servient estate (neither done violently, nor secretly, nor by his permission). The content of the nuisance must be capable of existing as an easement. Whether it is or not is a question that the law of real property decides. It was stated *obiter* in *Sturges* v. *Bridgman* (1879) that the right to cause vibrations could be acquired by prescription, but this is open to doubt (and see Megarry and Wade, *Law of Real Property* (5th ed.), p. 908, where the case is criticised).

Conduct of the plaintiff

It is no defence that the plaintiff acquired the land with knowledge of the nuisance existing there, *i.e.* that he "came to the nuisance." In *Miller* v. *Jackson*, however, one of the reasons of Cumming-Bruce L.J. for refusing the plaintiff an injunction was that she had come to the nuisance, since she knew about the playing of cricket on the field adjacent to her property before she acquired it. But if coming to the nuisance is to have this effect, the properties of many persons who have not come to the nuisance will be rendered less marketable. The fact that they have a remedy at law does not appear a good answer to this. As *Sturges* v. *Bridgman* illustrates, the fact that the nuisance only arises because the plaintiff has put his land to some particular use is not a defence, provided that this is not a special use which nuisance would not protect. Once the nuisance has been established, the normal duty in tort to take reasonable steps to mitigate damage no doubt applies. But the plaintiff need only take such action as is reasonable and it would seldom lie in the mouth of the defendant to argue that the plaintiff could by the incurring of expenditure protect himself against the nuisance.

Consent may be a defence to nuisance. In *Kiddle* v. *City Business Properties Ltd.* (1942) it was held that the tenant of part of premises consents to run the risk of nuisances due to the condition of the premises retained by the landlord provided there is no negligence on the part of the latter; so in that case the plaintiff tenant could not succeed in nuisance when the landlord's gutter became flooded and water poured into the plaintiff's premises, damaging his stock.

The definition section of "fault of the plaintiff" in the Law Reform (Contributory Negligence) Act 1945 defines it as an act or omission which would, apart from the Act, give rise to the defence of contributory negligence. There is consequent doubt whether contributory negligence can ever operate as a defence to nuisance, since it does not seem to have been available prior to the 1945 Act. Even if it is capable in law of so operating, the facts upon which it is capable of doing so seem unlikely to arise. It is not contributory negligence to "come to the nuisance," nor to put the land to the use with which the nuisance interferes.

Act of God; act of a stranger

These defences assume a tort of strict liability and their general absence in cases on nuisance and presence in cases on *Rylands* v. *Fletcher* which is undoubtedly a tort of strict liability, tend to confirm the view that nuisance is not a tort of strict liability.

Statutory authority

The effect of the case law concerning the defence of statutory authority in nuisance was summarised as follows by Webster J. in *Northwestern Water Board* v. *Department of Transport* (1983):

(1) In the case of the statutory duty, the defendant is not liable in nuisance for carrying out the duty, in the absence of negligence on his part, and it makes no difference that he is made expressly liable for nuisance by the statute, or is expressly not exempted from that liability;

(2) In the case of the statutory power, the defendant is not liable, in the absence of negligence, for a nuisance created by the exercise of the statutory power if the statute expressly excludes liability in nuisance or is silent on the point;

(3) The defendant is liable for a nuisance created in the exercise of a statutory power even in the absence of negligence, where the statute expressly makes him liable in nuisance or expressly does not exempt him from liability in nuisance. This aspect of the judgment of Webster J. was expressly approved by the House of Lords on appeal, although his judgment was reversed on another point.

Clearly, statutory authority is no defence where the defendant has been negligent and the defendant who relies on statutory authority has the onus of showing that he took due care (*Manchester Corporation* v. *Farnworth* (1930)). The rules laid down by Webster J. assume that nuisance may operate as a tort of strict liability and it has been shown already that in private nuisance that is seldom if ever the case. It seems established that a statutory authority to execute public works conferred on a statutory undertaker will not be interpreted so as to confer discretionary power upon him to create a nuisance if it can be prevented by reasonably practicable means (*Manchester Corporation* case) This is so even if the undertaker purports to be acting in the public interest. The undertaker is therefore not immune from liability in relation to decisions which weigh in the balance the public interest in creating the nuisance against the private interests of the persons subject to it. In this respect the nuisance cases form an exception to the general case of powers conferred on public bodies (see, especially, the judgment of Lord Diplock in *Home Office* v. *Dorset Yacht* (1970) and of the court in *Fellowes* v. *Rother D.C.* (1983)). The reason for this exception was stated in *Fellowes* to be that an authority to execute works conferred by private Act of Parliament on statutory undertakers could not be interpreted as conferring a power to interfere with existing property rights even if the undertaker believed in good faith that this was in the public interest. It is nevertheless difficult to see the justification for this exception where the undertaker is a public body whose actions must be dictated by the public interest and there is earlier Court of Appeal authority to the effect that such a body may legitimately exercise its discretion to affect property rights if it believes it to be in the public interest to do so (*Marriage* v. *East Norfolk Rivers Catchment Board* (1950)). That case, however, seems to conflict with the principle accepted by the House of Lords in *Manchester Corporation* v. *Farnworth* (1930), which requires the defendant to show that the nuisance was the inevitable result of carrying out the statutory authority (a burden discharged in *Allen* v. *Gulf Oil Refining Co.* (1981)—specific power to operate oil refinery excused nuisance which was the inevitable result of that operation; *cf. Metropolitan Asylum District Hospital* v. *Hill* (1881)—a general power to construct hospitals did not authorise the construction of a smallpox hospital where it would create a nuisance).

Fires Prevention (Metropolis) Act 1774
The effect of this statute upon actions in nuisance will be considered in Chapter 17.

Remoteness of damage in private nuisance
In *The Wagon Mound* (No. 2) (1966) the Privy Council held that, in order to establish public nuisance, the plaintiff must show that the infringement of which he complains is a foreseeable consequence of the defendant's act. There seems little reason to doubt that the foreseeability test for deciding questions of remoteness of damage will apply also in private nuisance.

Remedies

Damages
The plaintiff is entitled to compensation for the damage he has suffered as a result of the nuisance. Thus he may recover for physical damage to his property, for depreciation in the value of his property, and for business loss resulting from the nuisance. In the case of the latter, the plaintiff may not recover the whole amount of the loss if the court considers that some loss would have been suffered even though no actionable nuisance had been committed. Thus in *Andreae* v. *Selfridge & Co. Ltd.* (1938), the court quantified the loss of custom which might have been

expected had the defendant's interference been reasonable, and this amount was deducted from the total damages. The reasoning of this case would also seem to apply to damages for depreciation of the plaintiff's land.

Where the nuisance is a continuing one, the award of damages in an action for the nuisance does not bar subsequent actions, since a cause of action in respect of the nuisance arises from day to day so long as it persists. It was not possible at common law for the court to award damages for anticipated future loss caused by a continuing tort, but this deficiency was made good by Lord Cairns' Act 1858 which allows the award of damages in addition to or in substitution for an injunction. The original Act has been repealed but its present day successor is section 50 of the Supreme Court Act 1981.

Injunction

It is common for the plaintiff in nuisance to ask for an injunction against further continuance of the nuisance by the defendant. This may be combined with a claim for damages. The injunction is a discretionary remedy and in some cases of actionable nuisance may be refused by the court (see, for example, *Att.-Gen.* v. *Sheffield Gas Consumers* (1853) where an injunction was refused on the ground that the nuisance would only be repeated at long intervals and would on the occasion of each repetition be of short duration—*a fortiori* where the nuisance is merely temporary). The court may grant a *quia timet* injunction in cases where no nuisance has actually been committed by the defendant, but the commission of one by him in the future is reasonably apprehended by the plaintiff. Damages may be awarded under Lord Cairns' Act 1858 in substitution for an injunction, even a *quia timet* injunction— although this leads to the startling conclusion that one who has suffered no tort may recover damages (*Leeds Industrial Co-operative* v. *Slack* (1924)). Generally, however, the courts are reluctant to countenance the compulsory expropriation of the plaintiff that an award of damages in lieu of an injunction against a nuisance represents. *Shelfer* v. *City of London Electric Lighting Co* (1895) which laid down restrictive conditions upon the exercise of the power, in particular that the injury to the plaintiff's rights must be small and capable of being adequately compensated by a money payment, is still regarded as stating the law.

PUBLIC NUISANCE

A public nuisance is, in the words of Romer L.J. in *Att.-Gen.* v. *P.Y.A. Quarries* (1957):

> "any nuisance 'which materially affects the reasonable comfort and convenience of life of a class of Her Majesty's subjects.' The sphere of the nuisance may be described generally as the 'neighbourhood'; but the question whether the local community within that sphere comprises a sufficient number of persons to constitute a class of the public is a question of fact in each case."

This definition makes it clear that no absolute line can be drawn between public and private nuisance so that overlapping between the two may exist. So, in the above case, a nuisance by the quarrying operations of the defendants which caused vibrations and dust to affect houses in the vicinity was held to be a public nuisance; clearly on the facts the individual householders could have sued in private nuisance. In fact an action in public nuisance by a private individual may not have succeeded on these facts because of the rule that the plaintiff in public nuisance must show damage to himself greater than that suffered by the public generally. The person who sues in public nuisance on the basis of special damage to himself arising from the nuisance is suing in tort, but there is also the possibility of bringing civil proceedings not based on tort but brought in the public interest to restrain the defendant by means of an injunction from committing the common law crime that public nuisance represents. Proceedings of that sort are brought either by the Attorney-General himself or by a private individual suing in the name of the Attorney-General and with his consent (on the "relation" of the person suing, hence the name, relator action).

Basis of liability

In order to establish liability for the creation of public nuisance it will be necessary to establish fault in the form of unreasonable conduct on the part of the defendant. It is not a public nuisance if, for example, one's car breaks down in the public highway and causes an obstruction there, if this happens without negligence on one's own part (*Maitland* v. *Raisbeck* (1944)). A question exists whether it is of any assistance to the plaintiff to establish the commission of a public nuisance when suing for damage allegedly caused by the defendant's negligence. In *The Wagon Mound* (No. 2) (*supra*, p. 144), the Privy Council found that, although the charterers committed the crime of public nuisance by discharging the oil into the harbour, their liability in tort depended upon whether they should have foreseen the risk of fire. Further, although Lord Reid appeared to regard the question of liability as turning on whether the fire was a foreseeable consequence of the nuisance, in deciding this question he took into account all the factors relevant to deciding whether a person has committed a breach of duty of care (*supra*, Chapter 7). On this approach, it seems that the "wrongfulness" of the conduct involved in committing a public nuisance is irrelevant to the question of liability in the tort. In order to succeed the plaintiff must prove the requirements of the tort of negligence, in particular, that of breach of a duty of care causing foreseeable damage. If that is so, the plaintiff appears to achieve nothing by relying on public nuisance—proving the nuisance merely goes towards showing that the defendant acted unreasonably. Even if this is so there may be advantages to suing in public nuisance. For example, there is no difficulty about recovering damages for purely economic loss as mere inconvenience as special damage, and in relation to buildings situated on the highway, liability under the tort is strict.

Special cases of public nuisance

(1) *Obstruction of the highway*

This is the most common type of public nuisance. The public have the right of passage along the highway. Interference with this right by obstructing the highway is a public nuisance. The defendant's use of the highway must be unreasonable in order to amount to an actionable nuisance. It is not an unreasonable use of the highway if an obstruction is created without fault provided it is not then unreasonably maintained in existence (*Maitland* v. *Riasbeck* (1944)). Nor is it unreasonable to create temporary obstructions in the course of exercising the right of passage, for example, by parking a car for a short time; not so, however, where the defendant parked a lorry for several hours at night on the public highway (*Dymond* v. *Pearce* (1972)). Whether the causing of a crowd to collect on the highway constitutes a public nuisance depends upon the circumstances of the case. Where the collection of the crowd is merely testimony to the success of the defendant's business and there is no other way of conducting that business, there is no public nuisance (*Silservice* v. *Supreme Bread* (1949)— daily queues to buy the defendant's fresh bread). Where the accumulation of people is avoidable, for example, by the defendant's opening his doors earlier to a theatre queue (*Lyons* v. *Gulliver* (1914)), or by his selling ice-cream inside his shop rather than through the shop window (*Fabbri* v. *Morris* (1947)), public nuisance will be established.

(2) *Buildings and projections on or over the highway*

In *Wringe* v. *Cohen* (1940) the Court of Appeal held that "if owing to want of repair, premises on a highway become dangerous and therefore a nuisance, and a passer-by or neighbouring owner suffers damage by their collapse, the occupier, or the owner if he has undertaken the duty of repair, is answerable whether he knew or ought to have known of the danger or not." The defendant landlord was therefore held liable for the collapse of the demised premises, which he had covenanted to repair, on to the plaintiff's premises. It seems fairly certain that the ratio is limited to public nuisance, and that where there is no element of danger to the highway the decision does not apply. This is supported by the fact that liability exists under the rule for personal injury (*Mint* v. *Good* (1951); *Wilchick* v. *Marks* (1934)) whereas private nuisance does not allow the recovery of damages for personal injury. The strict liability laid down by the case is of a somewhat special kind, since it only applies where the danger arises through want of repair, not through some secret, unobservable process of nature, nor through the act of a trespasser (*Cushing* v. *Walker & Son Ltd.* (1941)—enemy action caused tile to fall from the roof). Liability is strict, therefore, only where the need for repair accrues faster than a reasonable man would appreciate. It would follow logically from *Wringe* v. *Cohen* that the same liability should exist in respect of defects arising from want of repair in artificial constructions projecting over the highway, and *Tarry* v. *Ashton* (1876), although the ratio of this case is disputed, appears to impose such liability on the occupier of the house to which the construction is attached.

In the case of projecting trees, however, there is no liability for the fall of the tree in the absence of negligence, whether the trees are planted by the defendant, by a predecessor-in-title, or are self-sown (see *Noble* v. *Harrison* (1926); *Caminer* v. *Northern and London Investment Trust* (1951); *British Road Services* v. *Slater* (1964)).

(3) *Failure to maintain highway by highway authority*

The nonfeasance rule applied to the maintenance of highways by highway authorities. This meant that they were liable only for negligence which worsened the condition of the highway (misfeasance), not for negligence which merely failed to improve it. That liability lay in public nuisance or negligence. Nor were they under any positive duty to act to keep the highway in repair. This position changed with the enactment of (present) section 41 of the Highways Act 1980 which creates an absolute obligation on the highway authority to "maintain" the highway, and (present) section 58 of the Highways Act 1980 which removes the immunity of the highway authority for nonfeasance but also establishes a defence to an action against an authority for failure to maintain the highway that it took reasonable care to discharge its obligation. Five criteria are provided by the section to determine whether reasonable care has been taken.

The liability of a highway authority for failure to maintain the highway is no longer brought in public nuisance or negligence but is for breach of the absolute statutory duty in section 41. The plaintiff must therefore establish a failure to maintain the highway causing him injury or damage, and the failure to maintain is established by showing that the state of the highway is a danger to traffic, vehicular or pedestrian (*Littler* v. *Liverpool Corporation* (1968)). The defendant authority then escapes liability if it shows that it took reasonable care to maintain the highway (*Griffiths* v. *Liverpool Corporation* (1967)—the views of Goff and Shaw L.JJ. in *Haydon* v. *Kent C.C.* (1978) that the plaintiff must show that the existence of the danger points to negligence on the part of the defendant cannot be supported in that they require the plaintiff to lead evidence on an issue on which the defendant has the burden of proof.)

The following further points are of significance. The words of the 1961 Act refer to a failure to "maintain" the highway, and in

Haydon the majority in the Court of Appeal (Geoff and Shaw L.JJ.) accepted that this was wider than failure to "repair," and might encompass a failure to keep a highway clear of ice and snow. In both *Griffiths* and *Haydon*, the authority's failure was accounted for on the ground that insufficient men were employed to keep the highway in its correct condition—indeed, in *Griffiths*, that was the reason negligence was established against the defendants. Nevertheless a failure to employ sufficient workmen to maintain all stretches of the highway may derive from a legitimate policy decision based on lack of resources of the authority. This was relied on by Lord Denning M.R. as a reason for not holding the defendants liable in *Haydon* in relation to a claim based on common law negligence for failure to keep a subsidiary road clear of ice and snow, the defendants employing a task force only sufficient to keep major roads clear. A policy factor of this sort seems to be also capable of establishing a defence to a claim brought under the Act that the authority took reasonable care under the criteria applying under section 58 of the Act of 1980. Finally, if the defendant authority when relying on the statutory defence fails to show that it took reasonable care, it does not help it to show that even had it done so the highway would still have been dangerous. Diplock L.J. in *Griffiths* speculated that the common law defence of inevitable accident might be available to the authority here.

Special damage

In order to succeed in the tort of public nuisance, the plaintiff must prove special damage to himself arising from the nuisance. He must show greater damage to himself than that suffered by the public in general from the nuisance. Personal injury which is recoverable in public nuisance, and damage to property are clear examples. But the tort is liberal in allowing recovery for other less substantial damage. Purely economic loss is recoverable in public nuisance, for example, loss of business profits arising from an obstruction to the highway. Where, for example, the nuisance consisted of an obstruction of the highway, the plaintiff was able to recover loss of profits arising from the interference with the access of the public to his shop. (*Wilkes* v. *Hungerford Market* (1835)). So also in *Tate & Lyle* v. *G.L.C.* (1983) the plaintiff company was able to recover in public nuisance additional dredging costs that it

had to incur because of the obstruction of navigation in the
Thames caused by excessive siltation by the defendants' works in
that river. The ability to sue for economic loss in public nuisance is
one clear case in which the tort possesses an advantage over
negligence. Special damage may also be proved by showing the
type of interference that enables a person to succeed in private
nuisance, for example, intrusions into domestic premises of noise
or smell, provided this exceeds in degree that suffered by the
public generally (in *Halsey* v. *Esso Petroleum* (1961) the plaintiff
succeeded in public nuisance in relation to the noise created on the
public highway by the defendants' oil tankers travelling to and
from the depot). Even a mere inconvenience has been found to
constitute special damage (*Boyd* v. *G.N. Ry. Co.* (1895)—a delay
of 20 minutes at a level-crossing was found to justify a claim for
damages on the ground that a doctor's time has a monetary value.
In the Australian case of *Walsh* v. *Ervin* (1952) the same
assumption was not thought necessary to justify the court's
conclusion that a farmer's inconvenience in having to take his
sheep by a longer route constituted actionable special damage).
The special damage must not be too remote, which means that it
must be foreseeable under the rule laid down by the Privy Council
in *The Wagon Mound* (No. 2).

RELATIONSHIP WITH PRIVATE NUISANCE

Differences between the two forms of nuisance do exist. Thus
prescription is no defence to an action based on public nuisance. In
public nuisance it is possible to claim for personal injury. But the
rules applicable to the two torts are generally speaking treated by
the courts as similar, if not identical. The rules concerning who is
liable for a nuisance, for example, do not differentiate between
private and public nuisance.

STATUTORY NUISANCES

The above account does not exhaust the rights of the citizen to
complain of a nuisance. Various nuisances have been created by
statute under which the individual may bring a complaint, though
this is not quite the same thing as bringing a civil action for
damages. Statutes deserving particular mention are the Public

Health Act 1936, Part 31 (*cf. Coventry City Council* v. *Cartwright* (1975); *Salford City Council* v. *McNally* (1975)) and the Clean Air Act 1956.

16. THE RULE IN RYLANDS v. FLETCHER

THE DECISION IN RYLANDS V. FLETCHER

The facts in *Rylands* v. *Fletcher* (1868) were as follows: the defendant, a millowner, employed independent contractors to build a reservoir on his land for the purpose of supplying water for his mill. In the course of making excavations upon the defendant's land, the contractors came upon some disused mine-shafts which, unknown to them, connected with mines underneath adjoining land. The plaintiff had taken a lease of this land in order to work the mines. The contractors negligently failed to seal up these shafts and when the reservoir was filled with water, the mines were flooded.

The case came upon appeal to the Court of Exchequer Chamber, where the plaintiff succeeded, and this decision was upheld by the House of Lords. The ground for the Exchequer Chamber's decision is contained in this extract from the judgment of the court, delivered by Blackburn J.:

> "We think that the true rule of law is, that the person who for his own purposes brings on his lands and collects and keeps there anything likely to do mischief if it escapes, must keep it in at his peril, and if he does not do so is prima facie answerable for all the damage which is the natural consequence of its escape."

This sentence makes it clear that the defendant's liability was personal, not a mere vicarious liability for the negligence of his independent contractor, and that such liability was strict.

In the House of Lords, a qualification was put by Lord Cairns upon this statement of the rule by Blackburn J. to the effect that the defendant was only liable if he brought the thing on his land in the course of non-natural use of the land. This qualification has been accepted by later cases as an essential part of the rule.

The importance of Rylands v. Fletcher

At the time of the decision *Rylands* v. *Fletcher* did not appear to lay down new law. In the course of his judgment, Blackburn J. drew analogies from recognised cases of cattle-trespass and nuisance to justify his decision. Thus he compared the plaintiff's case to that of the person whose grass or corn was eaten by escaping cattle of his neighbour, or whose land was invaded by smells from his neighbour's alkali works or filth from his privy. He stressed that the defendant was liable for the escape of the thing even in the absence of any personal fault on his part but there is nothing to suggest that he thought there was anything new about this; such strict liability existed also in the examples which he gave of cattle-trespass and nuisance. What was important at the time about the decision in *Rylands* v. *Fletcher* was that a comprehensive rule was laid down governing the incidence of strict liability in the case of the escape of dangerous things from a man's land. This rule was accepted by the courts and applied by them in numerous cases following *Rylands* v. *Fletcher*, but it still remained doubtful whether the rule was merely a special branch of the law of nuisance or whether it established a separate tort. Now that the courts are moving away from the conception of nuisance as a tort of strict liability, it seems that a real difference may exist between it and *Rylands* v. *Fletcher*. The difference may be summed up by saying, that whereas in nuisance the defendant is only liable if as the result of a state of things he has created on his land an escape of something on to the plaintiff's land is foreseeable, in *Rylands* v. *Fletcher*, the defendant is liable even if the escape of the thing which he has brought on his land is unforeseeable.

At one time it was thought that the decision in *Rylands* v. *Fletcher* might have introduced into English law a general principle of strict liability for the carrying on of dangerous activities. In

Read v. *J. Lyons & Co.* (1947) it was necessary to examine the question whether such a principle had been established. The defendants operated a munitions factory as agents of the Ministry of Supply. The plaintiff was an inspector appointed by the Ministry. In the course of her duties she was in the shell-filling shop in the factory when an explosion occurred in the shop causing her serious injuries. She based her claim against the defendants on *Rylands* v. *Fletcher*, making no assertion that the defendants had been negligent. The House of Lords held that she could not succeed under *Rylands* v. *Fletcher* because her injuries had been suffered *on the premises of the defendants*; the explosives had not escaped within the meaning of the rule. The case is important because it shows that the courts treat the rule in *Rylands* v. *Fletcher* like a statute, and have applied to it the literal rather than the mischief rule of statutory interpretation.

Requirements of the rule in Rylands v. Fletcher

(1) *The defendant must bring the thing on his land; he must do this for his own purposes*

The first point to note is that the defendant need not own the land on to which he has brought the thing. A temporary occupier of land such as a lessee, or a person physically present on the land but not in legal occupation of it such as a licensee, is equally within the scope of the rule (*Rainham Chemical Works Ltd.* v. *Belvedere Fish Guano Co.* (1921)). In *Charing Cross Electricity Supply Co.* v. *Hydraulic Power Co.* (1914) the rule was applied to one who had a statutory power to lay water-mains under the highway. In *Rigby* v. *Chief Constable of Northamptonshire* (1985) the court stated *obiter* that the rule applied to cases where the defendant was in no sense in occupation of the land, for example, by firing a canister of CS gas from the highway into private premises. This is difficult to reconcile, however, with the language used by Blackburn J. It has been decided that where the thing is brought on to the land by a licensee, the licensor is also liable under *Rylands* v. *Fletcher* at least where it is brought there for his purposes (*Rainham* case, *supra*). Whether this would be extended to an owner of land out of occupation is uncertain.

The requirement that the thing must be brought on the land for the purposes of the defendant does not mean that it must benefit the defendant, according to *Smeaton* v. *Ilford Corporation* (1954), where it was stated *obiter* that a local authority which was under a statutory duty to collect sewage collected it for its own purposes within the rule in *Rylands* v. *Fletcher*. On the other hand in *Dunne* v. *North Western Gas Board* (1964) it was doubted *obiter* whether the defendant Board which was under a statutory duty to supply gas collected it for its own purposes within the meaning of the rule.

Where the thing is naturally present on the land of the defendant, he cannot be liable for its escape under *Rylands* v. *Fletcher*. The escape of such things as weeds, vermin, rocks, and flood water is thus normally outside the scope of the rule (*Giles* v. *Walker* (1890); *Stearn* v. *Prentice Brothers Ltd.* (1919); *Pontardawe Rural District Council* v. *Moore-Gwyn* (1929); *Whalley* v. *Lancashire and Yorkshire Ry. Co.* (1884)). Recent decisions, however, have established the possibility of an action in nuisance in such circumstances (*Davey* v. *Harrow Corporation* (1958); *Goldman* v. *Hargrave* (1967); *Leakey* v. *National Trust* (1980); *Solloway* v. *Hampshire County Council* (1981)).

(2) *The thing must be likely to do mischief if it escapes*

The rule does not require that the thing should be both likely to escape, and likely to do mischief on escaping. If this were the rule there would be little difference between *Rylands* v. *Fletcher* and negligence. Furthermore, the *Rylands* v. *Fletcher* "thing" need not be a thing dangerous in itself. The most harmless object may cause damage on escape from a man's land. The rule has been applied to a large class of objects including gas, electricity, explosives, the poisonous leaves of trees, a flag pole, a revolving chair at a fair ground, and acid smuts from a factory (*Batcheller* v. *Tunbridge Wells Gas Co.* (1901); *National Telephone Co.* v. *Baker* (1893); *Rainham Chemical Works Ltd.* v. *Belvedere Fish Guano Co. Ltd.* (1921); *Crowhurst* v. *Amersham Burial Board* (1878); *Shiffman* v. *Order of St. John* (1936); *Hale* v. *Jennings Bros.* (1938); *Halsey* v. *Esso Petroleum Co. Ltd.* (1961)). *Musgrove* v. *Pandelis* (1919) applied the Blackburn test literally where the collected thing did not itself escape but caused the escape of something else. Thus the defendant was held liable under *Rylands* v. *Fletcher* for the escape of a fire which started in the carburettor of his car and spread to the defendant's premises. The car was found to be an object likely to do mischief if it escaped. The artificiality of this approach was rejected in *Mason* v. *Levy Auto Parts* (1967) in relation to a fire which began in wooden packing-cases stored in number on the defendants' land. The test applied was whether the objects were likely to catch fire and the fire spread outside the defendants' premises. Liability was strict if this occurred but the result is a hybrid between *Rylands* v. *Fletcher* and negligence rather than true *Rylands* v. *Fletcher. A.-G* v. *Corke* (1933) in which a landowner was held liable under *Rylands* v. *Fletcher* for permitting the camping on his land of gypsies who trespassed and committed nuisances on neighbouring land has received general disapproval in applying the tort to human beings. There can be no question of being bound to keep human beings in at one's peril since that would be false imprisonment. Liability should be based on the original fault in permitting entry and should therefore lie in nuisance or negligence.

(3) *The defendant's use of the land must be non-natural*
Non-natural use of land was explained by the Privy Council in *Rickards* v. *Lothian* (1913) as follows:

> "it must be some special use bringing with it increased danger to others, and must not merely be the ordinary use of the land or such a use as is proper for the general benefit of the community."

Ordinary use cannot simply be equated with domestic or agricultural use; the working of mines is a natural use of land (*Rouse* v. *Gravelworks Ltd.* (1940)). Most domestic and agricultural uses of land are in fact outside the rule, for instance, the planting of trees (*Noble* v. *Harrison* (1926); but the planting of a poisonous tree is a non-natural use; (*Crowhurst* v. *Amersham Burial Board* (1878)). The lighting of a household fire (*Sochaki* v. *Sas* (1947)), the installation of water pipes for a water closet (*Rickards* v. *Lothian* (*supra*)), the wiring of a building for the supply of electric light (*Collingwood* v. *Home and Colonial Stores Ltd.* (1936)) are examples of natural use.

Non-natural use of land is constituted by such activities as the storage on the land in bulk of water, gas or electricity and the collection of sewage by a local authority (*Smeaton* v. *Ilford*

Corporation (1954)). It is arguable that all the above examples should be saved by the second part of the Privy Council's definition as being for the general benefit of the community. The opinion of certain members of the House of Lords (*e.g.* Viscount Simon in *Read* v. *Lyons* (1947)) that running a munitions factory in wartime was a natural use of land may be supported on this ground although this was not the reason advanced in the judgments. This is supported by the judgment of Lawton J. in *British Celanese* v. *A. H. Hunt* (1969) in which he held that the benefit derived by the community from the defendant's business of manufacturing electrical components made the use of land for this purpose and the storing of strips of metal foil thereon a natural use of the land. If this case is followed it seems to mean that the rule in *Rylands* v. *Fletcher* can only be applied in exceptional circumstances. Some of the earlier cases seem in any case due for reconsideration, especially the holding in *Musgrove* v. *Pandelis* that keeping a car in a garage is a non-natural use of land.

(4) *The thing must escape*
    This requirement has already been illustrated by *Read* v. *Lyons*.

Status of the plaintiff: type of damage recoverable
    In the judgment of Blackburn J. in *Rylands* v. *Fletcher*, there was no requirement that the thing should escape on to land in which the plaintiff had an interest. However in *Read* v. *Lyons* (1947) the opinion was expressed by Lord MacMillan that the doctrine of *Rylands* v. *Fletcher* "derives from a conception of mutual duties of adjoining or neighbouring landowners." In *British Celanese* v. *A. H. Hunt*, however, Lawton J. refused to limit the rule in this way, holding that there is liability provided there is an escape from a place over which the defendant has occupation or control to a place which is outside his occupation or control. So, in that case, liability would have existed for the escape of strips of metal foil from the defendants' land which caused a power failure and consequent damage to machinery in the plaintiff's factory by being blown on to a power station owned and operated by a third party (but for the fact that there was natural use of land).
    This divergence of opinion also affects the question of what damage is recoverable. If Lord MacMillan's view is correct, only damage to land occupied by the plaintiff and his chattels on that

land is recoverable, by analogy with nuisance, *supra*, pp. 255–256). On the view that the plaintiff need not be an adjoining landowner, it appears that personal injury is recoverable provided it is not too remote. There is a certain amount of authority suggesting that the latter view is correct. Thus successful actions have been brought under *Rylands* v. *Fletcher* for personal injuries, both where the plaintiff had an interest in the land on to which there was an escape (*Hale* v. *Jennings Brothers* (1938)) and where he had no such interest (*Shiffman* v. *Order of St. John* (1936)). These cases support Lawton J.'s view in *British Celanse* v. *A. H. Hunt*. It seems probable that the damage recoverable under the rule is limited to damage to person or property (*Cattle* v. *Stockton Waterworks Co.* (1875) in which it was held that purely economic loss was not recoverable—*cf. Weller* v. *Foot & Mouth Disease Research Institute* (1966)).

There must be proof of actual damage. This appears to mean actual physical damage to person or property, and to exclude a mere interference with the plaintiff's enjoyment of his land, such as would ground an action in nuisance. In *Eastern & S.A. Telegraph Co.* v. *Cape Town Tramways Co.* (1902) an interference caused by the emission of electricity by the defendants with the plaintiff's receipt of telegraphic messages through a submarine cable was thought to be capable of giving rise to an action under *Rylands* v. *Fletcher*. The plaintiff's action failed because this was an extra-sensitive use of his land, but the damage in question seems to be difficult to classify as damage to property. Although this case suggests that the rule concerning extra-sensitive use may be the same in *Rylands* v. *Fletcher* as it is in nuisance, the court refused to apply the rule in *Hoare* v. *McAlpine* (1923), in which vibrations emitted by the pile-driving activities of the defendants caused the collapse of the plaintiffs' old and unstable house, on the ground that the possession of such property did not constitute an extra-sensitive use of their land by the plaintiffs.

Defences to Rylands v. Fletcher

(1) *Act of God*
The basis of this defence, and of act of a stranger, is that the defendant ought not to be held responsible for an escape which is caused by something beyond his control. They show that the

obligation of the occupier is not an absolute one. Act of God has been defined as an operation of nature "which no human foresight can provide against, and of which human prudence is not bound to recognise the possibility." (*Tennent* v. *Earl of Glasgow* (1864)). The definition of act of God in terms of human foresight tends to assimilate *Rylands* v. *Fletcher* with negligence and this has been criticised (Goodhart, *Current Legal Problems* (1951) 177). However, not every event which is not reasonably foreseeable may constitute an act of God since the requirement is that the event be one against which no human foresight can provide. The defence was successful in *Nichols* v. *Marsland* (1876) where an extraordinary rainfall caused flooding from some artificial lakes on the defendant's land. It was rejected in very similar circumstances by the House of Lords in a Scottish case, *Greenock Corporation* v. *Caledonian Ry. Co.* (1917), on the ground that rainfall, however heavy, is not sufficiently unprecedented to be an act of God.

(2) *Act of a stranger*

If the escape is caused by the unforeseeable act of a stranger, and not by such persons as the occupier's servants, independent contractors, members of his family and possibly guests, this is a defence to *Rylands* v. *Fletcher*. Thus, where the plaintiff's premises were flooded because an unidentified person had turned on a water tap in the defendant's premises there was no liability under the rule (*Rickards* v. *Lothian* (1913)). Where the act of the stranger, whether it is deliberate or negligent, is foreseeable, there is liability under *Rylands* v. *Fletcher*, although here it will normally co-exist with negligence (*Perry* v. *Kendricks Transport Ltd.* (1956); *Hale* v. *Jennings Brothers* (1938)). In relation to the defence of act of a stranger, there seems greater force in Goodhart's criticism that its effect is to assimilate *Rylands* v. *Fletcher* with negligence. Even so, there may be a difference since it may be that the burden of establishing that the stranger's act was unforeseeable rests on the defendant, but the matter is unclear (in *North Western Utilities* v. *London Guarantee & Accident Co.* (1936), the Privy Council appeared to assume that the defendant must prove both that the escape was due to the act of a stranger and that this act was unforeseeable. In *Perry* v. *Kendricks Transport* (1956) the Court of Appeal regarded the burden of proof as resting on the plaintiff to prove that it was foreseeable).

(3) Contributory negligence

Exactly the same considerations apply to this defence as did so to the case of private nuisance (*supra*, pp. 264–265).

(4) Statutory authority

In the absence of explicit guidance from the relevant statute as to whether *Rylands* v. *Fletcher* liability applies, the following rules apply. Where the activity is carried out under a statutory duty as opposed to a power, *Rylands* v. *Fletcher* is excluded (*Dunne* v. *North Western Gas Board* (1964)). This is so even if, as in *Dunne's* case, the statute expressly preserves liability in nuisance. Where the activity is carried on under a statutory power, *Rylands* v. *Fletcher* is available where the statute expressly preserves liability in nuisance (*Charing Cross Electricity Supply* v. *Hydraulic Main Co.* (1914)). This is so even though the activity in question is within the terms of the power and there is no negligence. In the absence of a "nuisance clause," however, the person acting under a power is not liable under *Rylands* v. *Fletcher* (*Green* v. *Chelsea Waterworks* (1894)). Statutory authority is not available as a defence to *Rylands* v. *Fletcher* if the defendant has been negligent and the better view is that as in nuisance (*Manchester Corporation* v. *Farnworth* (1930) the burden of proving that he took due care rests on the defendant. The majority in the Australian High Court decided otherwise, however (*Benning* v. *Wong* (1969)).

Whether statutory authority is available as a defence is a more critical question in the case of *Rylands* v. *Fletcher* than in the case of nuisance since it is clear that the former tort imposes strict liability for the isolated escape whereas in nuisance this now seems unlikely to be the case. The present law tends to exclude from the operation of the rule numerous statutory bodies such as Gas and Electricity Boards to whose activities the type of liability created by *Rylands* v. *Fletcher* might seem particularly appropriate. In *Pearson* v. *North Western Gas Board* (1968) the plaintiff, who suffered personal injury and whose husband was killed and house wrecked following an explosion caused by an escape of gas from the defendants' gas main was able to recover no damages, since negligence was not established and the defendants were under a statutory duty to supply the gas.

(5) *Consent of plaintiff*

Where there is an express consent by the plaintiff to the defendant's bringing the thing on his land, this will be a good defence to an action under *Rylands* v. *Fletcher* (*Att.-Gen.* v. *Cory Brothers & Co.* (1921)). Consent may also be implied. For instance, it has been held that an occupier of part of a building consents to the presence of the water-closet kept in another part of the same building by the defendant (*Ross* v. *Fedden* (1872)). So also a tenant is taken to consent to anything kept by his landlord on his premises at the time of taking the lease (*Peters* v. *Prince of Wales Theatre* (1943)—tenant of shop in defendants' theatre impliedly consented to the presence of a sprinkler system, kept in the theatre by the defendants to prevent fire, which froze and flooded the shop). The presence of a common benefit to plaintiff and defendant may be an element in justifying the implication of consent, but was not present in *Ross* v. *Fedden* and is not necessary (*Peters'* case). These cases could no doubt also be justified on the ground of natural use (*Rickards* v. *Lothian* (1913)—keeping of domestic water supply was natural use).

Remoteness of damage

The rule as to remoteness of damage in *Rylands* v. *Fletcher* has never been authoritatively settled. Blackburn J. spoke of liability for the "natural consequences" of the escape, which may suggest a similar rule to that laid down for negligence in *The Wagon Mound* (No. 1). On the other hand, it appeared to be assumed before the latter case that the Polemis rule of direct consequences would apply to *Rylands* v. *Fletcher* and the Privy Council in *The Wagon Mound* (No. 1) expressly excluded from the width of their remarks concerning remoteness the rule in *Rylands* v. *Fletcher*. It may be, therefore, that the direct consequences rule survives in relation to this tort.

Rylands v. Fletcher and other torts

In many cases *Rylands* v. *Fletcher* overlaps with other torts, especially nuisance and negligence. The differences between *Rylands* v. *Fletcher* and negligence are fairly obvious but it is quite common for both to be committed in a given case. Furthermore, where act of God or of a stranger is relied on as a defence, there is considerable similarity because act of God is defined in terms of human foresight and the act of a stranger is no defence if it is reasonably foreseeable.

The similarity between private nuisance and *Rylands* v. *Fletcher* has already been mentioned. The following are the more important differences between *Rylands* v. *Fletcher* and nuisance:

1. Certain activities such as the creation of noise or offensive sights may ground liability in nuisance but do not do so in *Rylands* v. *Fletcher*. The *Rylands* v. *Fletcher* "thing" nevertheless need not be tangible and includes vibrations caused by pile-driving (*Hoare & Co.* v. *McAlpine* (1923)).

2. In *Rylands* v. *Fletcher* the defendant is liable if he has brought the thing on the land in the course of non-natural use. In nuisance the requirement is that the defendant should have used the land or acted unreasonably.

3. It is settled that nuisance may be committed by one who is not in occupation of land. The matter is less clear in the case of *Rylands* v. *Fletcher*, although recent authority suggests that occupation of land is not a requirement of that tort either (*Rigby* v. *Chief Constable of Northamptonshire* (1985)).

4. In *Rylands* v. *Fletcher* there is always liability for an escape caused by an independent contractor. In nuisance liability is not invariably imposed for the act of an independent contractor.

5. Liability under *Rylands* v. *Fletcher* is strict, whereas private nuisance is not in any real sense a tort of strict liability.

6. Liability under *Rylands* v. *Fletcher* certainly covers the case of the isolated escape of a thing which causes damage. In nuisance there is liability for isolated escapes, but it may be necessary to show a state of affairs of some permanence leading to the escape.

7. *Rylands* v. *Fletcher* probably does not share the characteristics of private nuisance that the plaintiff must have an interest in land and that he cannot recover for personal injuries.

Status of Rylands v. Fletcher today

Rylands v. *Fletcher* is now recognised as a tort in itself, independent of, though resembling, nuisance. At one time it was thought it might form the basis for the incorporation of a greater measure of strict liability into English law, either in the form of liability for hazardous activities, or in the form of enterprise liability. Neither of these developments has taken place. Instead by a series of restrictive decisions, in particular the establishment of the defences of act of God, act of a stranger and statutory authority and the expansion of the concept of natural user, the rule has little part to play in the modern law of torts.

17. LIABILITY FOR THE ESCAPE OF FIRE

In so far as there are any special principles applicable to liability for damage caused by fire, it is because of the former existence of a particular form of the action on the case by which a person was liable for the keeping of a fire on his land which spread to and caused damage on that of his neighbour. It is a disputed question whether liability was strict. In any event, the occupier was liable for the acts of members of his own household and of his servants, agents and guests, *i.e.* of persons who were not "strangers" to him. (*Beaulieu* v. *Finglam* (1401)). In 1774 the Fires Prevention (Metropolis) Act afforded a protection to the occupier on whose land a fire "shall accidentally begin." The courts have given to this Act the interpretation that, unless there is intention or negligence in causing the fire to spread or the constituent requirements of a tort of strict liability are present, the occupier is not liable.

Negligence
Filliter v. *Phippard* (1847) decided that the Act of 1774 was no defence when the fire began through the defendant's negligence. Furthermore, the fact that the fire began accidentally and is allowed to spread through negligence does not make the statutory defence available (*Musgrove* v. *Pandelis* (1919)). In *Sochaki* v. *Sas* (1947) it was held that where a lodger left a fire in his room unattended and without a fire guard for a few hours, and the fire spread, *res ipsa loquitur* did not apply to prove his negligence. This case makes it clear that negligence must be proved even where the

fire is intentionally lit, even though this appears to contradict the
wording of the 1774 Act.

Vicarious liability

The occupier is liable for an escape of fire caused by the
negligence of his servant or independent contractor. In the case of
the former, this is based on normal principles of vicarious liability
but in the case of the latter continues to be based on the old
liability under the action on the case, the contractor not being a
"stranger." (*Balfour* v. *Barty-King* (1957)). The continued existence of this ancient source of liability was recognised by the Court
of Appeal in *H. & N. Emanuel* v. *G.L.C.* (1971). The G.L.C. was
held liable in this case as occupiers of a site, for a fire caused by
the negligence of a contractor employed by the Ministry of Works
to clear the site of two prefabricated bungalows. The work was
done at the request of the G.L.C. The contractor as part of his
work of clearing the site had started a fire, although this had been
forbidden by the Ministry, and the fire had spread to and damaged
the premises and property of the plaintiffs. All three members of
the Court of Appeal found the G.L.C. liable under the *Beaulieu* v.
Finglam principle, the contractor not being a "stranger" to them.
Yet there was reluctance on the part of the Court of Appeal to
admit that liability in this instance was strict. Lord Denning M.R.
appeared to think that it was only because the G.L.C. should have
anticipated the lighting of a fire that the case fell within the
principle. Edmund Davies L.J. thought that the G.L.C. should
have supervised the clearing of the site and were personally
negligent. Phillimore L.J. appeared to think it necessary to find a
negligent failure to supervise the contractor on the part of the
G.L.C. or the Ministry of Works. He found it on the part of the
latter.

Strict liability

There is liability where the conditions of liability under the rule
in *Rylands* v. *Fletcher* are present and the Fires Prevention
(Metropolis) Act does not provide a defence.

18. LIABILITY FOR ANIMALS

Introduction

It is important to note that a person may be liable for the acts of his animals under the ordinary principles of torts not specifically associated with animals. Thus he may commit nuisance by keeping a noisy dog, or negligence by carelessly allowing his dog which he knows to be dangerous to mankind to escape and injure another person. The principles upon which a person will be held liable in negligence for the acts of his animals will be considered later in this chapter. First, however, it is necessary to consider those torts in which strict liability exists for the acts of one's animals. At common law, there were two, scienter liability (for knowingly keeping a dangerous animal which escaped and caused injury or damage) and cattle-trespass (for damage caused by escaping cattle and similar animals). The strict liability encountered in these torts has been retained by the Animals Act 1971 and the main features of the torts themselves have been preserved, although they have been entirely replaced by the statutory provisions. The reasons for the retention of the original strict liability differ as between the two cases. There seem to be good reasons both of justice and policy why a person who keeps a dangerous animal with knowledge of its characteristics should be an insurer in most cases against damage it causes. Original strict liability in cattle-trespass, however, received its primary justification by reason of its facilitation of the resolution of disputes within the agricultural community without recourse to law, and this remains the justification for the strict liability for trespassing live-stock that applies under the Act.

STRICT LIABILITY UNDER THE ANIMALS ACT 1971

Strict liability for dangerous animals was retained by the Animals Act. This seems sound as does the strengthening of strict liability by the abolition of the requirement of an escape by the animal and of the common law defences (if, in fact, such defences existed), of act of God and act of a third party. The Act has also left intact the common law position whereby some species of animals are conclusively presumed to be dangerous and some non-dangerous, so that in the case of the latter there is liability only where the particular animal has a known tendency to do harm. The basis chosen by the Act for classifying a species or a particular animal as dangerous seems questionable and likely to give rise to difficulties of interpretation.

Dangerous species

The dangerous species is defined by section 6 of the Act as follows: "A dangerous species is a species—

(a)   which is not commonly domesticated in the British Islands; and
(b)   whose fully grown animals normally have such characteristics that they are likely, unless restrained, to cause severe damage or that any damage they may cause is likely to be severe."

It may be noted that the dangerous species under this definition includes the animal such as the Colorado beetle which presents a danger only to property and also the animal likely to spread disease. Clause (a) of the definition shows that domestication of the species outside the British Isles is not relevant in determining whether it is dangerous. Difficulties of interpretation may arise, for example, the status of bees. The last words of section 6(2)(b) cause difficulty. They require the court to take an animal not likely to cause damage, to imagine it causing damage, and to assess the probable consequences of such damage as severe or otherwise. No guidance is given by the Act as to the meaning of severe. The courts are therefore free to adopt a purely quantitative test, or perhaps to treat personal injuries as more severe than damage to property. In view of the tortuous nature of this definition it is legitimate to wonder why the Law Commission Report, on which the Act of 1971 was based, did not give examples of the type of animals envisaged by the words. Is a giraffe such an animal? There is no definition of species in the Act, although section 11 provides that the word includes sub-species or variety.

Liability for animals belonging to dangerous species

Section 2(1) provides, "Where any damage is caused by an animal which belongs to a dangerous species, any person who is a keeper of the animal is liable for the damage, except as otherwise provided by this Act." It may be noted that, provided the animal has caused the damage, no further question of remoteness of damage can arise. If the animal is either likely to cause damage or if damage that it may cause is likely to be severe, it is irrelevant whether the damage it actually causes is the damage it is likely to cause or whether it is severe.

Liability for animals not belonging to dangerous species

Section 2(2) provides: "Where damage is caused by an animal which does not belong to a dangerous species, a keeper of the animal is liable for the damage, except as otherwise provided by this Act, if—

(a) the damage is of a kind which the animal, unless restrained, was likely to cause or which, if caused by the animal, was likely to be severe; and

(b) the likelihood of the damage or of its being severe was due to characteristics of the animal which are not normally found in animals of the same species or are not normally so found except at particular times or in particular circumstances; and

(c) those characteristics were known to that keeper or were at any time known to a person who at that time had charge of the animal as that keeper's servant or, where that keeper is the head of a household, were known to another keeper of the animal who is a member of that household and under the age of sixteen."

The following points may be noted about this subsection which has been the subject of serious criticism by the courts, notably in the recent decision in *Curtis* v. *Betts* (1990). The main problem seems to be the conflation of the concepts of likelihood to cause damage with that of the likely severity of damage that may be caused, with consequent unhappy results. The resulting uncertainty in a statute regarded as largely codificatory of the common law is undesirable.

1. It does not require the animal to be likely to inflict the damage in the course of an attack. It is thus wide enough to cover liability for infectious animals, for the animal which damages property or person without attacking it (*Wallace* v. *Newton* (1982)), and even for damage caused by a dog running into the highway and causing an accident. The wording of subsection 2(*a*) has strange results, in particular that the damage the animal actually causes does not have to be caused in the way it is likely to cause it provided it is of the kind it is likely to cause; also if the damage the animal causes is likely to be severe, then the defendant is liable even though that which it causes is not severe. The "damage likely to be severe" test is applied to the particular species of animal independently of the "particular times or circumstances" requirement in section 2(2)(*b*), although this contradicts the words of the Act (see Lord Denning M.R. in *Cummings* v. *Grainger* (1977)—Alsatians are likely to cause severe injury if they bite; Slade L.J. in *Curtis* v. *Betts* (1990)—so are bull mastiffs.)

2. Section 2(2)(*b*) enacts the common law rule imposing strict liability for the known likelihood of the particular animal to cause damage or the particular species to cause damage at particular times or in particular circumstances (established in *Cummings* v. *Grainger*—dog acting as guard dog in scrap-yard; and in *Curtis* v. *Betts*—dog defending territory which included rear of Land-Rover). But it extends that position in creating liability for the causing of damage that is likely to be severe. On the latter point, Stuart Smith L.J. (with whom Nourse L.J. agreed) criticised the wording of section 2(2)(*b*) on the ground that it could impose liability for damage caused by an animal outside the particular times

or circumstances in which it is likely to inflict that damage. They proposed that the words "likelihood of the damage or of its being severe" in section 2(2)(b) be replaced by "damage," thus creating a causal link between the damage caused and the characteristics of the animal in question.

3. Subsection (c) is based upon the common law rules which determine whether the knowledge of one person is treated as that of its keeper.

No necessity for escape

Neither subsection requires the animal to escape from the defendant's control in order that liability be established and the Law Commission Report makes it clear that this effect was intended.

Liability for damage done by dogs

Section 3 of the Animals Act which replaces liability under the Dogs Acts of 1906 and 1928 provides that where a dog causes damage by killing or injuring livestock (for the definition of this, see *infra*), any person who is a keeper of the dog is liable for the damage except as otherwise provided by the Act. The defences in section 5 of the Act therefore apply to this form of liability. Section 3 maintains the principle of the Dogs Acts that there is strict liability in the absence of *scienter* or negligence.

Section 9 provides a defence to an action for the killing of a dog which worries livestock (considered *supra*, Chapter 5).

Defences to actions brought under section 2 and section 3

Section 5(1) and (2) establish the defences that the plaintiff was wholly at fault and that the plaintiff voluntarily accepted the risk. Section 6(5) preserves the latter defence even where the risk is incidental to the plaintiff's employment. Section 10 of the Act makes it clear that the apportionment provisions of the Law Reform (Contributory Negligence) Act 1945 are applicable where the plaintiff has been contributorily negligent.

Section 5(3) deals with the problem of whether it is a defence to an action based on section 2 that the injury was inflicted by the defendant's animal while the plaintiff was trespassing on the defendant's land. Section 5(3) allows the defence if (a) the animal was not kept on the land for the protection of persons or property, or (b) the animal was kept there for the protection of persons or property and keeping it there for that purpose was reasonable. *Cummings* v. *Grainger* illustrates the operation of the defences under section 5(2) and (3). In that case the plaintiff was savaged by an Alsatian guard dog in the defendant's scrap-metal yard. The plaintiff had followed her friend into the yard, the friend having gone in to collect his car. The friend was a licensee but the plaintiff was a trespasser. The yard had warning notices outside it, and the plaintiff testified that she knew about the dog and was frightened of it. The Court of Appeal held that the defence under section 5(2) applied since the plaintiff had willingly accepted the risk of the dog's attack. The court's language suggests that any form of voluntary entry with knowledge of the risk is enough to establish the defence. It was also held that the keeping of the dog for the protection of property was reasonable, so that the defence under section 5(3) applied. This rather surprising attitude to the question of reasonableness may change in the light of the Guard Dogs Act 1975, which makes it a criminal offence to keep a guard dog roaming free without a handler. Section 5(4) gives a defence to an action under section 3 that the livestock was killed or injured on land to which it had strayed by a dog belonging to, or whose presence was authorised by, the occupier.

The omission of the defences of act of God and of a third party from section 5 means that these defences are not available to an action under sections 2 and 3. Liability is therefore stricter than, for example, under the rule in *Rylands* v. *Fletcher*.

Keeper

Liability under sections 2 and 3 of the Act is imposed upon the keeper of the animal. He is defined by section 6 of the Act as the person who owns the animal or has it in his possession; or is the head of a household of which a member under 16 owns the animal or has it in his possession. Section 6 also deals with the problem of wild animals in captivity which have escaped and returned to their wild state (particularly those indigenous to this country) by providing that the keeper of the animal at the time of its escape continues to be its keeper until another person becomes its keeper under the provisions mentioned above.

Liability under section 4 of the Animals Act for trespassing livestock

The former "cattle" is replaced in the Act by "livestock." These are defined in section 11 to mean any animals of the bovine species, horses, asses, mules, hinnies, sheep, pigs, goats, poultry and deer not in the wild state. Liability under section 4(1) for trespass by any of these species is strict, subject to the defences provided by section 5. Liability is that of the person to whom the livestock belong but section 4(2) provides that for the purposes of the section livestock belongs to the person in whose possession it is. The plaintiff in the action must be a person who has ownership or occupation of the land. It is necessary to prove damage as part of the cause of action and this is achieved under section 4(1)(a) by showing damage to the land itself or to any property on it which is in the ownership or occupation of the plaintiff, or under section 4(1)(b) by showing that expenses were reasonably incurred by the plaintiff while it cannot be restored to the person to whom it belongs or while it is detained in pursuance of section 7 of the Act, or in ascertaining to whom it belongs. Personal injuries, which were recoverable under cattle-trespass, are not recoverable under section 4.

Defences. Section 5 recognises three defences to liability under section 4. Section 5(1) excuses the defendant where the damage is due wholly to the fault of the plaintiff. Section 5(5) confirms the special defence formerly available to actions of cattle-trespass that the animal strayed from a highway which it was lawfully using. Section 5(6) provides the defence that the entry would not have occurred but for a breach by any other person (*i.e.* than the defendant) being a person having an interest in the land of a duty to fence (it). Contributory negligence of the plaintiff is also a defence to an action for breach of section 4.

New remedy. Section 7 abolishes the old right of distress damage feasant with regard to animals (as to objects see *supra*, p. 89), and replaces it with a new right of the occupier of land to detain any livestock which strays on to that land.

LIABILITY FOR NEGLIGENCE

There may be liability for negligence both in the case of dangerous and non-dangerous animals under the existing law. Negligence is particularly important however in the case of animals which are of the class of harmless animals and which individually do not have dangerous characteristics known to their keeper. Several cases have established that there might be liability for failure to control such animals when they are taken by a person in control of them on to the highway (*e.g. Deen* v. *Davis* (1935); *Aldham* v. *United Dairies Ltd.* (1940); *Gomberg* v. *Smith* (1963)). There might also be liability in negligence if such animals cause damage to other persons on the land of their keeper. There was however no duty of care, in the absence of "special circumstances" to prevent harmless animals from straying on to the highway (so held by the House of Lords in *Searle* v. *Wallbank* (1947)).

Impressed by the evidence about accidents on the highway caused by straying animals, the Law Commission recommended the abolition of the rule in *Searle* v. *Wallbank*. The abolition of the rule is accomplished by section 8(1). Now, therefore, an occupier of land owes a duty of care in relation to the straying of so-called harmless animals from his land on to the highway. But under section 8(2), no breach of duty is committed by a person by reason only of the fact that he has placed animals on land if: (a) the land is common land, or is land situated in an area where fencing is not customary or is a town or village green; and (b) he has a right to place animals on the land (*cf. Davies* v. *Davies* (1975))—right to place animals on common land included a licence to place animals on such land given by the person with the right to place them there.

19. BREACH OF STATUTORY DUTY

It is of course possible for torts to be created by statute. The term "breach of statutory duty" refers more particularly to those cases where an action in tort is found to be available for breach of a statutory duty even though no express indication is given in the statute that this is the case. Whether such action is available has been based by the courts upon an inference from the words of the statute of legislative intent, but as will be seen shortly such intent appears largely a legal fiction. As a tort, breach of statutory duty is something of a hybrid. In many cases, the behaviour which constitutes it amounts also to common law negligence, and for this reason it is sometimes called statutory negligence. This is particularly so in the case of industrial safety legislation passed for the protection of workers in factories, which is generally construed as conferring a civil action on a workman injured by its breach. The statute here serves the useful purpose of particularising the standard of reasonable conduct expected of his employer, so that the worker does not need to show that the employer acted unreasonably. But breach of statutory duty, even in those cases where the statute merely defines the employer's obligation to his employees to take reasonable care, is usually more than mere statutory negligence. If the statutory duty is construed as absolute, a non-negligent failure to comply with it will be a breach. Further, where the statute imposes an obligation which would not be required of the employer to discharge a duty of care deriving from common law negligence, liability is in every sense strict. Only where the effect of the statute is to impose an obligation upon the defendant merely to take reasonable care to do that which the ordinary law of negligence would in any case compel him to do can breach of statutory duty be entirely equated with negligence.

Requirements of the tort

The plaintiff in an action for breach of statutory duty must show: (i) that the statute was intended by Parliament to confer a civil remedy for its breach; (ii) that the statute imposed a duty upon the defendant; (iii) that the defendant was in breach of this duty; (iv) that the plaintiff suffered harm or damage which was a consequence of the breach of duty and which was not too remote.

Was the statute intended to confer a right of action in tort?

The difficulties of extracting any consistent approach from the decisions of the courts on this matter may perhaps be illustrated by indicating that though actions in tort are always allowed for breach of factory legislation, the same is not true of breach of road traffic regulations (*Phillips* v. *Britannia Hygienic Laundry* (1923); *Clarke* v. *Brims* (1947); but *cf. Kelly* v. *W.R.N. Contracting* (1968) in which an action for breach of a parking regulation was allowed); or by comparing *Read* v. *Croydon Corporation* (1938), in which an action was allowed for breach of a statutory obligation to supply wholesome drinking water, with *Square* v. *Model Farms Dairies Ltd.* (1939) which held that the supply of infected bottled milk in breach of statutory duty gave no civil action. One suggested criterion is that the statutory action would be "unusual" (*cf. Atkinson* v. *Newcastle and Gateshead Waterworks Co.* (1877)—no action for breach of statutory obligation to maintain water pressure so that fire brigade could not extinguish fire; and *Cutler* v. *Wandsworth Stadium Ltd.* (1949)—no civil action for breach of statutory obligation to admit bookmaker to dog track). But in *Monk* v. *Warbey* (1935) a successful action was brought against a motorist for breach of his statutory duty to insure his car. Other suggested criteria for finding that a civil remedy is intended are that the statute imposes no criminal or other sanction (*Reffell* v. *Surrey C.C.* (1964); *Booth* v. *National Enterprise Board* (1978); *Thornton* v. *Kirklees* (1979)); that the statutory sanction is derisory or inadequate (*cf. Groves* v. *Wimborne* (1898) on derisory penalties; *Meade* v. *London Borough of Haringey* (1979) on the "inadequacy" of the statutory remedy of complaint to a Minister); or that the statute is for the protection of a recognised class of persons. The first two suggestions can clearly have no general validity. The third explains some cases but not others. For example, although employees are a recognisable class of persons for whose benefit a civil action has been found to be conferred by safety legislation in factories and workplaces, the courts generally refuse to extend a similar benefit to road users who have suffered from breach of traffic regulations (*Phillips* v. *Britannia Hygienic Laundry* (1923)); or to tenants subject to the protection of the Rent Acts for breach of the latter (*McCall* v. *Abelesz* (1976)). The more general the duty and the more elevated the level at which it is imposed the less likely is the court to find a civil action to be conferred (but *cf. Booth* v. *National Enterprise Board* (1978) in which the court admitted the possibility of statutory government directives to the National Enterprise Board giving rise to civil actions). Although the decision is sometimes reached by a close examination of the relevant statute (*cf. McCall* v. *Abelesz*), very often the question looks to turn on matters of policy as much as of construction. (*N.B.* Occasionally the legislature solves the problem by expressly providing that the statute creates a civil right of action—*cf.* Guard Dogs Act 1975, section 5; Safety of Sports Grounds Act 1975, section 13).

Statutory duty laid upon the defendant

The statute must impose a duty rather than a power upon the defendant. The duty must be imposed upon the defendant (*Harrison* v. *N.C.B.* (1951)—duties imposed by Coal Mines Act 1911 in relation to shot-firing were imposed upon shot-firers rather than upon defendant employer).

Breach of duty

The defendant must be in breach of his statutory duty. Whether he is or not will raise, *inter alia*, a question of statutory interpretation. The court must decide whether the duty is a strict one, or whether it is one of reasonable care only. In *Galashiels Gas Co.* v. *Miller* (1949) it was held that the defendants' statutory duty to maintain a lift in good repair was strict, so that where the lift fell to the bottom of the lift shaft, injuring the plaintiff, there was liability even though no negligence by the defendants could be established. In *John Summers* v. *Frost* (1955) it was held that the duty to securely fence "every dangerous part of any machinery" was a strict one, so that the employers were in breach of this duty in failing to fence a grindstone, even though the effect of fencing the machine was to make it unusable. On the other hand, the duty arising under section 48(1) of the Mines and Quarries Act 1954, to take "such steps ... as may be necessary for keeping the road or working-place secure" is a duty based upon foreseeability of danger and is therefore one of reasonable care. (*Robson* v. *National Coal Board* (1968)). The wording "so far as reasonably practicable" qualifying the employer's obligation also means that the obligation differs little if at all from the employer's common law duty (*Levesley* v. *Thomas Firth* (1953)). The court must also be satisfied that the statutory duty, as precisely interpreted, applies to the case before it. Thus the plaintiff in *Eaves* v. *Morris Motors* (1961) failed to show a breach of section 14(1) of the Factories Act 1937, since that section only requires fencing of dangerous parts of machinery and not of materials that are inserted into machinery. Similarly, in *British Railways Board* v. *Liptrot* (1969) it was held that there is no duty to fence when what is dangerous is the machine as a whole rather than its particular parts—otherwise there would be a duty to fence vehicles.

Damage

Clearly some sort of infringement of the plaintiff's rights is necessary in order to mount an action in tort for breach of statutory duty. The action cannot serve as a private means of enforcing the criminal law (*cf. Gouriet* v. *Union of Postal Workers* (1976)). The type of infringement varies according to the nature of the statutory duty that has been broken. In the case of breach of the duties contained in factory legislation, actual damage in the form of personal injury is an essential part of the cause of action. In some cases it is not necessary for the plaintiff to show any form of temporal loss or damage. So an action for breach of statutory duty has been found to lie in relation to the duty under section 8 of the Education Act to provide schools, at the instance of parents whose children by reason of the breach are not receiving education (*Gateshead Union* v. *Durham C.C.* (1918); *Meade* v. *Haringey L.B.C.* (1979)).

The damage must not be too remote a consequence of the breach of duty

In order to establish a claim for breach of statutory duty the plaintiff must show that under normal principles of causation the damage he suffered was caused by the breach of statutory duty. The claim of the plaintiff in *McWilliams* v. *Arrol & Co.* (1962), for example, failed because the plaintiff was unable to show that the defendants' breach of statutory duty in failing to provide safety belts caused his injury since he was unable to satisfy the court that he would have worn a belt had it been provided. In addition, the plaintiff must show that the damage he suffered was not too remote. In relation to breach of statutory duty this means that he must show that that damage was of the sort contemplated by the statute and that it was foreseeable. These two requirements will be examined in turn.

(1) *The harm suffered by the plaintiff must be that contemplated by the statute*

In *Gorris* v. *Scott* (1874) the defendant, who was transporting the plaintiff's sheep on his ship, infringed a statutory order under which animals on board ship were to be divided into pens. The sheep were washed overboard and drowned and it was found that this would not have occurred had they been penned. The plaintiff's action for breach of statutory duty failed because the purpose of the statute was to prevent the spread of disease rather than to prevent the loss of animals in the manner that occurred. It is necessary to distinguish the rule in *Gorris* v. *Scott* from the rules relating to remoteness of damage, since the loss the plaintiff suffered in that case was clearly a foreseeable result of the defendant's breach of duty. This was recognised by the House of Lords in *Close* v. *Steel Co. of Wales Ltd.* (1962). An injury to the plaintiff through fragments of a shattered drill being flung against him would have been avoided but for the defendant's breach of statutory duty in failing to fence the drill. The House of Lords held that, even had the injury been foreseeable, the plaintiff would not have succeeded because the purpose of the statute was to prevent the machine operator's body coming into contact with the machine, rather than to prevent the risk of fragments being flung out. These cases emphasise a judicial tendency to confine breach of statutory duty within narrow limits. A different approach arose in *Donaghey*

v. *Boulton & Paul* (1968) (plaintiff's fall through hole in roof which would have been avoided by the provision of crawling boards which defendants in breach of statutory duty failed to supply was actionable though chief purpose of crawling boards was to prevent falls through fragile material in the roof).

Another manifestation of the *Gorris* v. *Scott* principle is that the plaintiff must show himself to be within the protection of the statutory provision. In general, employees of persons other than the employer subject to the statutory duty, and self-employed persons have been held to be outside the benefit of statutory duties in factory legislation for the purpose of suing in breach of statutory duty. Thus in *Hartley* v. *Mayoh & Co.* (1954) the plaintiff fireman was electrocuted in the course of fighting a fire at the defendants' factory, because of the defendants' breach of statutory regulations. It was held that he could not recover from the defendants for breach of statutory duty because he was not a "person employed" in the factory within the meaning of the regulation (*cf. Herbert* v. *Harold Shaw* (1959); *Kearney* v. *Eric Waller* (1967)). Something may turn upon the interpretation of the statute in question. Thus it has been held that the phrase "any person" in section 29 of the Factories Act 1961, extends to all those who enter a factory to work for the purposes of the factory, and that, therefore, a window cleaner who was employed as an independent contractor by the factory owner came within the ambit of the duty (*Wigley* v. *British Vinegars Ltd.* (1964)). Unless the wording of the statute appears clearly to envisage it, however, the courts will normally be reluctant to extend the benefit of statutory duties to outsiders. This may be explained either on the ground that courts believe in class benefit as the basis for allowing an action for breach of statutory duty, or as part of their general reluctance to impose duties on employers in respect of the safety of persons other than their own employees (*cf.* employers' common law liability, *supra*, pp. 241–242).

On the other hand, if the plaintiff is within the protected class, it does not matter that he is acting outside the course of his employment (*Smith* v. *Supreme Wood Pulp Co.* (1968)), nor that he is trespassing upon his employer's machinery (*Uddin* v. *Associated Portland Cement Manufacturers* (1965)) or premises (*Wedgewood* v. *Post Office* (1973)). Where such trespass shows an unreasonable failure to look after his own safety by the plaintiff, there will be a deduction for contributory negligence (to the extent of 80 per cent. in *Uddin*, though in *Wedgewood* no deduction was made since no danger was foreseeable to the trespassing employee).

(2) *The damage must not be otherwise too remote*

It is still not clear whether the foreseeability test laid down for remoteness of damage in negligence cases by the *Wagon Mound* (No. 1) applies to breach of statutory duty. Although liability in the tort may be strict, in practice it is largely concerned with fault by employers so that the *Wagon Mound* test would appear appropriate. However, in *Millard* v. *Serck Tubes* (1969) the plaintiff's arm was caught in a machine which the defendants had failed to fence. Although the way in which the accident occurred was unforeseeable, the defendants were held liable in breach of statutory duty. The result could no doubt have been easily explained in terms of the extended notion of foreseeability applied by cases starting with *Hughes* v. *Lord Advocate* (1963), but foreseeability was not mentioned by the Court of Appeal. Nor was it by the House of Lords in *Boyle* v. *Kodak* (*infra*, this chapter), a case expressly categorised as one where the foreseeable risk was insufficiently great to impose a duty of care. But in neither case was the matter discussed. In certain cases in which the plaintiff has received injury through contact between his person and unfenced machinery but the manner in which the contact occurred is not established, the court has assumed an act of inadvertence by the plaintiff and ignored the possibility of contributory negligence (*Thurogood* v. *Van Den Berghs* (1951); *Allen* v. *Aeroplane and Motor Aluminium Castings* (1965)).

Defences to the action

Volenti non fit injuria

For reasons of public policy this defence is not available to an employer in suits against him by his employees, since he should not be able to escape from his statutory obligations by obtaining his employee's consent. The defence is, however, available where the employer is being sued on the ground of his vicarious liability for a breach of statutory duty imposed upon and committed by his employee, provided that the employee who commits the breach is not of superior rank to and in receipt of habitual obedience from the plaintiff (*I.C.I.* v. *Shatwell* (1965)—two employees ignored statutory safety regulations imposed upon themselves and one was injured in consequence—held that *volenti* was a defence).

Contributory negligence

This defence is clearly available. Special rules relating to the defence in relation to breach of statutory duty have already been discussed (*supra*, p. 189).

Statutory duty delegated to or also laid upon the plaintiff

Where the performance of the employer's statutory duty has been delegated to the plaintiff employee, and he has failed to discharge it, with the result that he has suffered injury, a difficult causal problem arises as to whether the employer is liable. On the one hand, the employer is clearly in breach of his duty, because the statutory duty is non-delegable. On the other, a person ought not to recover damages for something that is entirely his fault. In *Ross* v. *Associated Portland Cement Manufacturers Ltd.* (1964) the House of Lords was concerned with the question whether delegation of the defendant's duty to the plaintiff was sufficient without more to enable the court to say that the plaintiff was entirely responsible for his own injuries. The employers in that case were held liable for two-thirds of the plaintiff's injuries, because they had delegated to him their statutory duty of making safe his work fence without giving him proper instructions, and he was not qualified to perform this task. The employer's fault thus was different from and went beyond that of the plaintiff in failing to make safe the workplace.

Where, however, the employer's breach of statutory duty is purely the result of the action of the plaintiff employee, no action will lie against the employer because the employee was the sole cause of his own injuries. This will be the case *a fortiori* where the statutory duty is also laid on the employee himself. Thus, in *Ginty* v. *Belmont Building Supplies Ltd.* (1959), the plaintiff failed to use a crawling-board while working on a roof, in breach of statutory regulations binding upon himself and his employers. He was injured as a result. His actions for breach of statutory duty against his employers failed because he was unable to show that they had committed any breach of the statutory regulations other than that committed by himself. Nor was the contributory negligence legislation of assistance to the plaintiff. The injury was "wholly the fault of the plaintiff and wholly the fault (vicariously) of his employers" (Pearson J.).

The House of Lords in *Boyle* v. *Kodak* (1969) held that the employer's duty to instruct an employee about the steps to be taken to avoid the commission of a breach of statutory duty binding on that employee applies whenever there is a risk that the employee will not be sufficiently familiar with the regulations imposing such a duty, and even if there is no foreseeable danger as a result of any breach. It is clear, therefore, that the doctrine whereby the employer may be found liable for a breach of statutory duty where his fault is not co-extensive with that of the employee reaches beyond the case where such fault would give rise to an action for common law negligence (in the *Boyle* case, the result was an apportionment of damages between the employer and the injured plaintiff who was also at fault in not performing the statutory duty).

20. VICARIOUS LIABILITY

This term used in connection with the law of tort refers to the situation where one person is liable for the commission of a tort by another. The outstanding case in English law is the liability of a master for the torts of his servant committed in the course of the latter's employment. Liability for the acts of an independent contractor is based upon the breach of a personal, non-delegable duty of the employer rather than on vicarious liability, although as we shall see, liability here is essentially vicarious. (The reader should note that in this chapter, for purposes of clarity, reference will be made to "master and servant" rather than to "employer and employee").

The relationship of principal and agent is, generally speaking, irrelevant for determining questions of vicarious liability for tort. The agent is employed to bring his principal into contractual relation with third parties. He may be either a servant or independent contractor (according to principles discussed below), and upon this will turn the question of the principal's liability for the torts he commits. An exception is the liability of car owners for the negligent driving of persons who drive the car at their request and for their purposes. This is rationalised in terms of agency, but there is no general principle of liability for the acts of a gratuitous agent, even though they comply with the same

307

conditions. Agency principles are also relevant to liability for misstatements made by servants or agents (*infra*).

The concept of vicarious liability, which refers to liability for torts committed by another person (the prime example being the master's liability for the torts of his servant committed in the course of the latter's employment) must be distinguished from personal liability in tort committed through the medium of another person. In the case of liability of an employer for the negligence of an independent contractor, liability is based upon the breach by the employer of a non-delegable duty of case binding himself. The non-delegable duty concept merely expresses a result—it gives no guidance as to which duties of care are non-delegable. Nor should it be allowed to disguise the fact that the employer's liability is essentially vicarious and strict, the fault element in the tort being supplied by the contractor. In some cases, however, liability in tort is essentially personal in that the defendant himself fulfils the relevant requirements of the tort and the fact that it is committed through a third party is irrelevant. Torts of strict liability are the best example of this. In *Rylands* v. *Fletcher*, the defendant was held liable because he had collected water on his land and it had escaped and caused damage. The fact that the escape occurred through the negligence of a contractor was irrelevant to liability. Again the employer's liability for breach of his own strict statutory duty is personal, and the fact that the breach occurs through the fault of another person to whom he has delegated the performance of that duty is irrelevant. Personal liability in tort may also be incurred by procuring the commission of the tort by a third party, for example, by instructing that person to do an act constituting a tort.

VICARIOUS LIABILITY IN THE CASE OF MASTER AND SERVANT

Rationale

It is now recognised that the reason for imposing liability upon the master for the torts of his servant committed in the course of his employment is one of policy. Vicarious liability achieves the dual purpose of providing a financially responsible person as defendant and of providing the master with an inducement to institute maximum standards of safety within the enterprise. At the

same time the limitation that the tort must have been committed
during the course of the servant's employment shows that this is a
form of enterprise liability, rather than that the master is an
insurer of the servant's wrongdoing.

Who is a servant? Servants distinguished from independent contractors

Several tests have been propounded by courts for deciding this
question. But it seems that these tests are for the guidance of the
court rather than principles of law, and that each case must be
resolved on its own special facts. No one test is paramount over
another and where different tests produce differing results, the
court must make up its mind on the evidence and its overall
impression. One test that was at one time regarded almost as
conclusive was whether the employer could determine the detailed
way in which the work was to be done, the test of control. With
the increase in technical knowledge and skill, this test has become
a great deal less useful, since in practice the employer will let the
servant alone in his performance of tasks demanding such
knowledge. If it is argued that the employer must be able to
control the overall manner in which the work is done, this element
would seem to be present also in the case of work done by
independent contractors. Other factors which will enter the court's
consideration are the method of payment (for example, wages or a
lump sum) and who supplies tools, premises, equipment. An
alternative test put forward by Lord Denning in 1952 has won
some acceptance today. He contrasted the servant who is normally
employed as an integral part of his employer's business (giving as
examples the ship's master, the chauffeur, and the newspaper
reporter) with the independent contractor whose services are
accessory to the business (examples being the ship's pilot, the
taxidriver, and the freelance contributor). The two tests of control
and integration may produce different results. Thus in *Morren* v.
Swinton and Pendlebury U.D.C. (1965) an engineer employed by a
local authority was held to be its servant though subject to no
control by it in relation to the carrying out of his work, on the
ground that the terms of his contract made him sufficiently
integrated into the business of the authority. On the other hand, in
Market Investigations v. *Minister of Social Security* (1969), a
woman interviewer, employed by the plaintiffs, who was subject to

exact control as to the method of conducting interviews, was held to be the plaintiffs' servant, though it seems doubtful whether she was sufficiently integrated into the employer's business to satisfy the integration test. In *Ready-Mixed Concrete Co.* v. *Minister of Pensions and National Insurance* (1968) it was stated that there must be sufficient control by the employer, and there must be no provisions in the contract inconsistent with service in order to establish a contract of service. However, it is not clear why control should be essential nor why the existence of certain terms pointing away from service should always outweigh a greater number of terms pointing towards it. The correct test of service seems to be whether a preponderance of the terms of the contract point towards it. Some may do this by establishing control, others integration, and others, such as the power of appointment and dismissal, may point to service though they establish neither control nor integration. It must be pointed out that it is not for the parties themselves to determine the nature of the contract they have entered into, so that express provision in the contract that a person is not a servant will not prevail against other factors which indicate service (*Ferguson* v. *Dawson* (1976)). A particular problem in relation to the police force has been removed by the Police Act 1964. A policeman is not in the position of servant to anyone. Section 48 of the Act makes the chief officer of police for any police area liable for torts committed by constables under his direction and control on similar principles to those determining the master's liability for the torts of his servant. Any damages and costs awarded are to be paid out of the police fund.

Cases on borrowed servants typify the problems of complicated factual analysis which have to be faced by courts. The servant may be so completely "taken over" that, at least as far as the doctrine of vicarious liability is concerned, he becomes the servant of the borrower; otherwise he will merely be his independent contractor (contractually speaking, however, he will remain throughout the servant of his original master). In *Mersey Docks and Harbour Board* v. *Coggins and Griffiths Ltd.* (1947), a crane driver employed by the Board had been hired together with his crane to another company and while with that company had by his negligence injured the plaintiff. The crane driver was held to be still a servant of the Board because of the following factors: he continued to be paid by the Board which alone had power to dismiss him; the borrower could give him directions as to the work to be done but could not instruct him in the operation of the crane. These factors outweighed the fact that the contract of hire provided that the crane driver should become the servant of the hirers, since this, as far as vicarious liability was concerned was for judicial rather than contractual determination. An easier case was *McDermid* v. *Nash Dredging Ltd.* (1987). There the servant of the parent company was working as the skipper of a boat belonging to the subsidiary company. The court held that he remained the servant of the parent company since he continued to be paid by them, the subsidiary was performing the parent company's work and the subsidiary gave him no instructions as to the performance of the work.

Master's personal duty

Little remains, nowadays, of the former theory of vicarious liability under which the master was liable because he had committed through his servant a breach of duty personal to himself, although it is true that some of the older cases seem to support it (*e.g. Broom* v. *Morgan* (1953); *Conway* v. *Wimpey* (1951); *Smith* v. *Moss* (1940)). It cannot meet the insuperable difficulty that if it were correct it would not matter whether the failure to discharge the duty was through the default of a servant or independent contractor, whereas there are numerous cases in which liability exists for the acts of a servant but not an independent contractor. The correct basis for vicarious liability is therefore that the master is liable for torts committed *by the servant* in the course of his employment. This is not to deny the possibility of the concurrent availability of a personal, non-delegable duty of care binding the master. If that is so, it makes no difference whether the person employed is a servant or independent contractor and this avoids difficulties that may arise in deciding whether or not to classify certain persons as servants. In cases of medical negligence in the course of hospital treatment, for example, doubts may exist whether the particular person negligent is a servant of the hospital. Thus although radiographers (*Gold* v. *Essex County Council* (1942)), house-surgeons (*Collins* v. *Hertford-shire County Council* (1947)), whole-time assistant medical officers (*Cassidy* v. *Minister of Health* (1951)) and anaesthetists (*Roe* v. *Minister of Health* (1954)) have been held to be servants of the hospital, a doubt remains about persons such as consultant surgeons. If, however, the hospital owes its patients a duty of care in their treatment which is personal to itself and is not capable of being discharged through other persons, it makes little difference whether the particular person at fault is classified as a servant or independent contractor of the hospital (apart from the difficulty over collateral negligence, *infra*, p. 321). No conclusive authority yet exists to show that hospitals owe such a duty, but there are supporting dicta in the case law (*per* Lord Greene M.R. in *Gold* v. *Essex C.C.* (1942); *per* Denning L.J. in *Cassidy* v. *Minister of Health* (1951)).

Morris v. *Martin* (1966) is another example of the way in which the imposition of a personal non-delegable duty upon the employer may avoid a problem as to whether vicarious liability for the act of servant exists in the particular case. The defendants were sub-bailees for reward of the plaintiff's mink coat for the purpose of cleaning it. They entrusted the cleaning of the coat to their servant who stole it. Difficulty existed at the time of the decision in establishing vicarious liability on conventional lines because of the doubt as to whether theft by a servant could be regarded as being within the course of his employment (in fact this difficulty was resolved in the plaintiff's favour (*infra*, p. 316)). Nevertheless, Lord Denning M.R. was able to hold the defendants liable on an alternative ground, that as sub-bailees for reward of the coat, they owed a personal duty of care in the safekeeping of the coat to the plaintiff which because of the action of their servant they had not discharged.

A final point needs emphasis. The "servant's tort" theory of vicarious liability does not require that the plaintiff must identify the tortfeasor, provided it is clear that the tort must have been committed by one of the defendant's servants acting in the course of his employment (*cf. Grant* v. *Australian Knitting Mills* (1936)). If it is merely shown that the tortfeasor must have been one of a number of servants or independent contractors employed by the defendant, liability will exist only if there is a personal non-delegable duty of care resting on the defendant.

Course of employment

The limitation has been established that the tort must be committed during the course of the servant's employment, and this requirement must now be examined. It may be noted that many of the decisions on whether a servant has acted in the course of his employment turn on questions of degree rather than logic. The present century has seen an extension of the limits within which the servant is recognised as acting in the course of his employment.

Substantive limits and duration of employment

The servant must be doing the work he has been employed to do. In *Rand* v. *Craig* (1919) the defendant employed servants to carry rubbish and deposit it in a named place. Instead they deposited it on the plaintiff's land. The defendant was held not liable to the plaintiff since the servants were acting outside the course of their employment. Here the area of employment was defined by the employer's express instructions. Similarly if the servant goes on a "frolic of his own" during his working hours he will be acting outside the course of his employment. By this term is meant some action of the servant which is so totally unrelated to the work the servant is employed to do that it cannot be understood to be a part of it. Whether the servant is on a frolic of his own or not is largely a question of fact and degree (*cf. Harvey* v. *O'Dell* (1958)—a journey of five miles during working hours to get lunch by servant who was paid a subsistence allowance and had no express instructions concerning lunch from his master was thought *obiter* to be within the course of his employment, with *Hilton* v. *Thomas Burton* (1961)—servants who knocked off early and repaired to a cafe were not acting in the course of their employment when driving back). In *General Engineering Services Ltd.* v. *Kingston* (1988) it was found that a fire-station crew which engaged in an industrial go-slow in proceeding to a fire was acting outside the course of employment. It is settled law that in the absence of special circumstances a servant travelling to work is not acting in the course of his employment. In *Smith* v. *Stages* (1989) it was held that travel by a servant back from a temporary place of work to the main workplace was within the course of employment where lost time through travel was paid for at the wage rate, even though the mode and to some extent the date and time of travel were left to the servant.

If the servant is performing work that he is employed to do in an improper way, he will be acting within the course of his employment. In *Century Insurance Co. Ltd.* v. *Northern Ireland*

Road Transport Board (1942) the House of Lords held that a lorry driver who caused a fire by striking a match to light a cigarette while transferring petrol from his lorry to an underground tank in the plaintiff's garage was acting in the course of his employment because he was doing in an unauthorised way that which he was employed to do. The distinction between doing an act which is no part of the servant's employment and doing authorised work in an improper manner is also relevant where the act in question has been specifically prohibited by the master. If the prohibition is regarded as delimiting the scope of the servant's employment, the prohibited act will be outside the course of employment. If what is prohibited is an improper method of carrying out the servant's authorised tasks, it will be within the course of employment (so in *Limpus* v. *London General Omnibus Co.* (1862) the defendants' bus driver who raced his bus with another belonging to a rival company despite the fact that the defendants had expressly warned their drivers not to race, was held to be acting within the course of his employment.) The case may be contrasted with *Iqbal* v. *London Transport Executive* (1974). The employee in question, a bus conductor, was found to be acting outside the course of his employment in driving the bus in breach of the express instructions of his employer.

The question of the effect of prohibitions on the servant's conduct causes difficulty in the case of the servant who gives unauthorised lifts to third parties in his employer's vehicle. If such a person is injured by the negligence of the employee, courts have based the non-liability of the employer on the fact that the servant was not acting in the course of his employment (*Twine* v. *Bean's Express* (1946); *Conway* v. *Wimpey* (1951) in which it was also explained by reason of the plaintiff's status as a trespasser on the vehicle). In *Rose* v. *Plenty* (1975) a milk roundsman had, contrary to the instructions of his employer, made use of the services of the plaintiff, a thirteen-year-old boy, for the purpose of assisting him in delivering milk. The plaintiff was injured by the negligent driving of the float by the roundsman. The Court of Appeal by a majority held the employer of the milk roundsman vicariously liable for his negligence to the plaintiff. All three members of the Court of Appeal treated the question as turning on whether the roundsman was acting in the course of his employment—the plaintiff's status as a trespasser on the float did not affect the duties owed to him by the servant and the vicarious liability of the employer depended upon whether the servant and not the employer had committed a tort. The majority were able to distinguish the earlier cases on the ground that in them the plaintiffs were receiving gratuitous lifts whereas here the plaintiff was being used for the purpose of the employer's business. Although the case seems rightly decided, the distinction it draws is not very satisfactory. In the earlier cases, it is not clear why the employer's prohibition is regarded as delimiting the sphere of the servant's employment since, apart from the prohibited act, the servant was carrying out his duties in a normal fashion. In any case it seems clear that the employer would have been liable in those cases had the servant's negligence injured a third party.

In some cases difficulty has arisen because the servant has performed some act which is not part of the servant's normal employment, but which by implication may be within the scope of his employment. Thus a servant may have an implied authority to defend his master's property, using physical force if necessary. If such a servant uses an unreasonable amount of force against one whom he reasonably suspects to be stealing from his master (so being deprived of the defence of defence of property), his master will be liable for the servant's act which is merely a wrongful way of performing something within the scope of the servant's employment (*Poland & Sons* v. *Parr* (1927)). On the other hand a servant, though he may have an implied authority to detain one whom he suspects to be obtaining his master's goods without paying for them, has no authority to do this when such payment has been made. So in *Warren* v. *Henley's Ltd.* (1948) the servant, a garage attendant, accused the plaintiff of attempting to leave without paying for petrol supplied to him. Later, after the plaintiff had paid, the servant assaulted him. The garage was held not liable because the servant had not acted in the course of his employment. (See also *Keppel Bus Co.* v. *Sa'ad Bin Ahmad* (1974)).

In order to be acting within the course of his employment, the servant must commit the tort during his actual hours of employment. For example, a servant who returned to his work without his master's permission after the premises had been closed would not be acting within the course of his employment. But a reasonable extension to normal working hours will be recognised by the courts as not outside the course of employment, for example, the servant who stays for a short time in order to finish a job, or one who leaves taps running in a washroom which he visits after completing his working day, so damaging the plaintiff's property (see *Ruddiman & Co.* v. *Smith* (1889)).

Criminal conduct by servant

The problem here is whether the servant who commits a crime or acts dishonestly entirely for his own benefit is acting within the course of his employment. The mere fact that the servant has committed a crime is clearly not enough to take his act outside the course of his employment—thus, the commission by a servant of a breach of statutory duty while performing his authorised work would be inside the scope of his employment. Even where the servant has acted for his own benefit the master may be held liable. Whether the servant's act will be regarded as within the course of his employment will depend upon whether it can be regarded as a wrongful performance of the work which the servant is employed to do. Thus in *Morris* v. *Martin* (1966), the master was held liable for the theft of the mink coat by the servant to whom it had been entrusted for cleaning (for this explanation of the decision based upon conventional principles of vicarious liability, see the judgment of Diplock L.J.). The Court of Appeal was in agreement that if the theft had been a servant who had no duties in relation to the coat, the master would not have been liable.

Vicarious liability for statements; apparent authority

Vicarious liability in tort may exist for the making of a fraudulent or negligent statement through a servant or agent which has been relied on to his loss by the plaintiff, provided the statement is made within the actual or apparent authority of the servant or agent. No problem arises of course in cases of actual authority. The first case in which apparent authority of a servant was used to establish vicarious liability in tort was *Lloyd* v. *Grace, Smith & Co.* (1912) and it was generally thought that the test of apparent authority was made use of by the House of Lords in that case to remove the difficulty as to whether a fraudulent servant acting for his own benefit could be said to be acting in the course of his employment. Now, however, the test of authority seems to apply to statements whether or not they are made fraudulently. In *Lloyd* the defendants, a firm of solicitors, were held liable for the fraud of its conveyancing clerk who had induced the plaintiff to convey to him two cottages which she wished to sell, representing that this was necessary for the transaction. The defendants had clothed the clerk with apparent authority in the matter, since conveying property was within the class of acts he was employed to perform. On the other hand in *Kooragang Investments Pty. Ltd.* v. *Richardson & Wrench Ltd.* (1982) the servant who worked for the defendants, a firm of valuers, had been told by them not to perform valuations for the plaintiff company. Nevertheless he performed certain valuations for the plaintiffs in his own time and, the valuations being negligent, the plaintiffs suffered loss. The Privy Council held the defendants not liable to the plaintiffs for this loss. Although valuations were clearly of the class of act the employee was employed to perform, the defendants had done nothing to hold him out as having authority in the transaction in question and indeed the plaintiffs did not know of his connection with the defendants. (See also *Armagas Ltd.* v. *Mundogas S.A.* (1986)—no apparent authority, in the absence of a representation by the principal, to communicate principal's approval of a contract known by the plaintiff to be outside the usual authority of the agent.)

Acts simultaneously inside and outside course of employment

Although there are only *obiter dicta* in support, it seems correct to say that the servant may be acting inside the course of his employment *vis-à-vis* one person, and outside it *vis-à-vis* another. In *Twine* v. *Bean's Express Ltd.* (1946) the defendants' servant, the driver of a vehicle belonging to the defendants, had given a lift to the plaintiff contrary to the defendants' instructions, and by his negligent driving of the vehicle had caused him injury. The employers were held not liable to the plaintiff because the servant's act was wholly outside the course of the servant's employment, rather than an improper means of carrying it out. But Lord Greene M.R. expressed the view that as far as persons other than the plaintiff were concerned the driving of the van was inside the course of employment, so that had they been injured by the negligent driving they would have had an action against the employer. This view appears sound in principle.

LIABILITY FOR THE ACTS OF AN INDEPENDENT CONTRACTOR

The liability of one who has employed a contractor to do work may be personal under the ordinary rules of tort, rather than vicarious. So, he may have instructed or authorised the contractor to commit a tort, or by his negligent instructions may have contributed to the contractor's commission of a tort, or he may have committed a tort of strict liability through the contractor (as in *Rylands* v. *Fletcher* (1868)). In certain cases there may be liability for the negligence of a contractor although the employer is not personally at fault and no tort of strict liability has been committed. Such liability has been based by English courts on a breach by the employer of a non-delegable duty of care binding on himself. Liability is therefore still personal rather than a vicarious liability for the contractor's negligence. This formulation is misleading in so far as it suggests that liability is other than strict. The employer of the independent contractor is not liable for his *fault* in delegating to the contractor. Indeed in many cases it would be negligent not to employ a contractor. Furthermore the liability of the employer of an independent contractor is in one respect stricter than the vicarious liability of an employer for the torts of his servant. The employer of the contractor has no detailed control of the way in which the work is done—the employer of a servant has such control.

There is no reason of policy comparable to the case of the employer of servants why liability should exist for the negligence of an independent contractor in every case. Contractors are usually financially responsible persons; their employers are often not. Policy reasons have dictated that liability should exist in two categories of case: (i) the person who has commissioned work involving exceptional risk is liable for the negligence of a contractor in carrying out that work; (ii) certain persons (who will in the normal course of events be financially responsible), and who have a duty of care for the protection of other persons by reason of their relationship to them, are not allowed to delegate the performance of that duty to a contractor. These two categories, and two additional categories less easily explained in terms of policy, will be examined in turn.

(1) *Exceptional risks*

The leading case on this category is *Honeywill and Stein* v. *Larkin Brothers Ltd.* (1934). The defendants had employed a contractor to take flashlight photographs inside a cinema. They were held liable for his negligence in starting a fire because the work commissioned was "extra-hazardous." This category also includes liability for work commissioned on the highway, which involves unusual hazards both because of the large number of people whom it may affect and because of the dangers of motorised traffic. Thus in *Holliday* v. *National Telephone Co.* (1899) the contractor, a plumber, was employed by the defendants to solder tubes through which the defendants' telephone wires were to be passed. The telephone wires were situated on the highway. The contractor carried out his work negligently and the plaintiff, a passing pedestrian was injured by molten solder. The defendants were held liable to the plaintiff. In an action for failure to maintain the highway brought against the highway authority, it is no defence for the highway authority to show that it had arranged for a competent contractor to carry out or supervise the maintenance of the highway (section 1(3) of the Highways (Miscellaneous Provisions) Act 1961). *Salsbury* v. *Woodland* (1970) held that the category of work done on the highway should not be extended to work done near the highway; also that the felling of a tree near the highway did not fall within the extra-hazardous category.

(2) *Non-delegability of duty of care for protection of a class of persons*

The master's personal duty of care to provide for the physical safety of his servants by providing proper plant, premises, staff and system of work is the most obvious, in fact the only clear, example of the duty of care falling within category (2). Policy dictates that the master, normally a financially responsible person, should not be able to escape from the duty of care by transferring it to another person, even one who may also be financially responsible (he may of course, have remedies in contract or by way of contribution proceedings against a negligent contractor). The duty of care which hospitals owe to their patients for their treatment may, as suggested above, be another example of this category but the law is not yet finally settled.

(3) *Nuisance*

Liability in nuisance for the acts of an independent contractor is considered in Chapter 15.

(4) *Duties analogous to contractual duties*

A number of amorphous cases are gathered together here, their common quality and the justification for doing so being that liability is close to or analogous to contract and it is clear that contracts must be personally performed and that the contractual duty may not be delegated. The bailee for reward, contractual or otherwise, owes a duty of care in the safekeeping of the chattel which is not capable of being discharged through the employment of a contractor (*B.R.S.* v. *Arthur V. Crutchley* (1968)). The same is true of a sub-bailee for reward in relation to custody of the goods of the owner (*Morris* v. *Martin* (1966)). In *D. & F. Estates Ltd.* v. *Church Commissioners* (1988), on the other hand, the House of Lords thought that a main contractor was not liable for negligence in the execution of plastering work by a sub-contractor, even though this might constitute a tort towards a future lessee or purchaser of the premises, where the main contractor was not in contractual relationship with that lessee or purchaser. A carrier of goods is liable to the cargo owner for loss of cargo which occurs through the negligence of a contractor employed by him (*Riverstone Meat Co.* v. *Lancashire Shipping Co.* (1961)). *Rogers* v. *Night Riders* (1983) is a case falling within this category although it takes the law further. The plaintiff hired a minicab by telephone from the defendants, thinking that the latter were providing both cab and driver. In fact the defendants merely booked the cab, the driver being independent of them. Nevertheless the defendants were held liable for injuries the plaintiffs received in an accident caused by the unroadworthiness of the minicab. The defendants had held themselves out to the plaintiff as a car hire firm and the plaintiff was entitled to expect personal performance by the defendants of the duty to provide a safe vehicle.

It should not be imagined that the four categories considered here are exhaustive of the cases in which the employee may be held liable for the negligence of an independent contractor.

Collateral negligence

The rule is generally stated to be that the employer is not liable for the collateral negligence of the contractor, even though the case is one in which liability for the acts of an independent contractor exists. It is not, however, clear what is meant by collateral negligence. One possibility is that it refers to negligence which is outside the risk created by the work commissioned and this view has much to support it. Another possibility, which is less satisfactory, is that it refers to casual acts of negligence by employees of the contractor not related to the execution of the work. The leading case seems, however, to support the latter view. In *Padbury* v. *Holliday & Greenwood* (1912) the defendants, who were having a building built by a contractor on the highway, were held not liable for the negligence of a servant of the contractor who rested a hammer on a window-sill from which a strong wind blew it causing it to fall on and injure the plaintiff. The defendants were held not liable on the ground that this was collateral negligence. The case seems unsatisfactory. There was no suggestion that the servant had acted outside the course of his employment. The reason for imposing liability for the acts of contractors in these circumstances is the risk to persons using the highway and that risk had materialised. (Where the servant's negligence is clearly in the execution of the work commissioned, the employer of the contractor will be liable (*Holliday* v. *National Telephone Co.* (1899)).

LIABILITY OF CAR OWNERS

It has been established for some time that a car owner who has delegated the driving of a car to another person while remaining a passenger in the car is liable for the negligence of the driver, on the ground that he has retained control over the vehicle. This is personal rather than vicarious liability. In *Ormrod* v. *Crosville Motor Services Ltd.* (1953) an extension to this rule was recognised, when the owner of a car which was being driven from London to Monte Carlo at the owner's request and for his benefit but in which he was not himself travelling was held liable for the driver's negligence. The ratio of the case is that where the driving is done at the request of the owner and for his purposes, the driver is the owner's agent, and the owner is vicariously liable for his negligence.

A latter case, *Launchbury* v. *Morgans* (1971) concerned the liability of the owner of a car whose husband borrowed it daily for work. She knew that the husband occasionally stopped out late for a drink, and acquiesced in this, provided he got someone else to drive him home if he was unfit to drive. After one such evening, the husband was killed and the plaintiffs, passengers in the car, were injured through the negligence of the husband's friend who was driving the car for the husband. In the Court of Appeal, the wife was held vicariously liable for the negligence of the friend on the ground that the car was being driven for her purposes, either on the ground that it was in the wife's interest that the husband should be driven home safely, or that in the case of a "matrimonial" car almost any journey undertaken by either spouse in it has a joint matrimonial purpose. The House of Lords refused to accept either argument. The fact that the wife had an interest in the driving did not mean that it was done for her purposes. Furthermore, the innovation of the "matrimonial" or "family" car was one for the legislature rather than the courts to make. The decision had unfortunate practical consequences for the plaintiffs since it meant that they could not recover on the wife's insurance policy which did not have a "named driver" clause. Now that insurance against liability to passengers in a motor vehicle is compulsory, the wife herself could be sued in similar circumstances for breach of statutory duty for permitting the car to be driven without insurance cover. More importantly, the plaintiffs would have an action against the Motor Insurers Bureau which by agreement among insurance companies pays out in cases where insurance against third party liability is compulsory but insurance cover does not exist. The House of Lords did not disapprove of *Ormrod* v. *Crosville Motor Services* and presumably the doctrine laid down by that case survives intact. Some of the other cases in which owners have been held liable for the negligence of those whom they have permitted to drive their cars must, however, be of dubious authority in the light of the judgments in the House of Lords (*cf.* especially, *Parker* v. *Miller* (1926); *Carberry* v. *Davies*

(1968)). Following *Launchbury* v. *Morgans*, the Court of Appeal in *Norwood* v. *Nevan* (1981) refused to make a finding of agency against the defendant husband where he permitted the use of his car by his wife for purposes including the family shopping and while on such a trip she by her negligent driving caused injury to the plaintiff.

21. DEFAMATION

The tort of defamation protects a person's interest in his reputation. Thus, if the defendant has made an untrue statement, or what amounts to a statement, which is defamatory of the plaintiff, the plaintiff has a right of action against him unless the defendant can establish one of the special defences available to an action for defamation. It is important to note that the tort protects the plaintiff's reputation as it appears to other people. This means that publication of the statement by the defendant to persons other than the plaintiff himself is an essential part of the tort—the purpose of the tort is not to protect the injured feelings of the plaintiff (on the other hand it appears to be accepted that there is defamation if the statement is made to a person who disbelieves it—see, for example, Lord Reid in *Morgan* v. *Odhams Press* (1971), the justification for this being, according to Lord Reid, the annoyance caused to the plaintiff). The tort goes beyond protecting the mere personal reputation of the plaintiff and extends to the protection of the reputation of his commercial and business undertakings.

The rules of the tort represent an attempt to strike a balance between two important and often competing interests, the public interest in freedom of speech (which is a private interest also), and the private interest in maintaining one's reputation. The difficulty of achieving this balance is perhaps indicated by the fact that, though liability for a defamatory statement is strict and substantial damages may be recovered from one who makes such a statement, a large variety of defences exist for the protection of one who makes such a statement. It is also the case that many of the rules of the tort, though reasonably well settled as matters of law, are notoriously uncertain in their practical application. This again supports the idea of the law treading a knife-edge between two conflicting positions.

The recovery of substantial damages for a defamatory statement, especially from one who is ignorant of the defamatory nature of the statement, has led to criticism. It is true that a few years ago damages awarded by juries in actions for defamation seemed disproportionately high when compared with damages awarded by judges for personal injury. In *Sutcliffe* v. *Pressdram Ltd.* (1990) the Court of Appeal reduced an original jury award of £600,000 damages for defamation to a tenth of the original on the ground that it was unreasonably high and must have contained an element of exemplary damages which the jury could not award on the facts of the case. Trial judges were advised to give homely and practical examples to the jury to indicate the purchasing power of the money it was awarding, so as to keep damages awards within reasonable bounds. The innocent defamer may still be liable to pay heavy damages for defamation despite the existence of certain defences that may operate for his protection and which are considered later in this chapter. Publication of an immediate retraction of the defamatory statement once the defendant becomes aware of it should, however, normally restrict the damages payable to a moderate amount. There is clearly no equity to limit the damages awarded against persons who calculatedly make use of defamatory statements as a means of selling newspapers and periodicals. This is one of the cases, and indeed the outstanding case, in which the power to award exemplary damages survives. The Faulks Committee Report on Defamation (Cmnd. 5909) recommended that the court's discretion as to whether to allow a jury trial in a defamation case should be the normal unfettered one (as to the present rule, see Chapter 1).

SLANDER AND LIBEL

Defamation comprises two torts, slander and libel. The distinction was formerly of purely procedural effect, slander being actionable in the common law courts while libel was purely within the jurisdiction of the Star Chamber. After the common law courts succeeded to the jurisdiction of the Star Chamber over libel, the distinction was maintained and unfortunately acquired substantive force. Broadly speaking, it can now be said that slander is committed by one who publishes the defamatory statement orally, libel by one who publishes it in writing. The effect of the distinction is that in the case of slander proof of special damage is, with four exceptions, an essential part of the plaintiff's cause of action; libel is on the other hand actionable *per se*. The distinction receives some justification from the greater triviality and lesser potentiality for doing harm of spoken rather than written words. But it still seems unfortunate for several reasons. In the case of slander which is not actionable *per se*, the plaintiff often has no means at all of vindicating his reputation. The distinction can also be criticised both for the difficulties that arise in drawing it and for its arbitrary nature. The line between slander and libel may be drawn on the technical ground that slander has its impact on the aural sense, libel on the visual. Thus libel would include defamatory pictures, statues, and conduct such as hanging the plaintiff in effigy. This distinction if based upon the greater permanency and therefore capacity to cause harm of writing and pictorial representations is not easily defensible in the light of modern methods of perpetuating sound, as in films, radio and television, gramophone records and tapes. But a distinction based merely upon the degree of permanence of the statement has at the moment no obvious acceptance in the English case law.

The only English case which suggests that the test is anything other than a mechanical one depending upon the mode of publication of the statement is *Forrester* v. *Tyrrell* (1893) in which it was held that reading out a defamatory written statement is libel. It is weak authority for a test of permanency, but does not distinguish according to whether the listener to the statement realises that a written statement is being read. It is contradicted by *Osborn* v. *Boulter and Son* (1930) in which two members of the Court of Appeal thought that the dictation of a letter to a typist and the reading out of the letter aloud after dictation amounted to slander alone, and the third thought that it amounted to libel. In *Youssoupoff* v. *Metro-Goldwyn-Mayer Pictures Ltd.* (1934) it was held that a film which suggested as a matter of historical fact that the plaintiff had at one time been raped was libellous, but as the defamatory meaning was conveyed by a combination of pictorial representations and sound, the case is no support for the view that a defamatory anecdote told in a film is libel. Defamatory statements made in broadcasts whether through radio or television are, under the Defamation Act 1952, to be treated as published in permanent form by which is meant that they are libel. So, under the Theatres Act 1968 are statements in theatrical performances. However, the uncertainty about other media such as films, gramophone records and recorded tapes, as well as statements made through trained parrots and skywriting, remains. The Report of the Committee on Defamation recommended abolition of the distinction between libel and slander. The Committee was satisfied that this would not lead to an undue increase in frivolous actions brought in respect of spoken words.

Slander actionable per se

In four cases the plaintiff does not have to prove special damage as part of his cause of action in slander:

(1) Imputation of crime

It is slander actionable *per se* to impute to the plaintiff the commission of a crime that is punishable by imprisonment.

(2) Imputation of disease

The disease imputed must be infectious or contagious and the imputation must be that the plaintiff is presently suffering from it.

(3) Imputation in respect of office, profession, calling, trade or business

At common law an imputation that a schoolteacher had committed adultery with a school cleaner was not actionable *per se* under this rubric—it reflected discredit on the schoolteacher as a man rather than on the man as a schoolteacher. But section 2 of the Defamation Act 1952 makes it slander actionable *per se* where the words are calculated to disparage the plaintiff in his office, profession, calling, trade or business, though not spoken of him in the way of such office, profession, calling, trade or business.

(4) Imputation of unchastity to a woman under Slander of Women Act 1891

Such imputation includes one of lesbianism (*Kerr* v. *Kennedy* (1942)).

Special damage in slander not actionable per se

Material loss such as loss of employment, loss of contracts through refusal by persons to contract with the plaintiff and loss of hospitality from friends proved to have provided food and drink on former occasions is special damage for the purpose of the tort. Nervous shock and illness arising from mental distress do not appear to be recoverable in slander, although the rule in libel and slander actionable *per se* is different, and no satisfactory explanation appears to exist for this difference.

Where the damage is suffered because of a third party's action, this may make it too remote (*Lynch* v. *Knight* (1861)—damage too remote where the husband made his wife leave home when he heard she had almost been seduced before marriage). But there is no rule of law that deliberate repetition of the defamatory statement renders the further damage it causes too remote. The matter is governed by the ordinary rule of remoteness relating to the deliberate acts of thirds parties, that is that the repetition must be the probable consequence of the original publication. Thus in *Slipper* v. *B.B.C.* (1991) the plaintiff was allowed to proceed with a claim for the further damage caused by press reviews of a B.B.C. film which had been shown by the B.B.C. at a preview to T.V. critics. The earlier case of *Weld-Blundell* v. *Stephens* (1920) was distinguished on the ground that the third party in passing on the contents of a letter known by him to be a confidential letter was acting as a mischief-maker.

PRINCIPLES OF DEFAMATION

It now remains to consider those principles which are applicable to both libel and slander. In order to establish the defendant's liability in defamation, the plaintiff must show that the defendant has published a statement about him which is defamatory.

Defamatory nature of the statement

The requirement that the statement should bring the plaintiff into hatred, contempt or ridicule, formerly the accepted definition of a defamatory statement, is now recognised to be inadequate in the light of decisions that to impute to the plaintiff that she has been raped (*Youssoupoff's* case, *supra*) or is insane is defamatory. The test that the statement should lower the plaintiff in the esteem of right-thinking men also fails to explain these cases. These tests fail to appreciate that the reaction of society as a whole to the statement may be irrational and emotional and may make people inclined to shun the plaintiff when what is imputed to him is a misfortune rather than a misdeed. Thus to say of the plaintiff that he is illegitimate, impotent or has cancer is almost certainly defamatory.

Another problem arises where the statement is calculated to bring the plaintiff into disfavour with a certain section of the community which is not an ordinary cross-section of the community and whose reaction to the statement is questionably right-thinking. Although there is little English authority on the point it has been held that to call a person a German in time of war with Germany is defamatory; it also seems likely that it is defamatory to call a person a Communist. These problems become more intractable when the statement imputes something to the plaintiff upon which there are deep divisions within the country. Is it defamatory to say that a worker is a non-unionist, or is a "scab," or that a student is a demonstrator? The answer to each question is, it is submitted, yes, on the ground that the statement is calculated to bring the plaintiff into disfavour with a sufficiently sizeable section of the community. This must receive some qualification, however, in the light of the decision of the Court of Appeal in *Byrne* v. *Deane* (1937). In that case it was held that it was not defamatory to say of a member of a club that he had supplied the police with information about an illegal gaming machine kept at the club, because a person who supplies such information ought not to be less well-thought of by his fellows. The decision may be explained in terms of policy. While police informers are no doubt held in some disesteem by a possibly sizeable proportion of the population, it would be impolitic for a court to appear to indicate its agreement with this view.

Circumstances of time, place and occasion will often be relevant in determining whether a statement has a defamatory content. Thus it is only defamatory to say of a person that he is a German if a state of war prevails between Germany and this country. The relevance of occasion explains why mere vulgar abuse spoken in the course of quarrelling is normally not defamatory. To call another a bastard in the course of a skirmish would not be defamatory, since the listeners would understand that the statement was not intended to contain any substratum of fact. But if the statement was intended to convey that a factual basis existed for the statement, or if its listener would reasonably interpret it in his way, then the statement would be defamatory even if uttered as abuse.

Statements imputing incompetence to the plaintiff in his trade or profession are actionable in the same way as attacks upon his character. Thus to suggest that the goods manufactured by the plaintiff are of inferior quality or that a film critic is an incompetent member of his profession is undoubtedly defamatory. Equally it is possible for a trading association such as a company to sue in defamation (*South Hetton Coal Co.* v. *North Eastern News Association* (1894)). It has also been held that a trade union (*Willis* v. *Brooks* (1947)), and a local authority (*Bognor Regis U.D.C.* v. *Campion* (1972)) can be defamed, although under the present trade union legislation the trade union may not have sufficient legal personality to sue (*E.E.P.T.U.* v. *The Times* (1980)). It may be noted that dead persons cannot be defamed. The Faulks Committee recommended that corporations and associations should be allowed to succeed in defamation only if they could show special damage or the likelihood of pecuniary injury. The Committee also recommended a limited right of recovery in defamation for the estate of a deceased person (*infra*, p. 408).

In order that a statement be defamatory it must be untrue, but not every untrue statement is defamatory. To say that the plaintiff has ceased to be in business is not defamatory since this can have no damaging effect upon the plaintiff's reputation (*Ratcliffe* v. *Evans* (1892)). If such a statement is made maliciously and if it causes the plaintiff actual damage, the plaintiff has another cause of action against the defendant (*infra*, p. 386). Negligence is also a possible cause of action here.

Interpretation of defamatory statements: innuendo

The test to be applied is whether the words of the defendant in their ordinary and natural sense defame the plaintiff. The whole of the defendant's statement must be looked at, not merely that which the plaintiff relies on as being defamatory. This is important because what follows an *ex facie* defamatory statement may qualify or explain it (as in, "Lord X, you are a thief. You have stolen my heart"). Where the plaintiff is not relying on the words having a defamatory meaning which is not explicitly stated, but which can be collected from the words in their ordinary and natural sense, the plaintiff does not have the burden of proving such extended meaning, and it is for the judge to decide whether the words are capable of bearing that meaning. The plaintiff does not have to allege such extended meaning in his pleadings, though in some cases it may be prudent for him to do so. In this situation the plaintiff is said to be relying on a "false" innuendo, false in the sense that the burden of proving such innuendo does not rest upon him. In *Lewis* v. *Daily Telegraph* (1964) the defendant newspaper stated that the Fraud Squad of the City of London Police were investigating the affairs of the plaintiff's company. The House of Lords held that, though the natural interpretation of these words was that the plaintiff was reasonably suspected of fraud, and were therefore prima facie defamatory, they could not bear the interpretation that the plaintiff had actually been guilty of fraud, so that the defendant could justify the statement by proving the facts stated. If the defendant has stated therefore that A reasonably suspects B of fraud, this is only defamatory if it is not true; if on the other hand, he says that A has told him that B has committed fraud, this is apparently defamatory in the sense that B has actually been fraudulent (*M'Pherson* v. *Daniels* (1829)). The distinction though not difficult to draw is difficult to justify. (See also *Cadam* v. *Beaverbrook Newspapers* (1959)— statement that a writ had been issued for conspiracy to defraud could be defamatory even if true).

Where the defamatory meaning cannot be collected from the actual words used, and the plaintiff is relying upon knowledge by those who have received the statement of facts which render it defamatory, the plaintiff is said to rely on a "true" innuendo. In *Tolley* v. *J. S. Fry and Sons Ltd.* (1931) the plaintiff, a well-known amateur golfer, was depicted in cartoon likeness in the defendants' advertisement, the suggestion in the advertisement being that he had a fondness for the defendants' chocolate. The advertisement was held to be defamatory because it suggested that the plaintiff had infringed his amateur status by accepting payment for appearing in the advertisement. This meaning could not have been derived from the advertisement alone; the plaintiff therefore had to prove that there were persons who knew of him as an amateur golfer and who would read the meaning he alleged into the advertisement. Where the plaintiff is relying on facts not stated in the defendant's statement in order to prove its defamatory nature, he must give details of these facts in his pleadings. He must therefore also prove the existence of such facts on the balance of probabilities.

The interpretation of the statement is along with other matters of law for the judge rather than the jury. He must decide, *inter alia*, whether the statement is capable of being defamatory in the sense that it is capable of bearing the meaning that the plaintiff puts upon it. If it is, the jury, which decides questions of fact, then decides whether it is actually defamatory. The interpretative function of the judge allows him to exercise considerable control over the outcome of an action, and can be abused (see, for example, the surprising decision in *Capital and Counties Bank* v. *Henty* (1882) in which it was held that the defendants' statement to their customers that they would not receive in payment cheques drawn on the plaintiff bank was incapable of being defamatory, although it caused a run on the bank).

Reference to the plaintiff

There must be a sufficient reference to the plaintiff in the defendant's statement. In the absence of express mention of the plaintiff in the statement, this means that a reasonable man reading the statement and knowing the plaintiff, would take it to be referring to him. Where the defendant's statement is made of a large class of people which includes the plaintiff ("All lawyers are crooked," or "All West Indians are idle") an action in defamation will generally not succeed although the statement may constitute a criminal offence, for example, seditious libel, or an incitement to a breach of the peace. But if the class referred to is so small that the defendant's statement may be regarded as being defamatory of each member of it, then the defendant may be successfully sued by each member. Thus where seventeen defendants had been indicted for murder, the defendant's statement that all took part in the murder was actionable by each of them (*Foxcroft* v. *Lacy* (1613)). Furthermore, a statement made about a class which would ordinarily be too large to allow members of the class to sue may be actionable by individual members of that class if there is evidence that the statement particularly refers to them. So in *Le Fanu* v. *Malcolmson* (1848) a statement in an article by the defendant imputing cruelties to Irish factory owners was found by the court on a reading of the article as a whole to refer to factory owners in Waterford including the plaintiff.

Reference to the plaintiff by the defendant's statement need not be intentional. There is sufficient reference if the defendant has used a fictitious name to identify a person in a work intended to be fictional, provided that it is believed by certain persons to refer to the plaintiff (*cf. Hulton* v. *Jones* (1910) in which one Artemus Jones, a churchwarden of Peckham was said in a newspaper article to be conducting an amorous liaison with a woman not his wife— the real Artemus Jones, a barrister who was not a churchwarden and who did not live at Peckham recovered £1,750 damages because several people testified to the fact that they thought the statement referred to him). Equally a true statement about one person may be defamatory of another person with the same name (*Newstead* v. *London Express Newspaper* (1940)—a newspaper statement that Harold Newstead, a thirty-year-old Camberwell man had been convicted of bigamy was true of a Camberwell barman of that name but untrue of the plaintiff, a Camberwell barber aged about thirty. The statement was held to be defamatory of the plaintiff). Finally it is clear that the statement need not expressly refer to the plaintiff, provided persons reading it or hearing it would take it as so referring. In *Cassidy* v. *Daily Mirror Newspapers* (1929), a newspaper photograph of Cassidy with a woman, together with a statement that the two had become engaged was held to be defamatory of Cassidy's wife who would have been assumed by those reading the statement who knew her to have been living in sin. The result of this case has been confirmed by *Morgan* v. *Odhams Press* (1971). In that case an article in the defendants' newspaper stated that a girl, who had been an accomplice of a dog-doping gang, had been kidnapped by members of the gang. The girl in question had, to the knowledge of people who read the article, stayed with the plaintiff during the period mentioned in the article and in the area indicated by the article. The article was held to be defamatory of the plaintiff. This is an astonishing decision. It would not seem to matter whether the statement is true, provided that in the minds of certain people it implicates the plaintiff, and this implication is false. So a newspaper which publishes a correct statement that a certain person has been murdered may be held liable to anyone whose friends believe him to have committed the murder. (The decision of the House of Lords is difficult to reconcile with *Astaire* v. *Campling* (1966)).

Whether the statement is capable of being understood as referring to the plaintiff is a question of law for the judge. Whether it in fact refers to him is a matter for the jury to decide.

Publication

Publication of the statement to persons other than the plaintiff himself is an essential requirement of defamation. This requirement is clearly satisfied where the defendant has intentionally made the statement to another person, but it is enough if the defendant should have foreseen its publication. Several cases have turned on whether the sender of a letter should foresee that it will be opened and read by someone other than its intended recipient. There is no publication when a father opens his son's letter, nor when a butler opens a letter to his employer even though it is unsealed. But it is to be expected that a postcard will be read, that clerks employed by the plaintiff will open letters addressed to him at his place of business and which appear to be business letters, and that a husband will open a letter which though sealed and addressed to his wife looks like a circular (on the last point see *Theaker* v. *Richardson* (1962)). There will also be publication if a Post Office official opens the letter in the course of his duties, for example, to check that it was the class of mail which ought to be placed in an unsealed envelope. Where the defendant has no reason to suspect that his statement is being published, as in the case where the statement is overheard by one whose presence is not reasonably suspected by the defendant, there is no publication (*White* v. *Stone Lighting and Radio Ltd.* (1939)).

It is also relevant in deciding whether there has been publication to consider the person to whom the statement has been made. Where a statement has been typed or printed at another's request, there is no publication where the statement is handed back to its author (*Eglantine Inn Ltd.* v. *Smith and Smith* (1948), a Northern Ireland decision—the typist or printer may be liable for its subsequent distribution under principles to be discussed below).

Publication by the defendant to his wife is also not enough though publication to the wife of the plaintiff is. In general the person to whom publication is made must be able to understand the statement—there is no publication by speaking the words to a deaf person who cannot lip-read, nor to an infant who is below the age of understanding, though there apparently is to one who does not believe the statement (Lord Reid in *Morgan* v. *Odhams Press*). Where the defendant's words have some special sense which can only be appreciated by one who knows of facts not stated by the defendant, it must be shown that publication has been made to such persons, though it is not necessary that any of them should be called to give evidence that he did so understand the defendant's words (*Hough* v. *London Express Newspapers Ltd.* (1940)). Publication by dictating the statement to a typist is sufficient (*Pullman* v. *Hill and Co.* (1891)).

One who repeats a defamatory statement made by another person is liable if the repetition constitutes a publication even if he does not know that the statement is defamatory. The original maker of the statement is liable for such republication if he has authorised it, or, it seems, if it is reasonably foreseeable. On these principles, the author, publisher, and printer of defamatory material and even such mechanical distributors as newsagents, bookshops and libraries are liable in defamation for the dissemination of the material among the public (for the defences available in the case of innocent defamation, see *infra*, this chapter). The printers in *Eglantine Inn* v. *Smith* (*supra*) were held liable on these principles because they clearly envisaged the distribution of the defamatory material among the public, and could therefore be taken to have authorised it. Liability of the maker of the statement for its subsequent repetition depends upon principles considered earlier in this chapter. Failure to remove defamatory matter may constitute publication (held *obiter* in *Byrne* v. *Deane* (*supra*) where the court considered that failure to remove the libel from the club notice-board amounted to publication). But the limits of this rule are ill-defined. There must be control by the defendant over the place where the statement appears and an expectation that he will keep it under periodic review. *Byrne* v. *Deane* was followed in the American case of *Hellar* v. *Bianco* (1952) in which failure to remove a libel from the wall of a toilet was held to be actionable defamation.

Nature of the liability for defamatory statement

Liability for publication of the statement requires, as noticed already, fault, in the form of intention or negligence on the defendant's part. Furthermore it seems clear that the defendant must intentionally make a statement (for example if the defendant's computer produced a defamatory statement through some mechanical defect, the defendant would not be liable). The defendant need not, however, know of the defamatory nature of the statement. He is liable, for example, if he does not know of facts which make the statement defamatory of the plaintiff, or if he does not realise that the statement refers to the plaintiff. Defamation is therefore in this sense a tort of strict liability (the "reference" cases, *supra*, make it clear that liability is strict).

DEFENCES TO DEFAMATION

Innocent defamation

The common law position whereby an innocent defamer could be held liable to pay substantial damages was clearly unjust. The rigour of the law has been mitigated in two respects.

(1) *Mechanical distributors*

Mechanical distributors of a libel, for example, newsagents, carriers, booksellers and circulating libraries are liable for publication of the libel despite ignorance of its existence. *Vizetelly* v. *Mudie's Select Library Ltd.* (1900) gives the mechanical distributor a defence if he can show that he neither knew nor ought to have known of the existence of the libel in the work he was distributing. *Vizetelly* indicated that in order to satisfy the latter requirement it might be necessary for the defendant to show both that there was nothing to put it on inquiry as to the existence of a libel in the work in question and that it employed staff to read for libels. The former is no doubt still the law but the latter seems unduly onerous at the present day.

(2) *Unintentional defamation*

Printers and publishers. The printer and publisher (other than a mere mechanical distributor) (the term "publisher" no doubt covers broadcasts on radio or television) of a defamatory statement cannot make use of the defence based on *Vizetelly's* case but may establish a defence based upon section 4 of the Defamation Act 1952. Under the terms of this section the publisher may make an offer of amends to the aggrieved party. This means an offer: (a) to publish or join in the publication of a suitable correction and apology; and (b) to take such steps as are reasonably practicable on his part for notifying persons to whom copies have been distributed that the words are alleged to be defamatory of the party aggrieved. If the offer of amends is accepted by the party aggrieved and duly performed, no proceedings for libel or slander may be taken against the party making the offer. If the offer of amends is not accepted by the party aggrieved, it is a defence to an action for libel or slander to prove that the words were published innocently in relation to the plaintiff. Innocent publication is defined in such a way as to include the various types of unintentional reference to the plaintiff in the cases considered above. It is also required, however, that the defendant must have exercised all reasonable care in relation to the publication and there must be some doubt whether each defendant in those cases could have established this. The defendant must also show that if he was not the author of the words, that the words were written by the author without malice. The difficulty of proving both the defendant's own lack of fault and the author's lack of malice has caused this section to be of little use to defendants. The Faulks Committee Report on Defamation recommended that the latter requirement should be dispensed with.

Justification

Defamation cannot be committed by telling the truth however deleterious an effect the truth may have on another's reputation. For the law protects the plaintiff against imputations about his actual character, rather than one he is generally thought to possess. The defendant, however, has the onus of establishing the truth of what he has said—he must justify the statement. The defendant justifying need only show that his statement was substantially accurate. A statement that the plaintiff had been sentenced to a fine or three weeks' imprisonment was justified by showing that he had actually been given the alternative of two weeks in prison (*Alexander* v. *North-Eastern Ry. Co.* (1865)). Further, section 5 of the Defamation Act 1952 provides that the defence will not fail if the truth of several charges is not established provided that, having regard to the truth of the remaining charges, the charge not proved does not materially injure the plaintiff's reputation. If, for example, the defendant states the plaintiff's conduct amounts to obtaining property and pecuniary advantage by deception under the Theft Act 1968, whereas in fact his conduct amounts to only one of these offences, the defendant could, it seems, justify by proving this. In such a case, however, there is nothing to prevent the plaintiff relying on his statement of claim on the one defamatory statement which the defendant cannot justify. Further, the defendant cannot adduce in mitigation of damages the fact that the plaintiff committed the other offence (*infra*, pp. 351–352). The Report of the Committee on Defamation recommended that section 5 of the Defamation Act 1952 should be amended to allow the defendant to refer to the whole of his statement in his defence of justification, so preventing the plaintiff from relying on a defamatory passage while omitting other material which the defendant can justify. Like other recommendations of the Faulks Committee, this recommendation has not been implemented, but the problem has to some extent been addressed by the decision of the Court of Appeal in *Polly Peck Holdings plc* v. *Trelford* (1986). In his judgment in that case O'Connor L.J. laid down the following rules: (a) where the plaintiff selects words from an article and pleads a false innuendo arising from those words, the defendant is entitled to refer to the article as a whole in order to show that the alleged innuendo does not exist; (b) where there are two separate and distinct defamatory statements, the plaintiff is entitled to select which one he wishes to complain of, though where the statements have a common sting (which is a matter of fact and degree), the defendant is entitled to succeed by justifying the sting; (c) section 5 of the Defamation Act 1952 only applies to distinct charges (*i.e.* imputations) in the words complained of by the plaintiff and therefore does not allow the defendant to justify with reference to other words of his of which the plaintiff does not complain—the defendant is better served by relying on the principles laid down under (a) and (b).

The defence of justification is integrally bound up with the interpretation of the statement since the defendant's justification must relate to the meaning finally put upon the statement by the jury, subject to the guidance and control of the judge (for a recent refusal to allow a case of justification to go to the jury because the natural and ordinary meaning of the words could not be that contented for by the defendant, see *Bookbinder* v. *Tebbitt* (1989). In *Lucas-Box* v. *News Group Newspapers Ltd.* (1986) the court required that a defendant who relied on justification make it clear in his pleadings the meaning of his words he is intending to justify. This does not of course pre-empt the jury's interpretative function nor need it necessarily prevent the defendant from urging another meaning at the trial. Its main purpose is to provide clarity and expedition in the course of the trial by removing misunderstandings between the parties.

A partial abrogation of the defence of justification has been provided by the Rehabilitation of Offenders Act 1974. The Act has introduced the notion of a "spent" conviction. Where a person has received a sentence for a crime, which generally speaking must not exceed 30 months' imprisonment, and where a certain period of time varying from five to 10 years has elapsed since the conviction (the rehabilitation period) the conviction becomes spent and the convicted person is entitled to be treated in law as though he had not been committed, charged with, prosecuted for, convicted of or sentenced for that offence. A person who publishes any of these facts may nevertheless rely upon the defence of justification (or any of the other defences to defamation). In the case of justification the Act expressly provides that this defence cannot succeed if the publication is proved to have been made with malice. The Act thus establishes the first infraction of the principle that truth is an absolute defence to the publication of defamatory material. It is worthy of note that section 13 of the Civil Evidence Act 1968 prevents the convicted person re-opening the issue of his guilt in proceedings for defamation by providing that the conviction is conclusive evidence of this fact.

Fair comment

It is a defence to an action of defamation that the defendant's words were fair comment upon a matter of public interest. More latitude is allowed to the defendant in establishing this defence than the previous one. In so far as his words consist of comment he is not required to show the objective correctness of his views. Indeed it is the difficulty of determining what is the correct view on so many matters that has led to the recognition of this defence.

But the courts have placed on the extent of the defence a number of restrictions which must now be considered.

Matter of public interest

The matter commented on must be one of public interest. Thus, it may concern the conduct of public officials, the government of the country both central and local, works of art and other matters submitted for public consideration, and other matters of public concern (such as the running of religious institutions) of which an exhaustive list cannot be given. The private life and conduct of anyone is not a matter of public interest, unless it throws light upon such matters as his fitness to hold public office.

Comment on true facts

The basis of the defence of fair comment is that the defendant is stating his honest opinion about certain facts. It is essential, therefore that his statement must contain, or refer to, facts upon which a comment can be based. If no such factual basis is stated, the allegation itself is treated as one of fact and must be justified—fair comment is not available as a defence. If, for example, the defendant has stated that X is a coward without more, fair comment is no defence, and he must prove the truth of the allegation. If, however, he alleges X to be a coward because he failed to volunteer for military service during the war, this is comment, and is protected provided he honestly believed it. Fair comment is, therefore, an important bastion of freedom of speech, allowing persons commenting on public affairs to indulge in criticism of a virulent or outspoken nature. The factual content of the statement need not be expressly stated and may be derived by implication from its context. Also, provided the defendant has referred to facts upon which he is commenting, these facts themselves do not need to support the allegation. These points emerge from the case of *Kemsley* v. *Foot* (1952). The defendant, a journalist, had written an article in a newspaper condemning the newspaper, the "Evening Standard" (not owned by Lord Kemsley) for its unethical standards in publishing a certain story. The article was headed "Lower than Kemsley." The House of Lords held that, taken in conjunction with the article itself, the headline could be regarded as an intended slur on the journalistic standards of the Kemsley press, and that a sufficient factual content existed in it (*i.e.* that Lord Kemsley was the proprietor of certain newspapers) to allow the defendant to plead the defence of fair comment.

What facts must the defendant prove in order to establish the defence of fair comment? Three types of fact must be distinguished in order to answer this question. The first are facts necessary to establish the minimum factual content of the statement in order to make available the defence of fair comment. This minimum factual content must be accurately stated though, as *Kemsley* v. *Foot* indicates, the requirement is easily satisfied. Second are facts stated by the defendant in his statement which go to establish the fairness of the comment. The former rule was that the defendant had to prove every factual allegation in his statement—comment had to be on facts truly stated. Under section 6 of the Defamation Act 1952, however, this is no longer necessary. The section provides that a defence of fair comment shall not fail by reason only that the truth of every allegation of fact is not proved if the expression of opinion is fair comment having regard to such of the facts alleged or referred to in the words complained of as are proved. This section refers only to the defence of fair comment and not to justification. The defendant must prove the truth of every defamatory allegation of fact in his statement, even though he could establish fair comment in relation to the facts he can prove (see *Truth* (*N.Z.*) *Ltd.* v. *Holloway* (1960)). Third are facts which the defendant has not stated in his comment but which he relies on to establish the fairness of his comment. Clearly the defendant will not fail by reason of a failure to prove one or more of such facts—the only relevance of such failure is that it tends to show the comment could not have been made fairly.

Because the defendant may have to prove the truth of factual allegations, whereas in the case of comment need only show that it is fair, it is clearly important to distinguish between what is fact in the defendant's statement and what is comment. This may, however, be a troublesome question. If the defendant has criticised a certain play because of the inadequacy of its plot, this is comment and it is irrelevant that the majority of leading drama critics would disagree with the defendant's views. If, however, the play is based on true events, a criticism which failed to make this clear and at the same time castigated the weakness of the plot would be factually inaccurate and the plea of fair comment would fail for this reason. The mere fact that the truth of the defendant's comment may be tested either empirically or by hearing evidence on the matter does not necessarily deprive it of the status of comment, provided it is a fair comment in the light of what is known to the defendant. This is because what the defendant is expressing is an opinion as to the truth of the fact, rather than advancing it as fact itself. The defendant runs the risk, however, that the court will treat his statement as a factual allegation and require him to justify it. This is well illustrated by *London Artists* v. *Littler* (1969) in which the defendant, relying on the fact that the owners of a theatre wished to get a certain play produced by the defendant out of their theatre by a certain time, and the fact that the actors in the play all gave notice of termination of their contracts through the same agent at the same time and in the same form, alleged the existence of a plot between the artists and the theatre owners. The Court of Appeal treated this as a factual allegation and required the defendant to justify it.

A particular instance showing the difficulty of drawing the line between fact and comment is that in which the defendant imputes motives of dishonesty or self-seeking to the plaintiff. Such an allegation may be treated as one of comment, but in evaluating the fairness of such a comment the law adopts a stricter test than that applying generally in cases of fair comment. The defendant must here show a reasonable basis of fact for the making of such imputations. Such basis was not present in *Campbell* v. *Spottiswoode* (1863) in which the defendant alleged that the plaintiff's motive in attempting to organise a religious campaign to spread the doctrines of Christianity among heathens was to increase the sales of the plaintiff's own newspaper (*cf.* however, the remarks of Lord Denning M.R. in *Slim* v. *Daily Telegraph* (1968) to the effect that even in cases where dishonesty is alleged, the only test of the fairness of the comment is whether the defendant honestly believed it).

Where the defendant is relying on the proof of certain facts for the purpose of establishing the defence of fair comment, the plaintiff is entitled to be given particulars of those facts under the rules of pleading. But he is not entitled to be informed in advance by the defendant what aspect of the alleged defamatory publication is fact and what is comment. The so-called rolled-up plea (in so far as the statements are of fact they are true and in so far as they are comment they are fair) is throughout a defence of fair comment, not of fair comment and justification. It was used as a means of making clear that the defendant did not purport to distinguish fact from comment in his pleadings, but under R.S.C. Ord. 82, r. 3(2) he is required to do this very thing when making use of the rolled-up plea, and as *Lord* v. *Sunday Telegraph* pointed out, he is therefore better off by making use of the ordinary pleading for a defence of fair comment. The rolled-up plea has become effectively extinct (nevertheless the Faulks Committee recommended its formal removal from the law). The law has now altered the position laid down by *Lord* by requiring the defendant to spell out with sufficient precision, to enable the plaintiff to know what case he has to meet, what is the comment which the defendant says attracts the defence of fair comment (*Control Risks Ltd.* v. *New English Library Ltd.* (1989)). This seems to entail that the defendant needs to distinguish fact from comment in his statement, though again this does not pre-empt the jury's interpretative function, subject to the judge's controlling guidance.

Fairness of the comment

Given the truth of the facts on which the defendant has commented, the court must then decide on the fairness of the comment. Courts are loth to pronounce comment upon true facts unfair, since the defence of fair comment is an important bastion of freedom of speech. Lord Denning remarked in *Slim* v. *Daily Telegraph* that the defence of fair comment is available to an honest man expressing his honest opinion on a matter of public interest, no matter how wrong, exaggerated or prejudiced that opinion. The defence will only fail therefore if either the comment is so blatantly unfair that no honest man could have written it, or if it is proved that the defendant had no genuine belief in the truth of what he said. There are two exceptions to this principle. Where the defendant's comment imputes dishonesty or dishonourable motives to the defendant (as in *Campbell* v. *Spottiswoode, supra*), the comment must be one which could reasonably be made on the facts known to the defendant. Secondly, in the case where the defendant's comment is actuated by malice towards the plaintiff, this will render his comment unfair even if he honestly believed in the comment and even though the comment itself would have been fair if made by one who was not actuated by malice (*Thomas* v. *Bradbury, Agnew & Co.* (1906)). This rule appears to have the effect of precluding one who is proved to be malicious towards the plaintiff from commenting unfavourably on the plaintiff or his work. The Report of the Committee on Defamation made the satisfactory suggestion that the only test of the fairness of the comment should be whether the defendant believed it. This suggestion would apply to both the special cases considered in this section.

Burden of proof

The onus is on the defendant to establish that the facts on which he commented were true, that the comment was such as an honest man might make, and that the matter commented on was one of public interest. The plaintiff must prove malice on the part of the defendant. The judge decides whether the matter commented on is one of public interest. The other questions that arise in relation to the defence must be decided by the jury.

Privilege

It may be a defence to an action of defamation that the statement was made on a privileged occasion. Such privilege may arise in the public interest (for example, the public interest in the freedom of reporting certain matters to be considered shortly) or in the protection of a private interest which the law considers to be deserving of this protection. If the occasion is one of absolute privilege, this is a complete defence to proceedings for defamation, however irresponsible or malicious the statement may be. If the occasion is one of qualified privilege, the privilege may be defeated by proof that the defendant was malicious.

Absolute privilege

The following are subject to absolute privilege:

(i) Statements made in the course of Parliamentary proceedings; this privilege extends to all reports, papers, votes and proceedings published by, or under the authority of, either House of Parliament. It is not possible to refer to a speech made in Parliament in order to establish malice in relation to a speech made outside Parliament (*Church of Scientology*

of California v. *Johnson-Smith* (1973)). Nor was it possible
to refer to the plaintiff's removal from one Parliamentary
select committee and his non-appointment as chairman of
another one in order to prove the consequences of a
defamatory letter, not itself subject to privilege, since this
fell within the impeachment or questioning of proceedings
in Parliament under section 9 of the Bill of Rights. The
Register of M.P.s' interests, however, is not a Parliamentary document protected by privilege (*Rost* v. *Edwards*
(1990)).

(ii)   Communications between high-ranking officers of state;
(iii) Statements made during the course of judicial proceedings,
       whether by the judge, counsel or witnesses, at least where
       they bear some relevance to those proceedings;
(iv)   A fair and accurate report in any newspaper or in a wireless
       broadcast of proceedings publicly heard before any court
       exercising judicial authority within the United Kingdom, if
       published contemporaneously with the proceedings;
(v)   Communications between solicitor and client; the privilege
       may be limited to communications made with reference to
       forthcoming litigation, other communications enjoying only
       qualified privilege.

Qualified privilege

On occasions of qualified privilege there is for various reasons
not the same paramount need to protect the freedom to make the
statement as in the cases considered above. Accordingly proof of
malice by the maker of the statement will destroy the privilege.

Occasions of qualified privilege

Qualified privilege may arise when a statement is made for the
protection of the public interest, or for the protection of the
private interest of one or more persons. Examples of the former
category are a statement made to the police by a member of the
public giving information about the commission of a crime, and a
complaint about misconduct or neglect of duty by a public officer
made by a member of the public to the proper authority.

Qualified privilege in the public interest also attaches to a
number of reports of the proceedings of public bodies. For
example, at common law qualified privilege exists in respect of fair

and accurate reports of Parliamentary proceedings and of judicial proceedings. The latter privilege is wider than the statutory absolute privilege in respect of such reports in that it is available by whatever medium the report is made and no matter at what time it is made. Various newspaper reports receive qualified privilege under section 7 of the Defamation Act 1952 and Parts I and II of the First Schedule to the Act: for example, reports of the proceedings at public meetings, of the proceedings of a local authority, or of the proceedings at the general meeting of a public company; a copy or a fair and accurate report or summary of any notice issued for the imformation of the public by or on behalf of any government department, officer of state, local authority, or chief officer of police (*cf. Blackshaw* v. *Lord* (1983)). (The privilege is forfeited if the publisher has unreasonably refused to publish a reasonable statement by the plaintiff by way of explanation or contradiction of the published statement); or, *e.g.* of public legislative proceedings in any of Her Majesty's Dominions, of proceedings of international organisations such as the United Nations or its constituent bodies, or of the proceedings in public of the International Court of Justice (in these cases the privilege is not lost by refusal to publish a statement on behalf of the plaintiff by way of explanation or contradiction). These are examples of cases where the public not only has an interest in the making of the statement but also in receiving the statement. This is not true of all statements made in the public interest. Thus information about a crime alleged to be committed by the plaintiff should normally be supplied to the police rather than to the public at large. Nor does the press have qualified privilege in the public interest to communicate its suspicions about the identity of a civil servant, allegedly transferred or dismissed for misconduct in office, to the public in its pages (*Blackshaw* v. *Lord* (1983)).

Qualified privilege may also be bestowed in the protection of private interests, especially those of the maker or the recipient of the statement, although the protection of the private interests of third parties could also be a reason for conferring qualified privilege. Where the interest is that of the speaker alone, the recipient must have a legal, moral or social duty to protect the interest. Where it is that of the recipient alone, the speaker must have a legal, moral or social duty to communicate the statement. It seems clear, also, that qualified privilege applies when each party has an interest to be protected by the making of the statement, whether the interests are distinct or common to both parties. Equally, where one party has a duty to make and the other to receive, the statement, qualified privilege applies (*Riddick* v. *Thames Board Mills* (1977)). The cases very often do not fit easily into one category. The chief requirement is that the statement should be made for the genuine protection of an interest or the performance of a duty.

A case which illustrates the operation of these principles is *Watt* v. *Longsdon* (1930). In that case the defendant, a company director, received some defamatory allegations about the plaintiff, an overseas employee of the company, in a letter. The allegations were of drunkenness, dishonesty, and sexual immorality. The defendant showed the letter to the chairman of the board of directors of the company, and to the plaintiff's wife. The former communication was held to be subject to qualified privilege because of the common interest of the defendant and the chairman in the plaintiff's conduct. The communication to the wife was, however, held to be not subject to qualified privilege because although the wife had an interest in her husband's conduct, the defendant had no duty of any sort, moral, social or legal to make communications about such conduct to her, nor did he have any interest of his own to protect. The case does not rule out the possibility of a third party having a duty to communicate to one spouse details about the behaviour of the other; on the facts however the defendant was behaving as an officious intermeddler in the plaintiff's marital affairs.

Excess of privilege and malice

It is necessary to distinguish these two matters because the House of Lords' decision in *Adam* v. *Ward* (1917) has made it clear that they are different. The defendant may exceed the privilege by publishing the statement to persons other than those to whom publication is necessary for the protection of an interest. For example, it will not normally be necessary for the protection of a private interest to publish a statement in the press and if this is done the privilege will be forfeited. Similarly, the privilege may be forfeited if extraneous matter not germane to the privilege is included in the defendant's statement (as in *Tuson* v. *Evans* (1840) in which the defendant's statement that the plaintiff owed him rent included the further statement that the plaintiff was dishonest). The prohibition upon publication of an otherwise privileged statement to third persons without an interest in receiving the communication does not mean that any publication of this sort automatically causes the forfeiture of the privilege. Publication to clerks and typists of the defendant is within the privilege provided it is reasonable and within the ordinary course of business. A difficulty arose, however, in *Osborn* v. *Thomas Boulter* (1930) in which the defendants had written a letter to the plaintiff defending the quality of their beer which the plaintiff had criticised, and making defamatory allegations about the plaintiff's keeping of it in his pub. The letter had been dictated to a typist. The publication to the typist was held by the Court of Appeal not to be defamatory on the ground that the occasion was privileged, since although no publication to anyone other than the typist had been proved, the sending of the letter to the plaintiff himself not being a publication, the publication to the typist was privileged because the letter had been sent to the plaintiff to protect the interests of both plaintiff and defendant. The case seems not unsatisfactory in its recognition of an ancillary privilege even where actual publication of the defamatory statement cannot be established. Nevertheless, doubt about the correctness of the decision has been created by the later case of *Bryanston Finance Co.* v. *De Vries* (1975), a case involving in its essentials the same factual situation as in *Osborne*. All three members of the Court of Appeal found the publication to the typist privileged but differed as to the reasons for this. Diplock L.J., dissenting, followed *Osborne* in holding the privilege to be ancillary upon the sending of the letter to the plaintiff, though finding the privilege to be forfeited by an improper motive in the defendant; Lord Denning M.R. found the publication privileged because of the common interest that existed between secretaries and their employer in their receiving normal business letters; Lawton L.J. thought that common interest of that sort could arise only where the letter was intented to benefit the business—nevertheless he found the publication to be privileged without giving a clear reason.

Qualified privilege may also be lost where the defendant has published a statement which does not exceed the privilege but can be proved to have been actuated by malice towards the plaintiff in making the statement. Malice for the purposes of qualified privilege means that the defendant has no honest belief in what he has said. However prejudiced, irrational or wrong-headed he may be, his belief in the truth of the statement prevents a finding of malice (recently affirmed by the House of Lords in *Horrocks* v. *Lowe* (1974), *cf.* the similar principles governing fair comment). There is an exception to this where the defendant has made use of the privilege for some improper purpose other than the legitimate protection of an interest. Here the defendant's honest belief in the truth of the statement will not protect him (*e.g. Winstanley* v. *Bampton* (1943)—the defendant who in publishing the statement was motivated by feelings of spite or anger towards the plaintiff was malicious though he honestly believed its truth (*cf.* also *Angel* v. *Bushell & Co.* (1968)).

In view of the emphasis upon the need for dishonesty or collateral purpose to defeat the privilege and of the purpose of the protection from legal liability that qualified privilege provides, the decision in *Lawton* v. *B.O.C.* (1987) that an employer owes to his employee a duty of care when providing a reference to another employer is rather surprising. But the qualified privilege point is not raised in the judgment.

Public interest privilege

Hasselblad (G.B.) Ltd. v. *Orbinson* (1985) held that a letter of complaint written to the European Commission enjoyed a privilege which was not qualified privilege, since it was not defeated by malice, but was not within any of the existing heads of absolute privilege since the Commission was not a court.

Malice and joint publication

The question of the effect upon the liability of joint publishers of the malice of one of them arises in connection with the defences of fair comment and of qualified privilege. Where each joint publisher has a separate and independent privilege, he will not be affected by the malice of one joint publisher. Thus in *Egger* v. *Viscount Chelmsford* (1965) members of the Kennel Club came to a decision that the plaintiff should not be allowed to officiate as judge at a dog show and communicated this in a letter to a third party. The letter was covered by qualified privilege but it was found that several members of the committee had been malicious in reaching their decision. The Court of Appeal held that their malice did not affect the privilege of the other members of the committee since each had a separate, independent privilege. Where the privilege of each joint publisher is not a separate privilege, but is a privilege derivative from one of their number the position is less clear. Are the printer and publisher of a work, who enjoy the same privilege as its author, affected by the malice of the author if the privilege is qualified? In *Egger* v. *Viscount Chelmsford* it was held that the secretary of the Kennel Club who wrote the letter on the instructions of the Committee and who was found to be not personally malicious was not liable, (by Lord Denning M.R. and Harman L.J. because an innocent agent should not be "infected" by his principal's malice, by Davies L.J. because the secretary had a separate and independent privilege). It may be assumed that the reasoning of the majority applies to protect all other innocent agents of the author. On the other hand, a principal is liable for a malicious statement made by an agent on ordinary vicarious liability principles, *i.e.* the agent must have acted within the scope of his apparent authority (*Egger* v. *Viscount Chelmsford*); so also, an employer is liable for the malicious statement of his servant made in the course of his employment (*Egger*; *Riddick* v. *Thames Board Mills* (1977)).

Whether the same principles apply to the defence of fair comment is unsettled. Lord Denning in *Egger* thought that they did, but Davies L.J. thought that the test for malice in fair comment was indivisible, and that, therefore, in particular, malice on the part of the maker of the statement would render innocent agents responsible for its publication. The latter was assumed to be the law in *Thomas* v. *Bradbury, Agnew & Co.* (1906) but the matter was not argued.

Consent

It is a defence that the plaintiff has consented to the publication of the defamatory statement. In *Cookson* v. *Harewood* (1932) the defendants had published in the Racing Calendar that the plaintiff had been warned off all pony racing courses under their control. This they were entitled to do under the Rules of Racing to which the plaintiff had consented. The Court of Appeal held that the plaintiff's consent prevented him from complaining of any defamatory innuendo that might be drawn from the warning-off notice.

Apology

In order to establish the defence of apology under section 2 of the Libel Act 1843, the defendant must show that the libel was inserted in a newspaper or other periodical "without actual malice" and "without gross negligence" and that the defendant inserted a full apology for the libel either before the commencement of the action or at the earliest opportunity afterwards. The apology must be accompanied by a payment into court of money by way of amends. Apology is a complete defence to the plaintiff's action, but if it fails the defendant will be penalised in costs even though his payment into court exceeded the amount of damages awarded by the jury (though the apology may still go in mitigation of damages). This has meant that apology is an unpopular defence, since the effect of a payment into court under Order 22 of the Rules of the Supreme Court is to make the plaintiff responsible for costs incurred after the payment if the damages awarded by the jury do not exceed the payment, and this procedure is therefore generally preferred though in the nature of a gamble.

REMEDIES

The primary remedy for defamation is the action for damages. Libel is actionable *per se*, as are certain forms of slander. In the case of defamation actionable *per se*, damages are at large. Therefore aggravated damages (*i.e.* increased damages arising from the circumstances of the tort's commission, *infra*, pp. 411–412) and parasitic damages (*i.e.* for injury to interests other than reputation, for example, injured feelings, *infra*, p. 414) may be awarded. Furthermore, in the case of defamation actionable *per se*, the plaintiff does not need to prove his loss—general damages may be awarded in respect of damage which is presumed to have occurred from the fact of the tort's commission (though sometimes the court will refuse to presume such damage. Contemptuous damages of a farthing were awarded to the plaintiff in the *Newstead* case, (*supra*, this chapter)) and this normally entails that the plaintiff is penalised as to costs (*Pamplin* v. *Express Newspapers* (1988)). The award of exemplary damages in defamation cases is dealt with in Chapter 28. The defendant is entitled to plead in mitigation of damages that the plaintiff's reputation is bad, but the court is here concerned with the plaintiff's reputation as it is and not as it ought to be. The defendant cannot therefore adduce specific events by way of detraction from the character the plaintiff is generally thought to possess (*Plato Films* v. *Speidel* (1961)). The law does, however, recognise a principle referred to as partial justification under which the defendant, if he is able to establish the truth of a less serious version of the libel contended for by the plaintiff, is able to rely on this in mitigation of damages (*Prager* v. *Times Newspapers* (1988)—not open to the defendant in that case because the libel the defendants wished to justify (incautionness by plaintiff in choice of business associates) was not a mere less serious libel than that complained of by the plaintiff (use in business of stolen money)). Partial justification differs from the principle established by section 5 of the Defamation Act 1952 in that it applies to an unsuccessful defence of justification. The Faulks Committee Report in one of its more controversial recommendations advocated the abolition of the rule in *Plato Films* v. *Speidel*. This if done would allow a quite unacceptable amount of muck-raking in defamation actions and would unduly protract litigation.

The courts are reluctant to issue an interlocutory injunction in cases of defamation, and will not do so when the defendant intends to plead a defence of justification, fair comment or qualified privilege (*Khashoggi* v. *I.P.C. Magazines Ltd.* (1986); *Harakas* v. *Baltic Exchange* (1982); *Herbage* v. *Pressdram* (1984)). Nor will the law of contempt of court be automatically invoked against those, including the defendant, who comment on the case after the issue of the writ—*cf. A.-G.* v. *Times Newspapers* (1973) and *A.-G.* v. *News Group Newspapers* (1986). Where, however, the defamatory statement is made as part of a conspiracy to injure the plaintiff, an injunction will be issued even if the likelihood is that the statement is true (*Gulf Oil* v. *Page* (1987)).

22. THE ECONOMIC TORTS

There is no general principle of liability in tort for the intentional infliction of economic loss upon another person. It is no part of the purpose of the law to inhibit trade competition and every successful competitor inflicts economic loss upon his rivals. The law has gone further and, less defensibly, refused to find that it makes any difference where the intention to inflict loss is malicious (*Allen* v. *Flood* (1898)). The general principle of no liability yields to exceptions under which the intentional infliction of economic loss if coupled with the presence of certain other factors may be actionable in tort. These factors are essentially three, the presence of one or more of which may justify a remedy in tort. They are:

(i) An improper motive in the defendant. Though malice is generally irrelevant, it is not so where the defendants have acted in combination.

(ii) The existence of a right in the plaintiff. The courts are more ready to give their protection when the defendant has interfered with a right of the plaintiff or something analogous to a right. The tort of interference with contract protects the plaintiff's enjoyment of his contractual rights. Intangible rights of property such as copyright, patents, and registered trade marks are protected by actions in tort. The tort of passing-off recognises a right in the name and appearance of the plaintiff's goods or services, clearly an analogous right to that of the other forms of intangible property.

(iii) The means used by the defendant. The defendant may incur liability because the means he has used are unlawful (interference with contract, conspiracy, intimidation and unlawful means) or because he has told a lie (deceit and injurious falsehood).

In many cases of liability for causing economic loss the result is achieved by influencing a third person to act to the plaintiff's loss. This result is inherent in the notion of an economic interest which generally presupposes an advantageous relationship with another person. However, it is possible for the economic torts to be committed otherwise than through the medium of a third party, and in the case of deceit this is invariably true. Another point of importance is that although the intention of causing the plaintiff loss is not a sufficient condition, it is generally a necessary one of liability. Negligence in relation to an economic interest alone is generally not enough, apart from the obvious exception of liability for negligent misstatement.

There is legislation both at the domestic and E.C. level protecting competition and rendering unlawful agreements amounting to cartels or mergers of companies producing monopolies, or the abuse of power that a monopoly position confers. It has been generally assumed that this legislation would not confer a private right of action for breach of statutory duty, but in *Garden Cottage Foods Ltd.* v. *Milk Marketing Board* (1984) Lord Diplock expressed himself firmly of the opinion that Article 86 of the Treaty of Rome which renders abuse of a dominant market position unlawful and which forms part of English law confers a private right of action for damages. It was unnecessary for the House of Lords to decide this question, however, since the matter was a mere interlocutory application, and the language used by Lord Diplock is in sharp contrast with his speech in *Lonrho* v. *Shell Petroleum* (*infra*, p. 362).

INTERFERENCE WITH CONTRACT

In *Lumley* v. *Gye* (1853) the principle was established that an action lay, at the instance of the other party to the contract, against one who induced, *i.e.* persuaded a party to a contract to break it.

The facts in *Lumley* v. *Gye* were that the defendant persuaded a singer, who was under contract to sing at the plaintiff's theatre, to sing at the defendant's theatre instead. The defendant knew of the singer's contract with the plaintiff. The court held that these facts disclosed a cause of action in tort.

Previous to this case, although it was recognised that a master could sue one who enticed his servant away from his services, there appeared to be no general principle of protection of contractual rights. The case is, therefore, an important milestone in the recognition and protection by the courts of purely economic interests. As long as *Lumley* v. *Gye* marked the boundaries of the tort, the law was reasonably clear. Developments which have taken place since *Lumley* v. *Gye* have made the basis of liability less apparent. It is now clear that action which is not persuasion but has the effect of preventing a contractual party from performing his contract may be actionable under this tort and it is also settled that in the case of such action a breach of contract is not a necessary requirement though it seems essential that the means used by the defendant should have been unlawful. Where, however, the defendant has used mere persuasion to induce a party not to perform his contract, the requirement that this should be a breach of contract still applies.

Where the breach of contract has been brought about by direct persuasion of a contracting party, the case is normally described as "inducing" a breach of contract. Where it has been brought about by prevention of performance it is described as "procuring" the breach. Both words have a causal connotation—whichever form the defendant's action takes, it must cause the breach of, or interference with the contract.

Elements of the tort

Actionable interference with contract

Until recently, lip-service, at least, has been paid to the view that the defendant's act must induce a breach of contract. If, for example, A persuades B to terminate lawfully his contract with C, C could not sue A under *Lumley* v. *Gye*. The view that the defendant's act must induce a breach was difficult to reconcile with cases in which the defendant's act had made it impossible for the other party to the contract to perform it, the consequence being that there was no breach of contract, although there may well have been a frustration of it (see *G.W.K. Rubber Co.* v. *Dunlop* (1926); *J. T. Stratford* v. *Lindley* (1965); *Torquay Hotel Co.* v. *Cousins* (1969)—for the facts of the *G.W.K.* and *Stratford* cases, see *infra*). Nevertheless the courts continued to talk in terms of breach until in *Merkur Island Shipping Co.* v. *Laughton* (1983) the House of Lords recognised the reality of the situation and accepted that certain interferences with contract not constituting a breach by either party were actionable in this tort. In the *Merkur* case the plaintiff shipowners had chartered their ship on a time charterparty to the charterers who had chartered it to sub-charterers and the ship was lying in port. The defendants, an international trade union, ITF, who had an industrial dispute with the plaintiffs, persuaded tugboat employees to break their contracts of employment by refusing to move the ship which remained berthed in harbour for a considerable period of time. The plaintiffs lost hiring charges because a term of the charterparty provided that no hire was due if the ship was stopped by industrial action; nor under the terms of the charterparty was there any breach of contract by the charterers. Nevertheless, the House of Lords held that a prima facie case of interference with contract had been made out by the shipowners since the defendants had used unlawful means, namely the inducement of breaches of their contracts of employment by the tugboat employees and this had caused an interference with the performance of the plaintiffs' contract with the charterers, even though no actual breach of contract had been committed. The House of Lords stated explicitly that the tort did not require the procuring of a breach of contract and that an act of interference whereby one party is prevented from performing the contract is sufficient.

Act constituting an interference

In deciding what acts amount to an actionable interference with contract, a distinction is sometimes drawn between direct interference and indirect interference. Examples of the former are persuasion of the other contracting party, and physical restraint aimed against him; of the latter, industrial action taken against him. It is suggested, however, that the more fundamental distinction is between persuasion of one of the parties to the contract to break it, and the doing of an act which, whether directly or indirectly, has the effect of preventing performance of the contract. The latter category would include both physical and industrial action against a contracting party. In the case of prevention of performance, it seems probable that the defendant is liable only if he has used unlawful means. Indeed it is possible to view the use of unlawful means to prevent the performance of a contract as part of the wider tort of causing loss by unlawful means (*infra*, this chapter). On that view, the original *Lumley* v. *Gye* principle applies only to persuasion and continued to be limited to the case in which the persuasion has induced a breach of contract. The necessity for a breach of contract continues to be paramount in this case, despite the view expressed by Lord Denning M.R. in *Torquay Hotel Co.* v. *Cousins* (1969) that this requirement no longer applies. (The two other members of the court in Torquay found a breach but one which was protected by an exclusion clause in the contract).

(1) *Persuasion.* The defendant's persuasion must induce (*i.e.* cause) a breach of contract. It is not necessary that the defendant should stand to profit from the breach, nor is the line that is drawn between persuasion and mere advice to break the contract a sound one, since it simply restates the issue as to causation. If the defendant, whether through persuasion or advice, has induced a breach of contract, he is liable. The defendant's persuasion may take the form of a dealing with a party to the contract which the defendant knows to be a breach of that contract (as in *B.M.T.A* v. *Salvadori* (1949)). In principle there ought to be liability only if the dealing has induced the breach. If the party to the contract had already decided to break his contract before the dealing, the latter has not caused the breach. This derives a measure of support from *Batts Combe Quarry* v. *Ford* (1943)—acceptance of a gift known to be given in breach of contract was not actionable under *Lumley* v. *Gye*.

Finally, in relation to persuasion, further mention must be made of *Torquay Hotel Co.* v. *Cousins*. In that case all three members of the Court of Appeal thought that there was direct interference with the contract where the defendants had blacked the plaintiffs' hotel through industrial action and had thereby caused an interference with a contract between Esso and the plaintiffs under which Esso supplied and delivered oil. There was found to be a direct interference here on the ground that Esso was informed by telephone call by the defendants that its employees would not be allowed to deliver the oil to the plaintiffs. This seems quite wrong. The telephone call did not bring about the interference with contract. The case belongs within the second category.

(2) *Prevention of performance of the contract.* In the first place, the defendant may have physically prevented the performance of the contract. In *Lumley* v. *Gye*, for example, had the defendant unlawfully detained the singer, thereby falsely imprisoning her, the result in law would have been the same. In *G.W.K. Co.* v. *Dunlop Rubber Co.* (1926) a car manufacturer contracted with the plaintiff that tyres manufactured by the plaintiff should be displayed on his cars appearing at an exhibition. The defendant replaced the plaintiffs' tyres on cars on show at the exhibition with tyres of his own manufacture. He was held liable to the plaintiff under the *Lumley* v. *Gye* principle. Also coming within this category is the use of industrial action against a contracting party which has the effect of making it impossible for him to perform his contract. In *J.T. Stratford & Co.* v. *Lindley* (1965) the defendants were officials of the Waterman's Union which had a dispute over the recognition of negotiating rights for the union with a company, Bowker & King, of which J. T. Stratford was chairman. In order to further the dispute, the defendants instructed their members to refuse to handle barges belonging to J. T. Stratford & Co. of which J. T. Stratford was chairman and controlling shareholder. The result was that the company's barge hiring business was crippled, contracts already made not being capable of being honoured by the company and its customers being unable to return barges already out on hire. The House of Lords held that these facts disclosed a prima facie case of procuring breaches of contract (*i.e.* the contracts for hire of the barges) by unlawful means (*i.e.* the inducement of breaches of the bargemen's contracts of employment with their employers). Since the action taken rendered performance of the barge hiring contracts impossible by either side, it is clear that an actionable breach could not have been established. This conceptual difficulty now disappears with the ruling in *Merkur* that an interference with contract not amounting to a breach is sufficient.

Until the *Stratford* decision it had generally been thought that where the interference took the form of prevention of performance of the contract rather than direct persuasion, the defendant must have used unlawful means. The means used might be a tort (for example, the tort of trespass in *G.K.W. Co.* v. *Dunlop Rubber Co.*), or a breach of contract (assumed to be the case in *D. C. Thomson & Co.* v. *Deakin* (1952), although in that case since no breach of contract had been committed it was not possible to establish unlawful means). The judgments of the House of Lords in the *Stratford* case, however, are curiously equivocal on the question whether unlawful means are necessary in the second category of interference. Lord Pearce actually said that it was unnecessary to decide whether the refusal of union members to work the plaintiffs' barges was a breach of their contracts of employment so as to constitute unlawful means. Lord Reid and Viscount Radcliffe thought that a breach of the contract of employment had been committed, but appeared to think this was relevant only to liability for causing loss by unlawful means rather than to liability under the *Lumley* v. *Gye* principle. Viscount Radcliffe and Lord Donovan seemed to treat the case as essentially one of causing loss by unlawful means rather than of interference with contract. Only Lord Upjohn treated the case unambiguously as one of interference with contract and he clearly thought that there was a requirement of unlawful means in this tort. With the recognition in *Merkur* that an actionable breach of contract is not necessary, the need for unlawful means is all the more apparent. *Merkur* affirmed the existence of the requirement in finding it necessary for the plaintiffs to establish breaches of their contracts of employment by the tugboat company employees.

Knowledge of the contract by the defendant
The requirement of knowledge of the contract by the defendant is illustrative of the requirement of the economic torts generally that the defendant must intend to cause loss. The rule is generally stated in terms of actual knowledge (*British Industrial Plastics* v. *Ferguson* (1940)), though there has been some relaxation of this requirement. Thus where, as in *J. T. Stratford & Co.* v. *Lindley* the existence of a contractual relationship between the company and the hirers of its barges must have been obvious to the defendants together with the fact that their action would bring

about a breakdown of those contracts, sufficient knowledge existed. In *Emerald Construction Co.* v. *Lowthian* (1966) it was held that where the defendant knows of the existence of a contractual relationship, he commits the tort if he intends to bring that contract to an end even if he assumes that it can be lawfully terminated.

The question at issue in the *Merkur* case was the different one of whether the defendant knew of the existence of a contract at all. In fact the defendant had received a copy of the charterparty at some time during the ship's immobilisation but Lord Diplock thought this to be irrelevant. In the case of a laden ship about to leave port, the almost inevitable inference was that it was carrying out some contract of carriage—the wholly exceptional case would be that of the ship carrying its owners' own goods. A final question is whether the plaintiff need be "targeted" by the defendant, as in the above cases, or is it sufficient that there is an inevitability of a degree of interference with contracts of which the plaintiff's happens to be one. The better view is that even here, granted the inevitability of the interference, there should be liability (supported by *Falconer* v. *A.S.L.E.F.* (1986)—rail strike caused booked tickets to be unusable at the booked time). The contrary authority, *Barretts & Baird (Wholesale) Ltd.* v. *I.P.C.S.* (1987) (intention of strikers was to cause employers to improve their conditions of service rather than to interfere with contracts) seems to confuse intention with motive. It is clear that along with the other economic torts apart from conspiracy, the defendant is not excused by the fact that he claims to be acting in his own economic interests rather than to injure the plaintiff. It is of course clear that mere reasonable foreseeability of the interference is not sufficient.

Justification

This defence is normally considered in connection with interference with contract but could arguably arise in connection with other economic torts, especially intimidation and the use of unlawful means. This, however, points to the doubt as to whether the defence is ever available where the defendant has used unlawful means, a doubt which affects the tort of interference with contracts itself—in other words it may be limited to direct persuasion as a means of committing the tort. In the case of direct persuasion the defence has been recognised in three cases:

(a) *Brimelow* v. *Casson* (1924) allowed the defence where the defendants persuaded theatre proprietors to break their contract with a theatre manager who was paying his chorus girls such low wages that they were forced to resort to prostitution. *Brimelow* v. *Casson* stands alone and it is difficult to decide on what legal basis it rests. In particular, if the main contract is one which would be upheld and enforced in a court of law, what justification is there for inducing its breach?;

(b) where the defendant has induced the breach of a contract made by the plaintiff with the contract-breaker which is inconsistent with a previous contract made by the contract-breaker with the defendant, justification is a defence. So if X has sold his land to D for £10,000 and then sells it to P for £15,000, D may lawfully induce a breach of the contract between X and P;

(c) where the defendant has an equal or superior right to that of the plaintiff. This case merely takes (b) a little further. In *Edwin Hill* v. *First National Finance Corporation* (1989) the defendants had lent money on mortgage to a property developer who had contracted to employ the plaintiffs as architects. The development failed but instead of exercising their power of sale under the mortgage the defendants joined as parties to the development, stipulating that the developer employ a different architect so that plaintiffs' contract was terminated by the developer in breach of that contract. The defendants succeeded in their plea of justification to the plaintiffs' action. The defendants' power of sale was a right which if it has been exercised would clearly have defeated the plaintiffs' contractual rights—it made no difference that the defendants had adopted another proposal which did not require its exercise. The difference between (b) and (c) is that the plaintiffs' contract was not necessarily inconsistent with the mortgage contract.

Damage

It is the law that the plaintiff must prove that he has suffered damage arising from the interference.

Only the party not in breach can sue under the *Lumley* v. *Gye* principle itself. In the prevention of performance cases there seems no reason why either party should not be able to sue, at least where no breach has been brought about.

CONSPIRACY

General Features

Subject to the problem of definition to be discussed shortly, conspiracy as a tort may be regarded as an agreement between two or more persons intended to inflict damage on the plaintiff, and that damage has occurred. An actionable conspiracy may occur between, *inter alia*, husband and wife, the directors of a company and the company, and, in the case of a "one man company," between the company and the one man (*R.* v. *McDonnell* (1965)— a criminal conspiracy), but not between an employer and his employees when acting in the course of their employment.

Problem of definition

The definition of conspiracy causes problems in the light of the House of Lords decision in *Lonrho* v. *Shell Petroleum Co.* (1981). Before that case it had been thought that an actionable tortious conspiracy might be proved in one of two ways; either by showing that the defendants had conspired to commit an act, whether lawfully or not, with the predominant purpose of injuring or causing damage to the plaintiff and had achieved that purpose; or, intending to harm the plaintiff they had conspired to do so by the use of unlawful means and had achieved their purpose. Unlawful means for the purposes of the second type of conspiracy would include torts, crimes and breaches of contract. In *Lonrho* v. *Shell Petroleum* (1981) the House of Lords held that only one type of actionable conspiracy existed, that in which the predominant purpose of the defendants was to cause injury or damage to the plaintiff. An allegation of the use of unlawful means by the conspirators, therefore, did not disclose a cause of action in conspiracy in the absence of an allegation that a predominant purpose existed to cause harm to the plaintiff. In *Lonrho* itself the allegation by the plaintiff was of damage caused to it by a conspiracy between the defendants, Shell Petroleum, and other persons to infringe an Order in Council, imposing sanctions on Southern Rhodesia, by causing oil to be delivered to that country and thereby causing damage to the plaintiffs by prolonging the period of sanctions and preventing the lawful use by the plaintiffs of their oil pipeline to Southern Rhodesia. The House of Lords held that these facts disclosed no cause of action in conspiracy since no predominant purpose of causing loss to Lonrho had been alleged. Nothing it seems could be clearer than the terms of Lord Diplock's judgment (in which all the members of the House of Lords concurred) rejecting as a separate form of the tort of conspiracy the conspiracy to use unlawful means. Nevertheless, New Zealand and Canadian courts continued to recognise this form of conspiracy (*Lintas N.Z.* v. *Murphy* (1986); *Canada Cement La Forge Ltd.* v. *British Columbia Lightweight Aggregates Ltd.* (1983) and the matter was reargued before the Court of Appeal in *Metall und Rohstoff A.G.* v. *Donaldson Lufkin Inc.* (1989). A company which operated as the plaintiffs' broker on the London metal exchange had incurred financial loss through the fraudulent dealing of a third party. In order to cover itself against this loss it conspired with the defendants, its parent company, to falsely assert that the losses were the financial responsibility of the plaintiffs and also to unlawfully seize some metal warrants belonging to the plaintiffs. The plaintiffs' action for conspiracy against the defendants failed. *Lonrho* v. *Shell Petroleum* was quite unambiguous as to the non-existence of a separate form of conspiracy by using unlawful means, and the defendants here had no predominant purpose of injuring the plaintiffs but were acting in their own interests—the fact that those interests were unlawful was irrelevant.

The question whether the "unlawful means" conspiracy is a separate form of conspiracy subject to different rules seems now for the moment settled by the judgment of the Court of Appeal but the question arises as to the desirability of the result. Lord Diplock's views in *Lonrho* were clearly inspired by his opinion of conspiracy as an anomalous tort because of its acceptance of the dubious logic that that which is lawful when done by one person becomes unlawful when done by two, based on the possibly naive premise that a combination can always exercise more economic force than a single individual (sometimes of course, it can). Granted the anomalous nature of the tort, it should be maintained within the confines originally dictated by the reasons for its existence, *i.e.* it should be limited to the doing in combination of acts, lawful if done by individuals, for a purpose which is an abuse of the power wielded by the combination, *i.e* solely or predominantly to cause damage to the plaintiff. Whether the use of unlawful means by persons acting in combination to injure the plaintiff is tortious would depend, therefore, in the absence of a predominant purpose of injuring the plaintiff, on whether the use of those means by the individual conspirators amounted to a tort.

Lord Diplock himself recognised the existence of a tort of causing loss by unlawful means in the *Merkur* case decided two years after *Lonrho*, and there is now ample support for its existence. If so, it may well appear that the controversy over the existence of a separate unlawful means conspiracy is purely academic. It is true that it is sometimes asserted that it is easier to prove the existence of a conspiracy to use unlawful means since it is unnecessary to show the commission of the individual tort by any one conspirator. Certainly, at least one person must be shown to have fulfilled all the requirements of the individual tort, but there seems no reason why other persons should not also be held liable for commissioning or inciting it. Conspiracy would also have an advantage if it could be shown that the unlawful means it comprised were more extensive than those comprised by the individual tort. But there is no reason to think this to be the case and *Lonrho* v. *Fayed* (1989) shows at least the possibility that unlawful means for the purpose of the individual tort are not narrowly defined. (for the facts, see *infra*, pp. 366–367).

The "predominant purpose" conspiracy

Conspiracy became a potentially important tort when it was decided that it lay even where the conspiracy was to perform a lawful act, provided the defendant intended to injure or damage the plaintiff. In the sphere of economic interests in particular, conspiracy appeared to be a means of getting round the rule of English law that an act done intentionally to infringe the economic prosperity of another person was not *per se* tortious. Despite the dubious logic which accepted that what is done by one person is not actionable but will be actionable if done by two, this did seem to promise some redress in cases where people suffered damage caused intentionally by their trade competitors. However, it eventually became established that a combination to cause economic damage to another person is not actionable unless the predominant purpose of the defendants is to cause that damage. If, for example, they are acting in the furtherance of their own interests, no action for conspiracy will lie against them. Thus, in *Crofter Hand Woven Harris Tweed Co. Ltd.* v. *Veitch* (1942) the defendant union officials instructed dockers to refuse to handle yarn sent from the mainland of Scotland for delivery to the plaintiffs' factory in the Outer Hebrides. The plaintiffs depended entirely upon these supplies in order to weave cloth. The defendants had no trade dispute with the plaintiffs but wished to reduce the competition provided by the plaintiffs' business for other mills on the island which employed union labour, so that the employers could increase wages. The House of Lords held that this was not conspiracy since the defendants' predominant purpose was the protection of members of their union. The case may be compared with *Quinn* v. *Leathem* (1901). The plaintiff had been employing non-union labour, but was willing for his men to join the union and was willing to pay their fines and entrance money. The defendant union officials refused this offer and ordered that the men be discharged and compelled to walk the streets for 12 months. The plaintiff refused to do this, and the defendants then brought pressure to bear on a customer of the plaintiff as a result of which he stopped dealing with the plaintiff. The plaintiff recovered for this loss in conspiracy. In view of the plaintiff's offer, the defendants had acted vindictively and not in protection of their legitimate interests. The interests furthered by the combination need not be economic nor need the action be in the private interests of those combining in order to come within the protection of the *Crofter* case (*Scala Ballroom* (*Wolverhampton*) *Ltd.* v. *Ratcliff* (1958)—legitimate combination aimed against the plaintiff who operated a colour bar). But the courts have a power to say whether the interest is one that can legitimately be protected. Thus, in the *Crofter* case, Viscount Maugham thought that a conspiracy aimed against the religious views, or the politics or the race or colour of the plaintiff would be actionable. Viscount Simon thought the same would follow where those combining did so because of a bribe offered to them by a third party. *Gulf Oil Ltd.* v. *Page* (1987) shows that the predominant purpose conspiracy, though an unusual tort nowadays, may still be of use to plaintiffs. In that case, the defendant, having won a contractual battle with Gulf Oil, hired a plane to fly over a racecourse towing the sign, "Gulf Oil exposed in fundamental breach." Although the words were true, this amounted to a conspiracy since it was done for no purpose other than to injure Gulf Oil. The case has been criticised by Weir, *Casebook on Tort* (p. 532), but his criticism amounts to no more than the same criticism of the anomalous nature of conspiracy as a tort we have already encountered from Lord Diplock.

It appears that the burden of showing that the predominant intention of the defendants was to injure him lies on the plaintiff (a majority of the law lords in the *Crofter* case were in favour of this view). Where damage disproportionate to the purpose of the defendants has been inflicted upon the plaintiff, this does not in itself make the defendants liable, but is evidence that their primary intention was to injure the plaintiff.

INTIMIDATION

The tort of intimidation consists in a threat to commit an unlawful act (or that an unlawful act will be committed), intending as a result of the threat to produce damage to the plaintiff, and actually producing such damage. "Unlawful act" includes a crime, a tort or a breach of contract. The existence of this tort, long in doubt, was finally confirmed by the House of Lords in *Rookes* v. *Barnard* (1964). The defendants were three officials of the A.E.S.D. Union, two of whom were employed by B.O.A.C. A branch of the union had, at a meeting at which the defendants were present, passed a resolution under which it was agreed that all union labour would be withdrawn unless the plaintiff, who was not a member of a union, was dismissed by B.O.A.C. The union had an agreement with B.O.A.C. providing for 100 per cent. union membership. There was also in the agreement a "no strike" clause which the defendants later conceded to be incorporated in the contracts of employees subject to the agreement. The defendants notified B.O.A.C. of the union resolution and B.O.A.C. thereupon lawfully terminated the plaintiff's contract of employment. The plaintiff was held to be entitled to damages for his loss from the defendants. The ground for the decision was that the individual acts of the defendants amounted to the tort of intimidation, since each had threatened B.O.A.C. with an unlawful act, namely, a withdrawal of labour in breach of the "no strike" clause (or in the case of the official not employed by B.O.A.C. the commission of an unlawful act by other persons). The combination to utter such threats was therefore an actionable conspiracy. It may be noted that the defendant in *Rookes* v. *Barnard* threatened merely that breaches of contract would take place, in the case of two of them, by the defendants themselves, not that they would induce breaches of contract by the other employees. The House of Lords found that since the acts of each individual defendant constituted the tort of intimidation, their doing so in combination constituted a conspiracy to utter unlawful threats not protected by the section of the Trade Disputes Act 1906 then in force (for its present reenactment, see *infra*, p. 371). More controversially, the House of Lords held that the defendants were liable for the coercive effect upon B.O.A.C. of a threatened general withdrawal of labour, even though the loss of the services of those two of the defendants employed by B.O.A.C. could not have produced that effect. After *Lonrho* v. *Shell Petroleum* (*supra*), the same decision could not now be reached, since the defendants were clearly acting to protect their own interests rather than to punish Rookes.

The House of Lords went to some trouble in *Rookes* v. *Barnard* to reject an argument that the plaintiff if he succeeded would be subverting the doctrine of privity of contract, but in truth that argument had little foundation. Rookes was not complaining of not receiving benefits due under the contracts of employment made with B.O.A.C. but of the infliction of loss upon him by his employer in response to the defendants' unlawful threat. There is continuing debate about whether the tort of intimidation would be available in the situation where there is no third party, *i.e.* where the unlawful threat is aimed at the plaintiff himself. There is no real authority, Lord Reid merely observing *obiter* in *J. T. Stratford* v. *Lindley* (1965) that different considerations might affect this case. Those considerations clearly turn upon the fact that the plaintiff may have an effective remedy against the defendant for the making of the threat or the carrying of it into effect, and therefore there is no need to provide him with a remedy if he yields to it. So if he is threatened with violence, he may obtain a *quia timet* injunction and if he is actually assaulted he has an action for damages. If threatened with a breach of contract, he has remedies for anticipatory breach of contract or for breach of contract if the threat is carried out. This, however, seems too theoretical. The legal remedies may not be effective in fact to protect the plaintiff, or, rather more important, they may not be seen as effective by him. What really matters is whether the threat is seen as so potent by the plaintiff that he has no option but to comply with it. If that is the case, there seems to be no reason to deny him a remedy in intimidation for the loss caused to him (in *Pao On* v. *Lau Yiu Long* (1980) the Privy Council in determining whether a threat of the commission of a breach of contract constituted improper duress against the other contracting party, thereby invalidating his agreement to a variation of the contract, applied the test of whether that party's action in response to the threat was truly voluntary. That test would appear to be a satisfactory one for intimidation).

Intention in intimidation

Rookes v. *Barnard* shows that the defendant need only intend to inflict harm upon the plaintiff. This need not be his predominant purpose. In *Rookes* the defendants were motivated not by a desire to injure *Rookes* but to establish a closed shop at B.O.A.C.

CAUSING LOSS BY UNLAWFUL MEANS

By way of introductory definition this tort is committed when the defendant by the use of unlawful means intentionally inflicts loss upon the plaintiff. The tort now appears to have survived the judgment of Lord Diplock in the House of Lords in *Lonrho* v. *Shell Petroleum* (for the facts, see *supra*), even though the possibility of liability under that tort existed on the facts of the case and was not mentioned. Lord Diplock's judgment established incontrovertibly the following points: (a) a claim for breach of statutory duty as regards breach of the sanctions Order in Council failed because no civil action was intended to be conferred by the Order; (b) a claim for conspiracy to break the sanctions Order failed because it was not the predominant purpose of the defendants to cause loss to the plaintiffs; (c) Lord Denning's principle in *ex p. Island Records* (1978) that "whenever a lawful business carried on by any individual in fact suffers damage as the consequence of a contravention of any statutory prohibition, the former has a civil right of action against the latter for such damage," formed no part of English law; (d) nor did the principle laid down by the High Court of Australia in *Beaudesert Shire Council* (1966) that "a person who suffers harm or loss as the inevitable consequence of the unlawful, intentional and positive act of another is entitled to recover damages from the other."

None of these holdings would have ruled out a claim based on the ordinary tort of unlawful means which requires that the defendant actually intended by the use of unlawful means to inflict loss upon the plaintiff (and on the extended notion of intention that may apply by analogy with the tort of interference with contract, Shell actually had this intention since they must have known of oil pipelines that had been operating lawfully in Rhodesia prior to the sanctions Order). The possibility of this tort arising on the facts of *Lonrho* was not considered by Lord Diplock in *Lonrho* but in two later House of Lords decisions (*Merkur Island Shipping Co.* v. *Laughton* (1983) and *Hadmor Productions Ltd.* v. *Hamilton* (1983) he referred to the tort without disapproval and as if it had a present existence. There were a few earlier indications of the tort's existence, all arising in interlocutory proceedings and therefore not conclusive evidence (*Brekkes* v. *Cattel* (1971)—void agreement under Restrictive Practices Acts could constitute unlawful means for purposes of the tort (difficult to reconcile with House of Lords decision in *Mogul S.S.* v. *McGregor* (1892) holding to the contrary in relation to an agreement void under common law rule about restraint of trade); *Acrow Automation* v. *Rex Chainbelt* (1971)—conduct which was a contempt of court and aimed at the plaintiff might be tortious; so also might inducement of breaches of contracts of employment of bargees causing plaintiffs loss of future hiring business (*per* Lord Reid and Viscount Radcliffe in *J. T. Stratford & Co.* v. *Lindley* (1965)). Inconclusive also is the decision of the Court of Appeal in *Lonrho* v. *Fayed* (1989) refusing to strike out a cause of action based on an allegation that the defendants by making fraudulent statements to the Secretary of State for Trade had deprived Lonrho of an opportunity to make a take-over bid for another company. All three members of the Court of Appeal seemed reasonably clear that the tort existed. Of interest also is the nature of the illegality alleged. The court thought that it made no difference that the fraudulent statements had caused no loss to the Secretary of State so that a completed tort was not present. A final point to be made is that it would be an odd state of the law if the threat to use unlawful means is tortious whereas their actual use is not.

Lonrho v. *Fayed* is also relevant to the intention requirement in the tort of unlawful means. Common to all three members of the

Court of Appeal is the absence of the need to establish a predominant purpose to injure the plaintiff—that requirement is limited to conspiracy. Not so certain is whether there must be proved an actual intention to injure the plaintiff (to "target" him) or whether the injury to the plaintiff need merely be a consequence whose likelihood the defendant must appreciate. Targeting of the plaintiff may well not be necessary in the tort of interference with contract and Woolf L.J. in *Lonrho* v. *Fayed* clearly favoured a less stringent requirement. He said: "If a defendant has deliberately embarked upon a course of conduct the probable consequences of which to the plaintiff he appreciated, there is no reason why the plaintiff should not be compensated."

As mentioned earlier, the House of Lords disposed without difficulty in *Rookes* v. *Barnard* of an argument based on privity of contract by pointing out that Rookes was not claiming a right arising from the contract, but an independent right in himself arising from the use by the defendants of the threat of breaches of contract with the intention to cause him damage. Precisely the same considerations seem to apply to the tort of unlawful means. Where the breach of contract is committed with the intention to cause the plaintiff loss, a right to sue in tort, therefore, may arise. As in the case of intimidation, there is a problem with the two-party situation. There is, perhaps, some difficulty in accepting that one party to a contract may sue the other in tort where it has been breached, but, provided it is clear that the defendant intended to commit the breach in order to cause the plaintiff loss, there seems to be no absolute reason for excluding such an action. It has the advantage for the plaintiff that he could then recover damages for the loss the defendant intended to inflict on him, whereas that loss might not have been one contemplated by the parties to the contract at the time of contracting as a likely result of breach, and therefore, if the plaintiff were to bring his action in contract, it would be regarded as too remote under the rule in *Hadley* v. *Baxendale* (1854).

The trade disputes defence

In certain circumstances, persons, whether individuals or trade unions (which now have capacity to commit torts (*infra*, pp. 446–447)), may establish a defence to one of the torts consider-in this chapter that they were acting in the contemplation or furtherance of a trade dispute. The limits within which a dispute may legitimately be regarded as a trade dispute are set out in section 29(1) of the Trade Union and Labour Relations Act 1974 (T.U.L.R.A.) as amended by the Employment Act 1982. The words have also received much judicial interpretation so that the ultimate question whether they apply to the case before the court is a question of both law and fact.

Section 13(1)(*a*) of T.U.L.R.A. 1974 provides: an act done in contemplation or furtherance of a trade dispute shall not be actionable in tort on the ground only: (a) that it induces another person to break a contract or interferes, or induces another person to interfere, with its performance; or (b) that it consists in his threatening that a contract (whether one to which he is a party or not) will be broken or its performance interfered with, or that he will induce another person to break a contract or to interfere with its performance. Section 13(4) provides that an agreement or combination to do or procure the doing of any act in contemplation or furtherance of a trade dispute shall not be actionable in tort if the act is one which, if done without any agreement or combination, would be actionable in tort.

The following points may be noted about these subsections. Section 13(1) clearly deals with the torts of interference with contract and intimidation. It may be noted that sections 13(1)(*a*) and (*b*) apply to all contracts, not just contracts of employment, an extension introduced by T.U.L.R.A. Amendment Act 1976. Despite the use of the word "only" in section 13(1), it appears to be the law that the conduct referred to in the two subsections cannot be regarded as unlawful means so as to establish the tort of that name as regards the causing of other loss than the various interferences with contract mentioned in sections 13(1)(*a*) and (*b*) (*Hadmor Productions Ltd.* v. *Hamilton* (1983)). Otherwise the protection conferred by section 13(1) could be easily sidestepped. The force of the word "only" is to make it clear that the defence will not avail where additional wrongs are committed producing the same result, for example, trespass or nuisance. The protection accorded by section 13(4) to conspirators seems unnecessary, since they are only acting to protect their own interests in acting in furtherance of the trade dispute and an additional allegation of unlawful means adds nothing. On the other hand, section 13(4) does nothing to legalise the acts of the individual conspirators, so that where these fall outside the protection of section 13(1) the tort of unlawful means will be available. Strikes or industrial action carried out in breach of the balloting provisions in Part II of the Trade Union Act 1984 (extended by sections 12–18 of the Employment Act 1988) do not receive the protection of section 18 T.U.L.R.A. (section 10 Trade Union Act 1984)).

Secondary action. The House of Lords decisions in *Express Newspapers* v. *McShane* (1980) and *Duport Steels Ltd.* v. *Sirs* (1980) recognise that immunity may exist in relation to action taken against non-parties to the trade dispute, provided it is believed that this action will conduce to an eventual favourable resolution of the dispute. Such action is referred to as secondary action. In *Express Newspapers Ltd.* v. *McShane*, for example, a dispute existed between the National Union of Journalists and the Newspaper Society, a body representing proprietors of provincial newspapers. The NUJ called a strike among its members in the Press Association, a news agency which supplied news copy to both provincial and national newspapers. The strike response was only partial. The defendant NUJ officials therefore instructed its members working for the national press (including the plaintiff newspaper) to "black" copy emanating from the Press Association. This action was held to be within the protection of the "contemplation or furtherance" formula, since the defendants had a bona fide belief that the solidarity of the strike at the Press Association would be increased thereby, thus increasing pressure on the Newspaper Society.

In order to restrict the immunity attaching to secondary action, section 17 of the Employment Act 1980 was passed. The section is complex, but its broad effect may be stated as follows. The immunities conferred by section 13(1)(*a*) and (*b*) and the consequential immunities in section 13(3) and (4), that exist in relation to action taken to "interfere" with contracts of employment with employers not party to a trade dispute are abolished where the effect of the action is to produce "interference" with contracts which are not contracts of employment. Certain secondary action, however, remains within the protection of section 13. Section 17(3) excepts secondary action designed to directly prevent or disrupt the supply of goods or services between an employer who is a party to the trade dispute, and the employer under the contract of employment to which the secondary action relates. The secondary action has to be likely to achieve that purpose. Section 17(6)(a) provides that references to the supply of goods or services between two persons are references to the supply of goods or services by one to the other in pursuance of a contract between them subsisting at the time of the secondary action and section 17(6)(b) provides that references to directly preventing or disrupting the supply are references to preventing or disrupting it otherwise than by means of preventing or disrupting the supply of goods or services by or to any other person.

Merkur Island Shipping Co. v. *Laughton* (1983) provides an example of secondary action that is actionable under the section (for the facts of the case, *supra*, this chapter). The relevant persons in that case were the shipowners who had let the ship under a time charterparty to the charterers, who had sub-chartered the ship to the sub-charterers; the tugboat company who had a specific contract with the sub-charterers to move the vessel; the tugboat company employees and the defendant members of the ITF. There was an admitted trade dispute between the shipowners and ITF. The defendants' action of inducing breaches of the contracts of employment of the tugboat company employees was found to constitute prima facie the tort of interfering with the main contract of charterparty, except for the fact that ITF was acting in the furtherance of a trade dispute. This defence failed, however, if the defendant's action was secondary action not falling within, in this case, section 17(3). The House of Lords held that the secondary action did not fall within section 17(3) as extended by section 17(6) since the contract pursuant to which the tugboat services were to be supplied was not made with the shipowners who were party to the trade dispute but with the sub-charterers who were not. It will be appreciated that this could easily have been otherwise and the shipowners could have been the parties to the tugboat contract, the result being that what is secondary action may turn on issues that have no substantive importance.

INTERLOCUTORY INJUNCTIONS

An important weapon in the trade dispute is the interlocutory injunction. By means of this a party to a trade dispute may obtain an immediate injunction against industrial action taken against him pending trial of the action. Because of the nature of trade disputes, the interlocutory proceedings almost invariably constitute the real trial of the action, though that may change now that the trade union itself may be sued for damages. The plaintiff in order to obtain an injunction in interlocutory proceedings needs to show that the balance of convenience lies in his favour (which normally he is able to show by proving that he might suffer irreparable damage before the action came to trial) and that he has a prima facie case of proving an actionable wrong. The House of Lords decision in *American Cyanamid Co.* v. *Ethicon* (1975), however, had changed the latter requirement to one that the plaintiff need only establish that there was a serious question to be tried. In response to this decision, the legislature passed section 17(2) of the Trade Union and Labour Relations Act 1974. This requires the court, in exercising its discretion whether to grant an interlocutory injunction to have regard to the likelihood of the defendant establishing a defence under the trade dispute provisions. The intention seems to have been to re-establish the previous rule that the plaintiff must establish a prima facie case of the defendants' liability to succeed. In *N.W.L. Ltd.* v. *Woods* (1979) the *Express* case and the *Dupont Steels* case, all members of the House of Lords were agreed that this is now the law, although opinions differed as to whether section 17(2) had changed the law established by *American Cyanamid*, or was merely declaratory of the position in relation to trade disputes which that case did not affect. Certain reservations were made. Lord Diplock in *N.W.L. Ltd.* v. *Woods* thought that the defendant would have to establish a high degree of likelihood of a "trade dispute" defence succeeding where the consequences of his action were likely to be disastrous to the employer, to third parties, to the public or to the nation. Lord Fraser in the *Dupont* case thought that the court might grant an injunction even where no prima facie case existed where the health or safety of the public was threatened; Lord Scarman in the *Express Newspapers* case where the freedom of the press was seriously threatened.

23. THE ECONOMIC TORTS: PASSING OFF AND ANALOGOUS TORTS

PASSING OFF

The tort known as passing off protects primarily the person whose trade competitor passes off his goods or services as that person's. It is often said that in this tort the courts are recognising a proprietary right in the description or appearance of the goods or services, a right of intangible property akin to such things as copyright, patents, and design (which now receive the protection of statute). In a way all rights protected by the law of torts are proprietary in the sense that the protection they enjoy is universal—they are *iura in rem*. But it seems true to regard passing off as a proprietary type of tort, in a particular sense, since in it the plaintiff is complaining not of damage inflicted upon himself or his property by the defendant, but of the defendant's unauthorised use of something which belongs to the plaintiff. In this, passing off strongly resembles conversion, the other tort with a predominantly proprietary purpose. Passing off is the "purest" of the economic torts. Its purpose is almost exclusively the protection of economic interests. Furthermore, passing off has become of increasing importance since the courts by allowing numerous extensions of it have used it as a means of controlling unfair trade competition. This has meant, however, that the boundaries of the tort and its extensions are somewhat ill-defined. Lord Diplock's definition of the tort in *Warnink* v. *Townend* (1979) in terms of a misrepresentation

made by a trader in the course of trade to prospective customers of
his is true in the sense that the ultimate effect must be a misrepresentation, but conceals the fact that passing off is almost entirely
concerned with the deceptive selling of goods or services in such a
way as to suggest they are the plaintiff's or have some connection
with the plaintiff. The former case is passing off in the strict sense.
The latter is protected by an action analogous to passing off.
Passing off is also not limited to trade in the narrow sense.

Passing off; main methods of commission

(i) *Use of plaintiff's trade name*

In *Powell* v. *Birmingham Vinegar Brewery Co.* (1896), the plaintiff
sued to protect the name "Yorkshire Relish" which the plaintiff used
for the sauce he manufactured. The action was successful.

The trade name may be derived from the area in which the
goods are manufactured. Thus, successful actions have been
brought to protect the trade names "Stone Ales," "Chartreuse"
liqueurs and "Champagne." The last case (*J. Bollinger* v. *Costa
Brava Wine Co. Ltd.* (1961)) concerned an action by a manufacturer of champagne against the defendants who described their
wine, produced in Spain, as "Spanish Champagne." It was held
that the word "champagne" was still generally regarded as
referring exclusively to wine produced in the Champagne district of
France, that the prefix "Spanish" did not prevent the possibility of
purchasers being misled into thinking they were purchasing such
wine; that the plaintiff could obtain an injunction to prevent the
defendants' use of the name, although he was only one of the wine
producers in the Champagne district.

The Spanish Champagne case has been approved and extended
by the House of Lords in *Warnink* v. *Townend* (1979). The
plaintiffs were one of a number of producers of advocaat, a drink
consisting of a mixture of eggs and spirits. The defendants
manufactured a drink in England which they marketed as "Old
English Advocaat," and which was made from dried eggs and
Cyprus sherry. Because of the sherry base it sold at a cheaper
price than the plaintiffs' product. The House of Lords granted the
plaintiffs an injunction against the defendants' use of the name
advocaat for their product. That name had acquired an exclusive
meaning that spirits and not wine were used in its manufacture.
Thus the Spanish Champagne case *ratio* protecting a name

exclusively associated with a particular region has thus been extended to products exclusively associated with a particular process.

When the plaintiff is alleging that he alone has the right to use words which simply describe the goods or their characteristics, he has a difficult burden of proof to discharge in that he must show that these words have acquired the status of a trade name. This was achieved by the successful plaintiff in *Reddaway* v. *Banham (George) & Co. Ltd.* (1896) where an injunction was obtained to protect the name "Camel Hair Belting."

(ii) *Use of defendant's own name*

It is sometimes said that there is nothing to prevent a person trading by or describing his goods by his own name. But it is clear that this is not so where the use of the name is fraudulent (*Croft* v. *Day* (1843)), nor where, though innocent, it creates avoidable confusion with that of that plaintiff (*Baume & Co. Ltd.* v. *A. H. Moore Ltd.* (1958)). Where confusion is unavoidable, the defendant is not entitled to use his own name as a description of his goods, though he is entitled to trade in his own name and use that name for his business as a whole (*Parker-Knoll* v. *Knoll International* (1962)). Where the plaintiff and defendant are not in competition with each other, the plaintiff may still succeed against the defendant for using a name identical with or similar to his own, provided the use of the name is calculated to cause him damage. The action is for a tort analogous to passing off (*Harrods Ltd.* v. *R. Harrod* (1923) is one of a number of examples).

(iii) *Imitating appearance or get-up of plaintiff's goods*

There are common-sense limitations to this method of committing the tort. Thus, where the similarity between the goods is in their functional rather than their decorative aspects, the courts are normally unwilling to interfere. In *Cadbury-Schweppes* v. *Pub Squash* (1981) the Privy Council took the law a little further by holding that passing off might be committed by imitating the main features of the advertising campaign for the plaintiff's product (in this case the attempt to associate it with a virile, sporting image) if the plaintiff could show that in the mind of the public those features had become exclusively associated with that product. On the facts, however, the plaintiff failed to prove this and the Privy

Council upheld the trial judge's finding that the public was not deceived, despite another finding that the defendants had deliberately imitated the features of the plaintiffs' advertising and evidence to show that the plaintiffs had suffered loss of sales after the introduction of the defendants' product on to the market.

Reckitt & Colman Products v. *Borden* (1990) is an example of passing off protecting the get-up of the plaintiff's goods. The plaintiffs sold lemon juice in lemon-shaped containers and there was evidence to show that they had originated this practice and that the lemon-shaped container was specifically associated in the minds of the public with the plaintiffs' product. The defendant then began to sell their lemon juice in similarly shaped containers although there were other distinguishing features. The House of Lords held that the plaintiffs were entitled to succeed against the defendants for passing off their product as that of the plaintiffs. The average member of the public was capable of being deceived and it did not matter that there would have been no such deception had that member been "more careful, more literate or more perspicacious." Nor was it legitimate to compare the shape of the containers to a word in common use, since the plaintiffs had sufficiently appropriated that shape to their juice.

Action for torts analogous to passing off

The courts have also allowed actions in some cases where no action for passing off would lie, if the case is analogous to passing off. For example, though no action for passing off will lie where plaintiff and defendant are not in economic competition (see *McCulloch* v. *May Ltd.* (1947)—plaintiff, a children's broadcaster who used the name "Uncle Mac" unsuccessful in action of passing off against defendants who manufactured a cereal, "Uncle Mac's Puffed Wheat"), it seems to be accepted that an action for a tort analogous to passing off will lie if the defendant's act is calculated to cause damage to the plaintiff's reputation or livelihood (held so in *Sim* v. *H. J. Heinz Co. Ltd.* (1959) and *Borthwick* v. *Evening Post* (1888)—in that case an injunction by the proprietor of the *Morning Post* against the defendants to prevent them calling their evening newspaper the *Evening Post*, was refused only because the defendant's act was not calculated to cause the plaintiff damage). The plaintiff was also held to be entitled to succeed in *Associated Newspapers* v. *Insert Media* (1990) in an action for the analogous action for inserting without permission into the plaintiff's newspapers advertising material organised by the defendants. This implied an association with the plaintiffs which did not exist and was calculated to harm the plaintiffs' goodwill since the plaintiffs strictly controlled the advertisements in their newspapers. Some cases have found the requirement that the defendant's use of the plaintiff's name must be calculated to harm the plaintiff's goodwill or reputation easily satisfied (for example, *Hilton Press* v. *White Eagle Youth Holiday Camps* (1951)—"Eagle" comic might be damaged by possibility of accidents at training camps; *Henderson* v. *Radio Corporation Pty. Ltd.* (1969)—use of dancing group's picture on record could diminish future ability to obtain sponsorship fees). Other cases have taken a sterner position (*Lyngstad* v. *Anabas Products* (1977)—pop group unable to restrain use of name and likeness on non-musical goods). The more lenient cases may represent a view that it should not be possible to appropriate the goodwill attaching to the plaintiff's name and imply association with him in order to sell the defendant's product even though the likelihood of damage is not apparent.

Sales Affiliate Ltd. v. *Le Jean Ltd.* (1947) represented another extension to the existing tort of passing off. The plaintiffs marketed materials which were used in a permanent wave process known as "Jamal." There was evidence that this process was exclusively associated in the trade with the plaintiff's materials. The defendant hairdressers used other materials when asked by their customers for the "Jamal" treatment. This was held to be a tort analogous to passing off, the latter not being available because the defendant had not sold goods or services to the public which they had represented as those of the plaintiffs. Granted the correctness of this decision the earlier case of *Cambridge University Press* v. *University Tutorial Press* (1928) seems wrongly decided. The defendants claimed that a book published by them was the book prescribed for study by an examination board for an examination. In fact the book published by the plaintiffs had been prescribed. The plaintiffs' action against the defendants failed. Clearly people could not have been misled into thinking they were buying the plaintiffs' book, but as in the *Sales Affiliates* case, the defendants were marketing a quality as their own which exclusively belonged to the plaintiffs.

Protection of ideas

Passing off does not protect bright ideas or information as such. Legal protection may exist under the law of copyright or breach of confidence (as to the latter, see *infra*, p. 399).

Strict liability

Like conversion, passing off may operate as a tort of strict liability, since the defendant is liable even if he has acted in good faith and without negligence, but this has a somewhat illusory quality. The primary remedy sought in cases of passing off is the injunction, and liability to this remedy is of course not strict. It is doubtful whether damages will be awarded against an innocent passer off (left open in *Marengo* v. *Daily Sketch* (1948)), though no doubt the court would be more willing to allow the plaintiff an account of profits.

Damage

It is usually stated as a requirement of the tort that the plaintiff must prove damage. But there is no need for the plaintiff to prove special damage in the form of actual business loss—the court may award general damages on the basis of a presumption that damage will flow from the mere fact of the tort's commission. Furthermore, where the plaintiff seeks only an injunction, there is no need to ask the court to presently presume damage—only that the damage is likely to occur in the future.

Remedies

The primary remedy is the injunction. The plaintiff may also claim damages or an account of profits. The latter yields to a more precise calculation than damages and is appropriate in cases of passing off, where only the vaguest estimate of damage may be possible.

Other requirements of passing off and the analogous torts

Act calculated to deceive

The test here is an objective one, *i.e.* whether the average member of the public is foreseeably likely to be deceived. This is a fundamental requirement in all actions for the true tort of passing off though less clearly in the case of the analogous tort. The basic issue is one of fact. Evidence may be received from persons actually deceived but is not necessary. An actual intention on the part of the defendant to deceive is very likely to produce a decision that his act is calculated to deceive, but this does not follow automatically.

24. THE ECONOMIC TORTS: DECEIT AND INJURIOUS FALSEHOOD

DECEIT

The tort of deceit is committed by one who makes a fraudulent misrepresentation to another who acts upon it to his detriment. The tort is not limited to the recovery of financial loss (in *Burrows* v. *Rhodes* (1899) the plaintiff recovered for physical injury suffered through his participation in the Jameson raid which he joined on the strength of a false representation by the defendant). Deceit has become of reduced importance since a duty of care in respect of statements was recognised by the House of Lords in *Hedley Byrne* v. *Heller and Partners Ltd.* (1964). But differences in the measure of damages in deceit (*infra*, this chapter) may mean that it is still worthwhile to attempt to prove fraud rather than negligence. It is still necessary to prove fraud in the making of the statement where either the requirements of *Hedley Byrne* or of the Misrepresentation Act 1967 cannot be met.

Requirements of deceit

The requirements of deceit are as follows:

(i) The defendant must make a false representation to the plaintiff or a class including him;

  (ii)   He must either know that it is false or make it recklessly, not caring whether it is true or false;

 (iii) He must intend that the plaintiff act or fail to act on the representation;

 (iv) The plaintiff must suffer damage as a result of his acting on the representation.

False representation

The term "misrepresentation" is not limited in the same way as that term when used in connection with equitable rules concerning rescission of contracts for innocent misrepresentation. That sort of misrepresentation had to be one of fact, representations of intention, opinion or law being excluded. It is quite different where the defendant is fraudulent as in the tort of deceit. So one may fraudulently misrepresent one's intention or opinion if at the time of making the statement one does not have that intention or opinion. "The state of a man's mind is as much a state of fact as the state of his digestion." (*Edgington* v. *Fitzmaurice* (1885)). And a fraudulent misrepresentation of law is clearly actionable, at least if made to a non-lawyer, now that it is clear that negligent misstatements of law are actionable under the *Hedley Byrne* case. There is indeed authority in support of this in *West London Commercial Bank* v. *Kitson* (1884) (misrepresentation about the effect of a private Act of Parliament actionable as deceit). There is liability for stating half-truths and ambiguities (*Briess* v. *Woolley* (1954)), for positive action taken to conceal the truth (*Schneider* v. *Heath* (1813)), and possibly for failing to correct a false statement originally believed by its maker to be true but discovered to be false before the plaintiff has acted on it. (Since the tort is not complete until the plaintiff has acted (*Briess* v. *Woolley*), liability should arguably exist in principle in this case.)

Knowledge of the falsity

There is some difficulty where the representation is made by a person other than the defendant. Where a servant acting in the course of his employment commits deceit, the master is vicariously liable. The same applies to a principal, where his agent has committed the tort, provided the agent has authority to make representations in the relevant matter. There is also liability if a fraudulent principal makes the representation through an innocent agent. But it is not possible to make the principal liable where his agent has innocently made a misrepresentation of whose untruth the principal would have known (*Armstrong* v. *Strain* (1952)).

Intention that plaintiff should act on the representation

It is not necessary that the representation should be made to the plaintiff himself. Thus, in *Langridge* v. *Levy* (1837), the plaintiff's father bought a gun from the defendant who knew that the father intended his sons to use it. The defendant fraudulently represented that the gun was sound. He was held liable to the plaintiff who was injured when the gun burst on firing. Here there was a continuing misrepresentation about the condition of the gun communicated through the father to the plaintiff with the defendant's knowledge. It was therefore legitimate to find that the defendant intended the plaintiff to act upon it. On the other hand, in *Peek* v. *Gurney* (1873) it was held that statements in a prospectus issued by the defendant were intended by him to be acted upon only by those who acquired shares by subscription from the company (to whom the prospectus would have been issued) and not by subsequent purchasers of the shares on the market. The fact that it is foreseeable that the plaintiff should act on the representation is, therefore, not enough. After the decision of the House of Lord in *Caparo Inds.* v. *Dickman* (1990), followed by *Al-NaKib (Jersey) Ltd.* v. *Longcroft* (1990) the position in negligence is the same.

Plaintiff's reliance on the representation

It must be shown that the representation was at least one of the reasons for the plaintiff acting as he did. Thus, in *Smith* v. *Chadwick* (1884), the plaintiff had bought shares in a company on the faith of a prospectus which contained the untrue statement that a certain person was a director of the company. Since the plaintiff had never heard of this person, he could not show that he

relied on the statement in the prospectus and his action therefore
failed.

Plaintiff must suffer damage

The normal claim in deceit is for economic loss, but personal
injury and damage to property are also recoverable; also for
consequential distress and inconvenience (*Saunders* v. *Edwards*
(1987)).

Damages

An action for damages is the virtually invariable remedy for
deceit. In *Doyle* v. *Olby* (*Ironmongers*) *Ltd.* (1969) the plaintiff
bought a business from the defendants about which the latter had
made various fraudulent misrepresentations including one to the
effect that all the trade was over the counter whereas, in fact, the
employment of a traveller was necessary. The plaintiff recovered
the following items as damages; (i) the difference between the
price he paid for the business and its actual value; (ii) expenditure
incurred in the course of running the business, *viz.* rent, rates, and
the interest on a bank overdraft. In contract the plaintiff would
have recovered only the difference between the value of the
business as represented and its actual value, since in contract the
plaintiff is put into the position he would have been in had the
representation been made good; in tort he is put into the same
position as if it had never been made. The damages awarded for
the first item included the reduction in value through the plaintiff's
being unable to afford to employ a traveller. This suggests that in
deceit damages will be awarded even though they are caused by
the plaintiff's impecuniosity, a more favourable measure than in
tort generally (*cf. Liesbosch* (*Dredger*) v. *S.S. Edison* (*Owners*)
(1933)). Lord Denning went so far as to say that the defendant was
liable for all loss flowing directly from the fraud, whether
foreseeable or not. (The position regarding the award of
aggravated and exemplary damages in deceit is dealt with in
Chapter 28.)

Lord Tenterden's Act

Under the Statute of Frauds 1677 a guarantee was unenforceable
unless it was in writing and signed by the guarantor or his agent.

After the action for deceit was created in 1789, it became possible to circumvent the statute by suing in deceit rather than on the guarantee itself. This resulted in the passing of Lord Tenterden's Act in 1828 which provided that a false representation as to credit could not be sued upon unless made in writing and signed by the representor or his agent. The Act is limited to fraudulent representations—it does not apply where the representation is made negligently (*W. B. Anderson* v. *Rhodes* (*Liverpool*) (1967)). The curious result is produced that the defendant might be able to defeat an action brought in negligence in respect of an oral representation as to credit by establishing his own fraud, though whether the courts would allow him to succeed is not clear.

INJURIOUS FALSEHOOD

Injurious or malicious falsehood consists in the malicious making of a false statement by the defendant about the plaintiff or his property which is calculated to cause him damage and as a result of which the plaintiff suffers damage. The tort is a generalisation from specific cases. It was called slander of title to make a verbal attack on another person's title to land as a result of which the land lost value or a purchaser could not be found for it. Slander of goods consisted in a similar attack on the plaintiff's chattels. The close relationship of these torts to defamation itself is indicated by their name. In *Ratcliffe* v. *Evans* (1892), however, the Court of Appeal found that these torts formed part of a wider principle by virtue of which any maliciously false statement made by the defendant about the plaintiff or his property was actionable, even though it was not defamatory, if it resulted in damage to the plaintiff. In that case the defendant published a statement in his newspaper that the plaintiff's firm had ceased to exist, knowing that this was untrue. The plaintiff recovered damages from the defendant in injurious falsehood for the loss of custom he suffered as a result of the statement. The two torts may overlap, however (*Fielding* v. *Variety Inc.* (1967), *infra*, this chapter).

Elements of the tort
The following are the chief elements of the tort:

(1) *There must be a false statement about the plaintiff or his property*

Where the statement does not refer to the plaintiff or his property, this does not appear to be tortious even though the plaintiff suffers damage as a result. If, for example, on the facts of *Ratcliffe* v. *Evans*, another firm which enjoyed advantageous business relations with the plaintiff's firm had also suffered economic loss as a result of the loss of custom suffered by the plaintiff's firm, this would not have been recoverable from the defendant. This requirement of injurious falsehood is the reason why statements such as that made in *Cambridge University Press* v. *University Tutorial Press* (*supra*, p. 379) are not actionable as that tort.

(2) *The statement must be calculated to cause the plaintiff damage*

"Calculated" merely means here "forseeably likely." Because of the courts' policy whereby they will not allow advertising campaigns by rival business men to be conducted in court, the defendant is not liable if his statement is a mere puff, extolling his own product, even at the expense of the plaintiff's. Thus, in *White* v. *Mellin* (1895), the defendant sold infant food produced by the plaintiff in his shop. He affixed to the bottles in which the food was sold, labels stating that a certain food (produced by the defendant) was better in several respects for infants than any other. This was held not to be injurious falsehood. Where, however, the defendant has made a disparaging statement about the plaintiff which goes beyond a mere puff, the requirement that it is calculated to cause damage to the plaintiff is fairly easily satisfied. In *Lyne* v. *Nicholls* (1906) a statement by a newspaper proprietor that the circulation of his newspaper greatly exceeded that of the plaintiff's rival newspaper was held to be actionable. Again, in *De Beers Abrasive Products* v. *International General Electric Co. of New York* (1975), where the defendants had circulated in the international trade market a pamphlet which purported to give the findings of laboratory experiments concerning the effectiveness of an abrasive manufactured by the defendants and another manufactured by the plaintiffs, the experiments concluding that the defendant's abrasive was superior, this was held to be more than a mere puff and was capable of amounting to injurious falsehood.

(3) *The statement must be made to a third party or parties*

The gist of this tort is that third parties, influenced by the statement, act to the loss of the plaintiff. The plaintiff must therefore show that the statement has come to the knowledge of third parties. This requirement for publication of the statement is the same as in the tort of defamation. It is also a requirement that the defendant intended the publication or should have foreseen it.

(4) *The statement must be made maliciously*

To show an absence of belief in the truth of the statement on the defendant's part is the normal means of establishing malice, though whether dishonesty is necessary is not yet established. It is settled that malice may be established although the defendant was acting to further his own trade interests. Thus, in *Joyce* v. *Motor Surveys Ltd.* (1948), the defendants wished to evict the plaintiff from the tenancy of one of their garages, because they wished to sell their business with vacant possession throughout. They told the Post Office that he had changed his address, and told the tyre manufacturers' association that the plaintiff had ceased trading there (the plaintiff was a tyre dealer). This was held to constitute injurious falsehood. The burden of proving malice lies on the plaintiff.

(5) *Damage*

The plaintiff must show that he suffered damage as a result of the statement. In order that the damage should not be too remote, it must either have been intended to occur by the defendant or have been a reasonably foreseeable consequence of the statement. The damage in question will normally be pecuniary, though there seems no reason to exclude a claim for physical damage where this has occurred. Where he is claiming that he suffered loss of custom as a result of the defendant's statement, it is not always necessary to call the evidence of particular customers who have ceased trading with him as a result of the statement. In *Ratcliffe* v. *Evans* (*supra*), for example, the plaintiff was allowed to succeed on proof of general business loss, rather than the loss of particular customers. Whether the plaintiff is allowed to do this will depend largely upon the type of falsehood and the circumstances of its utterance. Section 3(1) of the Defamation Act 1952 further alleviates the position of the plaintiff by allowing him to succeed without proof of special damage at all; (a) if the words complained of are published in writing or other permanent form, and are calculated, *i.e.* foreseeably likely, to cause pecuniary damage to the plaintiff; or (b) if the words are calculated to cause pecuniary damage to the plaintiff in respect of any office, profession, calling, trade or business carried on by him at the time of the publication.

Since most actions for injurious falsehood occur when the plaintiff has suffered pecuniary damage, and the majority of these concern damage to the plaintiff's trading interests, the necessity to prove special damage will now only rarely arise. Where the requirements of the Act are fulfilled, the subsection places injurious falsehood in the same position as regards proof of damage as libel and slander actionable *per se*. The court may award general damages for actual loss to the plaintiff that is presumed to arise from the statement even though that loss is not actually proved. *Fielding* v. *Variety Incorporated* (1967) shows, however, that it may still be of advantage to the plaintiff to prove the defamatory nature of the statement. The defendants' magazine had published a statement that a play, "Charlie Girl," produced by the plaintiff had been a "disastrous flop." In fact the play had been a great success. The plaintiff recovered £1,500 for libel and £100 for injurious falsehood, the difference being due to the fact that damages for injury to feelings may be awarded in defamation but in injurious falsehood the plaintiff is limited to his actual loss.

Injurious falsehood and negligent statements

Ross v. *Caunters* (1980) shows that where A by a negligent misstatement causes B to act to C's loss, C may succeed in negligence against A only if a sufficient degree of proximity exists between A and C, and that, at least where the loss is purely economic, that proximity is not necessarily established by showing that the loss to C is foreseeable. In the absence of the requisite degree of proximity, C must

establish the requirements of injurious falsehood in order to make
A liable.

25. MALICIOUS PROSECUTION AND ABUSE OF PROCESS

MALICIOUS PROSECUTION

Malicious prosecution is commited by one who maliciously and without reasonable and probable cause institutes criminal proceedings against the plaintiff, the result of the proceedings being in the plaintiff's favour, and the plaintiff thereby suffering damage. The formidable series of hurdles the plaintiff must surmount in order to succeed in this tort accounts both for the rarity of actions for it and for the low proportion of those which succeed. It is questionable whether the public interest in the bringing of criminal prosecutions requires such extensive protection at the expense of the private interest in not being brought unnecessarily to court. The Court of Appeal in *Metall und Rohstoff A.G.* v. *Donaldson Lufkin* (1988) expressed considerable doubt whether the malicious institution of civil proceedings was a tort, apart from the recognised cases of the malicious institution of bankruptcy proceedings or proceedings for the liquidation of a company (*Quartz Hill Gold Mining* v. *Eyre* (1883)). Such proceedings may be struck out as an abuse of the process of the court.

Prosecution

The defendant must be the person "actively instrumental" in causing proceedings to be brought against the plaintiff. In the large number of prosecutions brought by the police, the prosecutor is the police officer who conducts the prosecution, even though he may have acted on the advice of his superior officers in deciding to

391

prosecute. A private person who gives information to the police or to a magistrate as the result of which a prosecution is brought is not the prosecutor, since the decision to prosecute is not his. If, however, he agrees with the police to prefer charges and later signs the charge-sheet, he is the prosecutor, although the decision to instruct counsel to prosecute was taken by the police (*Malz* v. *Rosen* (1966)). The mere laying of information before a magistrate does not apparently constitute a prosecution for the purpose of this tort, though it is different where the magistrate has begun to inquire into the merits of the case, since at that stage the necessary damage to sustain the tort, in the form of presumed damage to reputation, will have occurred (*Mohammed Amin* v. *Jogendra Kuma Bannerjee* (1947))—the case appears to confuse the issue of whether there is a prosecution with whether there is damage sufficient to sustain the action.

Termination of the proceedings in the plaintiff's favour

This requirement of the tort is satisfied even though the plaintiff has won on a technicality such as a defect in the indictment or excess of jurisdiction in the court.

Absence of reasonable and probable cause

The plaintiff has the difficult onus of proving the negative, that there was no reasonable and probable cause for the institution of proceedings against him. Such absence may be established in one of two ways: (i) the plaintiff may show that the prosecutor had no honest belief in the probable guilt of the plaintiff: (ii) he may show that despite the prosecutor's honest belief in the plaintiff's probable guilt, the facts which the defendant honestly believed would not lead a man of ordinary prudence and caution to that conclusion.

Both means of discharging the plaintiff's onus require the court to inquire into the prosecutor's state of mind. If dishonesty on the defendant's part is established, it is irrelevant that the facts as found by the jury would have led a man of prudence and caution to believe in the plaintiff's probable guilt. The second method involves an inquiry into the facts honestly believed by the defendant and then an objective determination whether these facts ought to have caused him to believe in the plaintiff's guilt. The jury as the tribunal of fact will answer the question whether the defendant was dishonest and if they find he was this will determine the question whether there was reasonable cause. If they find the defendant to be honest, the jury must determine what facts the defendant honestly believed, and it is for the court to decide whether these were capable of furnishing reasonable and probable cause.

The fact that the defendant took advice before instituting proceedings seems logically relevant only to whether he was malicious, not also to whether or not the facts he believed constituted reasonable cause. But several recent cases have indicated that this fact may be sufficient to determine both issues in the defendant's favour (*Malz* v. *Rosen* (1966)—private person prosecuting on advice of police; *Glinski* v. *McIver* (1962) (*obiter*)—police officer acting on advice of his superiors, for example, the legal department of Scotland Yard). To take advantage of this rule, the defendant must communicate all the facts which he knows to the other person.

Malice

The plaintiff must prove that the defendant was actuated by malice in bringing the prosecution. This is achieved by showing that the defendant's motive in bringing the prosecution was not the vindication of justice. If it can be shown that the defendant had no honest belief in the plaintiff's guilt, malice is easily enough established. Even where he has such belief, however, it is possible to establish malice if it can be proved that the defendant brought the prosecution for some ulterior purpose of his own rather than the desire to see justice done. It is apparently enough if the defendant prosecutes in order to make an example of the plaintiff to deter others (*Stevens* v. *Midland Counties Ry.* (1854)). Generalised ill-will towards the plaintiff will also point to malice, on the defendant's part, but feelings of anger and resentment arising from the facts on which the defendant based his decision to prosecute are not.

The judge decides whether there is evidence of malice to go to the jury. The jury decides whether there was malice in fact.

The two issues of malice and absence of reasonable and probable cause must be kept separate by the judge in advising the jury. Thus, though malice exists, there may still be reasonable cause for bringing the prosecution and no inference may be drawn of the absence of reasonable cause from the presence of malice. Where, however, reasonable cause is absent, this does not *ipso facto* establish malice but may justify an inference of malice (*Johnstone* v. *Sutton* (1786)).

Damage

Damages must be proved in this tort and it is arguable that this should preclude the award of aggravated damages to compensate the plaintiff for matters such as distress or humiliation arising from the prosecution. In view of the much greater willingness of courts to compensate for injured feelings generally, and in view of the award of aggravated damages in the comparable tort of deceit (*Archer* v. *Brown* (1984)) (*infra*, p. 412), it may be anticipated with confidence that they may also be awarded in a successful claim for malicious prosecution.

Actual damage may be proved under one or more of the three heads established by *Savile* v. *Roberts* (1698).

These are:

(i)   Damage to reputation. The charge against the plaintiff must be necessarily defamatory of him, not merely capable of being understood in a defamatory sense, malicious prosecution being narrower here than defamation. To accuse the plaintiff of pulling the communication cord in a train is not defamatory (*Berry* v. *British Transport Commission* (1962)).

(ii) Damage in respect of the personal security of the plaintiff. Mere exposure of the plaintiff to the risk of imprisonment because of the charge seems enough (*Wiffen* v. *Bailey and Romford U.C.* (1915)—*contra*, Diplock J. *obiter* in *Berry's* case).

(iii) Pecuniary loss. The plaintiff may recover the difference between actual costs awarded him and the amount of his defence costs (*Berry's* case), but not for other consequential pecuniary losses.

Malicious process

It is a tort maliciously and without reasonable cause to make use of a legal process against the plaintiff (apart from the mere swearing of false evidence in respect of which legal immunity from civil action exists—*Hargreaves* v. *Bretherton* (1958)) as a result of which the plaintiff suffers damage. The tort is merely another form of malicious prosecution. In *Roy* v. *Prior* (1970), for example, the defendant obtained a bench warrant for the plaintiff's arrest by giving evidence which the plaintiff alleged to be false that the plaintiff was evading service of a witness summons. As a result the plaintiff was arrested. The House of Lords held that the plaintiff had a good cause of action against the defendant if he could show that the defendant acted maliciously and without reasonable cause. Another recent example of this tort is the obtaining of a search warrant maliciously and without reasonable cause (*Reynolds* v. *Metropolitan Police Commissioner* (1985)).

In both malicious prosecution and malicious process, where the prosecution or process leads to the plaintiff's arrest, there is a need to distinguish false imprisonment by wrongful arrest. False imprisonment requires directness. Where this is present, there is false imprisonment without any requirement of malice or absence of reasonable cause. If the defendant wrongfully arrests the plaintiff, this is false imprisonment however genuine the defendant's belief in the plaintiff's guilt, though this belief may be relevant to the establishing of a defence of lawful arrest. If, however, he procures the arrest of the plaintiff by another person, by making use of a legal process, this is too indirect to be false imprisonment. It is only a tort if the defendant has acted maliciously and without reasonable cause or has abused the process (*infra*). Thus it is not false imprisonment to give false information to the police as a result of which they arrest the plaintiff (*Grinham* v. *Willey* (1859)). Where, on the other hand, the police are acting as mere agents of the defendant in effecting the arrest, as when they refuse to effect an arrest unless the plaintiff signs the charge-sheet, this is sufficiently direct to be false imprisonment (*Hopkins* v. *Crowe* (1836)).

Abuse of process

It is a tort to make use of a legal process to effect an object not within the scope of the process. In the old case of *Grainger* v. *Hill* (1838) the plaintiff succeeded against the defendant for swearing an affidavit of debt against him, not for the purpose of obtaining payment of the debt but of extorting security for the debt from the plaintiff. This case appears to be the only successful action for this tort in English law, but its existence has been confirmed and its characteristics defined in recent decisions at first instance and of the Court of Appeal (*Speed Seal Products* v. *Paddington* (1986); *Metall und Rohstoff A.G.* v. *Donaldson Lufkin Inc.* (1989)). The collateral purpose must be the defendant's predominant purpose in using the process. Malice and absence of reasonable cause do not have to be proved nor does the process have to terminate in the plaintiff's favour. The plaintiff must prove damage.

26. INNOMINATE AND DOUBTFUL TORTS

INNOMINATE TORTS

In this chapter will be discussed a number of cases which cannot be classified under previously mentioned categories. Innominate torts are those which escape classification either because the interest protected is an unusual one, or because they are analogous to although distinct from well-recognised torts. There is a large variety of torts of the former class of which only a few examples can be given. It is a tort actionable *per se* for a member of a common calling to refuse to provide services to the public. So an innkeeper is liable in tort for refusing to provide accommodation which he has available to the plaintiff (*Constantine* v. *Imperial Hotels Ltd.* (1944)). It is a tort actionable *per se* to interfere with another person's right to vote (held so far as the Returning Officer of a constituency was concerned in *Ashby* v. *White* (1703), although this person now has a statutory defence to such an action). It is tortious to interfere with a right of franchise enjoyed by another, an example of such a franchise being the exclusive right to carry for hire goods or passengers by means of boats across a river or arm of the sea.

One innominate tort whose existence has recently been affirmed and which may become of greater importance is that which concerns misfeasance in office by a public officer. It was clear law that a justice of the peace who maliciously abused his powers and thereby caused damage was liable in tort and this liability extended to other public officers (*Whitelegg* v. *Richards* (1823)); *Henley* v. *Mayor of Lime* (1828)). This ancient liability has recently been confirmed and an extension of it recognised in *Bourgoin S.A.* v. *Minister of Agriculture, Fisheries and Food* (1985). In that case the court refused to strike out a cause of action alleging a revocation by the minister of the plaintiff's licence to import turkeys and turkey parts into Britain, that revocation being a deliberate breach of Article 30 of the Treaty of Rome which forbade quantitative restrictions on imports. The Court of Appeal held that the statement of claim disclosed a cause of action in the tort of misfeasance in a public office by the holder of that office. It stated that in addition to malicious abuse of power, the tort might be committed by the defendant's knowingly exceeding the power vested in him, the relevant averment in the case itself. The tort has survived the scrutiny of the House of Lords in *Jones* v. *Swansea C.C.* (1990), though the plaintiff failed in the case itself because of failure to establish malice on the part of the defendant. The House also confirmed the ruling of the Court of Appeal that a public body may be held liable for the tort even though it is exercising contractual rather than statutory powers provided that it is acting as a public body in so doing.

Innominate torts which are analogous to nominate torts have been discussed in various sections of this book. So, for example, those with a reversionary interest in land or in chattels can sue in tort for damage done to such interests though they cannot comply with the strict requirements of trespass or conversion (*supra*, Chapters 3 and 4).

DOUBTFUL TORTS

In some cases there is doubt whether an existing civil remedy is based on tort. Two leading examples are discussed here.

Interference with occupation

Although the phrase "right to work" is an emotive one and although no such generalised legal right exists, it is undoubtedly true that courts will sometimes intervene to protect the plaintiff in the exercise of his occupation or profession. What is not clear is whether the type of intervention that the court makes justifies the view that the defendant has committed a tort. Many cases have concerned the expulsion of the plaintiff from membership of an association which controls the entry into or right to practice a given occupation. The courts will intervene here if the expulsion is *ultra vires* or otherwise in breach of the association's rules, by way of an injunction or a declaration that the plaintiff has been improperly expelled (*Lee* v. *Showmen's Guild* (1952); *Abbott* v. *Sullivan* (1952)). The remedy in such cases is often explained as resting on contract—the rules of the association have contractual force as between the members of the association. In *Abbot* v. *Sullivan* the Court of Appeal considered whether the expelled member had any claim in damages for breach of contract or in tort but decided against both. Since the right to claim damages is an essential characteristic of a tort, the case does not support the view that the right is based on tort. On the other hand it is clear that the situations in which the courts will protect a person's occupation are not limited to cases where there is a breach of contract. In *Nagle* v. *Feilden* (1966) the Court of Appeal refused to strike out a cause of action in which the plaintiff claimed that the Stewards of the Jockey Club had refused her a trainer's licence solely on the ground that she was a woman. In *David* v. *Abdul Cader* (1963) the Privy Council refused to hold that an allegation that the defendant, the chairman of a licensing committee, had maliciously refused the plaintiff a licence to run a cinema disclosed no cause of action. Nor did they rule out the possibility of damages being recovered. *David's* case could be rested on misfeasance in public office. Apart from that, the existence of tortious relief for interference with occupation must be considered doubtful.

Breach of confidence

Courts have for many years been willing to restrain by injunction the disclosure of confidential information, whether of a personal (see *Gee* v. *Pritchard* (1818); *Argyll* (*Duchess*) v. *Argyll* (*Duke*) (1967)) or of a commercial character (*Cranleigh Precision Engineering* v. *Bryant* (1965)). It is possible to obtain damages in lieu of an injunction in such cases under section 50 of the Supreme Court Act 1981, but the award of damages, like that of the injunction itself, lies within the discretion of the court. Furthermore, as the remedy is equitable, damages could not be awarded against a bona fide purchaser of the information for value and without notice. It is clearly therefore advantageous to show that the user of confidential information commits a tort, since in that case damages are obtainable as of right, and perhaps, from anyone who discloses or utilises the information in whatever circumstances he has obtained it. *Seager* v. *Copydex* (*No.* 1) (1967) suggests that a tort is committed by one who makes use of confidential information. In that case, damages were awarded against the defendants who had made use of the plaintiff's design for a carpet grip, which the plaintiff had entrusted in confidence to the defendants. The damages awarded were tortious in character, on the analogy of conversion, rather than equitable in lieu of an injunction (see *Seager* v. *Copydex* (*No.* 2) (1969)). A new tort may therefore have been created. Whether it has, and what are its features, must be left for resolution by the courts.

The Law Commission in its Report No. 110 accompanied by a draft bill recommended that there be a statutory tort of breach of confidence, available against persons who had obtained the information in circumstances where an obligation of confidence arose or they had obtained it improperly, for example by unlawful surveillance. Damages would be obtainable as of right for damage, whether pecuniary or in the form of mental distress, suffered as a result of the revealing of the confidence prior to the trial of the action; otherwise they would continue to be available in lieu of an injunction. An account of profits would be available as an alternative to a claim for damages.

PRIVACY

Privacy already receives a considerable degree of incidental protection under existing legal remedies, for example, nuisance (*cf. Lyons* v. *Wilkins* (1899)), trespass to land (*cf. Hickman* v. *Maisey* (1900)), defamation (*cf. Tolley* v. *Fry* (1931)), infringement of copyright (*cf. Williams* v. *Settle* (1960)), and the action for breach of confidence. There is, however, no tort of infringement of privacy itself, despite several abortive attempts to pass legislation creating one. (*Malone* v. *Commissioner of Police* (*supra*) is the latest decision to confirm this point). In this Britain is very different from the United States in which protection of privacy is comprehensive. The Younger Committee Report on Privacy (Cmnd. 5012), however, recommended no basic change in the law, although recommending that there should be a new tort of unlawful surveillance by technical device. Part of the problem with protection of privacy is that it interferes with freedom of speech, the view prevailing in this country that this should rule out a remedy for infringement of privacy altogether rather than that the publisher should be required to justify his publication on the ground that it was in the public interest or made without malice. Another problem with the protection of privacy is that there appears to be no consensus among those who support it as to the best method of achieving it and in particular whether this should be done through criminal sanctions or civil remedies. The Rehabilitation of Offenders Act 1974 is a good example of the complications that may be involved. It contains criminal penalties for the disclosure of spent convictions, a civil remedy for defamation against a person who reveals another person's spent conviction, and a number of exemptions from liability in relation to the non-disclosure or denial of a previous spent conviction (see further for statutory civil actions protecting privacy section 22 of the Data Protection Act 1984; section 85 of the Copyright, Designs and Patents Act 1988. The Interception of Communications Act 1985 creates only criminal offences).

27. DEATH IN RELATION TO TORT

The former rule was that the death of either party extinguished the defendant's tortious liability. It was also a rule of the common law that a third party could not bring an action in respect of the death of another person as the result of a tort (*Baker* v. *Bolton* (1808)). Both these rules could be productive of injustice and both have now largely been abrogated by statute. The major injustice was to deny third parties such as dependants an action in respect of the death. This was remedied by the Fatal Accidents Acts. The effect of these, since they allow dependants a tortious action in respect of the death of another, has been to create a new tort. The substantive effect of these Acts must be contrasted with the merely procedural significance of the Law Reform (Miscellaneous Provisions) Act 1934, which allows tortious actions to survive as part of the estate of the victim or against the estate of the tortfeasor. Despite the differing effects of these statutes, they are best treated in conjunction since claims under both are commonly made when actions are brought in respect of death as the result of a tort.

FATAL ACCIDENTS ACTS: DEATH CREATING LIABILITY

By a series of Acts now consolidated in the Fatal Accidents Act 1976, it is possible for a dependant to bring an action when the death of the person upon whom the dependency exists has been caused by the tort of another, provided the person killed would have been able to bring an action and recover damages for such tort. The list of dependants is now contained in section 3(1) of the

402

1976 Act as amended by the Administration of Justice Act 1982. Broadly speaking, a relationship to the deceased by consanguinity or affinity is required. In the former case illegitimate relationships and those of the half-blood are recognised. Step-children are children of their step-parent. The 1982 Act extends the list by including former spouses of the deceased, persons living with the deceased as husband or wife for at least two years prior to the death, and persons treated by the deceased as his parent or child. A person who can show that he falls within one of the recognised categories must also establish a relationship of dependency on the deceased.

The action is normally brought on behalf of the dependants by the executor or administrator of the estate of the deceased but where there is no one acting in that capacity or no action has been brought by the personal representative within six months of the death, any dependant may sue in his own name on behalf of himself and the others. This distinguishes further the dependants' action from the estates action under the 1934 Act which can only be brought by the personal representative.

Nature of the relatives' action

Clearly the Fatal Accidents Act creates an important exception to the normal rule that negligence causing purely economic loss is not actionable. The Act requires the death to be caused by the wrongful act, neglect or default of the defendant. These words are clearly wide enough to cover all torts, and in general the relatives' action is an action for tortiously causing the death of another person (though a breach of contract causing death is enough). As such, it has been said to be "new in its species, new in its quality, new in its principle, in every way new" (words spoken by the court in an 1884 case). It is, however, a requirement of the Act that the wrongful act of the defendant could have been made the subject of a successful action for damages by the person injured had he survived to bring such action (section 1(1)). This has been interpreted by the courts to mean that anything which has the effect of extinguishing the liability of the defendant to the deceased in his lifetime (for example, settlement of the action by the deceased, expiration of a limitation period on his action or judgement obtained by the deceased against the defendant (this could have unfortunate consequences for the dependants since if damages have not been fixed by the judgment, no amount may be awarded for the deceased's loss of earnings after death)), has the same effect on the relatives' action. It is also provided by section 5 that contributory negligence by the deceased operates to reduce the amount the relatives can recover. Though a new cause of action, therefore, the relative's action is treated as very similar to that of the deceased himself. But the relative's claim is not affected by any contract under which the deceased limits the amount payable by the defendant (*Nunan* v. *Southern Railway* (1924)). Similarly in *Pigney* v. *Pointers Transport* (1957) (*supra*, p. 174) the relatives' claim succeeded even though the deceased had died by his own hand. The death was not too remote because it was caused by the injury the defendant had inflicted on the deceased. The *ex turpi causa* defence was rejected in *Pigney*. This has recently been confirmed by the Court by Appeal in *Kirkham* v. *Chief Constable of Manchester* (1990) in which it ws held that since suicide was no longer a crime and since there was no moral turpitude involved in it, the defence failed. Where the nature of the dependency itself is *turpis causa* the action will fail (see *Burns* v. *Edman* (1970)—action by criminal's widow failed).

Nature of the dependency

The courts have in the absence of specific legislative provisions devised rules of their own about the interest of the relatives which is protected by the action. This interest will be described here as their dependency, although it is not so described in the Act itself. The dependency must be of a financial nature; the relative must suffer pecuniary loss as a result of the death. Thus the action is not available to give damages to the relatives for their mental suffering as a result of the death. The financial advantage must be actual or a reasonable probability; if it is too speculative the courts will reject it. Where the deceased was a child of four years to whom the father intended to give a good education, the action was not allowed. Where on the other hand the deceased had gratuitously assisted his father in his business in the past, and where the deceased had made gifts of money to his father during a period of unemployment, the action was allowed because it was reasonable to expect such charity would recur (*Barnett* v. *Cohen* (1921); *Franklin* v. *S.E. Ry.* (1858); *Hetherington* v. *N.E. Ry.* (1882)). In

Davies v. *Taylor* (1974) the court held that the dependant was entitled to be compensated for the loss of the chance of a benefit even though that was lower than 50 per cent. But since the plaintiff dependant must establish loss as part of the cause of action, it seems that this requires proof on the balance of probabilities and in this respect *Davies* v. *Taylor* is inconsistent with the recent decision of the House of Lords in *Hotson* v. *E. Berkshire H.A.* (1987). Chances of benefit of less than 50 per cent. will of course be allowed where the dependant can establish other loss on the balance of probabilities.

One case (*Sykes* v. *N.E. Ry.* (1875)) holds that the dependency must arise from a family rather than business relationship. So where a son was employed by his father under a contract of service, the father did not have an action for loss of these services when the son was killed. The father had not established any dependency on the son since he was paying him the going rate for his services. Where the dependant is being paid more than the value of his services by the deceased, he is entitled to recover the excess from the defendant (*Malyon* v. *Plummer* (1964)).

Although a pecuniary advantage is insisted on, this may be of a quite indirect nature. Thus the services of a wife or a mother in performing ordinary domestic tasks have a financial value, even though in their absence the employment of outside help would not be considered. So also do the mother's services in instructing her children in matters such as their upbringing and education (*Hay* v. *Hughes* (1975); *Mehmet* v. *Perry* (1977); *Cresswell* v. *Eaton* (1991)). But the services must have a pecuniary value—no damages may be awarded for loss of love and affection, and where a dependent child had been adopted by its aunt, the aunt's legal duty to maintain the child completely replaced the loss of dependency on the mother (*Watson* v. *Willmott* (1991)—not so, however, the loss of dependency in relation to financial gifts likely to have been provided by the father). In *Cresswell* v. *Eaton* (1991) a small reduction was made in damages for loss of the mother's services on the ground that she had had a full-time job and this affected the quality of those services. Also a reduction must be made to reflect the declining need for the mother's services as the child grows older (*Spittle* v. *Bunney* (1988)). The mother's services are valued on the basis of the net-in-hand wages payable to a nanny-housekeeper (*Corbett* v. *Barking H.A.* (1991)). An unusual benefit was recognised in *Davies* v. *Whiteways Cider Co.* (1974). The deceased's dependants had in his lifetime received gifts which because of his death within seven years of the gift attracted estate duty. The amount of this was held to be recoverable in the dependants' action. On the other hand, a plaintiff who can establish a loss of the normal type of dependency may fail on the ground that he is unable to establish any financial loss to himself arising from the death. So in *Malone* v. *Rowan* (1984) it was held that a working wife who continued to work after her husband's death could not recover damages for the increase in her dependency on her husband that she would have incurred through giving up her job and having children.

Assessment of damages

It is impossible to lay down firm rules on this matter: so much depends on the individual case and the nature of the dependency involved. Where the deceased's resources include earnings, the amount of future earnings lost is worked out on similar lines to those governing the assessment of such loss generally (see *infra*, Chapter 28) though a major difference is that the "multiplier" fixing the number of years of lost future earnings that is allowed for purposes of compensation is assessed from the moment of the death rather than, as in the case of a living plaintiff, the date of the trial. Lord Fraser's reason for this in *Cookson* v. *Knowles* (1979) that contingencies in the case of a living plaintiff only operate from the time of the trial whereas in the case of the dead person they date from the death is not entirely satisfactory and the rule can produce odd results—in *Corbett* v. *Barking H.A.* (1991) an 11½ year old boy still being looked after by a relative had only half a year left of an original multiplier of 12 years (but there had been inexcusable delay in bringing the action). Contingencies affecting both the deceased and the relatives must be assessed by the court, but statute now prevents the assessment of the likelihood of a widow's remarriage or actual remarriage to be used as a ground for reducing damages. However, in the case of the child's claim under the Fatal Accident Acts, the likelihood of remarriage of the widow may be a relevant factor and is one which the court is not precluded from taking into account. In assessing the damages payable to a person who has lived with the deceased as husband or wife for two years prior to his death, the court is required under section 3(4) of the Act as amended by the Administration of Justice Act 1982 to have regard to the fact that the dependant had no enforceable right to financial support by the deceased as a result of their living together. As in the case of the living plaintiff, the dependant who is looked after free by a relative or friend is entitled to claim an amount representing the pecuniary value of those services. Again, as in the case of the living plaintiff, the claim is that of the dependant, not the relative (*Cresswell* v. *Eaton* (1991) (*infra*, p. 419)). The claim is in addition to the claim for loss of the mother's services. The amount claimed may be based on the loss of the relative's wage, where it is reasonable for the relative to have given up employment; otherwise the cost of employing similar services (*Cresswell* v. *Eaton*).

Non-deductibility of benefits; section 4 Fatal Accidents Act 1976

Section 4 is a sweeping provision to the effect that all benefits accruing to the dependants in consequence of the death from the estate or otherwise are to be disregarded in assessing the damages to be paid. This includes property inherited from the deceased including damages payable by the tortfeasor to the estate in consequence of the death. It also includes pensions payable on death (*Pidduck* v. *E. Scottish Omnibuses* (1989)—though *cf. Auty* v. *National Coal Board* (1985)). In *Stanley* v. *Saddaqui* (1991) where the dead mother's services were, because of her personality, likely to be unsatisfactory and erratic and the child dependant was being much better looked after after her death by the mother's ex-husband and his wife, no deduction was made in respect of this "benefit," although the damages payable for the loss of the mother's services were discounted to reflect their unreliability. The rule as to deduction of benefits is far more generous in claims for wrongful death than that applicable to living plaintiffs, though the philosophy behind this is unclear.

SURVIVAL OF CAUSES OF ACTION AFTER DEATH

It has been already stated that the common law rule was that death extinguished causes of action in tort both vested in and lying against the deceased. The common law was totally changed by the Law Reform (Miscellaneous Provisions) Act 1934, section 1(1) of which provides that on the death of any person all causes of action subsisting against or vested in him shall survive against, or as the case may be, for the benefit of, his estate. Section 1(4) defines the concept of a subsisting cause of action to include the case where the defendant dies before damage necessary to establish the cause of action has occurred, but such damage has occurred thereafter.

Defamation is now the only tort to which the Act does not apply. The Committee on Defamation recommended that actions in defamation should survive against the estates of defendants, that in certain circumstances the estates of defamed persons should be allowed to bring the action, and that near relatives of deceased persons should have an independent right to sue for a declaration and injunction (but not damages) for defamatory statements about the deceased made within five years of his death.

Action on behalf of the estate of victim

The action differs from that brought under the Fatal Accidents Acts in that it is the deceased's own action which is brought. It is therefore brought on behalf of his estate by his personal representative, the amount recovered passing as part of his estate to those entitled under the rules of succession.

What damages may be claimed

Under the 1934 Act, all causes of action vested in the deceased at the time of his death survive for the benefit of his estate and this has been taken to mean that the estate may claim under the same heads of damages as the deceased himself during his lifetime. Thus there may be a claim for pain and suffering, loss of amenity and for loss of earnings until the death of the deceased (cf. *Murray* v. *Shuter* (1975). In *Watson* v. *Willmott* (1991) £4,000 damages were awarded to the estate for nervous shock suffered by the deceased caused by the death of the deceased's wife prior to his own suicide some months later). None of these claims would be sustainable where the deceased died instantaneously as the result of the tort. Here the only possible claim for non-pecuniary loss was for loss of expectation of life. The claim for damages for loss of expectation of life whether by the victim himself or by his estate, has been abolished by section 1 of the Administration of Justice Act 1982. A new claim for bereavement that is intended to take its place but is available only to certain close relatives is introduced by section 3 of the Act. Section 1(2)(*a*) of the Law Reform Act of 1934 (as amended by section 4(2) of the Act of 1982) precludes the award to the estate of: (i) any exemplary damages; (ii) any damages for loss of income in respect of any period after the deceased's death. The latter claim, which only became available after the House of Lords recognised in *Pickett* v. *British Rail Engineering* (1980) that a living plaintiff was able to claim in respect of the "lost years" of earning of which the tort deprived him, (*i.e.* during the period of lost expectation of life), and which it held in *Gammell* v. *Wilson* (1982) survived to the estate, now, therefore, no longer exists.

Funeral expenses

These may be claimed from the tortfeasor either by the estate under the Law Reform Act (section 1(2)(*c*)) or by the dependants under the Fatal Accidents Act (section 3(3) of the 1976 Act).

CLAIM FOR BEREAVEMENT

The new section 1A of the Fatal Accidents Act (introduced by the Administration of Justice Act 1982) provides a claim for bereavement caused by death where this is the result of the requisite wrongful act, neglect or default. The claim is available only to the wife or husband of the deceased or where the deceased was a minor who never married, to his parents if he was legitimate or to his mother if he was illegitimate. The amount claimable is £3,500 which is both the maximum and minimum award (subject to variation by the Lord Chancellor).

28. REMEDIES

DAMAGES

The most common and important remedy in the law of tort is the award of damages. The principles upon which damages are awarded have, where relevant, been discussed in connection with the individual torts. In this chapter the general principles relating to damages are considered, and a detailed examination is given to the award of damages for personal injury. The general rule governing the award of damages is that it should compensate the plaintiff for the loss he has suffered. In cases of tort this means that the plaintiff should be restored to the position he was in before the tort was committed against him. This is of course an impossibility in many cases of personal injury since no amount of money can restore a permanently disabled person to his previous position. This does not prevent the law from awarding monetary compensation for incommensurables such as loss of amenity. The award of exemplary damages does not satisfy the compensatory principle, since these damages do not compensate for any loss the plaintiff has suffered but are imposed as a punishment on the defendant.

Classification of damages

(1) *Contemptuous and nominal damages*
These types of damages are similar in that they signify the award of a token sum to the plaintiff equivalent in law to no damages at all. But they differ in purpose. Nominal damages are awarded in

order that the plaintiff's right should be vindicated although he has not suffered anything for which substantial damages could be awarded. Contemptuous damages are awarded where the court, though vindicating the plaintiff's right is also signifying disapproval of his having brought the action. The award is therefore of the smallest coin of the realm. There is the important difference between contemptuous and nominal damages that where the former are awarded the plaintiff is unlikely to be awarded costs (*Pamplin* v. *Express Newspapers* (1988)). Neither can be awarded where the tort is not actionable *per se*, since their award is tantamount to a finding that the plaintiff has suffered no damage.

(2) *Special and general damages*

Two senses of this distinction must be noted. First, "special damage" is used to denote that damage which the plaintiff must establish as part of his cause of action when suing for a tort not actionable *per se*. The term "general damages" as opposed to this sense of special damage, refers to damages which do not have to be precisely pleaded and proved but may be inferred from the fact of the tort's commission. Such damages include the damages payable for torts actionable *per se* in the form, for example, of aggravated damages payable for the outrage suffered by the victim of a trespass, or damages for the injury to reputation that may be presumed to occur upon publication of a libel. But general damages of this sort may also be awarded for damage that may be presumed to occur in the case of a tort not actionable *per se*, for example, nuisance passing off or injurious falsehood. The second meaning of the distinction is particularly related to actions for personal injury. The plaintiff's pre-trial pecuniary loss must be precisely pleaded and proved and the damages awarded for this are referred to as special. Future pecuniary losses for which the plaintiff is entitled to receive compensation are clearly incapable of the same precise pleading and proof though they may not be merely inferred—they are compensated by "general damages." Nevertheless, both forms of loss are special damage within the first meaning of the distinction drawn in this paragraph.

(3) *Aggravated damages*

Aggravated damages are awarded to compensate the plaintiff for his distress and humiliation arising from the commission of the tort against him. Their award is specifically associated with torts which are actionable *per se* and in which the damages are said to be at large. Trespass and libel are obvious examples. Recent authority shows, however, that the award of aggravated damages is not limited to torts of this nature. The starting point of this development was the award of damages for injured feelings in breach of contract (for example, in *Jarvis* v. *Swan Tours* (1973)). The courts have since then made similar awards in cases of negligence, where that negligence gave rise to a claim either for breach of contract or in tort (*Heywood* v. *Wellers* (1976)— negligence of solicitors in failing to apply for a non-molestation order against the plaintiff's husband; *Perry* v. *Sydney E. Phillips* (1982)—discomfort and distress suffered by the plaintiff from buying a house with defects in it which had been negligently surveyed by the defendants); and in the tort of deceit (*Shelley* v. *Paddock* (1980); *Archer* v. *Brown* (1984)). The present law appears to be that the award of aggravated damages is possible in an appropriate case for the commission of any tort involving an intentional wrong—they will not be awarded for negligence however extreme (*Kralj* v. *McGrath* (1986)).

(4) *Exemplary or punitive damages*

In all the cases discussed so far, the amount of damages the court may award reflects as far as this is possible the injury or damage inflicted upon the plaintiff. In the case of exemplary or punitive damages this is not the case; damages are awarded in order to punish or make an example of the defendant. The House of Lords in *Rookes* v. *Barnard* (1964) confined the award of such damages to three situations:

(i) Where the tortious action consists in oppressive, arbitrary or unconstitutional conduct by a government official (*N.B. Holden* v. *Chief Constable of Lancashire* (1987)—unconstitutional action need not also be oppressive).

(ii) Where the defendant has calculated to make a greater amount of money from his commission of the tort than he will have to pay in damages to the plaintiff (*Drane* v. *Evangelou* (1978)). It is not necessary that the defendant should have attempted a precise calculation of profit and

loss to be liable under this category (*Cassel & Co.* v.
Broome (1972)). The category is particularly apt to apply to
newspaper publishers who knowingly print libels in the
confident belief this will boost circulation.
(iii)   Where statute authorises the award of such damages.

Libel is the obvious and prime example of category (ii). To show
that the defendant is in the business of publishing for a profit is not
enough to bring the case within the category, though it is not
necessary to show that the defendant has precisely calculated the
gains and losses expected to arise from publication of the libel
(*Cassell & Co.* v. *Broome* (1972)). Precautions must be taken by
the trial judge against excessive awards of exemplary damages by
juries. Thus the jury should be warned that their award is of an
exceptional nature and to consider the question whether the
aggravated damages awarded already constitute sufficient punishment (*Riches* v. *News Group Newspapers* (1985)). Where there are
several plaintiffs each must receive the same award by way of
exemplary damages and the proper way to assess this is to assess
total damages payable by the defendant and to divide it by the
number of plaintiffs, rather than to decide on the individual award
and multiply it as the jury had done. More controversial is the
limitation in the *Cassell* case that where there are several
defendants, each must pay the lowest sum which the conduct of
any of them deserves. So the serious offender gets the lightest
possible sentence (The High Court of Australia took a different
position in *XL Petroleum* v. *Caltex Oil* (1985)). A deceit case,
Archer v. *Brown* (1984), decided that where the defendant has
been convicted and sentenced for the same conduct as that
constituting the tort, an award of exemplary damages is not
appropriate.

   For what torts may exemplary damages be awarded? There was
at one time an assumption that they could be awarded only for
torts actionable *per se*, but there is no hint of this in Lord Devlin's
categories. At the same time Lords Diplock and Hailsham in
Cassell & Co. v. *Broome* warned *obiter* that Lord Devlin's
categories were not intended to extend the cases in which
exemplary damages could be awarded. Previously, Lord Widgery
C.J. and Sachs L.J. had differed *obiter* as to whether exemplary

damages could be awarded in the tort of deceit (*Mafo* v. *Adams* (1970)), and Pain J. would have awarded them in *Archer* v. *Brown* but for the reason mentioned above. It is virtually certain that they cannot be awarded in the absence of intentional wrongdoing and Lord Devlin's categories may limit them to cases where there is unlikely to be a criminal prosecution—prosecution arising out of libel or unconstitutional action is highly unusual.

(5) *Parasitic damages*

These are damages given for the infringement of some interest which is not protected at all or not primarily protected by the tort in question. So, in an action for conversion, damages have been awarded for loss of reputation (*Thurston* v. *Charles* (1905)). In a woman's action for negligence causing her personal injuries, damages were awarded in respect of the loss of her husband's consortium, even though no action could have been brought in respect of this alone (*Lampert* v. *Eastern National Omnibus Co.* (1954)). This case shows that the "parasitic interest" may be one not protected by other torts.

Damages for personal injuries

Two types of "loss" are inflicted upon one who suffers personal injuries. He may suffer actual financial loss such as loss of wages or reduction in his earning capacity. And he may suffer reduction in his enjoyment of his life, through pain and suffering and inability to participate in his usual activities, whether of a temporary or permanent nature. It is clear that the latter loss is incompensable in monetary terms. To allow a plaintiff £1,000 for the loss of a leg is assuagement rather than replacement. Nevertheless, English law compensates the injured person for both types of loss. The latter type of damages is often referred to as non-pecuniary damages, the former as pecuniary damages.

(1) *Non-pecuniary damages*

With the abolition of damages for loss of expectation of life by section 1(1) of the Administration of Justice Act 1982, there are now two heads of non-pecuniary damages. These are damages for pain and suffering and for loss of amenity.

Pain and suffering. This is pre-eminently the head of damages which reflects the subjective effect the injury has upon the plaintiff. He is entitled to be compensated both for pain and suffering he has experienced up to the date of the trial and for such as he will experience in the future. The sum awarded may be in respect not only of the physical pain involved but also the mental anguish the plaintiff experiences, for example, in knowing that his expectation of life has been reduced or that his capacity to enjoy life has been reduced. No award for pain and suffering may be made where the plaintiff is rendered permanently unconscious by the injury and does not regain consciousness (*Wise* v. *Kaye* (1962)).

Loss of amenity. There was doubt for some time whether in the case of injury such as loss of a leg, damages were given to compensate the plaintiff's subjective appreciation of the effect of the injury, or for the injury itself. If the former, damages for loss of an amenity would be merely part of damages awarded for pain and suffering. In *Wise* v. *Kaye*, however, the Court of Appeal awarded £15,000 damages for loss of amenity although the plaintiff could have had no appreciation of the effect of her injuries upon her, and this decision was followed by the House of Lords in *West and Son Ltd.* v. *Shephard* (1964). It is now clear, therefore, that loss of amenity is a distinct head of damages from pain and suffering. Cases such as *Wise* v. *Kaye* and *West* v. *Shephard* render the compensatory function of the award of damages almost a fiction, but have been recently confirmed by the House of Lords (*Lim Poh Choo* v. *Camden A.H.A.* (1979)).

(2) *Pecuniary damages*

The plaintiff will recover as special damages his loss of earnings up to the time of the trial, and medical expenses actually incurred by him (including the cost of private medical treatment). The plaintiff is also able to recover as general damages loss of future earnings through reduction in his earning capacity. The method of assessment is to take a number of years' purchase (corresponding to the number of years of working life that would have been left to the plaintiff but for his injury), to multiply this by the annual sum of earnings lost by the plaintiff, and to adjust the sum arrived at to reflect contingencies such as the shortening of the plaintiff's working life through other events, and the benefit the plaintiff receives from receiving an immediate lump sum. The method of adjustment is to shorten the "multiplier," *i.e.*, the number of years of working life left to the plaintiff. Even in the case of young working adults, the maximum multiplier is about 18 years (and it shortens rapidly for older persons—see the choice of a multiple of 11 for a healthy 41-year old man by the House of Lords in *Graham* v. *Dodds* (1983)). Courts refuse to admit in evidence actuarial tables showing the life expectancy of persons comparable to the plaintiff (*Taylor* v. *O'Connor* (1971); *Mitchell* v. *Mulholland* (1972)). Furthermore several cases have established that the possibility of future inflation is not to be taken into account in making the award (*Cookson* v. *Knowles* (1978); *Lim Poh Choo* v. *Camden A.H.A.* (1979)). It is of course impossible for courts to know in advance whether inflationary conditions will continue to exist in, say, 15 or 20 years' time. But the present fact of inflation has led to the possibility of serious under-compensation of plaintiffs. Some of the reasoning of the courts on the matter is based on the high interest rates obtainable on money compared with the low discount rate adopted to fix the multiplier (about four and a half per cent. produces a multiplier of 18). This ignores the fact that the major part of the interest rate obtainable is there to defeat inflation. And the courts themselves have assessed the real interest rate at two per cent. rather than four and a half per cent. (*Wright* v. *B.R.B.* (1983)), admittedly for a different purpose, that of assessing interest due on non-pecuniary loss damages, but why should this make a difference? The courts also find themselves presented with a Catch 22 situation in arguing the benefit of high interest rates to the recipient of damages, because they are then compelled to admit that he will move into a higher tax bracket and should receive compensation for this. The recipient may well be taxed thrice, because damages are paid net of tax (*infra*), interest on the invested damages will have to be paid, quite likely at a higher rate of tax, and capital gains tax may have to be paid on investments. The House of Lords has now reinstated the original rule in which the effect of tax on the invested sum of damages is completely ignored, overruling the short-lived decision of the Court of Appeal in *Thomas* v. *Wignall* (1987)—*Hodgson* v. *Trapp* (1988). It is suggested that two main arguments underlie the courts' refusal to take into account inflation or taxation. The first is that the courts are determined to retain control over damages awards in themselves, rather than to hand the matter over to accountants and actuaries, whose calculations will be incomprehensible to most lawyers. Secondly, the calculations of the majority of the Pearson Committee show that if tax and inflation were to be taken into account in full mathematically, exceptionally large sums would have to be paid in damages. It seems that both points could be met merely by adopting a modest increase in the multiplier, as was accepted for tax by the Court of Appeal in *Thomas* v. *Wignall* and the High Court of Australia in *Todorovic* v. *Waller* (1981).

In *Pickett* v. *British Rail Engineering* (1979), the House of Lords overruled earlier authority and held that a person who had suffered a shortening in his life expectancy through the infliction of a tortious injury on him, was able to recover compensation for loss of future earnings during the "lost years," *i.e.* those years of life of which he has been deprived by reason of the tort, even though the plaintiff himself would not be alive to enjoy the use of those earnings. The decision in *Pickett* is defensible in terms of the injustice to the plaintiff of depriving him of the benefits of his future earning power during whatever life is left to him, but there seems little doubt that the chief reason for the decision is the protection of the plaintiff's dependants. The bringing of an action by a living plaintiff bars a further action on behalf of dependants under the Fatal Accidents Act 1976, and there is no question that dependants suffered a real loss by being deprived under the law before Pickett of compensation for loss of the plaintiff's earning power during the lost years. The anomalies and injustices arising from the decision of the House of Lords in *Gammell* v. *Wilson* (1982) that the cause of action for lost future earnings descended to the estate of the victim have been removed by statutory reversal of that rule.

It may be expected that the principles laid down for assessing compensation during the lost years in relation to actions brought on behalf of the estate in a number of post-*Gammell* decisions (for example *Harris* v. *Empress Motors* (1983) will be followed in the case of a living plaintiff at least to the extent that compensation will not be awarded to him in respect of sums representing his own living expenses. Two decisions have ruled out altogether a claim by young children for damages during the lost years where their life expectancy has been reduced by the tort (*Croke* v. *Wiseman*

(1981)—child of 21 months; *Connolly* v. *Camden Area Health Authority* (1981)—child of five years). The speculative nature of the claim for the lost years and the fact that the plaintiff is likely to be saved living expenses during that time mean that the claim is met by a small increase in the multiplier (half to one per cent.— *Housecroft* v. *Burnett* (1986)).

The claim for damages for lost future earnings is perhaps best looked at as a claim for compensation for destruction or lessening of earning capacity. The plaintiff's present earnings merely provide the best evidence of the value of that earning capacity to him. There are a number of cases in which it is not possible to base an award of damages upon the loss continued into the future of the plaintiff's present earnings. The plaintiff may yet be entitled to an award for his loss of earning capacity. Children who have never worked are clearly entitled under this head, although the amount to be awarded is in the nature of guesswork by the court (*Croke* v. *Wiseman* (1981)—award of £25,000 to a boy of 21 months who would never be able to work; *Joyce* v. *Yeomans* (1981)—award of £7,500 to a 10-year old whose earning capacity was considerably impaired). The same problem would arise in the case of the plaintiff who is not utilising his earning capacity but might have done so in the future. There is also the case of the plaintiff who has retained his job but whose earning capacity is impaired. *Moeliker* v. *Reyrolle* (1976) approved a small award of damages in this situation.

In relation to medical expenses, the plaintiff is not compelled to take free treatment under the National Health Service, even though it is readily available (Law Reform (Personal Injuries) Act 1948, section 2(4)—*cf.* the huge amount awarded under this head to the plaintiff in *Lim* v. *Camden Health Authority* for the cost of private medical treatment in the future). The computation of future medical expenses where these will last indefinitely is based upon the same principle as that of future lost earnings. A suitable multiplier is derived from the amount of years the plaintiff is likely to live and then reduced to reflect the contingency of death through other causes (the only relevant contingency here) and the receipt of a present sum. There is of course no question of recovery of medical expenses for the period representing the lost years (for a typical case illustrating the award of future medical expenses, see *Lim Poh Choo* v. *Camden A.H.A.* (1979)).

Other losses

Other types of loss may be awarded, subject to the compensatory principle obtaining. Loss of marriage prospects of a woman were compensated in *Hughes* v. *McKeown* (1985) though only by not adjusting the multiplier to reflect the fact that the plaintiff would probably have lost earnings through marrying and having children, rather than to allow a claim for it as loss of amenity. Financial loss consequential upon a divorce caused by the plaintiff's injury was rejected as a valid claim on policy grounds in *Pritchard* v. *J. H. Cobden Ltd.* (1987), not following *Jones* v. *Jones* (1985). Since the tort damages and the financial settlement under the divorce would be interdependent, it would be impossible to fix tort damages if the divorce proceedings were continuing or had not been commenced.

Third parties

There is now, apart from the claim of dependants upon death, no case in which a third party has a right of action in respect of loss suffered through a tort committed against another person. Section 2 of the Administration of Justice Act 1982 has abolished the remaining cases in which this was possible, that is the husband's action for loss of his wife's consortium, the parent's action for loss of his child's services, and the employer's action for the loss of the menial services of his servant.

These actions were regarded as anomalous historical survivals. Only one had any continuing practical importance, that of the husband's claim for the loss of the domestic services of his wife (in a role-reversal case, no action lay to the wife, another anomaly (*Best* v. *Samuel Fox Ltd.* (1952)). The general absence of any right in a third party to recover for financial or other assistance such as gratuitous services rendered to the victim caused hardship and this has been met by allowing a claim by the victim which is the victim's own claim but has the effect of benefiting the third party. The breakthrough as regards the conceptual difficulty facing the courts was the case of *Donnelly* v. *Joyce* (1973), a case concerning the provision of gratuitous services to the victim by a relative. The Court of Appeal held that the need for services arising out of the accident was a loss for which the victim was entitled to damages which could in the case itself be measured by the loss of wages suffered by the third party in rendering the services. No undertaking was required of the plaintiff/victim to compensate the third party. No doubt the same principles are applicable to the provision of financial assistance by the third party to the victim (*cf. Schneider* v. *Eisovitch* (1960)), or to the cost of hospital visits which speed recovery (*cf. Wilson* v. *McLeay* (1961); not where patient unconscious—*Richardson* v. *Schultz* (1980)). In the case of domestic services the cost of these is recoverable even though they are of benefit in part only to the husband of an injured wife, the wife's action thus operating as a substitute for the former consortium claim (*Daly* v. *General Steam Navigation Co.* (1980)). The third party's loss of wages up to trial were allowed as damages in *Donnelly*, though it would no doubt be thought unreasonable to extend the period too long if the wages greatly exceeded the commercial cost of help, in which case the commercial cost will be awarded (*Housecroft* v. *Burnett* (1986)). The claim these cases recognise are almost certainly limited to the case of the provision of gratuitous services by relatives or friends of the victim. No such claim would be allowed on behalf of free providers of medical services such as National Health Service hospitals. Equally the benefit of the claim is unlikely to be extended to employers who have paid the wages of the victim or have rendered him other financial assistance during his incapacity (the employer also has no quasi-contractual action for recovery of the payments against the third party (*Receiver for Metropolitan Police District* v. *Croydon Corporation* (1957)).

Deductions for collateral benefits

The question that arises here is for what benefits which result from the accident to the plaintiff must deduction be made from damages. In certain cases the courts insist upon the compensatory principle, and that the plaintiff must not profit from the commission of the tort. So in *British Transport* v. *Gourley* (1956) it was held that damages for loss of earnings must be paid net of tax—the award itself is not taxable. In *Dews* v. *N.C.B.* (1987) the plaintiff received an injury at work for which his employer was liable and during part of the time he was off work he was not in receipt of wages. The result was that his and his employers' contributions to his pension scheme lapsed. Nevertheless, his pension rights were totally unaffected. The House of Lords held that he was not entitled to claim the unpaid contributions as damages from his employers—he had suffered no loss. Two cases in which the compensatory principle is departed from are continually reaffirmed by the courts. These are the cases of insurance money payable to the victim under a personal accident insurance policy (*Bradburn* v. *G. W. Ry.* (1874)); and money donated to the victim by way of charity (*Redpath* v. *Belfast and County Down Ry.* (1947)). There are differences of opinion as to the reasons for these exceptions to the basic principle, but in the end it is probably a matter of policy. To deduct might cause people not to take out accident insurance or to give to charity, and, because these benefits are available where no tort has been committed, this would be against the public interest. A competing principle and one which may produce different results is that where the benefit is clearly intended to compensate for a specific loss, no damages will be awarded for that loss. In *Hussain* v. *New Taplow Paper Mills* (1988) the plaintiff who had received a serious injury at work was entitled under his contract to sick pay for 13 weeks and thereafter to half-pay or half the difference between wages actually received and his former wage. These benefits he would continue to receive while still employed. The House of Lords held that the half-pay benefits as well as the sick pay were deductible from damages. These benefits were not in the nature of insurance or pension within the *Bradburn* case (even though the defendant was insured to provide them) since they were clearly intended to compensate for a specific loss, *i.e.* lost wages, and were provided only while employment lasted, so were not in the nature of a pension. The House of Lords distinguished its own earlier decision in *Parry* v. *Cleaver* (1969) in which it was held that a police disability pension payable to a policeman who had retired through injury was not deductible from damages. *Parry* v. *Cleaver* has recently been upheld by the House of Lords in a case in which the House was invited to overrule it—*Smoker* v. *London Fire and Civil Defence Authority* (*The Times*, April 18, 1991). *Parry* was supported in *Hussain* on the ground that the pension was payable after employment ceased and without reference to whether the plaintiff was earning in outside employment. Where actual wages continue to be paid to an employee while employment continues, these should, following *Hussain*, be deductible, whether paid under a term of the contract or *ex gratia*, though there is an argument that the latter case is charity (deductibility in both cases supported by *Graham* v. *Baker* (1961)); the non-deductibility in *Dennis* v. *L.P.T.B.* (1948) of *ex gratia* payment of wages by employer may be supported only because the court extracted an undertaking from plaintiff to repay employer, and of *ex gratia* payment of half-pay for life in *Cunningham* v. *Harrison* (1973) on the ground that this continued after employment. Within the spirit of *Hussain* are *Parsons* v. *B.N.M. Laboratories* (1963); *Foxley* v. *Olton* (1965); *Nabi* v. *British Leyland* (1980)—unemployment benefit deductible; *Lincoln* v. *Hayman* (1982)—supplementary benefit deductible; *Gaskill* v. *Preston* (1981)—family income supplement deductible; *Colledge* v. *Bass, Mitchells & Butlers* (1988)—payment for voluntary redundancy taken after accident deductible, since this was caused by the accident. It would have been different if the plaintiff was already being made redundant since that would have had no connection with the accident. Social security benefits not caught by section 2 of the Law Reform (Personal Injuries) Act 1948, such as mobility and attendance allowance, are nevertheless deductible from damages since they partake neither of insurance nor charity. On the other hand, where an employer had taken insurance in order to provide a lump sum payment to an injured workman, and where this payment was independent of whether the workman was receiving any wage or by reference to the value of the wage lost, this was not deductible from damages because it was charity (*McCamley* v. *Cammell, Laird* (1990)—the court ruled out insurance because the plaintiff had made no contribution to the policy, but this contradicts *dicta* in *Parry* v. *Cleaver*).

Section 2 of the Law Reform (Personal Injuries) Act 1948 makes specific provision for the deduction of certain social security benefits from damages for loss of earnings, including industrial injury benefit, disablement benefit and sickness benefit. These are deductible for a period of five years from the first payment. Section 2 is exhaustive of the power to deduct these benefits. (The latest confirmation on this point is *Jackman* v. *Corbett* (1987)). Although the Act uses the words "loss of earnings," deductibility applies also to damages for loss of earning capacity (*Foster* v. *Tyne & Wear C.C.* (1986)). Any benefit an accident victim gains through saving of living expenses by being maintained at public expense in a hospital or other institution must now be deducted from damages for loss of earnings (section 5 of the Administration of Justice Act 1982).

Damages for contingencies

It has for a long time been accepted that the plaintiff is entitled to be compensated for contingent loss arising from the defendant's wrong, even though he can prove a less than even chance of that loss occurring. "Loss" includes here both the deprivation of the future possibility of benefit (*cf. Chaplin* v. *Hicks* (1911)—damages awarded for plaintiff's loss of chance of winning a beauty contest through being deprived by defendant's breach of contract of right of taking part), and of the possibility of later, additional damage occurring after the trial of the action. The capacity to award damages for contingencies of which there is a less than probable (under 50 per cent.) chance of their occurring only exists where the plaintiff has established the tort on the balance of probabilities (*Hotson* v. *E. Berkshire H.A.* (1987)). So the plaintiff may be awarded damages for the 10 per cent. chance of arthritis in a broken leg caused by the tort of the defendant. It is, however, an imperfect solution. If the later deterioration takes place the plaintiff is under-compensated and if it does not he is over-compensated. A change in the law introduced by section 32A of the Supreme Court Act 1981 is intended to deal with this problem. This allows the court to make a provisional award of damages assessed on two alternative bases, *i.e.* that the plaintiff will or will not as the result of his injury develop some serious disease or suffer some serious deterioration in his physical or mental condition after the trial. The plaintiff may then apply to the court for the increased amount to be awarded to him should the relevant condition develop at a later date (see *Hurditch* v. *Sheffield H.A.* (1989); *Willson* v. *Min. of Defence* (1991)).

Itemisation of damages and overlap

In *Fletcher* v. *Autocar and Transporters* (1968) the Court of Appeal expressed its disapproval of a method of awarding damages under which individual amounts were assessed for the different heads of damages and the total sum was then awarded as damages. This they thought would tend to produce over-compensation, particularly if no account was taken of possible overlap between these heads of damages. It is clear that, to avoid overlap, where damages include the cost of living in a medical institution, some deduction must be made from damages for loss of earnings on the ground that the plaintiff is now saved the cost of food and accommodation (*cf. Shearman* v. *Folland* (1950)). Also, where the plaintiff indulged in an expensive pastime such as golf, the loss of amenity involved in not being able to play golf was to some extent compensated in the financial saving to the plaintiff (the *Fletcher* case itself). This approach was also manifested in *Smith* v. *Central Asbestos Co.* (1972) in which the Court of Appeal thought that a high award in respect of future earnings would to some extent compensate for the loss of amenity involved in asbestosis. There is some inconsistency in the Court of Appeal's approach to this problem since it is difficult to see how the question of overlap can be examined without the court making at least a notional itemisation of damages. In any case the court must now itemise its awards for the purpose of awarding interest. Different rates of interest apply to each head—*Jefford* v. *Gee* (1970)). The justice of the Court of Appeal's approach to overlap is also not readily apparent. If the plaintiff has lost one expensive amenity, this seems no reason to deprive him of the opportunity of replacing it with another expensive pastime which the injury does not prevent him from indulging. And the Law Commission and Pearson Commission have criticised the logic of *Smith* v. *Central Asbestos Co.* (Law Comm. No. 56, paras. 195–201; Pearson Commission Report, para. 159).

Interest

Since many actions in tort take years to resolve, the question of interest on damages is important. The court is now bound to award interest on damages where the plaintiff recovers more than £200 unless it is satisfied that there are special reasons why it should not be given (section 35A of the Supreme Court Act 1981). The principle adopted by the courts (see *Jefford* v. *Gee* (1970); *Cookson* v. *Knowles*; *Pickett* v. *British Rail Engineering*) is that interest is only awarded on money which the plaintiff has been kept out of by the defendant's wrongful act. Thus there can be no interest awarded on damages for loss of future earnings. In relation to loss of earnings up to the date of trial, the plaintiff is entitled to interest at half the short-term interest rates during that period on the whole sum, the justification for this being that interest on the first instalment of wages should bear the full interest and thereafter on a declining scale to the last instalment which should bear no interest at all. Interest on damages for non-pecuniary loss bears interest at 2 per cent., the reason for this low amount of interest being that the non-pecuniary loss is assessed at the time of trial, thus excluding any interest representing the inflationary fall in the value of money after the injury and including only interest representing the loss of use of the money (*Birkett* v. *Hayes* (1982); *Wright* v. *British Railways Board* (1983)). Where liability and damages are assessed in separate trials, interest only accrues from the date of the award of damages (*Thomas* v. *Bunn* (1991)).

Duty to mitigate damage

The so-called duty to mitigate damage is not a legal duty at all. The phrase conveniently expresses the fact that failure by the plaintiff to take reasonable steps to mitigate his damage results in his not being able to recover damages for the damage which taking those reasonable steps would have prevented. The defendant has the burden of proving that the plaintiff could have mitigated his damage by taking certain action. The burden is then on the plaintiff to show that his failure to take that action was reasonable (*Selvanayagam* v. *Univ. of the West Indies* (1983)—reasonable for the plaintiff to refuse an operation in the circumstances of the case). Reasonableness is a question of fact. In *London and South of England Building Society* v. *Stone* (1983) the court found that a refusal by the plaintiff to enforce a repair term in the contract of mortgage against its borrowers was reasonable in the circumstances since by this means it preserved its goodwill and business reputation, even though by enforcing the term it would have been saved the financial loss that the negligent survey of the mortgaged properties by the defendant had caused it.

The decision of the House of Lords in *Liesbosch Dredger* v. *Edison S.S.* (1933) has relevance to the duty to mitigate damage. In that case the defendants' ship had by negligent navigation sunk the plaintiffs' dredger. The plaintiffs, who were working under a contract with the port authority, could not afford to buy a replacement dredger, which would have been available, and in order to carry out their contract had to hire a replacement. Rates of hire were high and the substitute dredger was more costly to work than the Liesbosch. The plaintiffs claimed this extra economic loss as damages from the defendants, but the House of Lords refused to allow them anything beyond the normal measure of damages, *i.e.* the cost of buying a replacement dredger, and costs and loss of profit incurred until it could have been regarded as ready for work. The reasoning was that the plaintiffs' extra losses were caused by their own lack of means, which must be regarded as a new cause not flowing from the defendants' negligence. Lawyers have always been sceptical of the "new cause" theory. The impecuniosity of the plaintiff was a pre-existent condition rather than a subsequent development and the normal rule is that the tortfeasor takes the victim as he finds him. The rule looks therefore more like one of policy, no doubt deriving from the same source as the rule about negligence causing purely pecuniary loss—a desire to shield the defendant from having to meet all the financial consequences of his act. It is no doubt a rational argument that persons in the position of shipowners carrying out commercial contracts should foresee the disastrous financial consequences of the loss of the ship and the inability to buy a replacement, and should take steps to provide against the event. Against this it is arguable that where the plaintiff's lack of means is based upon the refusal by the defendant to pay him damages until a court has determined his liability, the extra loss should fall upon the defendant.

Dissatisfaction with the *Liesbosch* rule seems to underlie the distinguishing of it in the Court of Appeal decision in *Dodd Properties* v. *Canterbury C.C.* (1980) though the grounds for the distinguishing are not satisfactory. In *Dodd* the plaintiffs had received damage to their property through the negligence of the defendants in 1970. They could have effected repairs immediately by increasing their bank overdraft but were undergoing a period of "financial stringency" and put off doing the repairs until they were certain of the defendants being held liable for them which only occurred some eight years later. By that time the cost of repairs had almost tripled. The Court of Appeal allowed the plaintiffs the higher cost of repairs as damages. Financial stringency was not impecuniosity and the plaintiffs in postponing repairs had made a reasonable commercial decision. So the plaintiff who has a choice is judged by the reasonableness of his decision whereas one with no choice is barred from arguing that the further loss is recoverable. Donaldson L.J. in *Dodd Properties* suggested that the *Liesbosch* decision itself might now be justified only on the ground that the extra damage in that case was unforeseeable and the need for revision of the rule in the *Liesbosch* case in the light of the present rule for remoteness of damage based on reasonable foreseeability was supported by Kerr L.J. in *Perry* v. *S.E. Phillips* (1982) and by Pain J. in *Archer* v. *Brown* (1984).

Once-and-for-all assessment of damages

Damages are awarded in a lump sum and are not subject to review. The award of damages in respect of any one cause of action is therefore final. This causes hardship in the type of case of which *Fitter* v. *Veal* (1701) is an example, where the plaintiff's injuries are greater than appears at the trial. In that case the court refused to alter its original award on subsequent application to it by the plaintiff. This particular hardship is alleviated by the new power of the court to make a provisional award of damages (section 32A, Supreme Court Act 1981, *supra*). The principle established by this case does not apply when the plaintiff is suing in respect of a different cause of action (as in *Brunsden* v. *Humphrey* (1884) in which it was held that the defendant's negligence in causing the plaintiff personal injury and damage to his property gave rise to distinct causes of action so that action in respect of the latter did not prevent a subsequent action for the former). For the same reason, it does not apply where the defendant has committed a continuing tort since fresh causes of action arise in respect of such tort from day to day as long as it is being committed.

Pearson Commission Report

The Pearson Commission Report made a number of suggestions for change in the law relating to damages for personal injury. Some of its suggestions were made law in the Administration of Justice Act 1982 and have been dealt with already. Those suggestions which have not yet found favour are indicated below.

(1) *Heads of damage*

Damages for pain and suffering and for loss of amenity should continue to be awarded, but damages for non-pecuniary loss should not be awarded in cases of permanent unconsciousness of the plaintiff. No damages for non-pecuniary loss should be awarded for such loss suffered during the first three months after the injury. This proposal, which would eliminate a large number of small claims, is the less attractive in the light of the fact that the

Report favours the retention of fault-based tort compensation as a whole. It is presumed, in view of the Commission's terms of reference, that the recommendation is not intended to apply to injuries inflicted intentionally. In relation to damages for pecuniary loss, the Commission made two recommendations that have been anticipated by court decisions: that damages for loss of earning capacity, and for loss of earnings during the "lost years" should be recoverable. The repeal of section 2(4) of the Law Reform (Personal Injuries) Act 1948 was recommended; instead it should be enacted that the expense of private medical treatment should be recoverable as damages only if it was reasonable on medical grounds that it should be sought.

(2) *Periodic payments*

The Commission made important recommendations concerning periodic payments. In the case of future pecuniary loss caused by death or serious and lasting injury, the court must award damages in the form of periodic payments, unless the plaintiff satisfies it that a lump sum would be more appropriate. The court would have a discretion to award periodic payments where injury is not serious and lasting. This would not interfere with out-of-court settlements which could continue to be made on a lump sum basis. The plaintiff could apply to the court at any time for commutation of a periodic into a lump sum award. Periodic awards of damages would be subject to review in the light of changes in the plaintiff's medical condition, and would be revalued annually in line with the movement of annual earnings. The right to the periodic award should "descend" to dependants for the time the deceased would have lived but for his injury. If enacted these provisions should remove the injustices caused by the erosion of the value of damages by inflation; also by the rule in *Fitter* v. *Veal*.

(3) *Assessment of damages*

The Commission recommended that all social security benefits, whether past or future, should be fully deducted from damages, whether for pecuniary or, where relevant, non-pecuniary loss. Such a rule would further eliminate numerous small claims in tort. Otherwise the Commission favoured the retention of the somewhat illogical rules established by the courts as to the deductibility of collateral benefits. In relation to the assessment of damages for loss of future earnings, a majority of the Commission recommended a modification of the assessment of the "multiplier" to take into account inflation and the fact that different earnings attract different tax rates. The application of the "modified multiplier" would produce the result that highly taxed plaintiffs with large earnings losses over a lengthy period of time would be compensated on the basis of a multiplier exceeding the length of working life left to them (with a consequent vast increase in awards).

THE INJUNCTION

A court may, in addition to awarding damages to the plaintiff, or without awarding damages, issue an injunction. This is a peremptory order to the defendant (disobedience of which is punishable by imprisonment) to abstain from (prohibitory injunction) or to take (mandatory injunction) certain action. The injunction is a discretionary remedy and will be issued only where it is "just and convenient" to do so (the words are taken from section 37 of the Supreme Court of Judicature Act 1981).

Types of injunction

A prohibitory injunction takes the form of an order to the defendant to stop committing a tort such as, commonly, trespass or nuisance. The mandatory injunction orders the defendant to perform a certain act, for example, the pulling down of a building which infringes the plaintiff's right to light. An injunction of the former type may cause less hardship to a defendant in that it may afford him a large amount of choice as to how he complies with it. So an order to discontinue a nuisance caused by fumes may be obeyed in a number of ways, which is not true of an order to pull down a building. For this reason a stronger case has normally to be made for the grant of a mandatory than a prohibitory injunction.

An injunction which is a final one issued after the trial of the plaintiff's action is called perpetual. Other types of injunction which may be issued are the interlocutory and the *quia timet*. The former type of injunction is claimed by the plaintiff in interlocutory proceedings taking place before the actual trial of the action, the justification for its issue being that otherwise the plaintiff may suffer irreparable damage before the trial of the action takes place.

The interlocutory injunction has been heavily relied on in recent years by those who have been threatened with heavy economic losses as a result of strikes (*supra*, Chapter 22). The interlocutory injunction is distinguishable from the *quia timet* injunction on the ground that the plaintiff is alleging that the defendant is actually committing (or has committed) a tort against him. The *quia timet* injunction is available where no tort has been committed by the defendant but the plaintiff apprehends the possible future commission of a tort by the defendant.

Torts restrainable by injunction

There appears to be no tort against which an injunction will not be awarded, although some torts, notably trespass to land and nuisance, are particularly apt for the issue of the remedy, and others, such as assault and malicious prosecution will nearly always be redressed by damages. Where it is doubtful whether the wrong committed by the defendant is a tort, this does not mean that an injunction will not be granted. Examples have already been given (*supra*, Chapter 26) of the issue of injunctions in cases where the tortious character of the defendant's conduct is in doubt. Furthermore, under section 50 of the Supreme Court Act 1981 the courts may award damages in such cases (see *infra*). Eventually the courts may award damages as of right in cases of this sort, thereby treating them as torts. If this is the case, the injunction may be seen as a way of extending the boundaries of the law of tort.

Exercise of court's discretion

The issue of any type of injunction lies within the discretion of the court. Discretionary factors affecting all types of injunction are the availability of alternative remedies, the conduct of the plaintiff (for example, undue delay in bringing the action or acquiescence in the defendant's wrongdoing) and the effect of issuing an injunction upon the rights of third parties. In deciding whether to issue a final injunction, the court is particularly concerned with the question whether an award of damages in substitution for an injunction made under section 50 of the Supreme Court Act 1981 and allowing the court to compensate the plaintiff for future loss arising from the tort's commission will constitute an adequate remedy. The "working rule" provided by *Shelfer* v. *City of London Electric Co.* (1895) still holds good and lays down restrictive conditions under which the award of damages may be chosen in preference to the injunction. These are:

(1)   The injury to the plaintiff's legal rights is small; and
(2)   Is one which is capable of being estimated in money; and
(3)   Is one which can be adequately compensated by a small money payment; and
(4)   The case is one in which it would be oppressive to the defendant to grant an injunction.

It may be noted that the cost to the defendant may operate as a relevant factor under (4). The cost to the defendant of observing a prohibitory injunction is unlikely to weigh heavily with the courts in their decision, although there may be a cost factor, for example, in wasted expenditure. However, cost is more relevant in the case of a mandatory injunction, and the House of Lords in *Redland Bricks Ltd.* v. *Morris* (1970) refused to issue a mandatory injunction where the cost of remedial work to restore support to the plaintiff's land vastly exceeded the damage the plaintiff had suffered.

The exercise of the court's discretion in relation to an interlocutory injunction is rather different. The essence of the plaintiff's claim for an interlocutory injunction is that if the defendant's conduct is allowed to continue the plaintiff will have suffered irreparable damage by the time of the trial. The court is therefore not so much concerned with the possible greater suitability of the remedy of damages to that of the injunction as with the claim that damages awarded at the trial will in no way compensate the plaintiff for the damage that has then occurred. This exercise of discretion causes the court to examine the matter referred to as the balance of convenience. Broadly put, the court must consider which side will be the more inconvenienced by the issue of the interlocutory injunction—the plaintiff by reason of the allegedly irreparable damage that the alleged tort is inflicting on him, or the defendant who may allege that the issue of an injunction would interfere with his lawful business, for example, a defendant who is defending a claim of passing off or infringement of copyright. Sometimes the balance of convenience points in one direction only, and this is particularly so in the case of industrial action inflicting damage on business. The industrial action is generally carried out at small individual cost to its perpetrators. In those cases where the balance of convenience is convincingly arguable from the standpoint of both plaintiff and defendant, the court is likely to require an undertaking in damages from the plaintiff who has obtained the award of an interlocutory injunction. The effect is that if the defendant succeeds at the trial of the action, the plaintiff must then compensate him for damages that the interlocutory injunction has caused him. In order to obtain an interlocutory injunction, the plaintiff must show that there is a serious question to be tried (*American Cyanamid* v. *Ethicon* (1975)) (though see *supra*, Chapter 22 on the award of interlocutory injunctions in industrial action cases). The plaintiff must convince the court that there are in his allegations serious questions both of law and fact to be tried which if resolved in his favour will establish a remedy for the tort that is alleged.

Lord Cairns' Act; section 50, Supreme Court Act 1981

The court has jurisdiction under section 50 of the Supreme Court Act 1981, the present equivalent of Lord Cairns' Act 1858, to award damages either in addition to or in substitution for an injunction. Although originally intended for the purely procedural purpose of giving the Court of Chancery a power to award damages, Lord Cairns' Act also had a substantive effect in allowing damages to be awarded in lieu of an injunction in relation to the future, apprehended commission of a tort. Damages might even be awarded in lieu of a *quia timet* injunction where no tort had been committed prior to the commencement of the action (*Leeds Industrial Co-operative Society* v. *Slack* (1924)). The common law courts had no power to award damages in relation to torts not yet committed. This substantive effect of Lord Cairns' Act survives under section 50. The award of damages under the section, like the award of an injunction itself, lies within the discretion of the court.

OTHER REMEDIES

The plaintiff may choose in some cases to sue for an account of the profits the defendant has made through committing the tort. This is particularly the case where the tort is passing off or another of the torts involving trade competition. It has been mentioned in an earlier chapter (Chapter 3), that in detinue the plaintiff may claim restitution of his property in addition to or as an alternative to a claim for damages. The remedy of self-help has already been dealt with in Chapter 5.

29. EXTINCTION OF TORTIOUS LIABILITY

Tortious liability may be extinguished in any of the following ways.

DEATH

The two torts of defamation are now the only exceptions to the rule that causes of action in tort survive both for the benefit of and against the estate of a deceased person (section 1(1), Law Reform (Miscellaneous Provisions) Act 1934).

JUDGMENT

Judgment obtained against a tortfeasor has the effect of converting his liability on the cause of action into liability on the judgment, so that further actions cannot be brought against him in respect of that cause of action. Where the same facts give rise to distinct causes of action, judgment obtained in respect of one cause of action will bar the pursuit of any of the other causes of action. This situation must be distinguished from the case in which different facts occurring as part of the same incident give rise to distinct causes of action, for example, where the defendant's negligence causes both personal injury and damage to property.

Here judgment obtained in relation to one cause of action does not bar the remainder.

Satisfaction of judgment

Judgment obtained against one of several joint or concurrent tortfeasors does not release the others (*supra,* pp. 177–178). But satisfaction of the judgment by one of them releases the rest. Where tortfeasors are neither joint nor concurrent, satisfaction by one will not normally release the others except in special circumstances. If however A and B have successively converted C's chattel, satisfaction of the judgment by A will release B since C cannot obtain double compensation for conversion of the chattel.

WAIVER OF TORT

The problem here is whether the election by the plaintiff to pursue one of two alternative remedies means that he cannot go back on this decision and pursue the alternative remedy. At one time it was thought that by choosing one remedy the plaintiff must be taken to have waived the other. But the House of Lords in *United Australia Ltd.* v. *Barclay's Bank Ltd.* (1941) found that the cases relied on for this turned on the extinction of tortious liability through judgment rather than waiver. The pursuit of one remedy only constituted waiver where the remedies were inconsistent with rather than alternative to each other. So a landlord who chooses to sue for a forfeiture of the lease rather than for rent which is due cannot sue for rent due from the date of the forfeiture proceedings even though judgment in the latter is not obtained (*Jones* v. *Carter* (1846)). On the other hand in the *United Australia* case the plaintiff company's institution and subsequent discontinuance before obtaining judgment of proceedings in quasi-contract against another company for improperly obtaining the proceeds of a cheque payable to the plaintiffs was held to be no bar to an action in conversion against the defendant bank which cashed the cheque.

VOLUNTARY TERMINATION

1. *Accord and satisfaction*

Liability in tort may be extinguished by an accord and satisfaction. This means an agreement between the parties (accord) backed up by consideration (satisfaction), the intention being that liability under the agreement should replace the liability in tort. The normal "settlement" of a tortious action operates in this way, the plaintiff agreeing to accept a certain sum and in return agreeing not to institute proceedings against the defendant. The consideration for the accord may be executory or executed; the difference is between the plaintiff's agreement to release the defendant in consideration of his promise to pay £100, and in consideration of his actual payment of that sum.

2. *Release*

This term signifies an agreement binding the victim of the tort whereby the tortfeasor is released from liability though he provides no consideration. The usual form of a release in English law is by deed, although this does not appear to be essential.

LIMITATION

The principle

The principle of limitation is that by lapse of time a right of action becomes no longer enforceable. The effect of the expiry of a limitation period on an action is generally to render that right unenforceable rather than to extinguish it altogether. A limitation defence must therefore be pleaded by the defendant. The effect of expiry of the limitation period in this case of conversion of a chattel is substantive rather than procedural—the title to the chattel of the person with the right to sue in conversion is extinguished.

The relevant law is now contained in the Limitation Act 1980, an Act which both consolidates and amends the previous law.

The Limitation Act 1980

Section 2 of the Act sets up a general time limit on actions in tort of six years from the date on which the cause of action accrued. The limitation period on the action for breach of contract is the same (section 5). Section 11 sets up a special time-limit on actions for personal injuries. Under this section where the damages claimed by the plaintiff for negligence, nuisance or breach of duty consist of or include damages in respect of personal injuries, a three-year time limit from the date of accrual of the cause of action, *i.e.* the date of the injury applies (subject to what is said below about the plaintiff's knowledge). Despite the specification of negligence, nuisance and breach of duty by the section, it seems that the last phrase covers all torts (for example, an intentional battery (*Long* v. *Hepworth* (1968)) and that three years is the invariable limitation period on actions for personal injury. "Personal injury" is defined by section 38 to include any disease or impairment of the plaintiff's physical or mental condition. The time-limit under section 11 applies where the plaintiff's claim includes one for personal injuries, so that a person claiming for damage to property and personal injuries in the same action would have to bring it within three years of the accrual of the cause of action for personal injuries.

Section 11(4) provides in effect that the time-limit on the claim for personal injuries does not commence until the plaintiff has the relevant knowledge of his right to sue. That knowledge is defined by section 14(1). It is knowledge of the following facts: (a) that the injury in question was significant; (b) that the injury was attributable in whole or in part to the act or omission which is alleged to constitute negligence, nuisance or breach of duty; (c) the identity of the defendant; and (d) if it is alleged that the act or omission was that of a person other than the defendant, the identity of that person and the additional facts supporting the bringing of an action against the defendant. Section 14(1) goes on to provide that knowledge that any acts or omissions did or did not, as a matter or law, involve negligence, nuisance or breach of duty is irrelevant. Section 14(2) defines "significant" for the purpose of section 14(1), and section 14(3) provides instances of cases in which the plaintiff may be fixed with knowledge of facts of which he has no actual knowledge.

Certain special cases of limitation are dealt with later in this section.

Accrual of the cause of action

The date of the accrual of the cause of action is, in general, the date from which the limitation period commences.

In the case of torts actionable *per se* the date of accrual is the date the defendant acted, in the case of torts which require proof of damage, the date on which damage occurs. In the case of continuing torts, where a fresh cause of action arises *de die in diem,* each successive cause of action has its own limitation period (*Coventry* v. *Apsley* (1691)—nuisance and trespass to land are torts which often may give rise to continuing causes of action). In cases of breach of contract time begins to run from the date of the breach of contract, which renders of greater importance the modern development by which an action in tortious negligence is often available as alternative to an action in contract, the time limit on the tortious action not commencing until damage has been caused. In *Cartledge* v. *E. Jopling* (1963) the House of Lords held that in an action for negligence time ran when pneumoconiosis first affected the plaintiff's lungs even though he could not have discovered this at the time, even by X-ray examination. The effect of this decision as regards personal injury has been removed by legislation (see the present sections 11 and 14 of the Limitation Act 1980). As regards damage to property, the test established by *Pirelli* v. *Oscar Faber* (1983) prior to the Latent Damage Act 1986 was that the damage occurred when it first manifested itself externally, for example, in the form of cracks in a building produced through a defect in the building caused by its negligent construction, even though the existence of the cracks was neither known to the building's owner nor reasonably capable of being discovered by him. *Pirelli*, though laying down a general test, was particularly associated with the case of latent defects in buildings arising from their defective construction, damage caused by an external source seldom giving rise to problems of discoverability. The Latent Damage Act 1986 has changed the *Pirelli* test in a way shortly to be considered. Even more important, *Murphy* v. *Brentwood D.C.* (1990) in overruling *Anns* v. *London Borough of Merton* (1977) rejected a duty of care in tort owed by the builder of a building towards future purchasers of it, where the building has caused no subsequent damage to person or other property. Most of the problems of limitation that arose with the *Anns* decision will disappear with its overruling. Nor will the dicta in *Pirelli* to the effect that future purchasers form a class the members of which obtain a cause of action on the date on which the damage first occurred (rejected as far as the recognition of a cause of action was concerned by *Perry* v. *Tendring D.C.* (1984)) have any further importance.

A different problem to that in *Pirelli* exists in deciding what is the date of accrual of a cause of action where the plaintiff has been subjected through the defendant's negligence to a transaction imposing a contingent liability or later possibility of loss which may never materialise. A series of cases of which the most important is *Forster* v. *Outred & Co.* (1982) and of which the latest is *Bell* v. *Peter Browne* (1990) held that the damage occurs and the cause of action accrues when the transaction imposing the liability is entered into, not when the actual loss materialises. The hardship caused by this is best exemplified by *Bell* v. *Peter Browne* in which the plaintiff lost through limitation his cause of action against the defendant solicitors even though he had no reason to suspect that any negligence on their part had occurred at the time of the transaction, is dealt with by the Latent Damage Act 1986.

Latent Damage Act 1986

First, the Act adds section 14A to the Limitation Act 1980. Section 14A creates a new limitation period in the case of actions for negligence other than claims for personal injury. Negligence is, curiously , not defined by the Act and this may raise problems. Presumably occupiers' liability is covered, though statutory; possibly breach of statutory duty where the duty is one of reasonable care; almost certainly not the duty under section 1 of the Defective Premises Act 1972 to build in workmanlike fashion, which though probably one of care is subject to a specific limitation period in the Act itself; probably also, not purely contractual negligence. The limitation period provided by section 14A is either six years from the accrual of the cause of action or, if later, three years from the "starting date," defined in section 14A(5) as the earliest date on which the plaintiff has both knowledge of the material facts relevant to the bringing of the action and the right to bring the action. "Knowledge" and "material facts" are defined in section 14A(6)–(10). Next, section 3(1)(*a*) of the Act deals with the situation that arises where property has received damage through negligence and is then disposed of to a purchaser before the damage is discovered. It provides that a person who acquires an interest in the property obtains a cause of action on acquisition provided the material facts were not known at that time to any person having an interest in the property. The date of accrual of that cause of action is the date on which the original cause of action accrued or the starting date (determined as stated above, the only difference being that the later acquirer's knowledge is the relevant one). The net effect is that the action must be brought within six years of the accrual of the original cause of action or three years of the acquirer's acquisition of knowledge of the material facts if that is later. A backstop limitation period of 15 years independent of knowledge in the possible plaintiffs is set up by the added section 14B of the 1980 Act. The importance of the 1986 Act is of course vastly lessened by *Murphy* v. *Brentwood D.C.* which now denies the existence of a number of causes of action which would have existed at the time of the passing of the Act.

Dispensations from the normal rules

(a) *Disability*
    Section 28(1) provides in effect that where the person in whose favour the cause of action accrues is under a disability at that time, the limitation period is six years from the date when he ceased to be under a disability or died (whichever first occurred) and in the case of personal injuries, three years (section 28(6)). "Disability" is defined to mean being an infant or of unsound mind. This dispensation does not apply where the disability occurs after the date of accrual of the cause of action (section 28(2)).

(b) *Fraud, concealment, mistake*
    Section 32(1) provides that where: (a) the action is based upon the fraud of the defendant; or (b) any fact relevant to the plaintiff's right of action has been deliberately concealed from him by the defendant; or (c) the action is for relief from the consequences of a mistake, the period of limitation shall not begin to run until the plaintiff has discovered the fraud, concealment or mistake, or could with reasonable diligence have discovered it. Section 32(2) provides that, for the purposes of section 32(1), the deliberate commission of a breach of duty in circumstances in which it is unlikely to be discovered for some time amounts to deliberate concealment of the facts involved in that breach of duty. This subsection brings into force the principles established by cases such as *Beaman* v. *A.R.T.S.* (1949). In that case a bailee of property in wartime disposed of it without the bailor's consent and without making any attempt to communicate with the bailor. This was found to be a fraudulent concealment of the cause of action in

tort for the purposes of the section of the Limitation Act then in force, even though the bailee committed no legal fraud. Negligent wrongdoing by itself, however, is outside the scope of the section (*cf. Kitchen* v. *R.A.F. Association* (1958)). Section 32(3) and (4) protect the innocent purchaser of property from the operation of section 32(1) and (2).

(c) *Personal injuries and discretion to exclude time-limits*

The statutory power under section 33 to exclude normal time-limits on an action applies only to the time-limits applying under section 11 to actions for personal injuries and under section 12 to actions by dependants for wrongful death. Section 33(1) confers a power to exclude the normal time-limit in the court's discretion, having regard to the degree to which the provisions of sections 11 or 12 prejudice the plaintiff and the degree to which any decision of the court to allow the action to proceed would prejudice the defendant. Section 33(3) gives six factors to which the court shall have particular regard in exercising its discretion.

Brief comment, only, is possible here on the section. It is not limited to exceptional cases and confers a general power of excluding time-limits (*Firman* v. *Ellis* (1978), a decision of the Court of Appeal confirmed by the House of Lords in *Thompson* v. *Brown* (1981)). Prejudice to the plaintiff is clearly established by his inability to litigate a claim for a substantial injury. Prejudice to the defendant is commonly associated with the difficulty involved in defending a case the facts of which occurred many years ago (for a weighing in the balance of these two factors producing on the facts a decision in the plaintiff's favour, see *Brooks* v. *J. & P. Coates* (1984)). The discretion must be properly exercised. The House of Lords in *Thompson* v. *Brown*, for example, found a failure to exercise the discretion by the trial judge who had held that he was bound as a matter of law to find that there was no prejudice to the plaintiff where, because of his solicitor's negligence, a time-limit on the action had expired, on the ground that a cause of action existed against the solicitor. Finally, the only prejudice that is relevant is that caused by failure to meet the statutory time-limits in sections 11 and 12. There is no power to exclude time-limits where the plaintiff has complied with the time-limit in section 11 but has failed to serve her writ (*Deerness* v. *J.R. Keeble* (1982)). *Donovan* v. *Gwentoys Ltd.* (1990) shows that the discretion under section 33(1) is not limited to the factors specified in section 33(3). So the court in the case itself could have regard legitimately to delay *within* the limitation period.

Special cases

(1) *Conversion*

Section 3(1) has the effect that it bars the right of a particular person to sue in conversion in relation to a particular chattel six years after the date of the accrual of his original cause of action in conversion, and this is so even though there may have been later conversions of the same chattel by the defendant or other persons. Section 3(2) goes further in providing that the title of that person is extinguished at the time the limitation period expires.

Section 4 creates an exception to the rules laid down by section 3 in the case of theft. The time-limit on the action under section 3(1) does not run in relation to a conversion which is a theft, nor to any conversion which is related to the theft. A conversion related to the theft appears to be any subsequent dealing with the stolen chattel amounting to a conversion except the innocent purchase of it. Once conversion by innocent purchase of the chattel has occurred, time runs against the person from whom the chattel was stolen and his title may become extinguished under section 3(2). Even if this happens, he is allowed to sue in conversion for the theft or a conversion related to the theft provided it took place before the date on which time begins to run.

(2) *Death*

(a) *Under section 1 of the Law Reform (Miscellaneous Provisions) Act 1934.* The time-limit on causes of action in tort other than actions for personal injury which are transmitted to the estate under this Act is not affected by the death of the person in whom they are vested. In the case of a cause of action in tort for causing personal injury, section 11(5) of the act of 1980 provides that if the tort victim dies before the expiration of the three-year limitation period, the period then applicable shall be three years from the date of the death or the date of the personal representative's knowledge, whichever is the later. The personal representative's "knowledge" is established in the same way as it is in relation to a living plaintiff, by application of the conditions laid down by section 14.

(b) *Under the Fatal Accidents Act 1976.* Section 12(1) expressly provides that the action on behalf of the dependants shall not be brought if the action could not have been brought by the deceased on his own behalf during his lifetime, and this includes the expiration of a time-limit on an action in tort. Where the time-limit has not expired before death, section 12(2) requires that the dependants' action be brought within three years from the date of death or from the date of knowledge of the person for whose benefit the action is brought, whichever is the later. "Knowledge" is again governed by section 14. The effect of section 13 is that the requirements of section 12 must be applied separately to each dependant where there is more than one; that in general a dependant is excluded if shown to be outside the time-limit even though there are other dependants who are within them.

(3) *Contribution*

Under Section 10 of the Act of 1980, a claim for contribution under the Civil Liability (Contribution) Act 1978 must be brought within two years of the date on which that right accrued. Section 10(3) and (4) are provisions fixing that date according to whether the right to contribution arises from a judgment in the action or a settlement of it.

(4) *Consumer Protection Act 1987; Defective Premises Act 1972*

The time-limits for suing for personal injury under the Consumer Protection Act 1987 are brought into line with the general limits for personal injury claims discussed earlier in this chapter by section 11A(3) of the 1987 Act (*i.e.* a general limit of three years, an extended period where the plaintiff has not the necessary knowledge and a discretionary power to override the limits so applying). In the case of damage to property, section 5(5) of the 1987 Act brings the case into line with the limitation period established by the Latent Damage Act 1986. The Limitation Act 1980 (as amended), sections 11A(3), 28(7) and 32(4A), however, sets up a limit on claims under the 1987 Act of 10 years from the date the product is put into circulation. This bar is in every sense absolute. It is independent of the plaintiff's knowledge of the defect, it cannot be overridden under section 33 of the 1980 Act, and it applies even though no cause of action has come into existence during the 10-year period because no injury or damage has occurred.

The limitation period on claims for the building of a defective dwelling under section 1(1) of the Defective Premises Act is the normal one of six years but this period begins to run from the date of completion of the dwelling (section 1(5)), a date which may well precede the coming into existence of any cause of action under section 1(1)).

30. CAPACITY TO SUE AND BE SUED

In this chapter are considered a number of cases in which special rules govern the capacity of the legal person in question to commit torts or to have torts committed against it.

CORPORATIONS

It is clear law that a corporation, as a legal person distinct from its members, may commit torts and may have torts committed against it. The commission of torts by a corporation clearly requires some action on the part of the human agents of the corporation. Thus the corporation is vicariously liable for the torts of its servants committed in the course of their employment. The corporation may incur personal liability where the human agent is so much in control of the corporation that his actions may be regarded as those of the corporation itself. In *Lennard's Carrying Co.* v. *Asiatic Petroleum Co. Ltd.* (1915) it was found that the managing director of a company was the "directing mind and will of the corporation" so that fault on his part constituted "actual fault" on the company's part for the purposes of a statute. Where the personal liability of the corporation is concerned it does not seem to matter that the act is *ultra vires* the corporation (*Campbell* v. *Paddington Borough Council* (1911)). Where, on the other hand, a servant is acting *ultra vires* the corporation his action may be outside the scope of his employment. Thus in *Poulton* v. *L. &*

S.W. Ry. (1867) the defendants were held not liable for the act of a station master who had detained the plaintiff for non-payment of a fare. The railway company itself had no power to detain in these circumstances. It is unsafe to conclude from this case that corporations are never liable for the torts of their servants where the corporation is carrying out an *ultra vires* activity. In *Poulton's* case the station master clearly had no authority express or implied from his superiors to act in the way he did.

UNINCORPORATED ASSOCIATIONS

(1) *Generally*

Unincorporated associations in general have no legal personality distinct from that of their members. In theory, therefore, all members should be joined as co-plaintiffs or co-defendants in an action in tort. Where, however, all the members of the association have an identical interest in defending an action, it is possible to bring a representative action against certain members who are sued as representing the members as a whole. So in *Campbell* v. *Thompson* (1953) a representative action against two members of a club was held to be correctly brought, where the members were allegedly all individually in breach of their duties towards the plaintiff as his employers and as occupiers of the club premises. Where such an action succeeds, judgment can be enforced against the separate property of any member—there is no limitation to "club" property. The same considerations will determine whether members of an unincorporated association can bring a representative action in tort. However, the members of an unincorporated club do not as such owe each other duties of care in tort, and it makes no difference that the rules of the club cast duties on particular members, for example, as chairman or secretary (*Robertson* v. *Ridley* (1989)).

(2) *Trade unions*

Trade unions are a special type of unincorporated association. An early Act, the Trade Disputes Act 1906, created a complete immunity for trade unions from liability in tort. That immunity was removed by the Industrial Relations Act 1971 but was restored with some exceptions in 1974 by the Trade Union and Labour

Relations Act. The exceptions under section 14(2) were liability in negligence, nuisance or breach of duty where that arose from an act not done in contemplation or furtherance of a trade dispute and where it resulted in personal injury; and liability imposed in connection with the ownership, occupation, possession, control or use of property, whether real or personal, and again provided that the liability did not arise from an act done in contemplation or furtherance of a trade dispute. Section 15 of the Employment Act 1982 has now again abolished the immunity. Section 15(2) contains special provisions concerning the liability of trade unions where the liability in question is alleged to arise from an act referred to in section 13 of the 1974 Act, in effect, liability for inducing a breach of or interfering with contract, for intimidation and for conspiracy. Liability on the part of the trade union exists here only if the act giving rise to liability is authorised or endorsed by a responsible person within the union. Section 15(3)(b) defines "authorisation or endorsement" and "responsible person." Section 16 creates financial limits upon the amount trade unions may in general be made liable to pay in damages for their torts, the limits varying according to the size of the trade union. There is, however, no financial limit where liability arises under the exceptional cases of liability retained by section 14(2) of the 1974 Act; nor does the financial limit apply in those cases even where the act in question is done in contemplation or furtherance of a trade dispute.

THE CROWN

The effect of the Crown Proceedings Act 1947 was to remove the almost complete immunity which the Crown enjoyed from actions in tort being brought against it, and to render it liable, with certain exceptions, to the same liabilities as those of a private person. Section 2 provides that the Crown shall be liable as if it is a private person of full age and capacity: (a) in respect of torts committed by its servants or agents; (b) in respect of the breach of those duties which a person owes to his servants or agents at common law by reason of his being their employer; (c) in respect of breach of the duties attaching at common law to the ownership, occupation, possession or control of property. Section 2(2) imposes liability in tort upon the Crown for breach of statutory duty in the same way as liability under that tort is imposed upon private persons. This means that the statute in question must be interpreted as being intended to confer a civil action in tort for its breach, and in addition it is necessary to show that the statute binds the Crown whether by express provision or necessary implication (some doubt still exists about certain acts, for example, the Fatal Accidents Act 1976 and the Law Reform (Miscellaneous Provisions) Act 1934, although they are assumed to bind the Crown).

There are certain exceptions. Section 40(1) provides that the sovereign is not liable for torts committed personally by herself. Section 2(5) contains a saving in respect of anything done or omitted to be done by any person while discharging any responsibilities of a judicial nature vested in him. There is now no exclusion of liability on the part of the Crown towards members of the armed forces while on duty (section 2 of the Crown Proceedings (Armed Forces) Act 1987). There will nevertheless be difficulty in establishing a duty of care in relation to military operations (*Shaw Savill Co.* v. *Commonwealth* (1940)). Section 11(1) contains a saving in respect of acts done under the prerogative or statute where prior to the act no liability would have arisen for those acts. Acts done under the prerogative must be distinguished from acts of state. An act validly done under the prerogative affords a defence to an action in tort against all persons, British nationals and aliens alike (although there still may be an obligation to pay compensation—for example, in *Burmah Oil Co.* v. *Lord Advocate* (1965) the Crown was held to be liable to pay compensation to the plaintiff company in respect of the military destruction of its property in Rangoon for the purpose of denying its use to the Japanese army). Act of state is not available as a defence against British nationals nor even against aliens enjoying the temporary protection of the Crown as British residents (*Johnstone* v. *Pedlar* (1921)), but it is available against aliens at least in relation to acts committed abroad. In *Buron* v. *Denman* (1848) the defendant, the commander of a British man-of-war had caused to be destroyed certain property off the coast of Africa belonging to the plaintiff, a Spanish slave-trader, in purported execution of a treaty with an African king for the abolition of the slave-trade. His act was ratified by the British government and the court held him to be entitled to the defence of act of state.

THE POST OFFICE

The Post Office used to be a part of the Crown. The Crown
enjoyed immunity from liability in tort under section 9(1) of the
Crown Proceedings Act for any act or omission of a servant of the
Crown in relation to a postal packet or telephonic communication.
Under the Post Office Act 1969, the Post Office became an
independent statutory corporation but its immunity from liability
has been preserved (section 29—*cf.* section 23 of the British
Telecommunications Act 1981 for the immunity from actions in
tort of British Telecom and its employees), except that under
section 30(2) it is liable (as was the Crown under the Act of 1947)
for the loss of or damage to a registered inland packet when that
loss or damage is caused by the wrongful act, neglect or default of
an officer, servant or agent of the Post Office.

JUDICIAL PROCESS

(a) *Judges*
   The immunity of the judge of a superior court of record from
liability in tort (or any other cause of action) for acts done in the
purported exercise of his judicial office is sometimes stated in
absolute terms (*cf. Salmond on Torts*, p. 385). However, the
leading case of *Anderson* v. *Gorrie* (1895) does not put it as high
as this. Even a judge of a superior court may be liable in tort for
acts that are in excess of his jurisdiction. The difference between
the judge of the superior court and of the inferior court, as Lord
Esher M.R. pointed out, is merely as to the extent of their
jurisdiction, the jurisdiction of the former having no clear limits.
The only substantive difference then between judges of superior
courts and those of inferior is that the latter may be liable in tort
for judicial acts which are done maliciously and without reasonable
cause but are nevertheless within their jurisdiction. Most of the
case law on liability of inferior courts has concerned justices of the
peace and section 44 of the Justices of the Peace Act 1979
preserves their liability for acts done maliciously and without
reasonable cause though within jurisdiction. Nevertheless, three
members of the House of Lords in *McC* v. *Mullan* (1984)
expressed the view *obiter* that this liability had become obsolete
and was no longer available. *McC* v. *Mullan* also indicates the

conditions under which the judge of the inferior court is liable in tort for acts done in excess of his jurisdiction. Not every defect in the decision will cause this liability to apply, even though that defect is one which renders the decision liable to be quashed on the bringing of a certiorari remedy on the ground that it is void. In general it must be shown that the judge had no power to hear the case at all, or that if he did have such power that he had no power to make the order he made. In relation to the latter, there is a difference between exercising a power that the judge possesses in an irregular fashion (*cf. Sirros* v. *Moore* (1975)) and purporting to exercise a power that the judge does not possess (*cf. McC* v. *Mullan* itself). In all cases where the relevant excess of jurisdiction is proved, the judge, who bona fide believes he has jurisdiction, is liable only if the facts presented to and found by the court would reveal the absence of jurisdiction.

For a case in which justices were held liable in tort for exceeding their jurisdiction, see *R.* v. *Manchester JJ., ex p. Davies* (1989). Section 52 of the Justices of the Peace Act 1979 limits damages to one penny if the circumstances referred to in that section apply (*R.* v. *Waltham Forest JJ., ex p.* Solanke (1986)). There is also a right to an indemnity out of public funds under section 53 of the same Act to a justice who has acted reasonably and in good faith.

(b) *Participants in judicial process*

There is absolute immunity from liability in defamation for words spoken by persons in court during court proceedings. This will extend to barristers and solicitors, parties and witnesses. That immunity would no doubt be forfeited by making a remark quite irrelevant to the proceedings. The immunity of the advocate from liability in negligence for his conduct of the trial has already been mentioned.

FOREIGN SOVEREIGNS

Lord Atkin in *The Cristina* (1938) stated the position authoritatively in the following way: "The first (rule) is that the courts of a country will not implead a foreign sovereign, that is, they will not by their process make him against his will a party to legal proceedings, whether the proceedings involve process against his person or seek to remove from him specific property or damages.

The second is that they will not by their process, whether the sovereign is a party to the proceedings or not, seize or detain property which is his or of which he is in possession or control."

The propositions state customary international law which is applied by the English courts. Major exceptions to the general rule have been introduced by the State Immunity Act 1978. The most important in relation to tort is that established by section 5. This provides that a (foreign) State is not immune in respect of proceedings for death or personal injury or damage to or loss of tangible property caused by an act or omission in the United Kingdom. Section 6(1)(b) takes away an immunity in relation to obligations arising from the State's interest in, possession or use of land in the United Kingdom. Section 5 allows proceedings to be brought against the State in relation to infringement of copyright and trade-mark, and passing off.

DIPLOMATS AND DIPLOMATIC STAFF

The diplomat himself under customary international law accepted and applied in England enjoyed full immunity from both criminal and civil liability for his actions. Article 37, Schedule 1 of the Diplomatic Privileges Act 1964 has created certain exceptions to the immunity from civil liability. The only one that appears to have significance for tortious liability is 1(c) which renders non-immune any action relating to any professional or commercial activity exercised by the diplomatic agent in the receiving State outside his official functions. Members of the diplomat's family continue to enjoy the same immunities as the diplomat himself (Article 37). Members of the administrative and technical staff of the mission also have a similar immunity under Article 37 except that that immunity does not extend to acts performed outside the course of their duties. There would, for example, be no immunity in relation to negligent driving causing an accident while the staff member is taking a holiday in the United Kingdom.

HUSBAND AND WIFE

The special position of spouses, both as regards liability in tort *inter se* and towards third parties, has now been almost totally abrogated by statute. The Law Reform (Married Women and

Tortfeasors) Act 1935 puts the wife into exactly the same position as any other person when she has committed a tort against a third party and abolishes the husband's vicarious liability for his wife's torts. Husband and wife may be party to a tortious conspiracy (*Midland Bank Trust* v. *Green (No. 3)* (1982)). The Law Reform (Husband and Wife) Act 1962 removed the surviving anomaly, that of prohibiting actions in tort between the spouses. The court has power to stay the proceedings if no substantial benefit will accrue to either party or if the case can more conveniently be dealt with under section 17 of the Married Women's Property Act 1882.

PERSONS WHO ARE INSANE

Insanity is not a recognised defence to action in tort. Where a tort requires proof of a specific intention, it might be expected that inability to form that intention through insanity would preclude liability and this receives support from *Morriss* v. *Marsden* (1952) (schizophrenic held liable in battery because he intended to commit the attack although he did not know that what he was doing was wrong). It has been suggested that insane persons are less capable of committing torts requiring intention and a specific state of mind such as malice (Clerk & Lindsell, para. 2.39). Torts of strict liability can no doubt be committed by such persons, but whether they can commit negligence is an open question.

MINORS

There is no minimum age of tortious responsibility. Minors, like insane persons, are judged by ordinary principles of tort. There is no authority to indicate at what age an ability to form a tortious intention is acquired. Does a minor of tender years who tears up a pound note commit conversion? Contributory negligence cases (*supra*, p. 190) indicate that a minor of quite advanced years will not be judged by the same standards as an adult in deciding whether he was contributorily negligent. Different considerations may affect his liability for negligence—in *Gorely* v. *Codd* (1967) a 16-year-old boy was held liable for his negligence in the use of an air-rifle.

A minor cannot be sued in tort where the action in tort is a means of enforcing a contract which does not bind him. So, for example, in *Jennings* v. *Rundall* (1799) where the defendant hired the plaintiff's horse to be ridden for a short journey and rode it for a much longer journey with the result that it was injured, he was held not liable in trespass. But in *Burnard* v. *Haggis* (1863) where the minor hired a mare which was not to be used for jumping, and allowed a friend to ride and jump it, he was held liable in trespass. His action was not merely a wrongful performance of the contract—it went totally outside its terms.

PARENTS

There is no general principle whereby a parent is vicariously liable for the torts of his children. His liability exists, if at all, under the ordinary rules of tort. So, for example, he may be liable in negligence for giving a dangerous gun to his child who causes an injury by using the gun (*Newton* v. *Edgerley* (1959)—*cf. Donaldson* v. *McNiven* (1952)).

BANKRUPTS

The effect of section 30(1) of the Bankruptcy Act 1914, which provides that demands in the nature of unliquidated damages arising otherwise than by reasons of a contract, promise or trust are not provable in the bankruptcy, is that most tortious claims cannot be so proved. The bankrupt himself remains liable in tort and may be sued for the full amount of the claim. The bankrupt retains the right to sue in tort where the claim is for the infringement of a purely personal interest. Where the claim is for the protection of the bankrupt's property, it vests in the trustee in bankruptcy. Examples of the former are claims in defamation, battery and false imprisonment; of the latter, conversion and passing off.

ASSIGNEES

Rights of action in tort can generally speaking not be assigned. The rule reflects the personal character of causes of action in tort. There are certain exceptions to the rule, most importantly, the right of the insurer by way of subrogation to pursue rights of action previously belonging to the insured, after he (the insurer) has discharged his liability on the policy. It is also possible to assign a right of action on a judgment debt which arises from an action in tort. So also is it possible to assign the proceeds of what may be recovered in a tortious action (*Glegg* v. *Bromley* (1912)).

UNBORN PERSONS

English law has been slow to recognise the existence of legal personality in the unborn child between the moment of conception and birth. Finally, however, in *McKay* v. *Essex Area Health Authority* (1982) the Court of Appeal accepted *obiter* that such personality might exist for the purpose of the bringing of an action of negligence by the child in respect of deformities which it suffered during the pregnancy of the mother as a result of the negligence of those charged with the mother's care. However, the claim before the Court of Appeal was not that the defendants had by negligence caused injury, but that, injury to the child being highly probable because of the infection of the mother by German measles, the defendants failed to diagnose the infection and in consequence to advise the mother to terminate the pregnancy. The Court of Appeal held that as a matter of policy no action lay for negligently bringing the child into the world, even if the risk of the child being born deformed should have been known; that in any case no possible measure of damages could be found which would evaluate the difference between the plaintiff's present condition and non-existence. In a different factual situation to that presented by *McKay*, that where a medical operation has been performed on either parent for the purpose of preventing or terminating pregnancy, it now is settled that an action lies to the parent concerned if the operation is negligently performed and as a result a child is born. This is so even though the child is born healthy (*Udale* v. *Bloomsbury A.H.A.* (1984)). Damages are awarded in relation to pain and suffering occasioned by the pregnancy and items of temporal loss occasioned by the birth of the child (*Thake* v. *Maurice* (1984); *Emeh* v. *Kensington A.H.A.* (1984)).

The facts in *McKay's* case occurred before the Congenital Disabilities Act 1976 came into force. The Act deals in general with the case of disablement of the child through the infliction of a tort upon or the commission of a breach of a legal duty towards the parent of the child. The Court of Appeal expressed the opinion, with respect correctly, that the claim under the Act would have been of no assistance to the plaintiff in *McKay*. Furthermore the recognition in *McKay* of the possible existence of a common law duty of care to prevent injury to the unborn child during pregnancy is of little practical importance since the claim under the Act "replaces any law in force before its passing, whereby a person could be liable to a child in respect of disabilities with which it might be born." Under section 1(1) of the Act, where a child is born disabled but alive, a person may be held liable to the child if he is "answerable to the child in respect of the occurrence" which produced the child's disablement. "Occurrence" is defined by section 1(2) as one which—(a) affected either parent of the child in his or her ability to have a normal, healthy child; or (b) affected the mother during her pregnancy, or affected her or the child in the course of its birth, so that the child is born with disabilities. Under section 1(3) a person is answerable to the child if he was liable in tort to the parent, or if he was in breach of a legal duty to the parent without producing any actionable injury to that parent. Liability of the mother, though not of the father, to the child is expressly excluded, except where the mother is driving a motor vehicle when she knows or ought to know herself to be pregnant. The Pearson Commission was in favour of extending a similar immunity to the father as the mother enjoys.

The Act recognises certain defences. Under section 1(4), in the case of an occurrence preceding the time of conception the defendant is not answerable to the child if either or both parents knew the risk of their child being born disabled; if the father is the defendant, this subsection does not apply if he knew of the risk and the mother did not. The defendant is able to rely under section 1(6) on a contract term excluding his liability in a contract with the parent affected. Because of the Unfair Contract Terms Act 1977 this is of reduced importance. Negligence of the parent affected has the effect of reducing the child's damages under section 1(7). The Pearson Commission favoured abolition of this rule.

The recent case of *B.* v. *Islington H.A.* (1991) confirms the position taken by the Court of Appeal in *McKay* that a duty of care is owed by a person carrying out an operation on a pregnant woman to the foetus. So a child born alive may sue for injuries caused by negligence in the performance of the operation.

INDEX

457